The Problem of Solidarity

T0271846

The Freedom of Solitude

The Problem of Solidarity

Theories and Models

Edited by

Patrick Doreian

and

Thomas Fararo

University of Pittsburgh
Pennsylvania, USA

Routledge
Taylor & Francis Group

LONDON AND NEW YORK

Published by Routledge
2 Park Square, Milton Park, Abingdon, Oxon, OX14 4RN
711 Third Avenue, New York, NY 10017

Routledge is an imprint of the Taylor & Francis Group, an informa business

First issued in paperback 2016

British Library Cataloguing in Publication Data

The problem of solidarity : theories and models
   1. Solidarity 2. Social structure
   I. Doreian, Patrick II. Fararo, Thomas J.
   303.3

   ISBN   90-5700-533-6

Publisher's Note
The publisher has gone to great lengths to ensure the quality of this reprint but points out that some imperfections in the original may be apparent.

ISBN13: 978-90-5700-533-6 (hbk)
ISBN13: 978-1-138-98379-3 (pbk)

CONTENTS

PREFACE

In the world at large and in sociology, solidarity is a key problem. At present, the world is undergoing some sort of transformation we barely understand. Social systems thought to be secure have broken down. Old hostilities based on ethnic identities have been renewed. On the other hand, globalization of the economy seems to be driving a process of integration at the world level. For the sociology of this confusing situation, there is the challenge of arriving at a sound cognitive mapping. On the one hand, each nation-state is a kind of system of solidarities in terms of internal differentiation within a broader collective identity. The heightening of the salience of ethnic, religious and other internal boundaries puts a strain on the solidarity of the overall collectivity. On the other hand, the world has been deficient in overall solidarity and globalization of the economy may be producing the sort of organic solidarity that Durkheim analyzed at the nation-state level about a hundred years ago. However we map the situation, the problem of solidarity looms large as a problem both for participants in these processes and for those who take the role of dispassionate analyst. This latter step makes the whole process reflexive. In this book, we step back from the evident turmoil in the world to pose the problem of solidarity as a cognitive problem of basic science. What is solidarity? How is it produced and reproduced? How is it related to other social processes? How can we formalize such processes and create conditions for studying their properties fruitfully?

Part I, the Introduction, contains our introductory chapter that sets the stage for the varied chapters that follow. We frame the problem both in terms of some of its history within sociology and in terms of its current state in sociological theory, leading us to propose an agenda for theory-driven model building under the presupposition that formal models gain in significance by their connectedness to the current state of theory and research. In writing this chapter, our plan was to stimulate colleagues who might be interested in making some contribution to our knowledge about solidarity at a theoretical level, whether in mathematical form or not. We contacted American and European scholars, both sociologists and non-sociologists, including colleagues in mathematics and the natural sciences, sending each a copy of our draft chapter. We were fortunate that almost all agreed to write on the subject, even though some had not previously given it serious attention while others were acknowledged major theorists of solidarity. As a consequence, the book realizes our hope that theorists of solidarity would be led to more formal statements of their ideas, while mathematical model-builders would respond by turning their attention to this important theoretical problem. We hope also that the ideas generated in this enterprise will prove fruitful for empirical studies of solidarity.

One of our motives in writing this chapter was to stimulate the integration of theories of solidarity with, and through, a variety of formalizations of key theoretical ideas. From the outset, we recognized that this would be a long and difficult process. Indeed, most theorists did not attempt to connect their ideas to those of other theorists, and, in this sense, the outcome reflects the current condition of social theory more than it corrects it: diverse perspectives produce contrasting conceptualizations and formalizations. Even so, the foundations for integrative work are in place through the efforts of our contributors. Each chapter makes some theoretical contribution to our ongoing collective dialogue about the problem of solidarity, viewed as a fundamental problem for sociological science. This does not imply that each is free from conceptual, theoretical or methodological problems — indeed, our hope is that triggering an ensuing debate concerning these problems will be a major contribution of this book.

We asked Barry Markovsky and John Skvoretz to read and comment on all the chapters they received from us. Their chapters provide lucid assessments of the strengths and weaknesses of the other contributions. In addition, we adopted Skvoretz's partition of the papers into three predominant approaches to solidarity in organizing the volume into three parts that are bracketed by our introduction and the conclusion containing two assessment chapters.

Part II, Rationality and Solidarity, contains four chapters. We discuss Michael Hechter's major and influential work, *Principles of Group Solidarity*, in our introduction. In his book, Hechter addresses the solidarity problem via consideration of the problem of order: given scarcity of resources and rational actors with goals that require these resources, how is order in social life possible? Here, in chapter 2, Sun-Ki Chai and Hechter collaborate to produce both an extension of Hechter's theory and the beginnings of a mathematical formalization of it. Siegwart Lindenberg has been at the forefront of rational choice thinking in sociology, with important methodological and theoretical papers advocating this paradigm. In chapter 3, he first reviews and criticizes various microfoundational approaches to solidarity theory and then, drawing upon his own prior work, presents another explanation of how solidarity ties are built and maintained.

Game theory is a multi-person rational choice model, stressing strategic aspects of social interaction. Jeroen Weesie, Vincent Buskens and Werner Raub — a group of European sociological game theorists — draw upon their prior work in approaching the problem of solidarity through a rigorous analysis of the mechanisms producing trust in social relations (chapter 4). The field of mathematical sociology has been enriched recently by the involvement of some European-based physicists. Wolfgang Weidlich and Dirk Helbing, two leading members of this emerging scientific research effort, provide an elegant statement of their stochastic and dynamic model-building methodology, together with an application to the problem of solidarity, in chapter 5.

Part III, Affect and Solidarity, contains two chapters by leading theorists who have stressed the role of affect in social processes. David Heise's major research program has involved the creation and advance of the Affect Control Model (also discussed in our introduction). His model incorporates ideas from control theory and symbolic interactionism in sociology to formalize how affective meanings drive social interaction. In chapter 6, Heise brings his perspective to bear on the problem of solidarity, stressing the situated emergence of common consciousness, what he calls "empathic solidarity." Randall Collins, as a leading sociological theorist, has advanced an interactionist model based on Durkheimian ideas concerning the centrality of ritual in social life. This Interaction Ritual Chain model forms the basis for his collaborative chapter 7 with Robert Hanneman, whose own work has focused on the use of dynamic simulation models in theoretical sociology.

Part IV, Social Networks and Solidarity, features three contributions. Ronald Breiger is a major figure in the history of the social networks paradigm as it has developed during and since the 1970s. In chapter

8, Breiger, together with John Roberts, Jr., uses social network thinking to create a family of models that build on the writings of Durkheim.
These models are applied empirically. For some time now, the field
of social network analysis has been blessed by the involvement of
creative mathematicians like Eugene Johnsen. In chapter 9, Johnsen
takes up the challenge of working on the problem of solidarity,
making substantial use of Newcomb's ABX model and his own previous work on triadic micromodels. Evelien Zeggelink (chapter 10)
approaches the problem of solidarity in terms of an extension of her
previous work with dynamic social network models that focus on
friendship bonds.

Finally, Part V, Assessment, opens with the contribution of Barry
Markovsky. We asked him to comment on the prior chapters as well
as advance his own recent work on a formal network-based conceptualization and theory of solidarity. Chapter 12 is John Skvoretz's
overall summary and assessment of the other chapters.

We particularly want to thank David Knoke and Satoshi Kanazawa
for reviews that helped pursuade the publisher of the merits of the
overall project. More importantly, their incisive comments led to considerable improvements throughout the book. Counting the introductory and concluding chapters, we have twelve contributions that,
together, cover a wide scope from the history and current state of the
problem of solidarity in sociological theory to the frontier of new
nonlinear dynamic models. We believe this volume will strengthen
the link between social theory and formal model building by wedding
the analytical power of mathematics to the conceptual and represen-
tational needs of explanatory theory in what we hope readers will
agree is an exciting blend of form and substance.

Part I

Introduction

1 THE THEORY OF SOLIDARITY: AN AGENDA OF PROBLEMS

THOMAS J. FARARO and PATRICK DOREIAN

University of Pittsburgh

1. INTRODUCTION

Our aim in this chapter is to stimulate the construction of theoretical models that employ formal ideas and techniques to advance the theory of solidarity.

Early formal models in sociology largely consisted of isolated efforts that were regarded with suspicion or indifference in the discipline. Yet these works did play a role in terms of stimulating further developments. For instance, diffusion studies (Dodd, Rainboth and Nehnevajsa, 1955) stimulated by the ideas of Dodd (1942) provided the empirical basis for mathematical models developed by Rapoport (1956). Rapoport was part of the research group in mathematical biology and general sociology organized by Rashevsky and publishing in *The Bulletin of Mathematical Biophysics*. The work of Rashevsky (1959) did not "catch on" in social science but was folded into an emerging zeitgeist that led to the establishment of the journal *Behavioral Science* in the late 1950s. In the 1960s, this journal provided an organ for publication not only of work by Rapoport but for other model-building ideas by such people as Ashby and Boulding, as well as a number of sociologists with formal model-building interests such as the paper on an algebra of shared awareness by Friedell (1969).[1]

James Coleman encountered the work of Rashevsky and Rapoport as a young researcher at Columbia studying under Paul Lazarsfeld and Robert Merton in the 1950s. Some of his early work consisted of expository reviews of such early efforts in mathematical model-building in sociology (Coleman, 1954, 1960) and helped to shape his and the field's perception of what was needed. This led him to a framework of birth-and-death type stochastic processes augmented with contagion terms (Coleman, 1964; see also, Jaeckel, 1971). Thinking in terms of the social survey methods being worked out by Lazarsfeld and others, as well as sociometry and diffusion processes, Coleman took an individual trait or attitude as a dependent variable (e.g., voting disposition) and tried to show, by a process model, how the evolving distribution of such a disposition and its equilibrium, could be derived from assumptions about the birth and death of such dispositions as affected by interpersonal influences. The logic of the method takes social structure as given in the form of a complete network. In both its original or a generalized form, the social structure would not really be the analytical focus of interest. The focus is on a process constrained by a network structure taken as given.

A rather different and influential research program was initiated by Harrison White in the early 1960s. Working with anthropological descriptions of the form of kinship systems, and with earlier work done by mathematicians, White (1963) worked out the group-theoretic (in the sense of abstract algebraic group) method for classifying such systems. In a sense, this was a type of measurement: kinship system K was described in terms of a group $G(K)$ that depended upon an idealized description of K. By the early 1970s, Lorrain and White (1971) had worked out a generalization of this procedure using category theory and taking up hints from the work of Boyd (1969). Not long after, the White group published a pair of papers that connected the abstract algebraic ideas to bodies of structural data with the proposal of defining "blockmodels," homomorphic reductions of matrices of structural data familiar to sociologists from sociometry (White, Boorman and Breiger, 1976). This work, in turn, has led to a proliferation of conceptual and technical developments concerned with concepts of equivalence of actors in a network, the definition of the equivalence yielding a partition of the network into substructures, examples of which include cliques and non-equivalent positions. Thus, in contrast to the Coleman line of research, in the White line of research, social structure is the analytical focus of interest. However, there is no process model.

A vital problem these two lines of research posed is clear: to integrate structural and process analysis to study *how structural forms emerge and change.* The very definition of the state of the system needs to be in terms of such forms. But since forms are not agents, any change of such forms needs to be derived from models that involve human activities: actions and interactions. Work on this problem is exhibited in what is called E-state structuralism (Fararo and Skvoretz, 1986). The linkage of agency and form is made by defining a relation in terms of actor's expectation states and the form of such a pattern of relations is the entity exhibiting emergence and change. For instance, deferential or dominating expectation states constitute the "stuff" of which dominance relations and structures are made. Axioms describe a stochastic process that recursively generates the changing state of the system of interaction, i.e., the succession of forms of dominance relations. The E-state model's derived stochastic equilibrium state then has zero-probability for all but the "really possible" forms (if the theory is correct) assigning a probability to each of these that depends upon the parameters of the stochastic process. For instance, for a triad, only the cycle and the transitive triad are really possible dominance forms. Even by chance, the transitive triad would arise 75% of the time, but with a "bystander bias," an element of process introduced to reflect recent empirical research findings (Chase, 1982), the probability of his sort of hierarchy rises nearly monotonically with the magnitude of the bias. Note that this method combines the White and Coleman foci: (1) there is process that relates actors, formulated "in the small," from t to $t + dt$ (actually in discrete time in the earliest models); (2) there is an analytical focus on structural form as the entity that emerges or changes; and (3) there is a linkage of these two elements, because the *state* of the process is described in terms of logically possible structural forms. Thus, structural form is endogenous, dynamic, emergent. Process is stochastic, involves actors in interaction and the consequences of their encounters in terms of change of state of the system of interaction.

   Let us say that the heritage of mathematical model-building in sociology thereby includes these three aspects of the problem of social structure: (1) how a social structure shapes or constrains some process (as in the Coleman work), (2) how the forms of social structure are defined and analyzed (as in the White work) and (3) how social structure forms and transforms over time (as in the Fararo–Skvoretz work). Models can be formulated that include all these features. Even with this done, however, there is another problem closely related to these problems of social structure that has received even less formal attention.

   Let us agree that whatever else a group is, some sort of social structure is involved. (See Freeman, 1992.) But if the structural form is built only on the relations among the parts – such as sentiments of the actors toward each other – something is missing. Namely, there is the empirical fact that people objectify the entity comprised of their interactions, name it and have a distinct feeling about it, and often incorporating this name and feeling into their identities. Patriotism is a key example, as is ethnicity and clan membership. In everyday life, teams representing social organizations engage in competitive sport events that produce and reproduce feelings of solidarity within the respective social organizations. The phenomenon relates to structured bases of inequality. Class consciousness may evolve, collective actions can be organized and in the process produce a novel unit to which people feel loyalty. In a sense, what is problematic is the very "groupness" of the group itself.

This is another problem to place on the agenda for formal theoretical work in sociology that can go beyond the current state of the field: the problem of solidarity. There may be a generic process involved here, one that builds a sense of common membership and "lifts" the network of interactions to what is, for the actors, a higher-order social entity. In other words, a *part-whole* cognitive, affective and moral relation emerges. The network N of interactions generating a structural form of relations among the actors also generates a conception of N as an entity, this conception linked to some symbolization (cognitive element) and this entity is the object of some sort of sentiment (a moral-affective synthesis). The "group" that emerges is *both* a social network with a structural form *and* a higher-order social entity constituted by the cognitive-affective nexus focussed on it but, for the actors, transcending them as individuals. When actions are taken in the name of the collectivity – perhaps with specific internal organization of member acts as part-acts of the whole action in an environment – the group is an emergent actor in a wider system of action.

Exactly how this generic process works is the theoretical problem. A related problem is how to represent this process and its outcomes, including what we can think of as the "lifting" of the social network to a new level in which the actors that are part of the network have a cognitive-affective feeling about the network as a whole. Here too, we require a combination of an analytical focus on structure, expanded to include emergent part-whole relations, and on the processes generative of changes of state of a system described in terms of possibilities for such relations. Some of our prior work (Fararo and Doreian, 1984) deals with the purely structural aspect of multi-level inclusion relations, with membership of a person in a group as one particular level. From the present point of view, this structural focus needs to be related to the process by which such inclusion relations are constructed.

Our purpose in this essay, however, is not to set out any kind of unique solution to this problem of solidarity. Instead, our aim is to survey a number of developments, old and new, in theoretical and mathematical sociology that *might* be brought into play to work out a set of formally expressed models related to the problem. As was indicated at the outset, our motivation is really to help stimulate such work. For this purpose, we will describe both non-formal theoretical work as well as potentially relevant mathematical ideas and formalisms. Our aim is not to consolidate all this work at one fell swoop, but to set out an agenda of potential consolidations or interconnections among theoretical and mathematical efforts not ordinarily juxtaposed and considered in the way we intend. Thus, the overall "big problem" of solidarity proliferates into a series of problems that might be developed within the community of researchers interested in the advance of theoretical sociology on a formal basis.

In the next part of this chapter, we introduce some important ideas and developments in general theoretical sociology as these may be helpful for work on the problem of solidarity. These ideas are not formal but they are a fundamental resource in grappling with any formal theory to deal with the problem set out earlier. Indeed, this problem is not fully understood without this theoretical background. In the following part, we formulate an agenda of formalization problems that emerge from this theoretical background.

2. THE PROBLEM OF SOLIDARITY IN SOCIOLOGICAL THEORY

Durkheim, Parsons and Collins

We start with how theoretical sociology has approached our problem. In his early work, Durkheim (1964[1893]) focussed on societal solidarity and its transformation in history. Employing a two-stage evolutionary description, he analyzed the basis of the wholeness or integration of industrial societies as based on the division of labor: units are interdependent. They need each other. The basis of the society is the obligation of each unit to "do its part." By contrast, the pre-industrial societies, with comparatively low division of labor, are said to be held together by the similarity of the units. They are like each other in thought and behavior. The basis of the society is "to be like others." Thus, the earlier type of society is integrated by common culture and the later type by structural interdependence.

In his later work, Durkheim (1973[1898]) modifies this approach. In an argument with those who thought that individualism would destroy the moral basis of society, he argued that one must distinguish between egoism and institutionalized rights of individuals. The second form of individualism, the institutionalized individualism, is actually a source of solidarity in modern societies. Adopting his religious model of society (Durkheim, 1915), he argues that the individual has become sacred. Thus, modern societies have an element of the older type of solidarity, since the culture includes a "cult of the individual," a kind of religion that, like any religion, unifies its members around common beliefs and practices. Thus, in the later viewpoint, Durkheim is saying that modern societies with their institutionalized individualism have two sources of solidarity: both arise from the division of labor, but one involves structural interdependence while the other involves respect for the rights of individuals as a common value.

When Parsons (1937, 1951, 1967) analyzed Durkheim's theories and tried to consolidate them with other classic theories, he treated the basis of solidarity of any society – indeed, any social system – as a matter of both Durkheimian elements, in all generality. Any social system has an integrative problem or dimension dealing with the relations among the parts of the system. If the parts are taken to be people in roles and also subcollectivities, then two levels of normative culture are the sources of integration. First, there is the level of common normative culture shared by all members of the social system considered as a single collectivity. An empirical instance would be Durkheim's individualism as a moral idea, a conception of the sacred character of the individual. This corresponds to Durkheim's first mode of solidarity, the one he had originally associated with simpler societies as the basis of their integration. Parsons calls any element of such common normative culture a *value*. Second, there is the level of differentiated normative culture, including laws. At this level, certain forms of action are prescribed or proscribed, depending upon the functional or situational nature of the structural unit. For instance, a law regulating contracts applies to people and collectivities in certain roles, e.g., employer and employee roles. Any element of such differentiated normative culture is called a *norm*. The fundamental relation between the two levels is that values serve to justify norms and that norms specify the values to particular functional or situational contexts. In this sense, for instance, there are norms of economic freedom, of political freedom, of freedom of association and of freedom of learning and teaching that are all specifications of a value, "freedom," in American society. This level of differentiated normative culture corresponds, for Parsons, to Durkheim's second source of integration. Every social system, then, has a social structure whose structural elements are roles, collectivities, norms and values.

At this point, an historical note is required. Durkheim's sociology gave rise to multiple lines of research and further theory. One wing of this Durkheimian sociology involved the efforts of Parsons (and his associates and students) to combine Durkheim with Weber to create a sociology grounded in a theory of action. Another wing, as described by Collins (1985), extended over time within anthropology and sociology in a number of countries, especially France and the United States. Familiar names in this wing are Mauss, Radcliffe-Brown, Lloyd Warner, and Goffman, as well as Collins himself in recent times. For Collins, the second wing is important for its focus on what he calls "ritual solidarity," while the first wing is characterized as structural-functionalist.

The highlight of the development of the second wing is the more explicit use of the religious model worked out by Durkheim. This means a focus not just on beliefs but also the rites, or practices, that unify the community of believers and, very importantly, the symbolism involved in these activities. In the work of Goffman (1967), Durkheim's analysis is adopted and applied to social interaction itself. The argument is couched in terms of the special case of "the modern world" (and it remains a matter of dispute to what extent Goffman's analysis of social interaction has greater generality). Namely, given institutionalized individualism as Durkheim characterized it in the modern world, the implication is that since individuals are sacred entities, there must be corresponding appropriate forms of action toward them: one does not behave toward sacred things as one does toward the mundane. In face-to-face interaction, two or more sacred beings confront each and show each other proper ritual behavior. This ritual behavior can be analyzed in terms of underlying rules of conduct bearing on demeanor and deference.

Finally, in the work of Collins (1981, 1988) the interaction ritual model of Goffman is combined with Durkheim's focus on solidarity to create a generalized and abstract (although not formal) model of the production of solidarity, a process that simultaneously creates a group, a morality, and a symbolism. Durkheim had cited occasions of effervescence in which great ideals take hold and embody themselves in persons and practices, periods of social creativity. The French Revolution was an example. In Collins' general model, these dramatic occasions are only special cases of the generic process.

The basic model has the following elements:

(1) physical co-presence of a set of individuals;
(2) common focus of attention and mutual awareness;
(3) common emotional mood.

These elements enter into a dynamic process such that the second and third elements are mutually amplified with the result that the common focus of attention becomes a membership symbol, a sacred object representing the emergent group feelings and such that the attachment to the symbol enters via a feedback loop into the process. There is also an enhancement of "emotional energy" and confidence for individuals who participate in the ritual and/or who respect its symbols. Finally, given the product of the process, persons who show disrespect for the sacred objects are subject to righteous anger and punishment. Adapting these ideas to some of Durkheim's other work as well as to common situations in contemporary life, Collins analyzes court trials, political rallies, wedding ceremonies, athletic events, and the like to show how the ideas apply.

This model is analytical and generalized in the sense that any social situation can be analyzed in its terms, provided we agree that some elements can be negligible, resulting in little build-up of group feeling. For instance, Collins mentions a routine urban street scene with people passing each other on sidewalks. There is little by way of common focus, so no solidarity is generated. Thus, not all ritual interactions operate with the same intensity. Both Durkheim's dramatic occasions and Goffman's everyday life encounters are special cases. Collins goes on to refine and extend the model and to link it back to Durkheim's two types of solidarity. He does this by using the notion of "type" in a precise way. An analytical "type" is a combination of values of a set of variables. Having set out his elements of the ritual model, he then regards them as a set of variables, the ritual variables: copresence (how dense); focus of attention (how diverse); common emotion (how strong); membership symbols (how concrete or reified); reactions of symbolic violations (how punitive); and attitudes toward nonmembers (how distrusting). The "early" mode of solidarity, Durkheim's "mechanical solidarity" corresponds to high density, low diversity, strong conformity pressures, concrete reified symbols, righteous anger and punitive ritual, and distrust of strangers. This is a polar form of society not in the sense that low density occasions never arise with high diversity of attention and the like, but that in a somewhat imprecise sense this "type" of ritual combination summarizes a basic macrosociological property of the society. But more importantly, Collins' model allows the possibility that Durkheim himself discussed: that any group may have a cycle of activities and interaction such that there are periods of high ritual intensity that revivify the meaning of group membership with periods of dispersed existence in which the ritual variables are in a different phase in the state space, all assuming values that do not remind people of their common membership with its common emotions and morality.

The important point about Collins' model, even if the ideas are still expressed in rather a loose way, is that it highlights a central problem of theoretical sociology: What are the processes by which groups are generated? As noted earlier, a group has some structural form. This structure can be represented in network terms: the actors and their social relations. However, this "social network" is a limited conceptualization as it does not invoke any idea of the novel entity, the emergent social unit symbolized in some way and concerning which the individuals have some feeling of bondedness.[2] Even if we map internal and external interaction patterns for a "group" and discern differences, we need to know that the ritual interaction processes generate a level of solidarity beyond the behavioral interaction patterns exhibited by the group members. Emergent solidarity changes the character of the membership relation and the social relations among the members. The central problem here is how groups and their levels of solidarity are generated jointly.

In general, a formal model corresponding to Collins' ideas would have to have the character of "recursive generativity (Fararo, 1989) in the sense that the basic state variables and events are framed "in the small" (from t to $t + dt$) and are re-applied to the very situation they generate until some "attractor" state of the ritual variables is attained, either a single state or a stable cycle.[3] We will return to this discussion in the second part of this paper.

Homans and Group Dynamics

Durkheim's focus on the group and the problematic character of its solidarity influenced a large number of subsequent social scientists, including anthropologists Lloyd Warner and Radcliffe-Brown, as well as Malinowksi. These authors, plus the Durkheim-inspired ideas of Elton Mayo, together with an attraction to Pareto's use of system concepts and emphasis on the role of sentiments in social systems, all led George Homans to a particular mode of theoretical synthesis of ideas about groups (Homans, 1950). It is not our aim to review this important work, but only to point out some key aspects of it that relate to Durkheimian sociology and to our problem.

First, Homans (1950: 82) defines the term "group" in abstraction from the problem of integration or solidarity, using the term merely to denote the concrete entity to be analyzed: a set of persons who in some interval of time interact with each other more than with persons we, the analysts, do not include in "the group." This means, for instance, that the people in an elevator can be readily be treated as a group. But this only means that we have designated some type of object for analysis, not that the analysis has really begun.

Second, the analysis of the dynamics of a group is conducted in terms of elements or variables referring to sentiments, activities and interactions, together with emergent group norms. These form a set of primitives for his theory. The states of these elements and their mutual interrelations is what Homans means by the social system (of the group).

Third, although he is not quite explicit on this point, he implies (and this is confirmed in his later writings) that by the social structure of the group he means an equilibrium state of the social system. This is an excellent way of linking dynamics and structure, because it implies, as he says quite explicitly, that the same mechanisms are invoked both to explain the emergence and maintenance of structure and the change of structure, usually called "social change."

Fourth, Homans very strongly focusses on the way in which the social system processes yield social bonds and social norms, as well as constitute social control relative to these norms when we analyze deviations from equilibrium in terms of restorative tendencies.

Fifth, Homans distinguishes between an "internal system" and an "external system." More or less explicitly, Homans is saying that any social system has two functional problems: adapting to an environment and integrating its units so as to form some sort of whole in that environment. These two problems are the basis of the two subsystems of the social system.

In all of this, Homans' basic problem is: "What makes customs customary?" He does not want to show how to explain people's behavior by saying that it conforms to a custom. The point is that anything that does emerge in social interaction – customs, practices, roles, positions, groups, communities – all these entities are to be accounted for. In other terms, he wants to specify the mechanisms that produce and maintain the entities typically said to comprise a social structure.

Since the latter is an equilibrium state of the social system, Homans wants to show how the processes of social interaction yield "solutions" that are the social structures observed. These are solutions in a double sense: (1) if formalized, he implies, the processes he specifies would comprise a system of differential equations that would have equilibrium solutions and these solutions would be those states of the system that are the social structure under the given parametric conditions (this is explored in more detail below); and (2) if we consider the adaptation and integration aspects of social life, then the social structure is an ongoing solution to these two functional problems. Thus, there is an implied structural–functional point of view analogous to that of Parsons.

We may note that this point of view is also not much different from that of Collins, who wants to generate the moral solidarity of a group from varying starting conditions. Like Homans, he recognizes that although groups are the fundamental entities that constitute our subject matter, for fundamental theory they cannot be simply taken as given. Homans implies a process of recursive generativity involving states of sentiments and activities, where the recursion is via interaction episodes in which these variables change state. But Collins is clearer on the Durkheimian focus on solidarity and the way in which a particular set of "ritual" variables, if treated dynamically, can help us to account for the "groupness" or solidarity of a system of interaction under given conditions.

Homans and Exchange

In his later work, Homans recognized that he had been somewhat deficient in his early theory about the dynamics of the emergent group. By asserting, for instance, that the more frequently persons interact, the more similar they become in sentiments, he had not really modelled the process of social interaction that would yield this relationship between variables. In passing to the conception of "social behavior as exchange" Homans (1958, 1974) intended to rectify this deficiency by starting with an actor-situation model and then coupling actors to arrive at an interaction model. To be sure, he did not quite state his procedure in this way, but this is what it amounted to. For the actor-situation starting point he took basic behavioral propositions, featuring the key variables of *value* of activity and *frequency* of activity. Social interaction is an exchange involving such valued activities. Phenomena of differentiation, such as status, power and authority, are to be derived on this basis. Their fundamental property that differentiates them from the spot transactions of markets (which are based on the very same behavioral exchanges, according to Homans' theory) is that they are *enduring* relations. That is, as in the prior book, Homans is trying to show how social relations of various sorts emerge in social interaction.

Homans draws upon the work in social psychology that had been accomplished since his anthropological–sociological synthesis of 1950. In particular, at one point he draws upon Heider's (1946, 1958) balance theory, which will be discussed later in connection with formal balance theory. However, this linkage has played little role in further work based on Homans' innovative ideas.

Homans' notion of social behavior as exchange and of the problem of generating social structure on that basis was employed by Emerson (1972) to create an influential theory that is represented in current work under the category of "network exchange theory" (Cook, Gilmore and Yamagishi, 1983) and "elementary theory" (Willer, 1987; Skvoretz and Willer, 1991). These theories, however, invert Homans' analytical focus. They take a structural form as given and try to derive how the implied distribution of power in that structure explains the outcomes of a set of exchanges and hence the distribution of the resources involved in these exchanges. In other words, the social structure is put in a parametric role and the state of the system is described in terms of resource distribution. Thus, it is not at all clear if any of this work is relevant to our problem, but we will have to see (making a start in our next part below.)

Somewhat similar remarks may be made about James Coleman's recent theoretical work. Coleman had studied the exchange theory formulated by Homans (1958) and in Coleman (1990) produced his own version of this idea. In one aspect, this work uses a general equilibrium framework from competitive market economics to derive resource distributions and the differential power implied in such distributions. Coleman treats problems such as the emergence of norms, interpersonal comparison of utilities, and the derivation of the interests of a collectivity from the exchanges among its parts.

But when Coleman invokes social networks, they are primarily in the role of givens, so that actors can use "social capital" (ties) to get things done. What this type of theorizing does not do is to take such a social network as endogenous, as that which is problematic as an emergent feature of reality. Thus, like the network exchange theories, much of Coleman's theory inverts the problems treated by Collins and

Homans. Yet, because this theory has such a strong mathematical component, because it has a consistent theoretical basis in rational choice thinking, and because its overall development goes in so many directions (that are difficult to integrate) it may yet be relevant to our problem.

Hechter's Theory

Recently, Hechter (1987) set out to construct a general theory of solidarity. He recognizes the conceptual problem that sociologists have rarely provided a definition of the basic terms, "group" and "solidarity" in the frequently used idea of group solidarity. His definition of group is somewhat windy (Hechter, 1987: 16) but is intended to differentiate groups from categories, crowds and corporations while formulating the intuitive notion that groups influence their members' behavior: "At a minimum, a group is a collection of individuals who are engaged in a specific type of mutually oriented activity (or set of interconnected activities), entry to which occurs according to one or more criteria of membership." Crowds have no membership criteria, categories lack the activity element, and corporations are defined by ownership rather than joint participation.

His next step is to treat solidarity as, in a sense, the "groupness" of a group: it is the extent to which members of a group willingly comply with their obligations to the group without explicit compensation. More formally, Hechter proposes that group solidarity $= f(ab)$, a function of the product of the two terms:

$a =$ extensiveness of a group's obligations,

$b =$ rate of member compliance with these obligations.

The simple formalism used here is to emphasize that *both* a and b must be present for the generation of solidarity.

Hechter suggests measuring a in terms of the proportion of a member's resources expected for collective ends. If we interpret parameter b in probabilistic terms as the likelihood that a member complies with a norm, then the product ab yields the average proportion of a member's resources contributed to collective ends.

So far we have only concepts. The theory of group solidarity takes the form of proposing a factor that influences parameter a and a factor that influences parameter b. First, there is a group property defined as the extent to which members are dependent on the group for benefits: the more dependent are the members, the more extensive will be the obligations. To test this proposition, Hechter looks at roll-call votes in modern legislatures and tests the derived hypothesis that the more dependent the legislator on the party, the greater the vote in the direction favored by the party leaders. Dependence here may consist of resources useful in re-election campaigns and also advancement in the legislature itself. So, in general, dependence has a positive effect on the first parameter of solidarity, the extensiveness of obligations.

The second factor presupposes a rational choice perspective. Members will be making choices about contribution of resources to the group in the fulfillment of obligations, e.g., time and effort. In making such choices, the free rider problem looms large: if an opportunity exists to gain from others' contributions without contributing oneself, the rational actor will not contribute. Hence, the rate of compliance depends on the extent to which the group can control – through monitoring and sanctioning – the conduct of members. So the general proposition is that the greater the control (monitoring and sanctioning) capacity by the group, the greater the compliance. For example, this proposition implies that among a set of communes, those with social arrangements making it easy to observe and sanction behavior will survive longer than those that do not.

One consequence of the propositions relates to group size: as size increases, it is easier for members to evade obligations and they are motivated to do so by rational considerations (free riding). Hence, large groups will have to employ formal control mechanisms. Establishment of these controls also implies costs for the group, again raising the free rider problem. We should note also that both the dependence of members on the group and the need to establish controls are driven by the individual demands for joint immanent goods, those that satisfy directly the utilities of group members. Other consequences of the theory depend upon a rather technical vocabulary we cannot elucidate here.

Thus, Hechter has set out a theory of solidarity that, in its presuppositions, appears very different from Collins' ritual interaction theory. Hechter argues *against* affective conceptions of solidarity. But his grounds are not really theoretical, but methodological. "However appealing an affective conception of solidarity might appear to be, it is no substitute for a more behavioral definition. Since the strength of sentiment that exists between individuals is so difficult to measure apart from actual behaviors – and is likely to be mercurial to boot – it is hard to conduct empirical research about it. One simply cannot explain variations in the solidarity of given groups without using an operational definition of the term" (Hechter, 1987: 19). The latter point is well-taken, but Hechter's viewpoint confuses the postulation of mechanisms to explain solidarity, the abstract conception of solidarity, and the empirical recognition of some other factor that varies with solidarity and may be used to indicate the state of solidarity.

We can further analyze the problem of solidarity by considering three perspectives, rather than two, bringing in Marx's theoretical ideas. Three questions can then be addressed in a comparative way: What is meant by solidarity? By what process is solidarity generated? How do solidarity outcomes depend on the parameters of the process?

For Marx, solidarity means class consciousness enabling action in concert of a class in opposition to another class. It presupposes a social relation $a\mathrm{R}b$ is given such that class $[a]$ is the set of all persons in the same position as a and class $[b]$ consists of all those in the same position as b. In a private enterprise system, for instance, $a\mathrm{R}b$ if a works for b, where b is the owner of the enterprise. For Marx, the process that generates such solidarity is class conflict. For instance, a wildcat strike is an instance of such a process, in which over time the actions of members of $[a]$ activate more and more other such members, making them aware of their joint membership and their common interests, and then (and here Marx needs supplementation with a resolution of the free rider problem) contributing to the ongoing collective action.

Finally, for Marx, a basic idea is that density of communication or interaction is a fundamental parameter of this conflict process. The less dense the interaction network linking members of a class, the lower the level of class action. For instance, an action in region A may fail before it can get the support of others in region B because of poor communication links. Historically, peasants represent the low density condition and urban factory workers represent the higher density condition.

For Collins, solidarity means a moral feeling of belonging together. The process, as indicated earlier, involves interaction rituals as a mechanism of production of solidarity, which is the outcome of the process. Finally, for Collins as for Marx, density is again a fundamental parameter: the higher the co-presence, the greater the solidarity (ceteris paribus).

Returning now to Hechter's theory, we see that he presents the most elaborate answer to the question of the meaning of solidarity but also that he has little or nothing to say about process. And the absence of a process conceptualization means that the distinction between parameters of the process and endogenous state variable is not clearly present in the discussion. It is possible to interpret such a static model in dynamic terms as follows. The endogenous state variable is simply solidarity, treated now as adjusted to its parametric conditions (i.e., equilibrated to them). Then the parameters of the (absent) process are dependence and control, the two "factors" that respectively influence the two elements of solidarity, extensiveness of corporate obligations and compliance with them. Thus, we now see that Hechter's theory is really a *comparative statics* model in the sense that it expresses the implied equilibrium state of solidarity as a function of these two parameters, so that as conceptual shift of a parameter produces (via the unexplicated process) a shift in the level of solidarity.

In terms of Marx's model, Hechter's theory does refer to the actual contribution to the collective action: at any time, the solidarity of class [a] in this action is the proportion of those in this class that are contributing to it in some way. However, Hechter presupposes some group, while Marx's concept starts from the more fluid conception of an aggregate of people who *come to recognize themselves as forming a collectivity* with common interests against another such aggregate.[4] This property is shared with Collins' model, which also does not presuppose a given group.

How can we sum up this rather complex state of affairs in regard to theories of solidarity? We can use Homans' (1950) four elements of the social system as a helpful device. Solidarity, like the related but different concept of cohesion, may be *analyzed* in terms of these elements: sentiment, activity, interaction, and norms. The analytical aspects of solidarity chosen for the *definition* do not exhaust its content. Thus, different theories may invoke the same elements and even some of the same relationships among them, but differ in which elements or relations they take as definitions. Hechter's concept of solidarity favors the activity element for the definition in order that it be an observable state of the system of interaction. But this definition includes the conception of a norm, because it presupposes a group with existing obligations of members to that group. The element of density of interaction enters into the theory, but it does so as a derived proposition concerning the control parameter (the more dense, the easier the control). What the theory is silent about, both in its definition and its propositions, is the element of sentiment. Yet when Hechter does raise the question of how groups solve the free rider problem, in his discussion of "friendly societies" (Hechter, 1987: 113–4) as a type of insurance group, he describes what amounts to a considerable amount of communal interaction. This suggests a Collins-Durkheim mechanism of solidarity production. The group begins as an instrumental means for each member to attain a private good (a sense of security) but acquires, in interaction, a value that goes beyond this purely instrumental aspect. This is precisely what Homans (1950) was saying about groups in his formulation of the emergent internal system. And, as Homans makes clear, this emergence is grounded in the simple idea that people who *repeatedly* interact "in the external system," (instrumentally) form bonds of sentiment. In his later work, he invokes exchange and balance to treat this process. The upshot is that a more complete theory of solidarity than Hechter presents would touch bases with all four of Homans' elements, whatever components it selected for definition and testing.

By contrast with Hechter's theory, Collins' theoretical model invokes the sentiment and normative elements in its definition. Interaction as density and as potentially or actually repeated episodes of co-presence is invoked directly in the idea of interaction rituals. Collins can assert that the element of activity is either an aspect of the co-presence, producing some level of common focus, or it is a mode of action that depends upon the generated solidarity (or both).

The upshot is that if we move toward a mathematical approach, we have to keep in mind both the more recent formulations (of Collins and Hechter) and also older and still useful formulations (such as those of Marx and Homans). It may not be possible to directly synthesize these theories until they are directly presented in formal terms. Experience with formal theories teaches that apparently very different "approaches" turn out to be complementary and, in fact, possible to coordinate and subordinate within a more comprehensive framework. This is one of the aims of the agenda of problems we are suggesting.

3. FORMAL FRAMEWORKS AND SOLIDARITY: AN AGENDA OF PROBLEMS

Our hope is that, at some point, a set of general dynamic models can be formulated to account for both the structural processes and the generation of solidarity of human groups. One step in this direction is to look at structural balance theory.

Balance Theory and the Solidarity Problem

Balance theory originated with Heider (1946, 1958). Taking the point of view of the actor or person p, the theory is said to be p-centric in that all relations are from p's point of view. Objects are either persons or non-persons. Other persons are denoted by, say, o, q, ... Two types of relations connect objects: cognitive links that constitute *unit formation* are one type and sentiment relations are the other type. For instance: p likes o and p believes that o made non-personal object x. Here $[o, x]$ is a unit by virtue of p's cognition. The sentiment relation that p likes o may be accompanied by a sentiment relation that p likes x. Then the unit $[o, x]$ has an unambiguous sign and the triad of p, o, x is said to be in a balanced state. By contrast, if p dislikes x, then there is an ambivalence toward the unit and the state is not balanced. The original state could be that no sentiment relation exists toward x. Then there is a tendency, if p forms sentiment relation toward x, for that relation to take the sign that produces a balanced state. Similarly, unbalanced states have a tendency to change, they are states of psychological disequilibrium. If congruence among signs is the criterion of balance – so that if p likes o, o likes x, and p likes x is a balance state, for instance – there is a scope restriction on its application, as pointed out in the literature (Berger, et al. 1962: 13, fn. 6). Sometimes there are rules or norms that make a common sentiment toward x by both p and o an unstable situation. A good example is romantic love: if both p and o like each other but love a third person x, the situation is not balanced, on the contrary it is the scene of complex emotional dynamics leading to a change of state.

Newcomb (1953) extends Heider's ideas to a system of social interaction in which the standpoints of all interactants are jointly considered. His *ABX* model has two persons A, B and an object X. By considering their attitudes toward X as well as toward each other, balance considerations arise in this system. The system is in a balanced state if each person is in a balanced state. The key factor that leads to changes in the configuration of signed relations is communication about X, which occurs if X is jointly relevant. What then occurs can be put in mathematical terms (not Newcomb's own) as a system in which all the relational elements adjust to each other, if this is possible under given conditions. Despite the apparent simplicity of the two-person *ABX* system, there is a hidden complexity when it is approached from the Heiderian p-centric viewpoint because the beliefs that one party has about the sentiments of the other have to be considered as well as the actual sentiments.

Cartwright and Harary (1956) formalized the concept of balance within a graph theoretic setting. Formally, there is a set of actors, A, and two social relations, R1 and R2, that are specified for pairs of actors in A, such that R1 and R2, have an empty intersection. The standard interpretation has R1 and R2 as positive and negative interpersonal sentiments, respectively. These are represented by signed lines in a graph representation, where the points represent the entities in set A. The concept of cycle is defined for such a graph and the sign of a cycle is the product of the signs on its lines. Then the signed graph is balanced if and only if all its cycles have a positive sign. (These ideas extend readily to directed ties using the concept of semi-cycles.) For example, the imbalanced 3-cycles have either one negative line or three negative lines. Cartwright and Harary proved the important Structure Theorem: *If and only if* the graph is balanced, then the set A can be partitioned into two subsets (one of which may be empty), such that all the positive lines are within the two subsets and all of the negative lines are between them. Treating triads with three negative lines as balanced, Davis (1967) generalized the structure theorem, showing that when balance holds, the structure breaks up into a finite number of clusters with positive lines within clusters and negative lines between them. In either form, this is a dramatic macro-level group property that is generated by the working out of all the imbalances in the various triads of group members.[5]

We need to note two points. First, social groups need not reach a balanced state. To deal with this, an extension of balance theory to a quantitative apparatus was made by Norman and Roberts (1972) who devised a scheme to compute the degree of balance of a network, since some cycles may be positive and others negative. Since negative cycles imply forces toward change, the lower the degree of balance the more likely it is that a sentiments and cognitions will change. Second, in many of the applications of the idea of structural balance, the subtle intricacies of Heider's balance model have been eliminated by fiat: namely, actors' perceptions of ties have been assumed to be veridical with the actual states of interpersonal sentiment.[6]

For purposes of treating the problem of solidarity, these ideas should be linked to the ABX framework. The X object plays the role of some distinctive entity for the attention of the actors $(A, B, ...)$. Thus, X is Collins' focal object. The actors are those in mutual co-presence. Dynamically, signed "lines" pointing from the actors to X form over time along with signed lines between the actors. Mutuality of awareness is cognitive knowledge, in Heider's sense, of the beliefs and sentiments of others. For instance, at a political rally, the speaker is the focal object. The initial state may possess little by way of signed lines toward the speaker and little knowledge of others' attitudes toward the speaker. An "exciting" speaker will activate positive signed lines and awareness of them will be spread, so that as attitudes are formed toward each other and toward the speaker they tend to do so in a way that balances each person's cognitive system.

The problem is to formalize this idea. We want to go from the system of interaction – persons in co-presence oriented to a common object X – to an emergent sense of unity, of common belonging. How can we get what Collins calls the "moral feeling," however? What makes the "rev'ed up" states of sentiments toward X in mutual awareness transmute into a feeling of what is right and wrong? What makes this potentially transient state of feeling into an enduring sense of belonging? Collins' model says that X becomes a symbol of the emergent group. The feeling about X endures to some degree, although without further ritual occasions it might die out. The process is episodic. As Collins puts it, there is a "chain" of interaction rituals.

We can distinguish three levels of analysis here. The first involves the details of social interaction as such and the way in which emotions are generated and feedback into the process. The most important mathematical development in this domain has been affect control theory (Heise, 1979; Smith-Lovin and Heise, 1987). This theory maps cultural types of actors, types of behaviors, types of social objects addressed by such behavior, and related typifications of actors and settings, into a vector space. Each cultural category, for instance, ⟨king⟩ or ⟨subject⟩ is mapped into three measures of semantic connotation involving evaluation, potency and activity. For instance, for a population of actors who are subjects of a monarch, ⟨king⟩ would map into a very high evaluation, a very high potency and perhaps a not as high activity measure.[7] One path of mathematical model building treating the problem of solidarity should be an effort to bring to bear on the Collins' informal ritual interaction model the formal mathematical theory and the associated measurement system employed by Heise, Smith-Lovin and others who are developing affect control theory. Indeed, this is an exciting possibility for the field as a whole in terms of integrating two important theories dealing with affective elements of social interaction.

The other two levels of the problem are structural. The first level is the "network" of people forming around focal object X. The second is an inclusion network that arises on the foundation of processes in this network. We can characterize each level and briefly describe one connection to work involving formal models.

At the first level, the network process could be very fluid, as in a crowd, or a wildcat strike, or very fixed, as in an audience in an auditorium or a classroom. Actually, we can bring in a process from Marx too. If we start from Marx, there are such assemblages on each side of the fundamental relation aRb that induces the two aggregates [a] and [b] that are the starting points for group construction.

This idea relates to the notion of equivalence mentioned earlier, a key concept in the tradition of structural analysis. Actors are equivalent if they are connected to others in the *same* way in terms of the patterning of ties. Based on ideas developed by Sailer (1978), White and Reitz (1983) proposed the concept of regular equivalence whereby actors are regularly equivalent if they are equivalently connected to equivalent others. (Two jurors on the same jury are structurally equivalent; two jurors on different juries are regularly equivalent.) This more general form of equivalence captures exactly the Marxian idea of aggregates (classes) standing in relation to each other, given the relations of production.

However, these formal ideas about equivalence remain silent about the processes that generate and maintain such a "class structure" and any emergent class consciousness. Among these processes are those whereby the actors in [a] develop a sense of identity and solidarity with each other, as do the actors in [b]. The events that involve interaction ritual process draw-in the two classes differentially and create, differentially, two more or less solidary groups amid the conflict process. These emergent groups are the next level "up."

This takes us to the second structural level that arises on the foundation of the first. This second level is an inclusion network in which each person *is a member of* one of the classes that has formed itself into a group, a class-for-itself. More generally, one social entity is *included in* another social entity. For instance, in providing an account of the social situation of persons in the American colonies in the mid-eighteenth century, Wood (1991: 11) points out:

> Like all Englishmen, the colonists continued to embrace deeply rooted assumptions about the order and stability of a monarchical society. Living in a monarchical society meant, first of all, being subjects of the king. This was no simple political status, but had all sorts of social, cultural and even psychological implications.... . The allegiance the English subject owed his monarch was a personal and individual matter. *Diverse persons related to each other only through their common tie to the king*, much as children became brothers and sisters only through their common parentage. (Italics added.)

Thus, a tie between two colonial persons was created, without direct social interaction, by virtue of common allegiance to the king. Let this "subject of" relation be designated by S. Then persons a and b stand in relation $aSS^{-1}b$. In turn, the royal emblem and royal arms, displayed especially in royal ceremonial occasions, kept the tie alive in the minds of the persons involved. Thus the king is symbolized by these entities and by relating to them, the persons are reminded of their tie to the king (or queen, of course). Also, when they interact, they recognize their commonness of linkage to the king as part of the definition of the interaction situation and any emergent interpersonal tie. We might suggest, with S now considered abstractly, that if S is a membership relation linking two levels of structure, then the induced relation SS^{-1} is a *solidary tie*.

Building on an idea of Breiger (1974) and Wilson (1982), some of our earlier work (Fararo and Doreian, 1984) has dealt with this type of solidary tie relation. It can be generalized to cover the relation between groups that are included in some wider collectivity. It is then a generalized inclusion relation within a hierarchy of inclusions. The patterning of such ties generated by a hierarchy of inclusions is subject to a mathematical analysis of connectivities implicit in the overall structure.

Thus, considering the two levels and the corresponding formal work, we see that two fundamental types of relations are involved: (1) a direct interpersonal tie in a social network and (2) a solidary tie that connects actors whether or not they interact directly with each other. We suggest that the problem of solidarity, in one aspect, is a problem of how these two types of relations are themselves related. One way to distinguish *cohesion* from solidarity, for instance, is to define it as a property of a network of interpersonal ties. Put another way, using Mead's (1934) terminology, an actor can orient to *particular others* and to *generalized others*. Each interpersonal tie is a pair of self-other orientations, each actor relating to the particular other. Cohesion is a property of a network of such ties. The set of ties to the generalized other, on the other hand, forms the basis of the solidarity of the emergent group which is a generalized other for each of its members.

Perhaps enough has been said here and in the prior part of this paper to indicate the nature of the first problem-set on our agenda:

Problem-Set #1. Model the formation of groups, as an interaction ritual process and/or conflict process, in which actors $A, B, \ldots$ are points with directed signed lines toward focal objects $X, Y, \ldots$ such that these points and/or lines are dynamic, i.e., subject to over time birth and death process. Derive the steady states of the process. Explore the conditions of stability. Show how the stable states vary with variations in parameters of the process. In this formalization, try to solve the related conceptual problem of how the moral element enters into the sentiments and also precisely in what sense objects function as symbols. Use the model to define/measure a precise notion of solidarity of the emergent group(s) and relate this idea to the concept of a solidary tie SS^{-1} (and the patterning of such ties with plural emergent groups). It is suggested, in particular, that one important route of such work will involve forging a connection between the conception of an interaction ritual process generating solidarity and the detailed mathematical theory of social interaction developed within the tradition of affect control theory.

Exchange, Rational Choice and the Solidarity Problem

Generating the extent of obligations In approaching the solidarity problem, the fact that Hechter's theory relates dependence to the extent of corporate obligations, one of two factors of solidarity, suggests an exchange-theoretic connection. In Emerson's (1972) influential theory, power is directly related to dependence of one actor on another. In turn, dependence varies directly with the need for the resources controlled by the other and the value of those resources to the actor. However, there has been a subtle shift here: in Hechter's formulation, members are dependent on the collectivity rather than on specific other individual actors. For a mathematical model that might incorporate an idea of this sort while, at the same time treating the problem in terms of the dependence of the member on the collectivity, we might be able to employ Coleman's (1990) model.

Coleman's model starts from two relations connecting two sets of entities: actors and resources (or events). Each actor has some level of interest in each resource and also some proportion of control over each resource. The interests are taken as parametric, while the control relation shifts from an initial state to a final state through exchanges. Actors are willing to give up some control over some resources to gain more control over other resources of interest. We can interpret interest as need for the resource, for instance. The exchanges occur via a maximization of utility by each actor subject to a constraint expressed in terms of the givens.

In the application to the treatment of dependence, we represent the initial situation as one involving the interaction of a member with the collectivity (which, in practice, will usually mean the leadership subgroup of that collectivity). For instance, the individual legislator interacts with the leadership of the party in the legislature. Thus, we have two actors. For resources, we can assume two types: one initially under more control by the individual actor and one under more control by the collective actor, and with the interests such that both actors have some motivation to exchange. For instance, the party leadership is interested in the legislator's voting along the lines it wants and the legislator is interested in help in financing a campaign and/or gaining certain committee positions. Of course, these interests are expressed, for theory, in terms of parameters that will substantially vary from one situation to another. For instance, the modern American legislator has much lesser dependence on the party than in earlier years in this century. This dependence is a function of the fact that there is less interest in financial support from the party, given alternatives outside the party. We let it be a sub-problem for the next problem-set as to how one should quantitatively define the dependence of the member on the collectivity in the context of the Coleman model, although it will certainly be some function of the two relations, control and interest.

Given this embedding of dependence in a formal exchange model, we can ask how to formally coordinate this to solidarity. In Hechter's theory, one may recall from our discussion, solidarity is a matter of compliance with obligations: the more compliance and the more obligations, the greater the solidarity. We are treating the extent of obligations component now in abstraction from compliance, which will be discussed below. Recall that our analysis of Hechter's theory showed it to be a comparative statics theory: the greater the dependence of the typical member on the collectivity (parameter), the greater the extent of corporate obligations (in an implied equilibrated state). Thus, we require a process formulation in which corporate obligations are constructed over time and such that the level of obligations, in equilibrium, depends upon the prevailing dependency, taken as a given. Hence, we are talking about the emergence of norms, a topic treated by Coleman (1990: Ch. 30) within his mathematical framework as also involving rational action. It follows that the formal problem is to try to link dependence to emergence of norms, considered together in the context of the formal framework of Coleman's model.

Problem-Set #2. Construct a theoretical model of the process by which corporate obligations arise in a collectivity and how the extent of these varies with dependence of the members on the collectivity by employing Coleman's exchange framework.

Then another problem arises if both Problem-Set #1 and this context of Problem-Set #2 are considered together: to relate the formal models and thereby address the fundamental theoretical question as to how ritual interaction, conflict processes and the like enter into the production of solidarity.

Problem-Set #3. Given two formal theoretical models addressing the first and second problem-sets, respectively, work on the problem of articulation of these two models. Initially, this is a conceptual problem because the exchange representation involves rational choice (in fact, maximization of utility by each actor) while the first problem-set involves ritual interaction. However, the first class of theoretical models will be generating an emergent group, while the second class starts from a given group. Yet the "moral feelings" of the first process must be somehow related to the rational action of the second (exchange) process.

The compliance element It will be apparent that we are treating the problem of solidarity in terms of three components in sequence: the emergence of a group, with some moral feelings and symbolism (the interaction ritual process possibly in a conflict process setting); the emergence of corporate obligations, given a group exists with members more or less dependent upon it (the exchange process representation); and, third, the generation of a rate of compliance, given a group and its corporate obligations. We turn now to this third component or stage.

As a reminder, recall that in Hechter's theory,

$$\text{solidarity} = f(ab)$$

where parameter a is the extent of corporate obligations and parameter b is the extent of compliance with them. In the formulation of Problem-Set #2, we were focussed on the production of element a as the outcome of a process in which dependence is a parameter so that we could retrieve the comparative statics principle that the extent of corporate obligations varies directly with the dependence.

The problem now concerns the production of element b as the outcome of a process in which episodes of possible compliance or "defection" arise in such a way that we obtain a generated rate of compliance as a function of the element of "control" in Hechter's sense: the monitoring and sanctioning of behavior.

Consider any one episode in which the member is rationally considering compliance with a corporate obligation. Such a consideration – following "control theory" in the deviance literature (Hirschi, 1969) – would not even arise unless there was some potential gain from defection. But there is always the chance of detection, involving monitoring. This can be represented as the probability that a defection is detected, given it occurs. It is actually the actor's subjective perception or belief that detection will occur, in the rational choice model we are suggesting. Then, given detection, there is some loss, the factor of sanctioning.

Assume that the status quo is compliance and has utility zero, a baseline value. Then the rational member will comply (in such an episode) if and only if the expected value of defection is less than zero. To find the expected value, note that if the actor defects the gain G is obtained but if the act is then detected a loss L is imposed. Thus, with p as the probability of detection, the expected value of the defection alternative is:

$$E(\text{defection}) = (1-p)G + p(G-L)$$

Since the actor complies if and only if this quantity is less than zero, we obtain:

$$\text{compliance if and only if } pL > G$$

Thus, if and only if the *social control* product pL of monitoring (yielding p) and sanctioning (L) is sufficiently great relative to the incentive to defect (G) will the actor not defect.

One problem with this version of the choice situation is that there is a potential second-order free rider problem: Other actors have to decide to apply the sanction to a detected defection from corporate obligations (a second-order free rider problem, see Heckathorn, 1992) because a choice may involve costs for the sanctioning agent, making it rational to let someone else apply sanctions. When this problem is included in the analysis, an appropriate model can be thought of as yielding a kind of probability mixture of L and zero for the prospective defecting actor, modifying the above simple model.

The key conceptual point is that any attempt to write down in a formal way how a rational decision is made to comply when a temptation to defect exists leads to a formal representation of Hechter's control element in terms of (a) detection probabilities as a consequence of monitoring aspects of the collectivity and (b) expected losses, as a consequence of the sanctioning capacities of the collectivity and of its mode of resolution (or not) of the second-order free rider problem.

By considering a conceptual aggregate of corporate obligations and a conceptual aggregate of occasions in which actors are tempted to defect, the final step is to derive the average proportion of compliance decisions over all the obligations and occasions. This corresponds to solidarity as a product of the extent of obligations and the rate of compliance with obligations in the given collectivity. Before stating the next agenda problem-set based on these considerations, we mention one conceptual problem that needs to be considered in the formal work as well. Namely, the phrase just above, "a conceptual aggregate of occasions in which actors are tempted to defect" is misleading if it suggests that we should consider only occasions in which the actor considers non-compliance and then accepts or rejects that possibility. The problem is that well-socialized actors will routinely exclude objective possibilities for deviance and this is an important element of the overall rate of compliance. Thus, in the presumed count of occasions, a problem exists in trying to specify exactly which situations should be counted. This is an old problem in the theory of deviance and social control (Gibbs, 1981). In the course of work on the next problem-set, it is possible that some solutions to the difficulty will present themselves.

Problem-Set #4. Construct a theoretical model of the process by which a rate of compliance is generated for each of the corporate obligations of a group. This can be done by starting with a rational choice to comply given a temptation to defect and applying "control theory" considerations from the theory of deviance. The terms in the choice model – detection probability and expected loss if detected – correspond directly to Hechter's two factors that determine the level of social control, namely, monitoring and sanctioning capacities.

Given this model element, the final problem is to assemble the whole set of formal models into the overall formalized theory of solidarity:

Problem-Set #5. Assemble the various models developed in addressing the earlier problems on the agenda so as to construct a comprehensive and formal theory of solidarity.

4. CONCLUSION

It is likely that there are other problem-sets that could be formulated, but the five outlined above emerge directly out of some of the most significant current literature of the field. There are other relevant literatures which we mention in concluding this paper. First, the connection between emergent solidarity and collective action suggests the relevance of critical mass theory (Marwell and Oliver, 1993). Second, the continuing importance of ethnicity in the world suggests a substantive connection to work on the emergence of new ethnic identities, as when Alba (1990) suggests that a "European–American" ethnic identity is emerging in a sub-population of the United States. At the same time, Alba argues that a conceptual distinction needs to be made between such ethnic identity and the notion of ethnic solidarity. This argument may have a more general relevance for theories of solidarity. Third, of considerable relevance to the topic of this paper are some recent strands of neofunctionalist work. In Alexander and Colomy (1990), for instance, there are papers on the creation of solidarity through trust in leaders and on social-integrative institutions, such as "the public" and the mass media. These ideas are framed within the AGIL functional scheme. They relate directly to societal solidarity in this Parsonian framework.[8] Fourth, and finally, we draw the reader's attention to a recent paper by Markovsky and Lawler (1994) that both provides a comprehensive review of the solidarity literature and goes on to construct a new theory of solidarity, defining the latter concept in terms of structural properties of a social network.

This chapter has presented an analysis of the "big problem" of solidarity in sociological theory and an attempt to translate it into an agenda of problems involving formalization. It is our hope that the agenda we have set out will not be viewed as some sort of private property of the authors. On the contrary, we have formulated it in the hope of stimulating contributions addressing this important problem in sociology through original formal-theoretical means building on the two traditions of sociological theory and mathematical sociology.

NOTES

1. The problem of shared awareness is relevant to the interaction ritual chain model discussed below. Another example of an algebra of shared awareness connected with human reflexivity is set out and developed by Lefebvre (1977).

2. To be sure, according to the Collins model, every enduring social relation may itself have its ritual interaction aspect that helps account for the intensity of that bond.
3. In a formal model, we could also look for chaotic attractors as solutions under certain parametric conditions.
4. In a comment to us, Hechter has argued that we have misunderstood his theory, that it does not assume groups, only individuals. We think his use of such concepts as "extensiveness of a group's obligations" and "dependence of member on the group," indicates otherwise. Note, for instance, that the concept of dependence used by Emerson (1972) is a directed relation between actor *a* and actor *b*, while Hechter's dependence relation is between actor *a* and collectivity *b*. For a recent statement related to his theory of solidarity, see Hechter (1994).
5. Doreian et al. (1996) use the Newcomb (1961) data (see Nordlie, 1958), to show the movement of a human group towards the macro-structural property of balance through time.
6. The Cartwright and Harary generalization invited this elimination by dropping the distinction between affect ties and unit formation ties. In the transformation of a relational structure to a signed graph, attention was focused on the signed graph. Distinctions between relational ties and the perceptions concerning those ties were eliminated also.
7. The notation used here was developed in the context of developing a formal concept of institution for sociology. See Fararo and Skvoretz (1984).
8. For a pioneering effort to conceptualize a solidarity system in terms of the AGIL scheme, see Baum (1975).

REFERENCES

Alba, Richard D. 1990. *Ethnic Identity: The Transformation of White America.* New Haven, CT: Yale University Press.
Alexander, Jeffrey C. and Paul Colomy. 1990. eds. *Differentiation Theory and Social Change.* New York: Columbia University Press.
Baum, Rainer. 1975. "The System of Solidarities." *Indian Journal of Social Research* **16**: 307–352.
Berger, Joseph, Bernard P. Cohen, J. Laurie Snell, and Morris Zelditch, Jr. 1962. *Types of Formalization.* Boston: Houghton-Mifflin.
Boyd, John P. 1969. "The Algebra of Group Kinship." *Journal of Mathematical Psychology* **6**: 139–167.
Breiger, Ronald L. 1974. "The Duality of Persons and Groups." *Social Forces* **53**: 181–190.
Cartwright, Dorwin and Frank Harary. 1956. "Structural Balance: A Generalization of Heider's Theory." *Psychological Review* **63**: 277–293.
Chase, Ivan D. 1982. "Dynamics of Hierarchy Formation: The Sequential Development of Dominance Relationships." *Behavior* **80**: 218–240.
Coleman, James S. 1954. "An Expository Analysis of Some of Rashevsky's Social Behavior Models." Chapter 3, pp. 105–165, in Paul F. Lazarsfeld (ed.) *Mathematical Thinking in the Social Sciences.* New York: Free Press.
———. 1960. "The Mathematical Study of Small Groups." Part One, pp. 7–149, of Herbert Solomon (ed.) *Mathematical Thinking in the Measurement of Behavior.* New York: Free Press.
———. 1964. *An Introduction to Mathematical Sociology.* New York: Free Press.
———. 1990. *Foundation of Social Theory.* Cambridge, MA: Harvard University Press.
Collins, Randall. 1981. "On the Micro-Foundations of Macrosociology." *American Journal of Sociology* **86**: 984–1014.
———. 1985. *Three Sociological Traditions.* New York: Oxford University Press.
———. 1988. *Theoretical Sociology.* Ch. 6. San Diego: Harcourt Brace Jovanovich.

Cook, Karen S., Mary Rogers Gilmore and Toshio Yamagishi. 1983. "The Distribution of Power in Exchange Networks: Theory and Experimental Results." *American Journal of Sociology* **89**: 275–305.

Davis, James A. 1967. "Clustering and Structural Balance in Graphs." *Human Relations* **20**: 181–187.

Dodd, Stuart C., E. Rainboth and Jiri Nehnevajsa. 1955. *Revere Studies in Social Interaction.* Public Opinion Laboratory, University of Washington. Seattle, WA.

Dodd, Stuart C. 1942. *Dimensions of Society.* New York: Macmillan.

Doreian, Patrick, Roman Kapuscinski, David Krackhardt, Janusz Szcypula. 1996. "A Brief History of Balance through Time." *Journal of Mathematical Sociology* **21**: 113–131.

Durkheim, Emile. 1964[1893]. *The Division of Labor in Society.* New York: Macmillan.

———. 1973[1898]. "Individualism and the Intellectuals." Ch. 4, pp. 43–57, in Robert N. Bellah (ed.) *Emile Durkheim on Morality and Society.* Chicago: University of Chicago Press.

———. 1915[1912]. *The Elementary Forms of Religious Life.* New York: Free Press.

Emerson, Richard M. 1972. "Exchange Theory: I and II." Chs. 3 and 4, pp. 38–87, in Joseph Berger, Morris Zelditch, Jr., and Bo Anderson (eds.) *Sociological Theories in Progress.* Volume Two. New York: Houghton Mifflin.

Fararo, Thomas J. 1989. *The Meaning of General Theoretical Sociology: Tradition and Formalization.* New York: Cambridge University Press.

——— and Patrick Doriean. 1984. "Tripartite Structural Analysis." *Social Networks* **6**: 141–175.

——— and John Skvoretz. 1984. "Institutions as Production Systems." *Journal of Mathematical Sociology* **10**: 117–181.

——— and ———. 1986. "E-State Structuralism." *American Sociological Review* **51**: 591–602.

Freeman, Linton C. 1992. "The Sociological Concept of "Group": An Empirical Test of Two Models." *American Journal of Sociology* **98**: 152–166.

Friedell, Morris. 1969. "The Structure of Shared Awareness." *Behavioral Science* **14**: 28–39.

Gibbs, Jack P. 1981. *Norms, Deviance and Social Control: Conceptual Matters.* New York: Elsevier North-Holland.

Goffman, Erving. 1967. *Interaction Ritual.* New York: Doubleday.

Hechter, Michael. 1987. *Principles of Group Solidarity.* Berkeley: University of California Press.

———. 1994. "The Role of Values in Rational Choice Theory." *Rationality and Society* **6**: 318–333.

Heckathorn, Douglas D. 1992. "Collective Sanctions and Group Heterogeneity: Cohesion and Polarization in Normative Systems." pp. 41–63 in Edward Lawler, Barry Markovsky, Cecilia Ridgeway and Henry A. Walker (eds.) *Advances in Group Processes.* Volume 9. Greenwich, CT: JAI Press.

Heider, Fritz. 1946. "Attitudes and Cognitive Organization." *Journal of Psychology* **21**: 107–112.

———. 1958. *Psychology of Interpersonal Relations.* New York: Wiley.

Heise, David R. 1979. *Understanding Events: Affect and the Construction of Social Action.* New York: Cambridge University Press.

Hirschi, Travis. 1969. *Causes of Delinquency.* Berkeley: University of California Press.

Homans, George C. 1950. *The Human Group.* New York: Harcourt, Brace & World.

———. 1958. "Social Behavior as Exchange." *American Journal of Sociology* **65**: 597–606.

———. 1974. *Social Behavior: Its Elementary Forms.* Revised Edition. New York: Harcourt Brace Jovanovich.

Jaeckel, Martin. 1971. "Coleman's Process Approach." pp. 236–275 in Herbert L. Costner (ed.) *Sociological Methodology 1971*. San Francisco: Jossey-Bass.

Lefebvre, Vladimir A. 1977. *The Structure of Awareness: Toward a Symbolic Language of Human Reflexion*. London: Sage.

Lorrain, Francois and Harrison C. White. 1971. "Structural Equivalence of Individuals in Social Networks." *Journal of Mathematical Sociology* 1: 49–80.

Markovsky, Barry and Edward J. Lawler. 1994. "A New Theory of Group Solidarity." pp. 113–137 in Barry Markovsky, Karen Heimer and Jodi O'Brien (eds.) *Advances in Group Processes*. Volume 11. Greenwich, CT: JAI Press.

Marwell, Gerald and Pamela Oliver. 1993. *The Critical Mass in Collective Action: A Micro-Social Theory*. New York: Cambridge University Press.

Mead, George Herbert. 1934. *Mind, Self and Society*. Chicago: University of Chicago Press.

Newcomb, Theodore M. 1953. "An Approach to the Study of Communicative Acts." *Psychological Review* 60: 393–404.

———. 1961. *The Acquaintance Process*. New York: Holt, Rinehard and Winston.

Nordlie, P.H. 1958. A Longitudinal Study of Interpersonal Attraction in a Natural Group Setting. Ph.D. Thesis, University of Michigan.

Parsons, Talcott. 1937. *The Structure of Social Action*. New York: Free Press.

———. 1951. *The Social System*. New York: Free Press.

———. 1967. *Sociological Theory and Modern Society*. Ch. 1: "Durkheim's Contribution to the Theory of Integration of Social Systems." New York: Free Press.

Rapoport, Anatol. 1956. "The Diffusion Problem in Mass Behavior." *General Systems Yearbook* 1: 48–55.

Rashevsky, Nicholas. 1959. *Mathematical Biology of Social Behavior*. (Rev. ed., original 1951). Chicago: University of Chicago Press.

Skvoretz, John and David Willer. 1991. "Power in Exchange Networks: Setting and Structural Variations." *Social Psychology Quarterly* 54: 224–238.

Smith-Lovin, Lynn and David R. Heise. 1987. *Analyzing Social Interaction: Advances in Affect Control Theory*. New York: Gordon and Breach.

White, Harrison C. 1963. *An Anatomy of Kinship*. Englewood Cliffs, NJ: Prentice-Hall.

——— and Scott A. Boorman and Ronald L. Breiger. 1976. "Social Structure from Multiple Networks, I. Blockmodels of Roles and Positions." *American Journal of Sociology* 81: 730–780.

Willer, David. 1987. *Theory of the Experimental Investigation of Social Structures*. New York: Gordon & Breach.

Wilson, Thomas P. 1982. "Relational Networks: An Extension of Sociometric Concepts." *Social Networks* 4: 105–116.

Wood, Gordon S. 1991. *The Radicalism of the American Revolution*. New York: Random House.

Part II

Rationality and Solidarity

2 A THEORY OF THE STATE AND OF SOCIAL ORDER

SUN-KI CHAI and MICHAEL HECHTER

University of Arizona

After a long period of neglect, the problem of social order has recently revived in social science discourse. This revival is largely due to the efforts of theorists attempting to explain the conditions under which rational egoists cooperate. One line of analysis offers invisible hand theories suggesting how cooperation may emerge spontaneously among rational egoists under anarchy (Axelrod, 1984; Ullman-Margalit, 1977; Taylor, 1987; Calvert, 1991; 1994). Another, drawn from the new institutional economics,[1] focuses on the state's role in creating and maintaining cooperative equilibrium between individual actors (North, 1981; 1983; 1990; North and Weingast, 1989; see also Hardin, 1991).

Although these two kinds of theories have proven insightful, neither can account for the emergence of order in large groups, let alone national societies. The former theories assume that the attainment of order in national societies is fundamentally similar to that in small groups. However, it is implausible that large numbers of atomized individuals can cooperate as the members of small groups do: the coordination and monitoring problems are simply too severe (Hechter, 1993: 2). The latter theories simply take the state's existence for granted. Yet if – as is likely – the state must be invoked to solve the problem of order, then its formation and maintenance should be part of the explanation.

If atomized individuals cannot produce social order on their own, one alternative is to assume that cooperation can take place at a higher level of analysis – among a few large groups that encompass many individuals. The apparently insuperable difficulty involved in coordinating the actions of many disconnected individuals then reduces to the more manageable problem of coordinating the actions of a relatively small number of groups. But what justifies the treatment of these groups as unitary actors? If the key to this solution lies in group solidarity, then how does it come about? And what is the interaction between the groups' internal dynamics and their external relations?

The notion that there is a relationship between group solidarity and social order has been broached for centuries (it dates at least from Althusius [1614], 1964), but evidence for such a link is contradictory. One body of literature suggests that highly solidary civic groups promote social order because they deflect potentially destabilizing popular grievances into more productive channels (Tocqueville [1848], 1945; Kornhauser, 1959; Putnam, 1994). Another suggests that quasi-kinship groups in post-Confucian societies promote social order and cooperative economic outcomes (Hsu, 1963; Nakane, 1970; Murakami et al., 1981; Murakami, 1984; Tu, 1984).[2] Finally, the "consociational" literature argues that social order is fostered when the state exercises control via the elites of large communal groups (Lijphart, 1972; 1977).

However, still other literatures come to the opposite conclusion. The "plural society" literature argues that societies containing more than one large, highly solidary group will be plagued by intense political conflict (Furnivall, 1939; 1943; Smith, 1965).[3] Likewise, studies of rent-seeking interest groups blame them for economic decline which may ultimately presage social disorder (Olson, 1980; Krueger, 1974; Bhagwati, 1982).

To understand why groups sometimes promote order and sometimes inhibit it, a theory of group solidarity is required. Such a theory is missing from all of these literatures.

We attempt to explain social order by redressing this lacuna. Building on earlier research by Hechter and his associates (Hechter, 1987; 1993; Hechter, Friedman and Kanazawa, 1992; Hechter and Kanazawa, 1993) we formalize the theory of group solidarity, paying particular attention to the influence of group size, the extensiveness of corporate obligations, dependence, and coercion. Then we show how highly solidary groups and their control institutions can act as the building blocks for the state in large societies, facilitating social order by mediating between the state and individual members. As a result, social order is attained *indirectly* at a lower cost than the state must charge for providing it *directly*. The relative size of groups helps determine their contribution to social order: those that are either too large or too small will not attain optimal levels of social order. Last, we discuss some differences between voluntary and coercive social orders.

Part I offers a formal, rational choice model of group solidarity. It analyzes how the incentives for free riding affect the cost of attaining group solidarity through enforcement of member compliance with obligations to contribute to a set of joint goods. Next we turn to *dependence* – in particular, the opportunity cost to members of exiting from a group. Dependence affects the cost of enforcement and determines the upper bound on the size of contributions to joint goods that can be maintained without having the group unravel. Finally, we discuss *coercion*, the forcible removal of the exit option. Although high levels of dependence are conducive to group solidarity, under certain conditions they also lead to coercive control by one subset of members over another.

Part II extends this model to explain the formation and maintenance of the state. It proposes that states maintain order between groups in a fashion isomorphic to that which group control institutions maintain solidarity among individuals. A high level of solidarity is a prerequisite to the consideration of groups as unitary actors at the state level, and thus to their capacity to contribute to social order. Hence, the state emerges either as the control institution of a *supergroup* created by a small number of highly solidary groups to prevent mutual predation, or as a means used by one set of groups to impose its will on others.

The arrangement of these groups has important implications for social order (Part III). Whereas some form of group mediation between individuals and the state is always necessary to minimize the costs of maintaining social order, the optimal configuration of groups varies across social forms. Sometimes complex structures made up of multiple layers of nested groups are optimal for attaining social order; at other times simpler structures will do the trick. The optimal configuration of groups for the attainment of social order is a function of environmental influences on monitoring costs. These, in turn, affect the optimal size of groups. Dependence affects both the ability of groups to contribute to social order and the coerciveness of the resulting order. A brief summary of the argument and its implications for further research concludes.

PART I: A MODEL OF GROUP SOLIDARITY

We view groups not merely as collections of rational individuals, but also as encompassing control institutions shaping interactions between members. For analytic purposes, our initial focus is on *voluntary* groups whose members are free to exit and yet who choose to remain.

If individuals are rational actors (that is, maximizers of expected utility), then they will form a group only if membership provides each with a higher level of expected net benefit than that attainable elsewhere.[4] Hence the original impetus for group formation is the prospective member's desire to obtain the group's joint goods. Absent institutionalized and enforced mutual agreements, individuals are likely to engage in mutual predation, even if this results in lower net benefits for all concerned.

To consume the joint goods that motivate membership, individuals must agree to a set of corporate obligations (or rules) that permit the goods in question to be produced. However, the mere formation of a group and agreement to a set of corporate obligations (including, but not limited to production rules) is insufficient to guarantee compliance to them. Even if all the members have agreed to honor these obligations, each will do better by ignoring them when doing so is expedient.

Because ensuring compliance with corporate obligations is necessary to gain access to valued joint goods, members have an interest in creating a group-level control institution for monitoring and sanctioning one another. This institution perforce constrains members' freedom of action to some degree. By deterring free riding, the control institution assures actual and potential members that their contributions to the group will redound to their personal benefit. Group solidarity will be defined as *the extent to which members comply with their corporate obligations to contribute to the group's joint goods* (Hechter, 1987).

Let n_s be defined as the number of members in group s and c_{sy} as the cost borne by member y when she complies with her corporate obligation to contribute to the group's joint goods. In essence, c_{sy} is the gap between the net benefit a member would receive from compliance with this obligation, and the net benefit she would receive were she to free ride with impunity.[5] We do not attempt to determine the exact level of contributions required to produce a particular group's joint goods; this is left exogenous to the model. For the sake of simplicity, we initially assume that members are faced with one of two alternatives: to comply and absorb the associated costs, or to fail to comply and face sanctions if detected. A group will be assumed to punish known free riders with a one-time set of sanctions, after which these members can continue to participate with no further punishment, barring future noncompliance.

Therefore, being rational actors, members will comply only if the probability of detection multiplied by the sanctions imposed given detection equals or exceeds the benefits from noncompliance. Hence, a condition for compliance of member y in group s is $p_{sy}\, d_{sy} \geq c_{sy}$, where p_{sy} is the exogenously determined probability of detecting noncompliance in group s by member y, and d_{sy} is the amount of punishment meted out to member y in the event of detection. Note that the benefits an individual gains from group membership do not enter directly into this particular calculation, since they will be enjoyed regardless of compliance unless withholding them is part of the punishment.[6]

Assume now that p_{sy} is a function of the size of the group n_s, is equal for all individuals in the group (and hence can be referred to as p_s), and is differentiable and monotonically decreasing, that is $\partial p_s / \partial n_s < 0$. This assumption is justified by the intuitive notion that visibility is decreased in large groups, resulting in greater difficulty in monitoring. The exact shape of p_s may vary depending on a number of additional factors relating to characteristics of the surrounding environment.[7]

Sanctioning will be carried out by a control institution, which is in turn funded by group resources. Hence resources above and beyond those necessary to provide the joint goods must be expended by the group to generate and maintain its sanctioning capabilities.[8] These resources can quite reasonably be assumed to be a monotonically increasing function of the sum of sanctions $d_{s1} + \cdots + d_{sn}$ that must be imposed on each noncompliant member. Since it is optimal, if sanctions are costly, to provide just enough sanctioning to yield compliance, the amount of sanctions imposed will for detected noncompliance equal the cost of compliance divided by the probability of detection. This implies that the amount of sanctions increases as the probability of detection falls, and therefore that they increase with group size, since the probability of detection is inversely related to group size. Formally, for each member y, d_{sy} will be equal to c_{sy}/p_s. Hence, it follows that $\partial d_{sy} / \partial p_s < 0$. Since $\partial p_s / \partial n_s < 0$, it follows that $\partial d_{sy} / \partial n_s > 0$, since n_s has no effect on d_{sy} other than through p_s.

Let γ_s^1 indicate the amount of resources needed to maintain minimal adequate sanctions to ensure contributions from all members of the group s. The superscript indicates "first-order" resources, to distinguish it from other levels to be introduced later. It can reasonably be assumed that γ_s^1 is equal to some differentiable function Φ of d_s such that $\Phi' > 0$ and $\Phi(0) = 0$, where d_s is defined as $d_{s1} + d_{s2} + \cdots + d_{sn}$. It follows that $\partial \gamma_s^1 / \partial n_s > 0$ and $\partial \gamma_s^1 / \partial c_{sy} > 0$ for all y. γ_s^1 represents a cost of control in group s that must be borne by the group's membership. Hence, the existence of a control institution creates additional obligations over and above those entailed in merely producing the joint goods, and the extensiveness of these additional obligations is a monotonically increasing function of the original ones. These additional obligations – to fund the control institution – can be considered to be second order. Since second-order compliance entails additional costs to members, this increases the amount of sanctions that must be imposed on members who fail to comply with their obligations, and the resources for these additional sanctions must be provided by the membership. This creates third-order obligations, which in turn entail still more costs, and so on indefinitely. In other words, costly obligations have a multiplier effect because they increase the cost of control institutions in a recursive manner.

Let γ_s^j stand for the aggregate jth-order costs for the control institution of the group – that is, the resources required for monitoring and sanctioning first- to jth-order compliant behavior. Let γ_{sy}^j be the portion of those resources provided by member y. By definition, $\gamma_s^{j-1} = \gamma_{s1}^{j-1} + \gamma_{s2}^{j-1} + \cdots + \gamma_{sn}^{j-1}$. Under these conditions, the aggregate amount of punishment that needs to be provided to ensure that member y engages in jth-order compliance is γ_{sy}^{j-1}/p_s, for $j > 1$. If so, then $\gamma_s^j = \Phi((c_s + \gamma_s^{j-1})/p_s)$ where c_s is defined as $c_{s1} + c_{s2} + \cdots + c_{sn}$. The aggregate cost of the group control mechanism is γ_s^∞, which for brevity can be called γ_s. Its value is $\lim_{j \to \infty} \Phi((c_s + \gamma_s^{j-1})/p_s)$. Provided that γ_s^j converges, this implies that $\gamma_s = \Phi((c_s + \gamma_s)/p_s)$. The value of γ_s in terms of c_s and p_s will depend on the precise form of Φ. If γ_s^j does not converge, then clearly γ_s will have no finite value, and it will be impossible to ensure compliance with group obligations. It follows that the condition for solidarity in a group is that, given a distribution of contributions $(c_1, c_2, \ldots, c_n)$, there exists a distribution of second and higher-order contributions for enforcement $(\gamma_1, \gamma_2, \ldots, \gamma_n)$ and a distribution of punishments $(d_{s1}, d_{s2}, \ldots, d_{sn})$ such that $\forall y: p_s d_{sy} \geq c_{sy} + \gamma_{sy}$ and $\Sigma \gamma_{sy} = \Phi((\Sigma c_{sy} + \Sigma \gamma_{sy})/p_s)$, where γ_{sy} is shorthand for γ_{sy}^∞.

One major conclusion of this analysis is that the creation and maintenance of a control institution raises the extensiveness (hence, cost) of corporate obligations, and, through a multiplier effect, does so by an amount that is positively related to the size of the initial obligations. Another conclusion, however, is that by causing shifts in p_s – and hence in the magnitude of the multiplier effect – changes in group size can lead to major shifts in the total sanctioning costs.

These two conclusions indicate that the extensiveness of (first-order) group obligations and group size interact in raising the cost of group solidarity. This helps explain why groups demanding particularly extensive obligations (including cults, communes, underground revolutionary cells)[9] tend to be relatively small. Even with modern technology, it is extremely difficult to enforce extensive obligations in large groups.[10] This becomes evident when we discuss the forces that bind members to groups, namely dependence and coercion.

Dependence and the Boundaries of Groups

To this point in the analysis, attaining group solidarity has involved the creation of a control institution sufficiently effective to ensure compliance with corporate obligations. As long as there is some level of sanctions at which the aggregate jth-order costs do not exceed the level of sanctions multiplied by the probability of detection, group solidarity can be maintained.

This seems to indicate that group solidarity can be maintained no matter how extensive corporate obligations are, if total sanctions for first- and higher-order noncompliance can be set high enough: γ_s^j converges to a finite number. Otherwise, there is no limit on the extensiveness of the obligations a group can demand of its members, even if the resulting marginal benefits do not outweigh the costs.

However, to this point the analysis has ignored the benefits that individuals gain from membership in the group. More specifically, it is clear that members will not voluntarily join a group unless the benefits to be gained from membership exceed the costs. Let b_{sy} stand for the benefits gained by member y from the provision of the joint goods of group s. In order for a voluntary group to be viable, not only must enforcement costs γ_s^j converge, but it must also be the case that joint benefits exceed aggregate first- and higher-order costs, that is, $b_{sy} > c_{sy} + \gamma_{sy}$ for all y. If this is not so, then even if it is possible to induce compliance in equilibrium, such an equilibrium will never be reached because members will refuse to form a group.

Yet the analysis needs to pay heed not only to the absolute level of net benefits gained from membership in a group, but also to the difference between these net benefits and those that can be gained outside the group. This brings up an important characteristic of groups, namely the *dependence* of their members.[11] Let the *dependence* of group member y on group s be defined as the opportunity cost of exit from group s. This is the difference between the net benefits gained from membership in the group – that is, benefits b minus the aggregate costs $c_{sy} + \gamma_{sy}$, – and the net benefits (the "reservation wage") that the individual can gain outside a group or as a member of some alternative group. So far we have only analyzed the relationship between the costs of compliance, the size of different groups and the cost of maintaining order within different groups, implicitly assuming that benefits were uniform across different groups.

The assumption of uniform benefits may not be justified, however. Some groups may be able to provide greater benefits than others relative to costs of first-order compliance c_{sy} and costs of monitoring and sanctioning γ_{sy}. Individuals will realize greater benefits to the extent that a particular joint good is widely valued by members; then the group can specialize in producing that good. Contributions for the production of goods that are valued only by a subset of members do not provide any benefit for the rest.

Another type of dependence can be created by shared altruism among group members. To the degree that members are altruistic, then they benefit from each other's consumption of joint goods, in addition to that derived from their own consumption. Formally, altruism can be regarded as a shared preference for the joint good that is comprised of increasing members' welfare (Chai and Wildavsky, 1994; Chai, forthcoming). These benefits must be foregone when a person exits a group.

Dependence may also be created by complementary skills and capabilities. These may include similar skills such as a common expertise in the production of a mutually valued good, or commonly shared language and other modes of communication. Conversely, they may consist of a distribution of different skills among members that are necessary for the production of a particular good. A final source of dependence, one that favors the status quo, derives from the costs of moving from one group to another.

Typically, dependence is strongest among groups with a long history of interaction. Members of long-lived groups have had the opportunity to develop friendships and shared preferences that bind people together.[12] Long-lived groups therefore are more effective at providing joint benefits given equivalent size and obligations than those formed more recently. This chapter will not attempt to analyze the differential consequences of various sorts of dependence. Instead, it will look at the effects of dependence in general on the maintenance of group solidarity.

Suppose b_{sy} is the joint benefit provided by group s for member y during each period. If y complies, then y's net benefits for membership in the group will be $b_{sy} - c_{sy} - \gamma_{sy}$. Then the expected loss y suffers per period on leaving y and joining another group will be $b_{sy} - c_{sy} - \gamma_{sy} - \max(t \neq s: b_{ty} - c_{ty} - \gamma_{ty})$. In that case, the dependence of

y on s will be based on this amount, presumably extended over an arbitrarily large number of future periods (for simplicity, we will not consider the possibility that y may rejoin s at some future period). If z_{sy} refers to this dependence, then $z_{sy} = (1 + \delta + \delta^2 + \cdots)(b_{sy} - c_{sy} - \gamma_{sy} - \max(t \neq s: b_{ty} - c_{ty} - \gamma_{ty})) = (b_{sy} - c_{sy} - \gamma_{sy} - \max(t \neq s: b_{ty} - c_{ty} - \gamma_{ty}))/(1 - \delta)$, where $0 < \delta < 1$ is the discounting factor for the benefit that y gains in future periods.

If they are rational actors, prospective members will not voluntarily agree to join a particular group unless the benefits that can be gained in that group are larger than those attainable in all other alternative groups, that is, $z_{sy} > 0$. This is in effect a more stringent condition than the condition that $b_{sy} > c_{sy} + \gamma_{sy}$, i.e., $b_{sy} - c_{sy} - \gamma_{sy} > 0$, since it is always possible for a member to eschew all groups (which is equivalent to forming a "group" consisting only of itself), in which case its benefits and costs b_{ty}, c_{ty} and γ_{ty} will all be equal to 0.

As noted above, a member will comply only if the expected punishment for noncompliance $p_s d_{sy}$ is greater than the cost of compliance $c_{sy} + \gamma_{sy}$. However, note that the dependence of member y on voluntary group s will be positive. Then another option is available besides forcible punishment, and that is the expulsion of the member from the group if the member fails to comply and is detected. The expulsion option is attractive in that it does not require the maintenance of a sanctioning force; thus it creates incentives for compliance to production rules without additional costs in the form of second- and higher-order contributions.[13]

Hence expulsion can be used, either alone or in tandem with forcible punishment, in order to ensure contributions to the joint good. The functional form of the second- and higher-order costs of maintaining order will then be $\gamma_s^j = \Phi((c_s + \gamma_s^{j-1} - z_s)/p_s)$, where z_s is defined as $z_{s1} + z_{s2} + \cdots + z_{sn}$. Hence $\gamma_s = \Phi((c_s + \gamma_s - z_s)/p_s)$ when $c_{sy} \geq z_{sy}$ for all y. If there exist y for which $c < z_{sy}$, then we have $\gamma_{sy} = \Phi(e_{sy}/p_s)$, where $e_{sy} = c_s + \gamma_s - z_s$ when $c_s + \gamma_s - z_s > 0$ and $e_{sy} = 0$ otherwise. If $c < z_{sy}$ for all y, then $\gamma_s = \Phi(0) = 0$; thus there will be no second- or higher-order costs.

As this implies, dependence lowers the cost of maintaining solidarity in a group by reducing the extent to which sanctions need to be used to ensure compliance with group obligations. In doing so, it increases the level of group obligations (needed to obtain the joint goods) that can be required of members within a group, while maintainining sufficient incentives for members to join and remain in a group.

Dependence therefore puts a ceiling on the extensiveness of obligations that groups can demand of their members. It follows that groups with high levels of member dependence can demand more extensive contributions than those whose members are less dependent. Clearly, more extensive obligations sometimes can more than compensate for their costs due to the greater joint goods they provide.[14] Thus members actually may gain additional benefit from increasing their dependence, thereby making their exit option more remote. Paradoxically, the reduction of outside options for group members can increase the absolute benefit they can gain by remaining in their group.[15]

Coercion and its Relationship to Dependence

Thus far we have only considered groups in which membership is entirely voluntary. However, in the absence or shortage of dependence among some subset of group members, one other option for preventing wholesale exit from a group exists – coercion. Groups may affect members' calculus of compliance by restricting their exit options rather than by changing their net benefits for remaining in the group. More specifically, a coercive group control institution may punish those who attempt to leave, and therefore may be able to demand more extensive obligations from certain members than a voluntary one.[16]

Coercion, however, requires the expenditure of additional sanctioning resources beyond those necessary to ensure compliance with corporate obligations in voluntary groups. This can be modeled by considering a given member's incentives to exit as a kind of *negative dependence*. If a subset of members feels that they can gain more outside a group than within it, they will free ride and simultaneously attempt to exit the group unless the expected amount of punishment exceeds both the gains from free riding and the gains from exit. This implies that the amount of resources required to coercively keep a member from attempting to exit is $\Phi((c_s + \gamma_s - z_s)/p_s)$, where in this case, however, $z_s < 0$.

The costs of the coercive apparatus designed to keep certain members in a group must be borne by the membership or some subset of it. This subset may be the coerced members themselves, who thus may be required to support the very structure keeping them trapped within a suboptimal group. This kind of system may be feasible as long as the marginal costs of maintaining sanctioning resources are sufficiently low (otherwise the feedback costs of second-order rule-abiding behavior created by the need to fund the coercive apparatus will create additional incentives to exit that more than offset the deterrent effect of the apparatus), and as long as coerced members form only a small portion of the group's population.

If coerced members contribute a large percentage of the resources expended on coercive controls, however, then the possibility of simultaneous coordinated exit threatens the entire edifice. If one member attempts to leave the group, that member's contribution to the coercive apparatus is foregone, at least during the period when the exit is attempted. This does not significantly affect the viability of the coercive apparatus. However, if a large number of members attempts to exit simultaneously, their failure to contribute during this period will render the coercive apparatus so weak that it may be unable to prevent their exit.[17]

For this reason, coercion affecting more than a small proportion of the membership of a group often will be based on the contributions of those who are not being coerced (this in turn implies differences among members in their levels of dependence). The additional demands placed on dependent members to support the coercive apparatus require higher monitoring and sanctioning costs, which will have recursive effects that raise the cost of maintaining solidarity in the group. These additional burdens may give some previously uncoerced members an incentive to free ride and exit if they are found out. This leads to a feedback effect – an even greater number of members will have to be coerced into staying in the group. Hence the resources that have to be devoted to coercion will increase apace.

If nondependent members comprising some large proportion of the group are to be coerced from exiting the group, then some core of voluntary members must tax themselves to contribute toward the coercive control institution. This core must be highly dependent, else its members will exit rather than bear the cost of the coercive control institution. Hence the only groups that can coercively restrict the exit of large proportions of discontented members are those with other members whose dependence is high enough (*superdependence*) to offset the (additional) costs of coercion. This analysis therefore shows how the factors responsible for group solidarity can also facilitate coercion in a group.

It may seem counterintuitive to say that dependent members of a group would ever be in a position to coerce nondependent members, since nondependent members, with an available exit option, would have greater power in any bargaining that takes place between them. However, this can be understood by examining the relationship between bargaining power and incentives for coercion. We define coerced membership as a condition in which a member is forced to stay within a group even though she could do better elsewhere. Hence nondependence is a precondition for coerced membership. Those who are dependent do not need to be coerced, because they are willing to stay within the group voluntarily.[18] It is precisely because they lack bargaining power that dependent members may be willing to resort to coercion of nondependent members rather than negotiation. We are discussing incentives for coercion, and do not imply that the dependent members will always have the resources to carry out coercion. Nonetheless, dependent members will better be able to ensure internal solidarity among themselves than nondependent members. Hence they may more credibly threaten to collectively use sanctions to enforce prevent nondependent members from leaving, even if the provision of these sanctions involve costs.

PART II: GROUP SOLIDARITY, THE STATE AND SOCIAL ORDER

Part I described the conditions for the creation and maintenance of solidarity in relatively small groups. Why does this analysis have any implications for the attainment of social order? Evidently, group solidarity is not a sufficient condition for social order. On the one hand, control costs increase dramatically with group size. On the other, there is no guarantee that a number of highly solidary groups coexisting in the same environment will interact peacefully. Instead, some of these groups may promote *dis*order by using force to appropriate resources from more vulnerable ones.[19] To interact cooperatively, these groups must remain solidary and at the same time establish an institution that binds them together externally.

By now, this problem should be familiar. We proceed to extend the previous analysis to include *supergroups* whose individual members are not persons but groups. Note that this upward shift in the level of analysis does not fundamentally change the mechanism of group solidarity. By what sleight of hand can we possibly consider groups to be unitary actors? By no sleight of hand: *the higher the solidarity of a group, the more it can behave as a unitary actor.* To the degree that groups can control their own members, they can be considered as unitary members of higher-level groups. The rationale behind this assumption is straightforward: if groups can maintain internal solidarity, then they can guarantee that their members will not violate obligations enacted at a higher level of aggregation. If groups are solely responsible for monitoring and sanctioning their members, higher-level control institutions need not deal directly with these members directly.

Thus initial state can be seen as the control institution of a super-group (society) encompassing the various highly solidary groups of a given territory. For our purposes, societies differ from solidary groups in that they are much larger in scale. States are formed for the self-same reasons that group control institutions are formed – either as a voluntary agreement among groups, or as a coercive structure used by one set of groups against another. In the voluntary case, a state emerges in an anarchical environment when a number of groups come together to form a single control institution that resolves intergroup conflicts and reduces their predation.

Up to a point, therefore, we follow the basic Hobbesian logic on the formation of the state – with the important proviso that *in this part of the theory highly solidary groups are the relevant units of analysis, rather than individuals.* Just as individuals who may have a common interest in a good are unlikely to obtain it without a group control institution, so highly solidary groups with a common interest in social order are unlikely to obtain it without the state.[20] In the coercive case, a state is used by a coalition of groups to harness its combined force to dominate another set of groups. However, *high* group solidarity is a precondition for the attainment of social order via the formation of a state, be it voluntary or coercive.

Group solidarity can occur at more than one layer below the level of the state. After all, the members of groups can themselves be groups. The state can be regarded as the top level of a hierarchy of nested groups control institutions extending down to the individual level.[21] The attainment of order can be viewed analogously at each level of nesting, with the unit that is macro on one level becoming micro on the next highest level (Alexander et al., 1987). Group members that are themselves groups will have to expend resources sufficient to maintain internal order for them to be treated as virtual unitary actors, or corporate individuals (Coleman, 1990; 1993), at the next higher level of analysis. This will hold true down to the atomic levels where group members are single individuals.[22] This analysis does not imply that individual rationality in groups *always* leads groups to act in a collectively rational manner. Such a claim is patently false (Hannan, 1992). Instead, the model specifies a set of necessary conditions (those promoting group solidarity) that are required for a group of individuals (or lower-level) groups to behave as virtual unitary actors. There are a number of ways in which a group can be considered to be a rational actor. The most restrictive is when the group maximizes the utility function of each of its individual members. This generally is impossible unless everyone in the group shares exactly the same utility function. In our model, solidary groups are seen as rational because they behave as if they were corporate actors having a single utility function. However, this utility function need not necessarily represent those of all its individual members (Coleman, 1990, Part III).

Hence, attaining solidarity in a group is analytically similar to attaining order in a territory composed of multiple solidary groups; both are instances of the same generic processes. Social order is simply group solidarity writ large. The idea that state control is isomorphic to lower-level group control is not a new theoretical insight (Eckstein [1966], 1992), but it has never before been incorporated in theories of state formation and maintenance.

Doing so raises three related questions. Why are pre-existing social groups necessary for the formation of state? Why do such groups remain extant even after the state has formed? And what prevents unattached individuals from forming and maintaining a state? The answers hinge on the cost of maintaining a state, which is minimized when groups intervene between individuals and the state.[23] Let the efficiency of maintaining social order be defined as the ratio between γ_s (where S refers to the society as a whole) and the number of individuals in the society. Then the more resources that must expended to maintain order, *ceteris paribus*, the less efficient the society's control institutions are. It then can be shown that efficiency increases with the size of constituent social groups, even if the total population of the society remains constant and the costs borne by the groups increase proportionately with the number of individuals they encompass.

Let N be the total population of the society in individuals, and n be the number of groups into which the society is divided. If no groups mediate between individuals and the state, then n will simply be equal to N. Otherwise, the average size of groups will be N/n. If each individual in the society is expected to contribute some uniform amount c through the auspices of her group, and all groups in the society are of equal size, then the total cost borne by the average group will simply be $c(N/n)$. Let γ_S refer to the (infinite-level) aggregated costs of order in the entire society S. Then $\gamma_S = \Phi(n(c(N/n) + \gamma_S/n)/p_S) = \Phi((cN + \gamma_S)/p_S)$. Since Φ is a monotonically increasing function, $\partial\gamma_S/\partial n$

has the same sign as $\partial((cN + \gamma_S)/p_S)/\partial n$. This is equal to

$$\frac{\partial \gamma_S}{\partial n} \frac{1}{p_S} + \frac{\partial(1/p_S)}{\partial n}(cN + \gamma_S).$$

The second part of this sum is positive, since p_S is a positive and monotonically decreasing function of n while c, N and γ_S are all defined to be positive. Since $1/p_S$ is by definition positive, the first part of the sum also has the same sign as $\partial((cN + \gamma_S)/p_S)/\partial n$. This calculation allows $\partial \gamma_S/\partial n$ to be decomposed to the sum of an infinite series of terms, each of which is positive. Thus the total is also positive, and $\partial \gamma_S/\partial n > 0$.

Hence, given equal individual-level obligations, the presence of groups mediating between individuals and the state reduces the state's costs of maintaining order (Hechter, Friedman and Kanazawa, 1992; Hechter and Kanazawa, 1993; Hechter, 1993).[24] Group solidarity contributes to social order by regulating members' behavior, thereby constraining their opportunities to engage in anti-social behavior. Further, states in societies with fewer and larger groups at the sub-societal level will be more efficient at maintaining order than those in societies containing several groups, because they require a smaller outlay of resources *per individual* for monitoring and sanctioning.

State-Level Versus Group-Level Costs of Order

A critic of the previous analysis might argue that it biases the results by only considering the *state's* costs of maintaining order. The state's savings from group mediation, this critic would note, are simply being passed down to the groups, which have to take responsibility for maintaining solidarity among their members. Hence, the cost to society as a whole may be affected differently by this group mediation than the cost to the state.

In response, we argue that the state's costs are particularly important because they are the final determinant of the existence of social order. In addition, highly solidary groups may be capable of demanding contributions from their members that the state cannot, particularly when it is a new entity on which individuals are not highly dependent (see Stinchcombe, 1965, p. 148 on the liability of newness). And due to their scale, groups are much more capable of monitoring and sanctioning than the state can ever be (Hechter, Friedman and Kanazawa, 1992; Hechter and Kanazawa, 1993). Nonetheless, the total social costs at all levels are important since they determine the overall burden borne by individuals. Rational egoists always seek to minimize these costs. Even when total social costs are taken into consideration, however, it can be shown that group mediation reduces the costs of maintaining order.

An appropriate measure of the total resources necessary to maintain order in society S is the total resources needed to maintain order between the various groups in society plus the total of the resources needed to maintain solidarity within each group. Let Γ_S be this quantity, which is defined recursively as $\Gamma_S = \gamma_S + \Sigma\Gamma_s$ for all members $s \in S$, and where $\Gamma_S = 0$ when s is a solitary individual. As the number of groups decreases in a society of fixed population, the average size of groups increases, and the cost of maintaining group solidarity rises as the cost of maintaining order between them falls.[25] By this logic, although incorporation into a few large groups lowers the amount of resources devoted to maintaining order at the societal level, it simultaneously raises the amount of resources devoted to maintaining solidarity at the group level.

Which scale of nested control institutions is most conducive to the maintenance of social order at the lowest total cost? The issue is complex, since no arrangement is most efficient at all levels of analysis. Consider the simplest case, where hierarchies are structured such that all groups at each level contain some uniform number of members. This number, n, can be seen as some measure of the shallowness of the chains of control in a society. Where $n = N$, a mass society having only a single level of authority between the state and atomized individuals obtains. At the other extreme, the deepest hierarchy will be one in which no group has more than a few subgroup members.

As noted earlier, the value of γ_S at the state level is $\Phi((cN + \gamma_S)/p_S)$. At the next layer of the hierarchy, the cost of maintaining order among subgroups within each group s is $\Phi((cN/n + \gamma_S)/p_S)$.[26] Hence the total cost of maintaining order at this level will be $n\Phi((cN/n + \gamma_S)/p_S)$. A similar logic can be used to calculate costs at lower levels of control. In general, Γ will be the sum of the costs at all of these levels.

While it is difficult to characterize the value of n that will minimize Γ, it is possible to show that there exist plausible Φ and p_S so that group mediation between the state and individuals can reduce Γ. For instance, suppose Φ is a linear function. Then $\gamma_S = \Phi((cN + \gamma_S)/p_S) = V(cN + \gamma_S)$, where V is simply the slope of Φ, divided by p_S. Then $\gamma_S - V_n\gamma_S = VcN$, and $\gamma_S = (V/(1-V))cN$. At the next layer of hierarchy, the cost of maintaining order among each subgroup will be $\gamma_S = V(cN/n + \gamma_S) = (V/(1-V))cN/n$. However, since there are n groups at this level, the total cost of maintaining order at the level will be $(V/(1-V))cN$, as well. A similar logic holds at lower levels; hence it can be concluded that such uniformly nested hierarchies will have equal total costs of maintaining order at each level all the way down the hierarchy, and that this cost will be equal to γ_S.

Thus the total (aggregate first- and higher-order) cost of maintaining order is simply equal to the number of layers multiplied by the cost at each layer, γ_S. Since each layer reduces the size of groups by a factor of n, the number of total layers will be such that $n^l = N$, where l is the number of layers. Therefore (ignoring indivisibilities) the total cost of maintaining social order will be minimized when $\log_n(N)\Phi((cN+\gamma_S)/p_S)$ is minimized. As a function of n, this is minimized when $(\ln(N)/\ln(n))\Phi((cN+\gamma_S)/p_S)$ is minimized, which in turn is minimized when $(cN+\gamma_S)/(p_S\ln(n))$ is minimized. Using a similar method as above, this can be seen as the sum of an infinite series of terms, each of which is minimized when $1/(p_S\ln(n))$ is minimized, that is, when $p_S\ln(n)$ is maximized. The first-order condition is $\partial(p_S\ln(n))/\partial n = 0$. This is true when $n\ln(n) = -d/(\partial p_S/\partial n) = (1/p_S)/(\partial(1/p_S)/\partial n)$. More concretely, it is clear that $n = 1$ is not optimal, since $\ln(1) = 0$. Hence, up to some point mediation between individuals in the state will reduce the total societal costs of maintaining order. However, for sufficiently steep d functions vis-a-vis n, it is clear that $n = N$ will not be optimal either, and there will be an interior solution.

The steepness of the relationship between group size and the cost of monitoring and sanctioning has a tendency to reduce the optimal number of members in groups at each layer. This implies that when groups grow larger and monitoring becomes more difficult, social order can be maintained most efficiently overall through narrow and deep chains of authority. When monitoring is less problematic, broad and shallow chains of authority are less costly.

Narrow, deep chains of authority seem to characterize the structure of small supergroups that are particularly difficult to monitor. This is one reason why underground political and military organizations tend to organize themselves into small cell structures (Chai, 1993). A similar structure characterizes societies lacking advanced communications, where distance and cultural diversity impede monitoring outside group boundaries. This analysis may explain how some societies are organized into a few groups just below the state level having narrow deep chains of control (as in feudalism), while others are divided into more numerous groups with broader and more shallow lines of control (as in modern unitary bureaucratic states). It may hence offer an explanation

for the transition from patrimonial to bureaucratic state forms as described by Weber ([1922] 1968) and Tilly (1990), among many others.

Finally, this analysis has a clear, if indirect, relationship to organizational theories on the span of control and the configuration of
hierarchies. For instance, it formalizes the idea that as monitoring
becomes more difficult (as a function of size, or due to the complexity
of tasks at hand), lines of authority tend to become longer and
narrower (Blau, 1968).

The upshot of this analysis is that *some* sort of group mediation – or
indirect rule – is always necessary to minimize the cost of order in large
societies.[27] Yet mediating groups that are too large given the constraints of the environment may actually have a negative effect on
order, primarily because of the large amounts of resources they must
expend to maintain internal solidarity.

Dependence, Coercion and Social Order

Given that a state is simply a group composed of members that are
themselves groups, the arguments developed above about the effects of
dependence and the possibilities for coercion in groups also apply here.
At the time of state formation, the level of dependence of groups on
the state will be equal to the difference between amount of net benefit
they gain from the given state and that to be gained from a rival state,
or under anarchy. This level of dependence puts an upper ceiling on
the amount of sanctions that the state can impose on noncompliant
groups, which in turn puts a ceiling on the extensiveness of obligations
that can be demanded from these groups. As is the case in a group,
higher levels of dependence can actually allow states to produce more
valuable joint goods for member groups. High levels of dependence
among one set of members also may promote coercion, however, as
such groups may be able to form a coalition and mutually enforce each
other's contributions towards coercing nondependent groups to remain
in the state.

Besides these society-level manifestations of simple group phenomena, however, further issues are raised by the complex, nested
structure of the state. Dependence is important to the maintenance of
social order and possibility of state coercion. Social order may not be
attainable unless the members of intermediate groups are superdepen-
dent (in the sense used above). Without superdependence, it is impossible to use group control to enforce individual compliance with
additional, societal obligations. Hence, social order should vary with

member dependence of mediating groups. In turn, dependence is fostered by a long history of interactions. Japan, the most ordered large industrial society, appears to be a case in point (Hechter and Kanazawa, 1993).

Likewise, coercion at the societal level depends on superdependence in coercing groups to ensure their members' contribution to the coercive apparatus. Coercion also can be fostered by insufficient dependence of the members of coerced or oppositional (Hechter, 1993, pp. 8–10) groups, since the inability of such groups to participate in a planned simultaneous exit (such as secession) can reduce the amount of coercion required to keep such groups under control. The major implication is that states in which there is high variance in member dependence across groups will be most prone to coercive rule. This analysis points out the need to distinguish between social order in general and voluntary order in particular. Dependence always fosters order, but the uneven distribution of very high levels of dependence can lead to coercive forms of order.

CONCLUSION

We have presented a formal model to investigate some aspects of group solidarity and its relationship to the attainment of social order. In doing so, we have also provided a parsimonious explanation of the formation of the state. Along the way, a number of hypotheses have been generated:

* High levels of group obligation interact with group size to raise the costs of maintaining group solidarity.[28] Hence groups that demand extensive obligations of their members will have fewer members than groups with less extensive obligations. The societal analog of this proposition is that states that demand extensive obligations – highly centralized ones – will tend to have deeper control institutions than those which demand less extensive obligations – federal ones. Because states that demand extensive obligations must employ more monitoring, they have to rely on smaller intermediate groups.
* Dependence sets an upper bound on the extensiveness of obligations any group can demand of its members. Further, dependence is a product of a long history of interactions. Since more extensive obligations often lead to more valuable joint goods, groups having long-standing, stable boundaries, and whose members have fewer exit alternatives, should produce the most valued joint goods.

Because a group's ability to contribute to social order is also a function of the dependence of its members, states are most likely to emerge on the shoulders of groups with long-standing boundaries and geographical and social impediments, such as ethnic groups.

- Whereas dependence is conducive to order, it is also conducive to coercion both within and between groups. Groups with highly dependent members are able to mobilize these members to exploit less dependent members by forcing them to stay in the group. Superdependence also enables some groups to coerce others to remain within a state control system. Thus coercive order should be most common in societies where part of the population belongs to long-standing communal groups and another part does not.

- The presence of solidary groups mediating between the state and individuals usually reduces the state's costs of maintaining order. Further, the larger the size of these mediating groups, the more the burden of maintaining order falls on groups rather than the state. This advantage is particularly important where individuals and groups have low dependence on the state and thus high autonomy from it; as a result, the state is incapable of imposing extensive obligations. Hence newer states with less autonomy (in general, those with fewer resources) will be particularly likely to be based on the mediation of larger groups and to rely on deeper lines of control.

- Finally, the total costs of social order are related in a complex way to the structure of nested control in a society, though some form of mediation will always be necessary to minimize costs. Apart from group dependence, the crucial factor determining the optimal structure for maintaining social order is the relationship between group size and the cost of monitoring group behavior. The steeper this relationship is, the deeper the optimal lines of control. Because this steepness is greatly influenced by the infrastructure of communication and surveillance, one should expect that socioeconomic modernization will tend to lead to shallower lines of control over time.

Thus, a model of group solidarity based on individual actors can not only account for the development of order among groups, but it can also explain the emergence of the state. This model generates new solutions to long-standing debates.

Much more work remains to be done, however. Most important, we have said nothing about how the benefits generated in a group or supergroup are distributed among its members. This modeling task lies ahead. We conclude by broaching few more substantive topics that will require analysis in the future: the development of state autonomy, the effect of the international system and the possibility of parallel membership in multiple groups.

State Autonomy

The state may originate as a set of agreements between social groups, but eventually it becomes an actor of its own that receives resources from groups, provides a wide variety of public goods and enforces laws (Skocpol, 1985; Krasner, 1984). The state not only interacts with groups; it can alter the nature of these groups. Whereas there is growing interest in the motives of the state as an actor and its effects on society (Levi, 1988; Bates, 1981; Magee et al., 1989), this literature generally takes the state as given rather than accounting for its origins.

The present model could incorporate state autonomy by positing that the formation of a state implies the creation of a special group that assumes responsibility for monitoring and sanctioning for the society. Initially this state-actor simply enforces agreements between a set of pre-existing groups. Later, however, the state-actor may attempt to modify the chain of authority, and to regroup the members of societies in a new set of sub-societal boundaries in order to maximize its own perceived utility (the creation of *départments* in Revolutionary France provides an apt example). Overall, the advent of the state transforms intergroup relations by creating a group that has special access to resources and coercive power. Thereafter, the remaining groups will attempt to provide sufficient resources to make the state effective, but not enough to allow it to coercively control them.

The International System

The present model provides a hermetically sealed view of social order. In common with most traditional models of social order, it considers a society to be a closed system insulated from exogenous forces. Despite this, the model can readily be extended to encompass interaction in the international system. Interaction between states in the international system quite properly can be considered isomorphic to the interaction of groups in a given territory. An analogous relationship exists between the internal order of societies and the ability of states to negotiate a common set of rules for interaction. In such a model, the difficulties of forming an all-encompassing world superstate can be linked to the initial inability of such a state to engender high levels of dependence among its member states, as well as the large number of existing states in the world, which makes the maintenance of order even at the top level relatively costly.[29]

Multiple Group Affiliation

Perhaps the most dramatic simplification in the present model is the assumption that social control institutions have a tree-like shape, with each individual and group located on a single line of control ultimately leading to the state. This is far from an accurate portrayal of most societies, particularly modern ones, where individuals simultaneously belong to several groups which are not nested in concentric rings or are only partially nested (Simmel [1922], 1955). The idea of a tree-like control institution was adopted as a simplifying assumption, one that presumably captures the fundamental characteristics of even more complex societies. Bringing more complex patterns of control into the model is quite possible, however, albeit with some loss in parsimony. In an altered model, compliance by individuals with obligations at the state level could take place through several parallel lines of mediation. In such a model it would be possible for compliance to occur along one line and not along another, thus allowing for partial compliance as well as compliance and noncompliance. This modification would make the calculation of optimal patterns of intermediation inordinately complex, but it would not change the basic calculus of obligations, monitoring and sanctioning that drive the results found here.

Group Member Heterogeneity

Much of the analysis above assumes for simplicity that all members of a group are identical in terms of the contributions they make and the benefits they receive from the group, the net utility that they gain from these, and the opportunitites they have outside the group. However, the model is quite compatible with extreme heterogeneity among group members, and indeed the assumption of heterogeneity is implicit in the discussion above of differential dependency and its relationship to coercion. Depending on the circumstances, group heterogeneity can have either a facilitating and inhibiting effect on member cooperation (Marwell and Oliver, 1993). Among the main points of interest for this model are the ways in which group heterogeneity affects variations in members' required contributions. While the model above treats required contributions as exogenously determined, they are clearly a product of bargaining that goes on among group members.[30] In particular, dependence can be seen to have a dual effect on the nature of that bargaining over relative contributions. Both nondependent and dependent members will have sources of leverage: nondependent members may credibly threaten to exit the group, yet dependent members may credibly threaten coercion in response. In order to determine how all this affects the nature of the control institution there is a need for a dynamic model of the bargaining process.

Although the present model offers far from the last word on these complex issues, it suggests that a host of significant questions can be explored through further formal analysis of the relationship between solidary groups, the state, and social order.

ACKNOWLEDGEMENTS

Earlier drafts of this essay were presented at the Conference on the Role of Institutions in the Public Sector, 9–10, November 1995, Netherlands Interuniversity Institute of Government, Oosterbeck, The Netherlands at the 1995 Annual Meetings of the American Sociological Association in Washington, DC, and in the Department of Sociology of the University of Stockholm. We are grateful to Göran Ahrne, Yoram Barzel, Patrick Doreian, Thomas Fararo, Satoshi Kanazawa, Edgar Kiser and Karl-Dieter Opp for their comments.

NOTES

1. This large body of literature focuses on the role of formal institutions in structuring interactions among rational actors. See, for instance, the review essays by Moe (1984) and Shepsle (1989).
2. For a rational choice application premised along these lines, see Hechter and Kanazawa (1993).
3. There have been some attempts to generate rational-choice models of such plural society arguments; see Rabushka and Shepsle (1972). More recent versions have stressed the problem of "commitment" among such groups experience in the absence of an effective state. See Fearon (1994) and Weingast (1994).
4. To this point in the analysis, we employ rational egoistic behavioral assumptions. Later, we consider the effects of altruistic preferences, but these are not fundamental for our results.
5. These contributions require groups to have more than one member, since a single member would be able to produce purely private goods and thus would face no free rider problem. A "group" of a single member is a trivial case, and such groups can be treated identically to the individual who comprises them.
6. Of course, it is implicit in the analysis that there be benefits b_{sy} exceeding c_{sy} in order for group membership to be worthwhile in the first place. We will discuss even more stringent conditions for voluntary membership in the section below on dependence.

7. A more precise model would account for the shape of p_s as a function of differences in the conduciveness of the environment to visibility, detection effort and monitoring technology. Even in such a more complex model, however, there would still be a negative relationship between the probability of detection and group size.

8. An alternative way of putting this is to say that the control institution is *itself* a joint good that is shared by group members. However, it is a special sort of joint good; one that is valuable because of its role in facilitating the production of other, more intrinsically valued joint goods.

9. The idea that rational choice principles of group solidarity can apply even in communes is pursued in Hechter (1991). An investigation of the dynamics of revolutionary cells can be found in Chai (1993).

10. This is evident in the case of the largest of groups, the state. Although modern technology has undoubtedly increased the state's ability to demand extensive obligations of its citizens, we are still some distance from the apocalyptic vision of Orwell's 1984.

11. For a detailed discussion of group dependence, see Hechter (1987, Chapter 3).

12. One way of understanding this type of dependence is as a particular kind of asset specificity (Williamson, 1985, pp. 53–63).

13. We are assuming here that loss of a member has neither costs nor benefits for the group. Under these conditions, there is no reason for the group to institute anything less than a permanent expulsion threat, since such a threat will be credible and will have the maximum deterrent effect. If loss of a member is not cost-free, there may be a reason for the group to use temporary rather than permanent expulsion as punishment. However, the complexity of such analysis will not change the basic point that member dependence will lower a group's enforcement costs.

14. In voluntary groups, greater obligations will not be demanded unless they produce joint goods of greater quantity or value.

15. This in effect is a multilateral version of the credible commitment phenomenon in bargaining theory. Each group member can, due to her dependence, credibly commit to contributing both to the joint good and to the control institution, as long as the others are doing so as well. As a result, the group can achieve a cooperative equilibrium that benefits all members.

16. Whereas the Soviet Union prohibited its citizens to exit (Reykowski, 1994), many intentional communities merely have confiscated the property of members who chose to exit.

17. Such a possibility requires disaffected members to have their own collective action mechanism, however.

18. Nor should we expand the definition of coercion so that a member's willingness to remain in a group due to dependence is seen as a case of dependency-induced coercion (as in wage slavery). This would imply that all choices which involve tradeoffs between costs and benefits are thereby coercive since the actor must bear costs to gain the benefits, regardless of whether they involve the threat of sanctions by other actors.

19. For a deeper discussion of predatory and oppositional groups that decrease social order, see Hechter (1993).

20. This does not deny the fact that states are more likely to be built around specialized institutions of control with significant autonomous power than are lower-level groups. We do not think that this difference is crucial for our central arguments about the effect of size on enforcement and the importance of intermediary groups. Further, there are cases, as in feudalism, where the state may sometimes be little more than a coordinating mechanism between the member realms. Likewise, even relatively lower-level groups of individuals, such as clubs or cooperatives, may designate certain members as those in charge of monitoring and enforcement. We do not analyze here the implications of any autonomous power of the state/control

mechanism – see discussion at end of paper for some suggestions on how such analysis might proceed. Thanks to Satoshi Kanazawa for bringing up this issue.

21. As implied by the term hieararchy, the nesting of groups follows a simple tree structure, where each group is a member of at most one group at the next highest level, and where group memberships at the same level do not overlap. Individuals will be at the bottom of this hierarchy, and the simple noncyclical nature of the hierarchy will imply that each individual will belong to only a single chain of group membership.

22. Incidentally, in this theory it is not necessary that this atomic level occur at the same level of the hierarchy for each chain of authority. Thus it is possible for some members at the same level of the structure to be individuals and others to be groups consisting of more than one individual.

23. In some historical circumstances, states created groups de novo in order to extend their control. Thus the Spanish Crown established the Mesta, a shepherd guild, to facilitate its revenue extraction (Klein, 1919).

24. What about predatory (organized criminal) and oppositional (potentially revolutionary) groups, whose very existence obviously represents a potential threat to social order? Recall that the possibility of predation is what motivates the establishment of the state in the first place. Predatory groups are best viewed as the consequences of incomplete social order, but due to monitoring costs in large societies it is unlikely that they can ever be eradicated (for an excellent analysis, see Barzel, 1995). Oppositional groups have a negative dependence on a society, and thus have an interest in overturing the prevailing order. Even then, however, their existence does not increase the cost of maintaining order in our theory, since absent these groups acting as mediating entities the state would have to impose compliance on a set of disaffected individuals directly, which would entail even greater monitoring costs. The cost of sanctioning in this model is related to ensuring positive contributions to the state, not preventing negative contributions, such as military rebellion. Note, however, that organization of individuals for the former does not necessarily entail organization for the latter, or vice-versa.

25. If this were not true, it would be possible to eliminate any cost of order in a society by creating a single all-encompassing group immediately below the state level. As long as within-group order must be maintained, however, such a step will have no effect on the cost of order, since it will effectively transfer all the costs from the state level to the group level without any other change in configuration.

26. Since the number of members at each level is the same, we can from here on refer to the probability of detection at all levels as p_s.

27. Tilly (1990) has an excellent discussion of the importance of indirect rule in the early development of the modern state, but he considers it irrelevant in the contemporary situation. This view is quite mistaken, however. For reasons that this theory elucidates, indirect rule continues to be essential to the production of social order even in the most developed states today.

28. The level of group obligation may be endogenous, however. Wherever it is easier to achieve more of it will be demanded, and the number of members will increase.

29. This may also explain why a super-state unit such as the European Community was formed as out of a smaller collection of mutually interdependent states.

30. Thanks to Yoram Barzel for bringing up this point.

REFERENCES

Alexander, Jeffrey et al. (1987) The Micro-Macro Link. Berkeley: University of California Press.

Althusius, Johannes ([1614] 1964) *Politica Methodice Digesta, Atque Exemplis Sacris et Profanis Illustrata*. Translated as *The Politics of Johannes Althusius* by Frederick S. Carney. Boston: Beacon Press.

Axelrod, Robert (1984) *The Emergence of Cooperation*. New York: Basic Books.

Barzel, Yoram (1995) Economic rights, legal rights and the evolution of the state Unpublished manuscript, Department of Economics, University of Washington.

Bates, Robert (1981) *Markets and States in Tropical Africa: The Political Basis of Agricultural Policies*. Berkeley: University of California Press.

Bhagwati, Jagdish N. (1982) Directly unproductive, profit-seeking (DUP) activities. *Journal of Political Economy* **90**: 5 (October), 988–1002.

Blau, Peter (1968) The hierarchy of authority in organizations. *American Journal of Sociology* **73** (January), 453–457.

Calvert, Randall (1991) Elements of a theory of society among rational actors. Unpublished manuscript, Department of Political Science, University of Rochester.

Calvert, Randall (1994) Rational actors, equilibrium and social institutions. In Jack Knight and Itai Sened (Eds.), *Explaining Social Institutions*. Ann Arbor: University of Michigan Press.

Chai, Sun-Ki (1993) An organizational economics theory of anti-government violence. *Comparative Politics* **26**: 1(October), 99–110.

Chai, Sun-Ki and Aaron Wildavsky (1994) Cultural theory, rationality and political violence. In Dennis J. Coyle and Richard J. Ellis (Eds.), *Politics, Culture and Policy: Applications of Cultural Theory*. Boulder: Westview Press.

Chai, Sun-Ki (Forthcoming) *Choosing an Identity: A General Theory of Preference and Belief Formation*. Ann Arbor: University of Michigan Press.

Coleman, James S. (1990) *Foundations of Social Theory*. Cambridge, MA: Belknap Press of Harvard.

Coleman, James S. (1993) The rational reconstruction of society. *American Sociological Review* **58** (February), 1–15.

Eckstein, Harry ([1966] 1992) A theory of stable democracy. In *Regarding Politics*. Berkeley: University of California Press, 179–226.

Fearon, James (1994) Ethnic warfare as a commitment problem. Unpublished manuscript, Department of Political Science, University of Chicago.

Furnivall, J.S. (1939) *Netherlands India*. Cambridge: Cambridge University Press.

Furnivall, J.S. (1948) *Colonial Policy and Practice*. London: Cambridge University Press.

Hannan, Michael T. (1992). Rationality and robustness in multilevel systems. In James S. Coleman and Thomas J. Fararo (Eds.), *Rational Choice Theory: Advocacy and Critique*. Newbury Park: Sage Publications.

Hardin, Russell (1991) Hobbesian political order. *Political Theory* **19**: 2 (May), 156–180.

Hardin, Russell (1990) The social evolution of cooperation. In Karen S. Cook and Margaret Levi (Eds.), *The Limits of Rationality*. Chicago: University of Chicago Press, 358–379.

Hechter, Michael (1987) *Principles of Group Solidarity*. Berkeley: University of California Press.

Hechter, Michael (1990a) The emergence of cooperative social institutions. In Hechter, Karl-Dieter Opp and Reinhard Wippler (Eds.) *Social Institutions: Their Emergence, Mainenance and Effects*. Berlin: Walter de Gruyter.

Hechter, Michael (1990b) The attainment of solidarity in intentional communities. *Rationality and Society* **2**: 2 (April), 142–155.

Hechter, Michael (1993) From group solidarity to social order. Unpublished manuscript, Department of Sociology, University of Arizona.

Hechter, Michael, Debra Friedman and Satoshi Kanazawa (1992) The attainment of global order in heterogeneous societies. In James S. Coleman and Thomas J. Fararo (Eds.), *Rational Choice Theory: Advocacy and Critique*. Newbury Park, CA: Sage Publications, pp. 79–97.

Hechter, Michael and Satoshi Kanazawa (1993) Group solidarity and social order in Japan. *Journal of Theoretical Politics* **3**: 4, 455–493.

Hsu, Francis L.K. (1963) *Class, Clan and Club*. Princeton: Van Nostrand.

Klein, Julius (1919) *The Mesta: A Study in Spanish Economic History*, Cambridge: Harvard University Press. 1273–1836.

Kornhauser, William (1959) *The Politics of Mass Society*. Glencoe: Free Press.

Krasner, Stephen D. (1984) Approaches to the state: alternative conceptions and historical dynamics. *Comparative Politics* (January), 223–246.

Krueger, Anne O. (1974) The political economy of the rent-seeking society, *American Economic Review* **64**: 3 (June), 291–303.

Levi, Margaret (1988) *Of Rule and Revenue*. California: University of California Press.

Lijphart, Arend (1969) Consociational democracy. *World Politics* **21** (January), 207–225.

Lijphart, Arend (1977) *Democracy in Plural Societies*. New Haven: Yale University Press, 1977.

Magee, Stephen P. and William A. Brock and Leslie Young (1989) *Black Hole Tariffs and Endogenous Policy Theory*. Cambridge: Cambridge University Press.

Marwell, Gerald and Pamela Oliver (1993) *The Critical Mass in Collective Action: A Micro-Social Theory*. Cambridge: Cambridge University Press.

Moe, Terry (1984) The New Economics of Organization. *American Journal of Political Science* **28**: 739–777.

Murakami, Yasusuke, Shumpei Kumon and Seizaburo Sato (1981) *Bunmei to shite no Ie Shakai*. Chuo Koronsha.

Murakami, Yasusuke (1984) Ie shakai as a pattern of civilization. *Journal of Japanese Studies* **10**: 2 (Winter), 281–363.

Nakane, Chie (1970) *Japanese Society*. Berkeley, UC Press.

North, Douglass (1981) *Structure and Change in Economic History*. New York: W.W. Norton.

North, Douglass (1983) A theory of institutional change and the economic history of the western world. In Hechter (Ed.), *The Microfoundations of Macrosociology*. Temple University Press.

North, Douglass (1990) *Institutions, Institutional Change and Economic Performance*. Cambridge: Cambridge University Press.

North, Douglass and Barry Weingast (1989) Constitutions and commitment: the evolution of institutions governing public choice in seventeenth-century England. *The Journal of Economic History* **46**: 4 (December), 803–832.

Olson, Mancur (1982) *The Rise and Decline of Nations: Economic Growth, Stagflation and Social Rigidities*. New Haven, Yale University Press.

Putnam, Robert (1994) *Making Democracy Work*. Princeton: Princeton University Press.

Rabushka, Alvin and Kenneth A. Shepsle (1972) *Politics in Plural Societies: A Theory of Democratic Instability*. Columbus: Charles E. Merrill.

Reykowski, Janusz (1994) Why did the collectivist state fail? *Theory and Society* **23**: 2, 233–252.

Rule, James B. (1988). *Theories of Civil Violence*. Berkeley: University of California Press.

Shepsle, Kenneth (1989). Studying institutions: some lessons from the rational choice approach. *Journal of Theoretical Politics* **1**: 2 (April), 131–147.

Simmel, Georg ([1922] 1955). The web of group affiliations. In *Conflict and the Web of Group Affiliations*, translated by Reinhard Bendix. New York: Free Press, pp. 125–195.

Smith, M.G. (1965) *The Plural Society in the British West Indies*. Berkeley: University of California Press.

Skocpol, Theda (1985) Bringing the state back in: strategies of analysis in current research. In Peter B. Evans, Dietrich Rueschemeyer and Skocpol (Eds.), *Bringing the State Back In*. Cambridge: Cambridge University Press, pp. 3–44.

Stinchcombe, Arthur L. (1965) Social structure and organizations, In James G. March, (Ed.), *Handbook of Organizations*. Chicago: Rand McNally.

Taylor, Michael (1987) *The Possibility of Cooperation*. Cambridge: Cambridge University Press.

Tilly, Charles (1990) *Coercion, Capital and European States, AD 990–1990*. Cambridge, MA: Blackwell.

de Tocqueville, Alexis ([1848] 1945) Democracy in America. New York: Alfred Knopf.

Tu, Wei-Ming (1984) *Confucian Ethics Today: The Singapore Challenge*. Singapore: Government Printing Office.

Ullman-Margalit, Edna (1977) *The Emergence of Norms*. Cambridge: Cambridge University Press. 19 October, 1995.

Weber, Max ([1922] 1968). Guenther Roth and Claus Wittich (Eds.), *Economy and Society*. New York: Bedminster Press.

Weingast, Barry (1994) Institutionalizing trust: the political and economic roots of ethnic and regional conflict. Unpublished manuscript, Department of Political Science, Stanford University.

3 SOLIDARITY: ITS MICROFOUNDATIONS AND MACRODEPENDENCE. A FRAMING APPROACH[1]

SIEGWART LINDENBERG

University of Groningen

1. INTRODUCTION

I get by with a little help from my friends (de Graaf and Flap, 1988). Having friends in important places is surely a useful thing, and one of the important changes in network analysis is the attention to the fact that people do not just have networks but actively build networks (Kaplan, 1984; Grieco, 1987). Ties are social resources, a network is social capital (Ben-Porath, 1980; Flap, 1988; Coleman, 1990; Burt, 1992). My social capital will provide me with important information, help me in need, get me favorable treatment, etc. There are stories abound how businessmen invite each other to expensive dinners, keep track of social events, like birthdays and quite generally invest in befriending those business partners whose trust they need most. Casson (1991, p. 20) speaks of "the engineering of trust". Heimer (1992, p. 143) even argues that organizational life is much about helping your friends and that relations in organizations are among named individuals who know one another as particular others.

Attention to this active side of people's pursuit of social ties connects nicely with sociology's most revered topic: solidarity. What it adds to this traditional topic is the possibility that solidary relations are not only "naturally" grown but also strategically created or maintained. In this way, it seems that traditional sociology is brought together with rational choice sociology in a very congenial way. The term "social capital" suggests that both sides have been covered: the social and the rational side. If this is correct, it would constitute a major advance because, as Hechter (1987, p. 30) argues at length, there is a severe problem with traditional sociology. Although much of the work in sociology is based on the concept of solidarity, neither normative, functional, nor structural explanations provide adequate accounts of when solidarity is likely to occur and how it is brought about. Hechter (1987, p. 31) goes on to argue that a satisfactory theory should be based on microfoundations and that the best elaborated theory of action in the social sciences is that of rational choice. Thus, if theories of social capital indeed provide us with the missing microfoundations of a theory of solidarity, we would have advanced a great deal.

I would like to argue here that rational choice theories of solidarity (including theories of social capital) do not offer these microfoundations, and that also the "classical" attempts which offer some microfoundations are seriously wanting. In this chapter, I would like to make an attempt to furnish such microfoundations.[2] Before I will get into the microfoundations themselves, I would like to do three things. First, I will turn to the question what kind of behavior patterns constitute solidarity. It is this kind of behavior that needs to be explained. Then I will briefly discuss why I think even the most sophisticated traditional sociological accounts of solidarity are wanting. Finally, I will try to show that the three kinds of rational choice theories developed to overcome problems with the traditional explanations have by and large not succeeded in doing so.

2. SOLIDARY BEHAVIOR: EXAMPLES

What is solidarity? How can it be defined in such a way that it covers the most important intuitive conceptions of the phenomenon? Hechter contrasts two basic ways to define solidarity:[3] through behavior or through sentiment (Hechter, 1987, p. 18f). The behavior refers to contributing private resources to collectively determined ends. The sentiment refers to love, fellow feeling or the feeling of brotherhood. He argues that the sentiments are much more difficult to measure than the proportion of an individual's private resources contributed to collective ends, and that therefore the behavioral definition should be used. It is perfectly legitimate to proceed like Hechter did but it is theoretically unsatisfactory to rest matters of conceptualization on the ease of measurement.[4] There is no discussion on the importance or unimportance of sentiment for solidarity, nor is there a distinction between kinds of solidary behavior that differ in other respects (for example, in the rules) than the individual's contribution to a collective end. For these reasons, I will proceed differently. I will begin with examples of what to me are instances of solidary behavior; I will then define solidarity more systematically in terms of five kinds of behaviors, with the claim that somebody who acts solidarily in some of the five situations but not in the others is not considered to act solidarily at all. Solidarity is thus a behavioral pattern *across* these five situations. Later on I will try to show why a definition of solidarity on the basis of sentiment is theoretically not satisfactory. Pragmatic issues of measurement do not enter this argument.

For convenience of the exposition, the examples that I will present are dyadic. This should not imply that there are no groups involved. The issue of groups will be dealt with later on. At this point, the reader might imagine Alter to be the representative of a group, and Ego to be a member of a group, but it is also possible to simply take them as two individuals.

First example: Ego and Alter are sisters, both very busy in their professional lives. Their old mother is ill. Alter goes there first to help her. Ego volunteers to take turns caring for the mother.

Second example: Alter is looking for a rare second-hand book and is willing to pay up to a hundred dollars for it. Ego knows this. He happens to find this book in a rummage sale for ten dollars. He buys it and will let Alter have it for the cost price: ten dollars.

Third example: Alter's house has been flooded by a rain storm. Ego helps him clean it up. There is no direct payment and even consideration of payment would be felt to be inappropriate.

Fourth example: Ego and Alter had agreed to pool their resources and start a restaurant together. They have worked out all the details of how they would do it. A third person turns up and proposes a different deal to Ego. At the moment, this new deal looks more attractive to Ego than the agreement with Alter but Alter would be disadvantaged if the agreement would not go through. Ego will stick to this agreement with Alter and not enter a deal with the third person, even though he thereby passes up a deal that looked better to him than the one he kept.

Fifth example: Ego has promised Alter to help clean up the mess from the rain storm but he does not show up. Later in the day, Ego calls Alter to say that he is sorry and explains why he was unable to come and even unable to notify Alter earlier.

In general terms, in each example, Ego contributes private resources without compensation, so all of them fall under Hechter's definition of solidarity. But in addition, each example stands for a type of situation in which Ego displays solidary behavior:

Common good situation   Ego and Alter both belong to a group that produces a common good. Ego will contribute to the common good even if he could free ride (the minimal amount of contribution in terms of money, effort, time etc. expected for solidary behavior varies).[5]

Sharing situation   If there are joint divisible benefits and costs and if Ego is the one who can divide them, he will not seek to maximize what he gets from the benefit and minimize what he gets from the costs but take his "fair share" of both (what the "fair share" is varies).

Need situation   Ego will help Alter in times of need (what constitutes need and how much help is minimally expected for solidary behavior varies).

Breach temptation   Ego will refrain from hurting Alter even at a cost to himself (the minimal amount of cost expected for solidary behavior varies).

Mishap situation   Acts can be intendedly solidary but factually turn out to go against the expectation of solidary behavior. In that case, Ego will show that he meant to act differently, that he feels sorry that it turned out that way, and he will make amends if the mishap has caused damage to others. Also, if Ego knows in advance that he will not be able to keep to the agreement, he will warn others in advance, so that they can mitigate the damage.

The claim is that these five situations cover all aspects of what one would intuitively call "solidary" behavior. Notice that solidary behavior is much more than just being cooperative behavior (i.e. behavior in common good situations). A theory of solidarity would have to explain why solidarity is not just cooperative behavior in common good situations and why it covers the other four situations as well. Each of the five situations asks for a sacrifice of Ego and there are trying times when the sacrifice may be expected to be particularly high. For example, when each member has to put in extra time to work on the common good, or when a number of members are struck by disaster and they need help. The *strength* of solidarity in a particular group can now be defined as the sum of the legitimately expected sacrifices (in terms of time, money, effort) in trying times (over all five solidarity situations). Let us call this sum *solidarity costs*. A theory of solidarity would also have to explain ordinal differences in the strength of solidarity.[6]

3. WHAT IS WRONG WITH DURKHEIM?

Everybody agrees that Durkheim is the major sociological theorist on solidarity. There is probably less consensus about elaborations after Durkheim and their relationship to what "the master" had done. I would like to maintain that Durkheim's theory of mechanical solidarity is still the most sophisticated theory of that phenomenon within traditional sociology, and elsewhere I have devoted considerable effort to reconstructing Durkheim's contribution in detail (see Lindenberg, 1975). In this chapter, there is only room to mention a few highlights of this complex theory.

The standard view, one that some of Durkheim's own formulations have helped to foster, is that mechanical solidarity is brought about by similarity, as if similarity by itself would somehow make people stick together. This is somewhat unfortunate because it leaves out the mechanism that connects similarity to the production of solidarity, and it is exactly in this point that Durkheim's theory is so interesting. The major point about the mechanism that brings about solidarity in Durkheim's theory is the dependence of the individual on the sentiments of others. The individual has one overriding goal: the coordination of energy of various physiological centers (Durkheim [1893] 1933, p. 97, mentions cortical centers, motor centers, sensorial centers and vegetative functions). Durkheim calls this coordinated energy "vitality". A sentiment is a belief with an affective (right/wrong) component. The stronger a sentiment the more it coordinates the energy of our various physiological centers. The individual is thus searching for strong sentiments that are congruent with the sentiment he or she already has. Because in interaction the strength of individual sentiments can fuse, collective sentiments (or what has come to be called "morality") are generally stronger than individual sentiments and individuals will seek out either exposure to these collective sentiments or exposure to a process in which individual sentiments can fuse. Sentiments contrary to our own weaken our vitality, and the stronger they are, the more they weaken it. Therefore, individuals will tend to avoid exposure to contrary sentiments and if they have been exposed to such sentiments, they will make extra efforts to strengthen their threatened vitality by interaction with others of similar sentiments. This can only be done by coming together face-to-face and expressing one to the other the adherence to the collective sentiments. This expressive behavior Durkheim called "ritual". Ritual interaction is the major vehicle of maintaining solidarity in the face of exposure to contrary sentiments. The more vitality individuals receive from collective sentiments, the more they value them and want to protect them from contrary sentiments. They become "sacred" and the rituals that protect them become more elaborate (Durkheim mentions alimentary communion, ritual sacrifice, dances, hymns, etc.) This, then, is the heart of mechanical solidarity. In recent times, Collins (1985) has followed this line of reasoning and Fararo and Doreian (see Chapter 1) discuss Collins' work in more detail.[7]

There are three important points that come out of this reconstruction of mechanical solidarity. First, mechanical and organic solidarity come much closer together than they seemed to be in traditional constructions of "similarity" (mechanical) versus "interdependence" (organic). Now it can be seen that, in both forms of solidarity, it is interdependence that creates the solidarity. In one case, it is the interdependence regarding the strength of sentiments and in the second, it is the interdependence through the division of labor. Second, mechanical solidarity is so important because the very organization of energy and motivation for the individual depends on the joint production of collective conscience. Third, because of the importance of joint production, solidarity is not a matter of dyads but of groups. Why would we need still another theory of solidarity, if Durkheim's theory is so powerful?

The answer to this question is that Durkheim had two major problems. First, his theory of action did not allow him to detect, let alone explain, problems of solidarity that come from the inside of the group. Second, his theory of action did not allow him to elaborate the relationship between mechanical and organic solidarity (i.e. the relation of internal and external threats to solidarity). The reason that a theory of solidarity has to be able to deal with threats to solidarity is that only then will it be able to explain the major puzzle: the behavior in solidary groups that is aimed at maintaining solidarity, i.e. aimed at mitigating these dangers. Let me briefly elaborate.

One can see right away that Durkheim's theory is not related to solidary *behavior*. There is no part of the theory that relates directly to the types of situations detailed above. This is serious because the action of maintaining solidarity (rituals) are not related to everyday actions. Maybe this lack might be repaired by adding assumptions on the link between solidarity and liking and then between liking and the various sorts of solidary behavior. But if one does that then solidarity is assumed to create a stable cooperative disposition. There is then no precariousness of cooperation. To me, a great admirer of the theory, the major flaw is exactly in this point. The theory is all about the benefits and contains nothing about the costs of solidarity. Therefore, the theory is very weak when it come to the description of the dynamics and precariousness of solidarity. Durkheim does not assume that solidarity is simply self-maintaining, because he had the anthropological evidence on periodic assemblies of tribes and the historical evidence of declining mechanical solidarity. But he has no clue where the built-in problems of solidarity lie. For him, the major threat to solidarity comes from the outside through contrary sentiments. Basically, as long as you stick to your own group, there should be no problem. Yet, what to do about the fact that tribes would assemble periodically for ritual activity? Durkheim's answers is as simple as it is unsatisfactory: Everyday life with its "utilitarian and individual avocations" is contrary to sentiments surrounding the sacred; and thus everyday life will slowly reduce the vitality coming from these sentiments (Durkheim [1912] 1965, p. 390), providing the impetus for periodic assembly. There is nothing in Durkheim's theory that would enable us to trace this impact of "utilitarian and individual avocations" of everyday life. It is completely *ad hoc*.

The division of labor comes in as the major external threat to mechanical solidarity and, at the same time as its replacement. But here Durkheim lacks a theory that could help him explain what problems arise within organic solidarity and how people deal with them. The theory of action (concerning the role of the collective conscience) that served him well with mechanical solidarity could not be applied to organic solidarity. Division of labor brings out individual autonomy: "the individual becomes more of an independent factor in his own conduct... the progress of individual personality and that of the division of labor depend upon one and the same cause. It is thus impossible to desire one without desiring the other." However, he has no theory for the individual as independent factor, and as if to reclaim the entire matter for mechanical solidarity, he added to the sentence just quoted: "But no one today contests the obligatory character of the rule which orders us to be more and more of a person" (Durkheim, 1933, p. 404f). Of course, even if society expects individuals to show autonomy, that does not explain what they will do, and certainly not what they will do in interdependence situations. In the end, Durkheim can deal with neither internal nor external threats to solidarity. This problem also shows up in the way he deals with sanctions. He assumes that there are very strong sanctions for deviating against the

collective sentiments and he even uses these sanctions as an indicator
for a society in which mechanical solidarity is strong. But why would
anybody deviate from the collective sentiments? They gain nothing
and lose everything from doing so. Thus, sanctions can only be leveled
at people who have contrary collective sentiments and they *must* be
members of another group. So why are there such strong sanctions
against group members?

Hechter has also observed the lack of theory on sanctions in the
normative explanations of solidarity (see Hechter, 1987, p. 23). The
theory of "internalization" which works with stable behavioral dispositions has a systematic problem of dealing with obligations and
sanctions at the same time. It creates what has been called "the sociologist's dilemma". Durkheim's (and thus the "classical sociological")
view on behavior is that through an elaborate process of socialization,
the individual learns to *want* to do what he *has* to do. There are moral
rules (norms) and they are "internalized" by the individual so that he
feels *obliged* to follow the rules. There is no weighing of costs and
benefits regarding the moral course of action; conformity to moral
rules is thus not a matter of *expedient* choice. Yet, according the same
orthodoxy, moral rules are *always* stabilized by "sanctions", i.e. by
costs for deviance and benefits for conformity. The absence of sanctions is a telltale sign that the rule is not a moral rule. How can
sanctions have any effect on conformity with moral rules if consideration of costs and benefits of this conformity is said to be absent? The
dilemma is this: either the sociologist drops the assumption that
cost–benefit considerations are absent from conformity to moral rules
or he drops the assumption that moral rules are always stabilized by
sanctions. In the first case, he would make conformity to moral rules
a matter of expedient choice, negating what is said to be *the* central
insight of traditional sociology. In the second case, he would negate
the empirical foundation of sociology, forcing him back to the purely
idealistic position. Clearly both horns of the dilemma are unacceptable
and a solid microfoundation of solidary behavior would have to deal
with this dilemma. Did rational choice theories of solidarity solve it?
Can these theories deal with internal and external threats to solidarity?

4. RATIONAL CHOICE VIEWS ON
THE EMERGENCE OF SOLIDARITY

Rational choice theorists have dealt with solidarity either as social
capital or as the result of dependency. Of the former, I can find two

kinds, both of them focusing on ties rather than groups.[8] I will briefly review all of these theories.

The Investment Theory

Ties come about because people invest in other people. The tie-forming mechanism itself has been gleaned from Marcel Mauss. It is the idea that gifts (investments) create obligations to be used later on. Prominent social capital authors who make use of this idea are Flap (1988) and Coleman (1990). Coleman asks: why do rational actors create obligations? His answer rests on the assumptions that obligations must be seen as "credit slips" which one can accumulate as a kind of insurance. According to him such credit slips work for goods that at any given time have different value to the actors. "When I do a favor for you, this ordinarily occurs at a time when you have a need and involves no great cost to me. If I am rational and self-interested, I see that the importance to you of this favor is sufficiently great that you will be ready to repay me with a favor in my time of need that will benefit me more than this favor costs me..." (Coleman, 1990, p. 309).

At this point, three observations must be made. First, the point that the goods can have different value to the helper and the helped and thus create an incentive to invest in low cost/high gain exchanges is a very interesting version of the gift idea quite different from the one presented by Mauss. For Mauss, this difference in value was decidedly not the issue of gift giving. Often, the opposite would be true. The gift might be a real sacrifice to the giver and only of symbolic relevance to the receiver. Second, why are obligations repaid? Coleman only points to the high value of the favor received now that would make me repay (at low cost) later. But there is no hint that the temporal gap between receiving and repaying may cause a problem. Most likely, Coleman tacitly assumes a preference change stable enough to last over longer periods of time. Against this idea, it is interesting to note that in the analysis of "archaic" societies, Mauss finds this temporal gap bridged with severe sanctions.[9] Third, it is possible that low cost/high gain situations are created by specialization. But then the goods (i.e. the results of specialized skills) can be traded and no obligation will evolve except if there are barriers to *quid pro quo* exchanges, as in high tax situations. What is at the heart of Coleman's low cost/high gain exchange *with* the creation of obligations is the fact that people can experience situations of need, i.e. of unpredicted increase in the value of certain goods, say through sickness or disaster, events for which they are not otherwise insured. His theory then only applies to need situations but does not cover breach temptations, common good, sharing, and mishap situations. The importance of solidarity is thus limited to unpredictable need, and internal and external sources of precariousness are not addressed at all.

By-product Theory

A second way in which some social capital theorists see solidarity ties emerge could be called the "by-product theory" of solidarity. People meet and either on the basis of increasing familiarity alone or on the basis of some attributes (such as similarity) they find each other attractive. There is good company for this assumption: interpersonal attraction has been a corner stone of theories of social cohesion in social psychology for a long time.[10] In contrast to the investment theory of solidarity, gift giving here is not meant to rationally create indebtedness in the other but meant as token gesture that indicates liking. Homans (1958) has given prominence to this view and he had found plenty of empirical evidence for it. Take for example his famous cash posters: "Girls who sat near one another then had many chances to interact and tended to become friends, and the friendships once made were apt to persists even after seating arrangements were changed..." (Homans, 1954, p. 729). Rationality does not come in in the emergence of the tie or in its maintenance. Rather, it is assumed that attraction changes somebody's preferences and as a consequence the rational pursuit of one's own preferences includes attention to the other's well being. Thus liking affects the utility function: the other's utility has become one of the arguments in Ego's utility function ("altruism through liking"). Examples of prominent authors of social capital working with this by-product theory of solidarity are Feld (1981) and Burt (Burt, 1992; Burt and Kñez, 1995). Related work is done by Lawler (see Lawler and Yoon, 1993; Markovsky and Lawler, 1994).[11]

The by-product theory does not address any particular situation of solidary behavior but with the appropriate auxiliary assumptions on what increases and decreases Alter's utility, one can make a case for need, common good and sharing situations. The theory also allows purposeful manipulation of liking (and thus of solidary behavior) by the influence on interaction frequencies. In that it seems to be the most general of the three. One big problem, however is that, similar to Durkheim's theory, the theory works with the assumption of stable solidarity preferences which exclude the internal and external precariousness of solidarity and this leaves out mishap situations and breach temptations.[12] As we will see, these two neglected aspects are vital with regard to the way solidarity is socially embedded in and with other groups and instrumentally embedded in opportunism-reducing arrangements.

Among the evidence contrary to the stable preference assumptions, the studies of categorization experiments seem to point to a situational influence (Tajfel, 1970; Tajfel et al., 1971). Solidary behavior in sharing situations is sensitive to experimenter induced categorization even against preexisting individual relations. There seems to be a situational sensitivity to solidary behavior that is incompatible with the assumption of transsituational preference effects. Another piece of evidence against the by-product theory is the fact that when individuals are confronted with two legitimate ways of showing solidary behavior *vis-à-vis* members of their own group, one being much more advantageous to themselves than the other, they tend to choose the one that is more advantageous to themselves, irrespective of the effect on the group (see De Vries, 1991). This does not point in the direction of altruistic motivations. Lastly, the fact that by all accounts sanctions are necessary for stable solidary behavior, does not make altruism through liking a theoretically stable basis for the explanation of solidary behavior. The by-product theory may thus seem more general than the investment theory. But it is also the more troublesome.

Group Solidarity

Next to these two dyadic theories of social capital, there is Hechter's theory of group solidarity, also based on rational choice. Here, social norms specify individual contributions to collective goods in groups, but other than for the normative theories of traditional sociology, conformity to norms is here related to expediency rather than morality. Rational individuals will be willing to follow these norms if there are effective sanctions against not following them. Hechter distinguishes between accepting a normative obligation to contribute to a collective good and complying with it. If Ego can get the same collective good with smaller obligations in another group, he will leave. But if he stays, he may still try to evade the obligations. "The more dependent a member on the group (that is, the more costly it is to leave the group in terms of opportunities foregone), the greater the tax that the member will be prepared to bear for a given joint good. However . . . compliance requires formal *controls*." (Hechter, 1987, p. 10f).

Without control and sanctions, the individual will try to free ride. Thus, one has to look at both control and exit effects. To the degree that observability of conformity diminishes (for example, through increasing size), or to the degree that exit costs decrease (for example, through new alternatives for the collective good), solidary behavior will diminish as well, *ceteris paribus.*

   This dependence/control theory of solidarity does deal with groups and the importance of solidarity is clearly linked to common good situations. This is clearly an advance. But Hechter does not work out the aspect of joint production, he only concentrates on dependency. A positive point is that there is some attention to internal (freeriding and control) and external (exit temptations) precariousness. But the theory views solidarity as solely a matter of a single group[13] and within that group solely a matter of cooperative behavior (common good situations), without specifying joint responsibility. It does not cover any of the other situations of solidary behavior. Mishap situations are not covered, even though mishaps can happen right under the eye of the guardian who has to decide whether he deals with a mishap or with motivated disobedience. Help in need situations is also ignored. Breach temptations are presumably no problem because they are curbed by observability and control so that there is no need for a member to voluntarily sacrifice in order not to breach. In sum, imagine that there is a prison with open doors and hell outside, then even that would fit Hechter's view of solidarity. In fact, in Hechter's theory, solidarity only works if people have no alternative outside and nothing escapes the eye of the watchful guardian inside. Yet, this is against common experience. In solidarity groups, people are expected and encouraged to cooperate even if nobody is watching, and the suspicion that somebody only cooperates when observed will in all likelihood lead to the exclusion from the group.[14] No wonder that Hechter laments that his theory "does not seem capable of accounting for the kind of solidarity that is so often celebrated in our own experience..." (*ibid.*, p. 183).

5. USEFULNESS AND PRECARIOUSNESS OF SOLIDARITY

Where do these developments leave us? I suggest that it is useful to have a closer look at the context in which solidarity arises and is maintained in order to get a grasp on the question when and why people would like to keep it going, what problems people have to overcome in order to do succeed in keeping solidarity going, and finally how people attempt to keep solidarity going. There are two theoretical pillars for this effort: sharing group theory (on joint production and use) and a theory of bounded rationality (myopia and framing). Both build on work done in a more concise language in the *Journal of Mathematical Sociology* (Lindenberg, 1980; 1982). In contrast, the purpose of this chapter is to add complexity in order to bring out the detailed preconditions (such as precariousness, self-signaling, formation of rules) as clearly as possible. Other theories are often only seemingly simpler in this regard because they leave important mechanisms implicit for the sake of simplification.

5.1. Sharing Groups

Solidary behavior will evolve where it is useful for people and where there are no major obstacles for its realization. If any kind of behavior is recognized as being useful by a number of interacting people and if that usefulness is fairly stable over time, then its occurrence will lead to regular expectations which, in turn, are governed by rules. The major interest here is with solidary behavior that is non-incidental and thus the first task is to look for an answer to the question under what conditions solidary behavior will be predictably useful, what rules are created to maintain this behavior, and under what conditions, the rules are observed.

The prime context of usefulness for solidary behavior is where people are face to face together to share in production and/or use of some goods. I have called these groups "sharing groups" (see Lindenberg, 1982).[15] For example, farmers may share the production and maintenance of a dike around their fields and they may share a combine which each can use on his own field. They need each other (for production and for cost sharing) but they also exert negative externalities on each other. If someone does not show up for the joint work on the dike, others may be greatly inconvenienced, and while one farmer uses the combine, the other cannot use it although rain may be coming soon and the wheat has to be brought in dry.

In such situations of combined positive and negative externalities solidary behavior is useful for the establishment of the rules for joint production and sharing and for the mitigation of the negative externalities. The more there is being shared (i.e. the higher the total value of what is jointly produced or consumed), the more positive the externalities, i.e. the less attractive the exit options. Also, the more is being shared, the higher the damage if negative externalities are not mitigated. Non-cooperative behavior thus engenders the more damage, the more is being shared. Therefore the usefulness of solidary behavior of each for all, at least as one solution among others to prevent non-cooperative behavior, will increase with the amount and value of goods being shared.

Because of this combination of positive and negative externalities, all kinds of sharing groups have one feature in common: the group *as group* is responsible for maintaining the conditions that are necessary for joint production or use. This feature of sharing groups can be simply called *joint responsibility*. This is different from a situation where an owner of capital hires (and pays) people to perform certain activities which jointly produce a marketable good. In the latter case, the owner is responsible for maintaining the conditions of cooperation.

Sharing Rules

One of the important issues that the group has joint responsibility for is to regulate the joint production and/or use and the sharing of joint costs and benefits by rules. The process of negotiating these rules may be quite difficult and conflict ridden, as the interests may not be homogeneous and there may be distributional disagreements.[16] The content of rules to these ends can be quite practical, depending on the goods jointly produced or consumed, such as division of labor for building the dike or regulating timeshares for the use of the combine, or delineating common property and allotting private property. Once the rules have evolved, non-cooperative behavior refers first and foremost to failure to conform to (the spirit of) these rules. The substantive claim I make at this point is that the question whether solidarity or some other solution to prevent non-cooperative behavior will be used depends on what we assume to be the sources of possible uncooperativeness. For example, if that source is only the tendency to calculatingly free ride, as Hechter assumes, then a group does not need solidarity (in the sense used in this chapter) but control and effective sanctions.

5.2. Internal Sources of Precariousness in Sharing Groups

No set of sharing rules can anticipate all contingencies, and the joint agreement on these rules as well as the handling of them *post hoc* will be subject to solutions to the precariousness of cooperation. In the very heart of a sharing group, the interests of an individual and the group are partially non-aligned because the individual could contribute less if others contributed more. Since the sharing groups we are talking about are face-to-face groups, Olson's logic of collective action for large groups (Olson, 1965) does not apply. But there is asymmetric information in the sense that surveillance (including surveillance of intentions) will be systematically limited. In sharing groups, most of the relevant contributions to a collective good consist of actions rather than money or material goods. There are typically many situations where failure to contribute (in terms of effort) or to comply with rules (in terms of intentions) cannot be determined unambiguously. If somebody is sick with a headache and does not show up for the joint work on the dike, what is going on? There are also many moments where a farmer is unobserved with the communal combine on his field. How careful is he in avoiding the bumpy rocks? In general there is likely to be a considerable regulatory interest in sharing groups but also the realization that monitoring is limited. Thus, the *regulatory interest* will prominently include the wish that individuals would effectively monitor themselves. However, there are two systematic problems: myopia and decay of solidarity motivation, both related to bounded rationality (framing). These points will turn out to be very central to the microfoundations of solidarity and I will go into somewhat more detail than would be warranted for the flow of the paper.

5.3. Myopic Versus Farsighted Rationality

If a human being really were the *farsighted* rational creature she is made out to be in neoclassical microeconomics then cooperative behavior by Ego *vis-à-vis* certain others would pay and thus be just another instance of maximizing behavior for certain need situations (insurance!) or it would be without object because breach temptations and mishap situations have been taken care of *ex ante* (through credible commitments[17]) or breach would be advantageous to both parties. This point is forcefully made by Williamson (1993) who does assume farsighted rationality and who chides Coleman and others for using the word "trust" (which leans on solidarity imagery) where what is really meant is "calculated risk." For example, if I lend a substantial amount of money to a friend without a formal contract then I calculate the risk that he will pay me back, considering that he is also far-sightedly rational, that the friendship is worth much to him and that he would lose it if he defaulted on the debt. To say that I trust the friend does not add anything to the explanation.[18] Coleman's investment view of helping fits perfectly into this calculated risk view of dealing with needy situations of certain others (i.e. when the calculated risk of default is small enough to make the investment attractive). Given the assumptions of farsighted rationality and continued interaction, this suggestion seems perfectly reasonable and it also applies to game theorists using the term trust. The jargon of solidaristic imagery is thus really quite superfluous, at least for repeated need situations and breach temptations.

For the explanation of cooperative behavior in common good situations we can do with Hechter's point that even farsighted rational people will not free ride if they have no alternative group for the production of the collective good and if there is observability with sufficient sanctions. What about solidary behavior in one-shot situations of need and sharing situations in general? The most far-reaching additions to rationality (in game theory) are being made for these kinds of situations in order to square solidary behavior with farsighted rationality. I just mention the introduction of emotions (Frank, 1988), fairness (Kahneman et al., 1986), altruism (Margolis, 1982) and empathy (Binmore, 1994). All these additions are considered to be theoretically "harmless" as long as they do not call into question farsighted rationality. For example, after introducing empathy, Binmore quickly adds that "this view can be defended without going outside the traditional optimizing paradigm of neoclassical economics" (*ibid.*, p. 57). Still, the additions thus bring in solidarity in the form of sentiments, and once they are admitted, they might as well be applied to the other situations. This reintroduces a meaningful solidaristic language (like trust) into situations in which Williamson wanted to ban this language as being superfluous. The further elaboration of these theoretical efforts clearly pulls in the direction of specifying the conditions under which emotions, fairness, and altruism operate, and we can expect a lot more research in this area.

All this would be very nice and an important lesson to sociologists were it not for the fact that there is overwhelming evidence that people are by and large not farsighted maximizers. Rather, *people are mostly myopic* (see, for example, Loewenstein and Elster, 1992). There are probably various reasons for this, but in our context here, one reason sticks out: the importance that goods have for an individual changes situationally, even if that individual had stable underlying preferences.

The reason for this is that attention is necessarily selective, some goals are focal, others are pushed into the background. Unless the value of goods related to background goals is quite high or very vivid, their importance momentarily escapes our attention. For example, a student had an important exam on January 10th, and on January 1st he received an invitation to a fun party to be held on January 4th. He remained officially undecided but for himself he was sure he would not go to the party in order not to lose valuable time for the preparation of the exam. A good party lasts late into the night and wastes the following day. On January 4th in the afternoon, the situation looked different. Now, the party looked more desirable and he told himself that he could leave early so not to waste the following day. He decided to go the party. At midnight, he decided to stay on for a little bit because just at that time, the party began to be really fun. Finally, he went home at four-thirty, went to sleep and got up at one o'clock with a terrible headache and a feeling of low self-esteem.

Action plans are often reversed without change in underlying preferences. Learning from such experience is limited by the fact that the next action plans feel very secure. "We always plan to be more farsighted in our future behavior than we are in the present" (Loewenstein, 1992, p. 30). In Section 5.4 below, a process that can generate such myopic behavior, called *framing*, will be described in some more detail.

For solidarity, this has one very crucial consequence: people may breach agreements, although this is against their long-term interest. They may also fail to fulfill obligations, although this is against their long-term interest. What threatens solidary behavior most is *myopic opportunism*, i.e. the tendency to give in to short-term temptations at the expense of long-term advantages. In a way, this is also rational, but it renders credible commitments much more limited than Williamson and others are willing to assume, and reciprocity over time becomes a theoretical puzzle. A long shadow of the future may help to curb myopic opportunism (for example, through reputation effects, see Ostrom, 1990; Raub and Weesie, 1990), but contrary to what is assumed on the basis of farsightedness, it will never eliminate non-cooperative behavior.

As Durkheim described, there is danger to solidarity lurking from the outside of the group. But that danger does the biggest damage when it feeds on what is produced inside: myopic opportunism. In this light, it is not an exaggeration to say that the main reason solidarity is an important topic in its own right is that human beings are myopic.

5.4. Framing, Rules and Decay of Salience

We are cognitively so limited that only some situational aspects will have our full attention while others only operate peripherally. This is called *framing* (see Lindenberg, 1993).[19] The focal aspects that capture the attention are related to the definition of the situation and the major goal in that situation. One defines a situation as a reaction to the action of others and part of that definition is the goal one will pursue in that situation, i.e. the definition of the situation drives the selection of the major goal. Or, one sets the goal to be pursued beforehand and lets the goal drive the definition. For example, you desperately need money and go to your colleague Fritz and ask him for money. For you the goal is getting money and as you considered Fritz to be not just a colleague but also a friend, you define the (potential) situation as one in which a friend in need asks a friend for money. This goal-related definition mobilizes in you the expectation that Fritz will help if he can, because that is what a friend does, if indeed Fritz still considers himself your friend. In any case it is your goal that drives your definition of the situation as you confront Fritz.[20]

For Fritz, by contrast, the definition drives the goal. He sees Ralph asking for money and, screening and rejecting the possibility that the purpose is frivolous, comes to the conclusion that this situation is "a friend in need." This definition mobilizes the goal "to help a friend in need" or, more precisely, "to act appropriately given a friend is in need, observing the situational constraints".[21]

With regard to the definition of the situation, this view is not much different from that advocated by Goffman (1974). What is different is the relation to rational choice theory, especially with regard to the structuring process, the evaluative process, and the choice process. May be the easiest way to summarize what is going on is to say that individuals are generally intelligent about pursuing one goal in any given action situation but that other potential goals in that situation are pushed into the background and only affect the strength with which the focal goal (frame) guides structuring, evaluation and choice processes. Rationality is thus strongly bounded by the fact that the various goals are not equally taken into consideration.

Specifically, the situationally focal goal together with the definition of the situation will govern the mobilization of knowledge chunks and expectations; the screening of further information; and the selection, evaluation and ordering of alternatives. Other goals in that situation do not vanish but affect the salience of the goal. Take the above example.

Fritz defines the situation as "a friend in need". Thus, other goals, such as "not losing valuable resources (such as money, time or effort)", will be in the background. Money in Fritz's pocket is at that moment much less worth to him than if the focal goal had been "not to lose valuable resources." *This situationally variable marginal utility of goods is the crucial framing effect.* The strength of this situational effect of marginal utility depend on the relative weight of the focal goal to the background goals. If Fritz had just lost $100 before he encountered Ralph, then the goal "not to lose valuable resources", though in the background, would be stronger and weigh more heavily against the salience of "helping a friend in need". This would translate itself in a higher probability for giving Ralph less than he asked for. In the extreme, the background goal could become so strong that it displaces the focal goal. Imagine Fritz had given Ralph already money for two days in a row. In that case, the definition of the situation might be driven by the goal "not to lose valuable resources" and Fritz might now see the situation as "Ralph, the colleague, using friendship to get money out of me".

We can now answer the question how opportunism, and a *forteriori* myopic opportunism, can be checked. The crucial point for checking opportunism is the fact that framing lowers opportunity costs of acting "appropriately" according to some rule by pushing some aspects into the background. The important difference to the standard theory of rational behavior is thus that the opportunity costs of, say, helping the friend are greatly reduced through the fact that the alternative uses for your money, your time and your effort pertain to the background goals and they affect the frame only indirectly through the salience. Potential temptations to deviate from the friendship norms on account of not wanting to spend the money or time or effort are thus considerably weakened and the ability to conform to rules is strengthened. In this sense one can say that there is no rational calculation of costs and benefits of norm conformity that includes both the frame and the background goals. On this point, traditional sociologists did have it right when they considered morality to be something that is outside the context of expediency. Still, the costs of deviance (sanctions from others for your not helping your friend) will increase the salience of the frame, and the costs of conformity (in terms of money, time, and effort) will lower the salience. In the first case the probability of conformity is pushed up, in the second, it is pushed down even though the costs were not directly taken into account. *Sanction thus do matter, even when expediency does not.*

The sociologist's dilemma described above can thus be solved by the theory of framing and solidarity frames in particular. The explanatory burden, then, is shifted to the question what (de)stabilizes such a solidarity frame? Or, what amounts to the same thing: what (de)stabilizes the marginal utility of cooperation across situations? One answer has already been given: prominent short-term advantages can lower the salience of the frame to such extent that the frame changes, leading to myopic opportunism. But there are still other dangers to the stability of a solidarity frame.

Decay

In many cases, the salience of the solidarity frame is the result of conflicting influences from the background, positive and negative ones. Let us say your frame is conformity to solidarity norms and you help a friend in need move. During your activity of lifting books into boxes, you receive periodic encouraging approval from your friend as he comes by to see what you have achieved. This approval increases the salience of your frame. At the same time, the effort of putting the books in the box goes against the background goal to avoid effort, which lowers the salience. What will be the net effect?

When there are fairly high costs involved in executing solidary behavior and when the situations are repetitive, then we are likely to observe, *ceteris paribus*, a decay in the overall salience of the solidarity frame. The reason for this lies in the different timing of costs and rewards which are both related to the background but still act on the salience of the frame. In repetitive solidary behavior, approval from others is likely to be much more intermittent than the costs made to execute the behavior. The higher the costs are, the more this difference in timing will pull down the salience over time. If you keep helping, or you keep resisting lucrative outside offers, or you keep contributing to the common good, or you keep dividing resources fairly, then at every single turn, you experience the cost of conforming to the solidarity expectations. When your behavior accords to the expectations, it does not attract special attention. Although there will be some positive feedback, it will be only at certain occasions while the costs are quite continuous, lowering the salience. This decay phenomenon is well documented for collective good contributions (see for example Andreoni, 1988).

It is also possible that the stability of the solidarity frame is endangered by *competition* or other conflicting interests internal to the group (see Ostrom, 1995). For example, positions in joint production may differ in attractiveness and members compete for these positions while cooperating with regard to the common goal. This competition may even help productivity in achieving the common goal, but then it may also interfere with cooperation (see Abell, 1996). Because competition is no inherent feature of sharing groups, I will only deal with it in passing (in the next section).

6. HOW SOLIDARY GROUPS DEAL WITH PRECARIOUSNESS

The basic point here is that the cognitive limitation that creates myopic opportunism and decay also drives the solutions to these dangers. There is a strong resemblance between, on the one hand, Durkheim's theory of vitality and collective conscience and, on the other hand, the theory of framing, except that the latter also specifies myopic opportunism and decay of salience whereas the former does not. Collective conscience can be interpreted as consisting of normative frames (i.e. situational goals tied to the intelligent conformity to rules), and the high salience of a frame is equal to vitality in the sense that a high salience makes a person very sure about the "right" course of action and sending all energies in the same direction.

With myopic opportunism and decay of salience as a threatening possibility, we can suspect virtually a universal interest among members of sharing groups in the stabilization of solidarity frames and in signals of that stability, i.e. signals that convey the continued disposition to behave solidarily. Members are not just interested in the stability of other people's frames but also in the stability of their own frames and this is due to the effect of *loss* on framing. There is a well-known preponderance of losses over gains (see Kahneman, Knetsch and Thaler, 1991). If a person experiences a loss, say due to uncooperative behavior of another, then the fact that losses quickly produce strong emotional reactions makes it likely that whatever frame a person is in, it will be replaced by a loss frame in which eradication of the loss is the focal goal. If nothing can be done to restore the loss, then "getting even" would be one way, although not a productive one, to balance the loss. For example, Uzzi (1997, p. 59) in investigating interfirm networks in the apparel industry found that "if the strong assumptions of trust and cooperation are exploited in embedded ties, vendettas and endless feuds can arise." Behavior in loss frames is rational only in a very limited sense and it can be very destructive. Uzzi reports a CEO as saying "If you screw a guy like that [a close tie] he'll stay in business just long enough to get even" (*ibid.*). Members would like to avoid bringing another person into a loss frame when they have to confront the consequences. Thus they are interested in not "slipping" into uncooperative behavior *via* myopic opportunism and decay.[22] *They are interested in their own frame stability.* In this sense, there is nothing altruistic about solidary behavior or rather, altruism is beside the point.

Sharing groups must be seen as ongoing social processes in which solutions to problems of frame stabilization are evolving over time in a collective learning process. Results crystallize in rules which can be taught to newcomers (including children), can be changed, refined, adapted. But the substantive claim here is that this process will be driven by problems which all sharing groups have in common. They are: getting people to cooperate in reaching the joint goal, sharing the joint costs and benefits, and taking joint responsibility for the conditions of maintaining joint production/use. Because there is limited observability of behavior and intentions, control and sanctions cannot solve problems that arise with regard to cooperation and sharing. Thus solidary behavior will always cover cooperative behavior and fair sharing. Because of joint responsibility in sharing groups, a situation which endangers a member's ability to contribute to the common goal is everybody's responsibility. Need situations are recognized as such in the group if they address themselves to this responsibility. Solidary behavior will thus also always cover need situations (just not any kind of need). Because of myopic opportunism and decay of salience and because people's behavior (and intentions) cannot be observed at all or not all the time, two extra problems arise universally in sharing groups: breach temptations and the ambiguity of mishaps. For this reason, solidarity will also always cover these two situations.

Thus, although concrete rules may differ in different groups, the underlying problems will be the same in all sharing groups as will be the range of solutions which have to address simultaneously the five solidarity situations listed above.

6.1. The Stabilization of Frames

Because of the close resemblance of solidarity frames and collective conscience, I look to Durkheim first for a theory of the stabilization of frames. As mentioned above, he had shown that collective rituals have the ability to reinforce the collective conscience and thus rituals must also stabilize frames. But Durkheim had not considered the relation of functional interdependence to the stabilization of the collective conscience, and therefore, his rituals do not relate explicitly to sharing groups. For example, in an industrialized country, he recognized only a need for collective conscience of professions, not within and between organization. Other work on rituals refers mainly to dyads (as for example Goffman's and Collin's work). Work done on intergroup relations (Sherif, 1966; Turner and Giles, 1981); on "collective identity" in the social movement literature (for example, Pizzorno, 1978, Melucci, 1989); and on "purposing" in organizations (see Veill, 1986) may be more closely related to frame stabilization in sharing groups even if they do not analyze processes in these terms.

The most obvious and well recognized focus of a frame-stabilizing ritual in a sharing group is the identification of the group as group, making membership easily recognizable,[23] and the celebration of a common goal that is abstract enough to cover all joint lower-level goals. For this purpose, symbols and periodic collective face-to-face gatherings are necessary. But equally important is the link to the outside of the group. Groups gain unity, i.e. the solidarity frames of their members gain stability, by defining themselves in relation to other groups and thereby increasing the salience of the solidarity frame. Remember, sustained cooperation is made possible by sustained low weights for its opportunity costs. The very point of framing was that a salient frame would greatly diminish the opportunity costs which are related to goals that have been pushed into the background of the frame.[24] How is this achieved?

The rites and rituals work directly on the salience of the frame by increasing the value of the focal goal, decreasing the value of conflicting background goals, increasing confidence in the efficacy of the joint effort, and making members alert to possible dangers. Quite typically, the worthiness of the group goal is enhanced by its relation to the realization of a still higher goal (i.e. the sharing group as unit being part of a larger sharing group). The group's ability to achieve the worthy goal is brought into relief by its relative superiority to other groups. The insignificance of internal divisions (i.e. the importance of not letting background goals become unduly important) is stressed by a collective definition of the dangers to cooperation, especially those stemming from certain other groups. Because of the decay of salience, these relations to other groups must be reflected in the daily activities of the group itself. This last point will be discussed again below when I talk about relational signals.

The *minimum number of groups* needed for the stabilization of a solidarity frame within a group is thus three if the groups of points two and three are identical, and four otherwise the ingroup; the encompassing sharing group (higher goal); the dangerous outgroup; the inferior group. This contrasts sharply with Durkheim's theory which would predict that a highly cohesive group does best without any other group in its environment.

Another instrument for the stabilization of frames in sharing groups is purely internal. It consists of rules which govern the way the negative sides of joint production or use (i.e. the negative externalities) are dealt with. These externalities either frustrate the joint production or the individual use. In either case, they create dissatisfaction with the cooperative arrangement and lower the salience of the solidarity frame.

There are mainly three kinds of *externality rules*: those dealing with identification of sources of disturbance, those dealing with the recognition of externalities, and those dealing with the size of externalities. Take an example regarding the first kind of rule. If my cattle grazes on your land, did I not watch my cattle or did you fail to fence your field? Clearly, if this question is unsettled, there will be escalation of conflict rather than amelioration. The classical question of tort already posed by Coase (1960) belongs here. Rules identifying the source of disturbance greatly reduce agreement costs on this point and thereby make it possible to deal with negative externalities more efficiently.[25]

Rules concerning the recognition of negative externalities are exemplified by the adage "fish and guests stink after three days". It conveys to those who might not know that one can easily overstay one's welcome. Sometimes this is also expressed in terms of putting yourself into the shoes of the other, or, even more general, as the golden rule. Of course, recognizing potential negative externalities before they have occurred greatly enhances the likelihood that their effects, and thus their negative influence on framing, are small.

For making up in mishap situations, here must be rules that roughly *measure the amount of damage* that arises from externalities. These rules will also be needed for control measures if making up did not work (see below). Here much collective learning is likely to take place before there are informal estimates of externalities which represent the damage to the joint effort. The reason for this is that framing either makes for individual underestimation of damage (if it is in the back-ground) or for an individual overestimation (if a person is in a loss frame). Leadership (or what may be called wisdom) is likely to play an important role in arriving at equivalences over time when there cannot be a market price for externalities.

6.2. Relational Signals

Because reliable cooperation depends on a solidarity frame and because this frame is precarious, individuals in a sharing group all have an interest to see whether the others still have a solidarity frame and to show to others that they themselves still have a solidarity frame. This is to say that the precariousness of framing engenders a process of mutual signaling with regard to solidarity frames. This process has been called relational signaling.[26] There is indeed much monitoring going on in solidary groups but it is a different kind of monitoring from the one assumed in the dependency/control theories.

What kinds of signals are being used? Goffman had aptly observed that when signals are important in interaction then they tend to prominently include what he called "expressions given off" (Goffman, 1959, p. 2f). These are expressions which are seemingly involuntary (like blushing). They are less open to manipulation and therefore are used to interpret the signals that are purposefully given by the interaction partner. Frank (1988) made use of these signals in order to show that emotions have an important role within rational behavior for creating credible commitments.[27]

Most ordinary everyday behavior acquires relational signal functions, including solidary behavior. For example, if the very first offer in bargaining is very low, this may be useful in getting a low price, but it is also likely to be interpreted as a sure sign of disinterest in the relationship. The offer you make in another context may signal right away your relational interest because you offer a "fair share".[28] People do not just judge the outcome but also the intention. A bad outcome may become more acceptable if it does not also signal relational disinterest. A good outcome may be worth much less if it is known that the indented outcome was much worse. There is also experimental evidence for these effects. For example, Kramer, Shah and Woerner (1995) showed that, in an experimental situation, people were very willing to accept a highly unequal division when they knew that the intended offer was equal and that "bad luck" had made the division unequal. Conversely, many people were dissatisfied with an equal division when they knew that the intended offer was highly unequal. Results in exchanges in which relational concerns matter are thus *judged simultaneously both for outcome and for*

the relational signal. Any theory that negates this double judgement
(as often happens in game theory) will be seriously off the mark in
explaining cooperation.

This argument also informs us why people would signal their "real"
intention in *mishap situations.* If you meant to display solidary behavior but for some reason you did not succeed, then it is important that
you avoid the impression that you are not interested in the relationship
between you and the others. You will go through the trouble and send
a relational mishap signal.

Self-signaling

Because, as Goffman suggested, purposeful relational signals are likely
to be judged against the background of more or less involuntary
signals, people learn about the importance of such signals and how to
handle them. Duplicity will very likely be betrayed by involuntary
signals. For this reasons, people will tend to avoid a situation in which
they signal relational interest to Alter while they interpret their action
as relational disinterest about Alter. In that case, the action would
inform the actor that he or she is somebody who deceives a person who
considers himself a friend. Such discrepancy will in many cases show
up in the involuntary signals, in pitch or tremble of voice, things said
or forgotten to notice etc.

Keeping the signals to Alter and to yourself compatible has a crucial
consequence in the way you treat situations with asymmetric information. For example, Ligthart (1995) could show that when Alter was
Ego's friend (in a scenario experiment), he would offer Ego a fair share
even if Ego had no way of knowing whether what Alter offered was
indeed a fair share. Thus, for solidarity relations (including acquain-
tances), the standard neo-classical assumption that asymmetric information would be exploited, does not generally hold.[29] Only if the
criteria for solidary behavior are ambiguous will the individual choose
the one more compatible with self-interest (see De Vries, 1991). Of
course, as stakes get higher, the goal in the background (to increase
your wealth) will increasingly lower the salience of the solidarity
frame, lower the probability of cooperation to the vicinity of 0.5 and
then abruptly switch to a different frame (in our example: to increasing
your wealth) with a very small probability of cooperative behavior. If
we were to include framing in general and self-signaling behavior in
particular in game theory, we would end up with very different experimental designs for behavior in non-cooperative games, even one-shot

games among people who are likely to perceive each other as belonging to some common sharing group.

People who have no relational concern can and probably will try to exploit relational signaling. This was found to be the case by Murnighan and Pillutla (1995). For example, subjects strategically created the impression of fairness. People can also create consonance between the signals by lying to themselves (see Goleman, 1985). Frank (1988, p. 131) suggested that if there are too many people who can lie to themselves, cooperative behavior will grind to a halt. However, the strategic creation of solidary ties, say through relational signals such as inviting business partners to dinner, inquiring about their family, etc., will work only under exceptional circumstances as an asymmetric relationship in which Ego simply exploits Alter's solidary behavior. The reason for this is that the very situations that are meant to rope in Alter also tend to rope in Ego, even if Ego lies to himself. Ego will fall into his own trap because of the way framing works: it pushes certain goals into the background and that can happen to the manipulator just as much as to the manipulated, especially if the manipulator tries to avoid giving off signals that would expose his plan. A confidence man must have considerable framing skills to avoid this trap.

The most powerful relational signals are those which (a) combine the signal with a direct contribution to the joint production and/or use; (b) are expensive to fake; and (c) cover the major *ex ante* and *ex post* problems of (re)alignment, as for example, in rule change and the interpretation of ambiguous information.

These signals relate to the solidary behavior in the five situations described above. In all five cases (need situations, common good situations, breach temptations, sharing situations, and mishap situations), sending the signal contributes at the same time to the cooperative effort and is costly to the sender. In *ex ante* situations of making sharing agreements, the behavior relating to need, common good, and sharing aspects signals the spirit within which the agreements are made. Once the agreements are in place, each one of these situations will come up *post hoc* again and again, as agreements or even joint products need to be adjusted and incomplete agreements made to apply to unforseen situations. There will also be various occasions to breach the agreement and even to breach the cooperative spirit about incomplete or lacking agreements, and each one offers the opportunity to signal cooperativeness (including making a plausible case for exceptions in a need or a mishap situation).

"Good standing" in a sharing group refers to the history of a members relational signaling. Members in good standing will be given the benefit of the doubt in mishap situations. By the same token, it is clear that the range of solidary behavior is always the full five situations. It is not possible to be extra solidary in one situation and little or not at all solidary in another. This is solely due to the fact that lack of solidary behavior in one situation signals to the other members that in all likelihood the conforming behavior was strategic rather than really solidary (i.e. really within a solidary frame). A "dear Abby" letter to a newspaper illustrates this point.[30]

> "*Dear Abby*. After nearly 20 years of marriage, my husband has asked me for a divorce.... Two years ago, in the middle of a heated argument I told my husband that his love-making did nothing for me – that I had only been putting on an act.
>
> Abby, it wasn't exactly the truth. I only said it to hurt him. He hasn't touched me or kissed me since that day. I would do anything to have my husband back the way he was."

In short, because of myopic opportunism and decay, relational signaling will be concentrated around these five situations and lack of positive signals in any one of these situations occasions a reinterpretation of behavior in the others.

An Example

As illustration of the five situations we can take an interfirm network such as the one described by Uzzi (1997) for the better dress sector of the apparel industry in New York. Uzzi makes a distinction between "arm's-length ties" (pure market relationships) and "embedded ties" (close or special relationships). The apparel industry contains simultaneously market and embedded relations, the former being a majority, the latter being the relations of special importance. Individuals (contractors, manufacturers, production managers etc.) would behave blatantly with self-interest in the market and cooperatively in the embedded relationships. The latter developed over a long time and showed typically solidary behavior in the five situations. The profitability for each was seen as a *common good*. "We are all in the same boat" Uzzi reports a contractor as saying. Uzzi found that extra effort was voluntarily given and reciprocated, there was joint problem solving, much communication and a very quick understanding of what adjustments had to be taken.

Signaling in *sharing situations* was also part of the routine interaction. Uzzi found a belief among partners of embedded ties that the other would not act in self-interest at another's expense; this showed up in concrete action such as resource pooling among partners and, when transactions had to be done fast, *post hoc* pricing. As one CEO put it: "we do first and fix price after;" another CEO would say "the contractors know that they will not lose." Help in *need situations* was taken for granted: "If there was a problem you knew you'd work it out and they'd help you" said a manufacturer of 30 years experience. A production manager even reports creating work for the contracting partners when there is a lull in the market. "We will put a dress into work to keep the contractor going. We'll then store the dress in the warehouse." By contrast, in arm's length relationships the other would "push the price down when the contractor tells his production problems."

Restraint *vis-à-vis breach temptations* was very evident in Uzzi's study. He reports that there is nondefection where defection clearly would serve the self-interest of a business partner. But then, there is also a watchful eye. Too frequent need situations are under suspicion of being covert breaches, putting the partner on the alert. Clear breaches are not forgiven. "If he switches to a new contractor then I won't work with that manufacturer again." This is in contrast to *mishap situations*. A manufacturer expressed it thus: "When you deal with a guy you don't have a close relationship with, it can be a big problem. Things go wrong and there's no telling what will happen. With my guys [his key contractors], if something goes wrong, I know we'll be able to work it out." One partner also warns the other about expected problems so the other can adjust in time. A production manager explains: "I tell them [key contractors] that in two weeks I won't have much work. You better start to find other work."

If the five solidarity situations come up routinely in the course of the daily activities of joint production and/or use, and if they are within the range of legitimate solidarity costs for Ego, then more and clearer signaling will be possible than if they happen rarely. For example, if there are regularly need situations which hit all members (but at different times) such that the other members can show their ability and willingness to help, the solidarity frame is more often reinforced and monitored, leading to a higher probability that the solidary behavior will be continued in the future. This deviates from the view that a solidary group does best if there are no problems. What makes some teams so solidary is exactly this combination of daily activities of joint production and the opportunity to signal cooperativeness. Regularly reoccurring minor crises and uncertain environments of the sharing group serve the same purpose and can at times even be manipulated by group leaders to this end. In this sense, frame stability should not be confused with stability of the circumstances of cooperation. On the other hand, even though the range of legitimate solidarity costs may increase in crisis situations, the need may be too high, the mishaps too often, the breach temptations too large, the windfall gains or unexpected joint losses too large to be handled by the signaling rules. I will come back to this point when talking about weak solidarity below.

Competition

There is a possibility that competition furnishes regular occasions for strong relational signaling and as such may even be beneficial for the stabilization of a solidarity frame. As mentioned above, Abell (1996) has recently suggested a model in which a productive balance between cooperation and competition could be achieved through the development of a team spirit which involves generalized reciprocity (i.e. the willingness to do something for someone in the expectation of getting something back *from somebody* at some other time). The problem is that for this to function, solidarity costs (i.e. the costs one is expected to incur in the five solidarity situations) must be quite high or the attractiveness of the prize for which one competes quite low. This may restrict the possibility of such a team spirit to situations of strong solidarity (see below) which in turn creates problems of cooperation with other groups. Abell had not considered this problem. It is more likely that competition and cooperation have to be governed by very clear relational signals. If that is possible, they can be combined, if not, they will constantly disturb each other. Arrangements for clear relational signals in such situations prominently include solutions to the question who can legitimately exert social control (see below).

Auxiliary Rules

The bulk of the rules concerning relational signals will be pegged to the five situations. However, there must be accompanying rules that finetune relational signaling to the specific context. One may call these *auxiliary solidarity rules*. There must be some rules of a social grammar, specifying what range of actions is considered to be a relational signal for certain classes of situations. For example, in many situations, relational signals allow quite a range of personal variance, as long as the signal is clear and unambiguous. If Fritz's cow eats Ralph's flowers, Fritz can help Ralph replant or bring him a present or help him dig a ditch around the flower bed. Paying money in mishap situations is often outside the range. "Shasta County landowners regard a monetary settlement as an arms' length transaction that symbolizes an unneighborly relationship" says Ellickson (1991, p. 61) in his landmark study of order without law. The reason for this is probably that unless the payment is very generous, it would symbolize a market transaction that leaves out all the costs of inconvenience, and thus be considered too little; and if it is very generous, it creates reverse indebtedness, symbolically also confusing the roles of the situation about who should feel sorry.

There are situations where signaling behavior would always be ambiguous unless there are clear conventions without much personal variance. For example, when people share small living quarters, it is quite important that the joint living room is relatively free to move about. What is the cooperative thing to do when one of the group members has a guest (which inevitably causes negative externalities)? Should everybody join in, or should he take him upstairs, or should he sit in a corner and whisper? No matter what he does, he might be giving the wrong signal. In such a case it is in his and everybody else's interest in a group that shares living quarters to agree on a preferred way of dealing with guests.

The more important it is that people act solidarily, i.e. the higher the total value of what is being shared in the group, the more likely that there will be additional rules about the importance of having and showing a cooperative attitude (i.e., signals), of keeping promises and of sticking to rules. In addition, there are likely to be common values that stress the importance of common goals. These are the social norms and values in the traditional sense. They function here a *metarules*. Notice however, that these norms and values are built on sharing rules and rules for relational signaling, not the other way around. As I will stress later on, if the productive context that brings about sharing changes, so will norms and values.

Sharing rules, relational signal rules, norms and values: all these point to a common culture that creates the grammar for relational signaling. Locally, the "spirit" of the culture will be heavily influenced by the relative balance of positive and negative externalities. For example, if the negative externalities weigh heavier than the positive externalities, then the culture will emphasise the importance of being considerate but separate, whereas a heavier weight of positive externalities will foster a spirit of togetherness. This cultural aspect of solidarity is another indication that it is only of very limited use to look at solidarity as a phenomenon between dyads or within single groups. I will come back to this point later time and again in this chapter.

6.3. Social Control

As mentioned above, sharing groups create internally a regulatory interest in every member because of the externalities. Thus, when things go wrong and they are not solved by mishap signals then the regulatory interest will turn into an interest of exercising social control. It should be clear by now that social control, like any behavior inside the group, will be subject to constraints set by relational signaling.

If Fritz takes Ralph to court, Fritz signals that he has no particular relational interest (anymore). Ellickson (1991) in his study of Shasta County found this very much to be true: "Being good neighbors means no lawsuits" (*ibid.*, p. 251). Litigation is only expected for parties "who lack the prospect of a continuing relationship" (*ibid.*, p. 274). There is likely to be a control hierarchy in which the more severe control instruments progressively indicate lack of relational interest (see Ellickson, 1991; Lindenberg, 1994).

At first the deviant will be informed that the act had been discovered, giving him a chance to take remedial steps and explain why the mishap signal had not been given or in which way it could be made more believable. If this does not help, negative gossip may be circulated about the uncooperative member. If this still does not help, the member may be shunned. Then physical intervention may be the appropriate fourth step. If this is still not enough, third parties (organizations or the law) and/or forced exit may be brought in.

Relational signaling thus governs the kind and calibration of social control efforts. It also influences *who does the controlling*. Whenever social control cannot be unambiguously distinguished from a negative relational signal between A and B, control is likely to be indirect and it will be exercised by somebody for whom control is not associated with a negative relational signal. For example, colleagues in a law firm earn joint income. They will of course also exert negative externalities on each other and even be in competition for positions in the firm. Say, that the slowness with which partner Fritz works on a case interferes with a case of partner Ralph. What will Ralph do? Because the legal work is very complex and it is difficult to prove lack of effort or even uncooperative intentions, there are few if any clear cut cases. Ralph is convinced that Fritz is not pulling his weight but he is in a bad position to complain to Fritz because in such a complex situation complaining by a direct colleague is ambiguous: it may be legitimate or it may be a strategic effort to get Fritz to earn more for the joint pot so Ralph might put in less effort or even get ahead of Fritz (both negative relational signals). In a situation like that, the control efforts would on the longer run cease to be direct and run instead *via* persons in the firm who have a neutral position, so that their control could not be interpreted as a negative relational signal; and/or *via* persons who earn so much for the firm that their control efforts would be beyond strategic suspicion (see Lazega (1995) for a case in point).

The substantive claim is thus that the clarity of relational signals will strongly influence all other arrangements in sharing groups, including social control.[31]

7. STRONG AND WEAK SOLIDARITY

The biggest difference how solidarity functions in a society depends on whether solidarity is weak or strong. While there are gradations within these categories they are qualitatively quite different.[32] Let us first look at weak solidarity.

7.1. Weak Solidarity

Take a sharing group that has been around for some time to have had the chance for individual and collective learning in terms of knowledge necessary for the sharing arrangements and in term of the formation of rules. When the value to the individual of what is jointly produced (or used) is high and non-solidaristic governance instruments considerably reduce myopic opportunism, or if the value is relatively low, then solidarity will be weak in the sense that the solidarity costs are relatively low and in the sense that the sharing group as group will influence but not dominate the framing of the individual. Examples of such weak solidarity groups are colleagues in a university department; an interfirm network; a tennis club; people sharing neighborhood space.[33] For *need, common good* and *mishap* situations, this means that the amount of money, time, or effort Ego may legitimately be expected to sacrifice for others is quite limited. In addition, the standards of evidence required for indicating need and for legitimate mishaps are also relatively easy to meet.

For *breach temptations*, solidarity costs will always be much higher than for the other situations because the regulation of these temptations is the basis for cooperative arrangements of the joint production or use. Still there are limits here too which play an important role in the mutual expectations concerning breach and, as I will discuss below, concerning the safeguards used against breach.

For *sharing situations* there is a special feature of weak solidarity that is very different from strong solidarity. In a weak solidarity situation, the group as group is not strong enough to override differences in investment in the joint production or use. A *fair share* in weak solidarity will thus be linked to the size of the input (i.e. equity). The group is not strong enough to suppress "gain" as a focal goal. One can do business in a weakly solidary group, one can make a profit of the other members of the group, one can become richer or acquire more status than the others in the group, given that input to the joint production or use can be measured, that this gain is related to differences in input and that it is accompanied by solidary behavior. From a framing point of view it is most easily modelled as a see-saw balance between two goals which keep replacing each other as frame: gain and solidarity. Imagine a person is in a solidarity frame. There are solidarity costs attached to solidary behavior. As the costs of being cooperative go up (i.e. as personal gain goes down due to solidary behavior) the salience of the solidarity frame will drop to a level where gain abruptly becomes the new frame. As the costs of increasing one's gain go up (i.e. as cooperative behavior decreases due to the pursuit of personal gain) the salience of the gain frame will drop to a level where the cooperation will abruptly become the new frame, etc. Subjectively, this may be experienced as ambivalence.

Because equity (rather than equality) is the basis for fairness in weakly solidary groups, solidarity will suffer less in such groups on the basis of a *division of labor* for the joint production than strongly solidary groups (see below). Division of labor introduces differences in input and unless these differences are legitimate, they will not be linked to output and thus will have no motivational basis for being sustained as a group-related activity. Authority in such groups must be legitimized in terms of the contribution to the common goal, and status difference are likely to develop on this basis (see Ridgeway and Walker, 1995). But, it is clear that such an authority structure can only function if solidary behavior is maintained even across hierarchical levels. The reason is not one of human relations *per se* and of being nice to one another, but of dealing with the precariousness of coopera-tion due to myopic opportunism and decay of the salience of a frame that ensures the motivation and flexible adjustments necessary for the joint production.

Embedding of Solidarity

Because in weak solidarity the group does not have a strong grasp on the framing of the individual, the range within which it can contain myopic opportunism and decay of the salience of the solidarity frame is also narrow. For some sharing groups of weak solidarity, this will not do because the curtailment of breach temptation is too important for its functioning and they have to be confident of a broader range within which breaches are unlikely to occur. In general this will be sharing groups in which economic transactions play an important role. The solution in these cases is to use other means than framing to reduce myopic opportunism, so that the temptation that is left is small enough to be governed by solidarity frames. Such means lower the real payoff for non-cooperative behavior, not just the perceived payoff through framing. Standard examples of such means are reputation, selection, credible commitment devices, and legal instruments (see Williamson, 1985; Raub and Weesie, 1996).

For this embedding to function, certain preconditions must be met. There is *reputation* in the sense of a good standing in the sharing group. This has everything to do with relational signaling and internal exchange of information. However, reputation effects in a wider circle will not work unless the environment of the sharing group has (a) some incentive to pass on negative and positive information and (b) shares the standards of judging misconduct. For example, Uzzi (1997, p. 55) relates that in the apparel industry in New York "generalized reputations are surprisingly weak control devices." In this case, the market is large enough for firms to escape bad reputations and – this is the important point here – positive information is hoarded and shared only very selectively in order to keep down the competition. Thus in this interfirm network, the reputational effects are mainly restricted to privileged expansions of the sharing group *via* "go-betweens" who transfer "the expectations and opportunities of an existing embedded social structure to a newly formed one." (*ibid.*, p. 48) These three forms of reputation effects are often not distinguished in the literature.

Related to the last two forms of reputation effects is *selection* as an instrument for flanking solidarity. For selection to work, it is not necessary to assume that there are stable personality traits in terms of virtues (such as trustworthiness). Selection is more likely to work on aspects which indicate greater ease for the stabilization of a solidarity frame, akin to the way Spence (1974) has looked at education as a signal in the selection process on the labor market. This ease may come from various sources. For example, a person who has talents and attitudes which fit well into the arrangements of joint production of the group would acquire more (less) social and self-(dis)approval in the group than a person without such talents or attitudes. As a result, outside opportunities would be smaller by comparison and the person would have less decay in the solidarity frame, offering less of a chance to myopic opportunism. Other aspects may indicate the alternative sharing groups a person has due to easily identifiable and stable characteristics, such as ethnic or racial characteristics. The fewer alternative sharing groups somebody has, the smaller the chance of myopic opportunism.

Credible commitments within the sharing group depend on the nature of the joint production or use. For example, two firms in an interfirm network may jointly pay for a machine which creates a hostage for each. In addition, credible commitments depend on differences in the (market) power of members. As Gál (1997) has shown, it is the strong party that will have to show credible commitments rather than the weak one because the weak partner has more to lose by defecting and is thus more reliable. If the judicial system works in such a way that its verdicts cannot be predicted on the basis of non-juridical characteristics (such as the relative market power of a contractual partner) and if the standards of evidence are in principle tied to those of science, then general *laws and regulations* can reduce myopic opportunism and dyadic relationships can be embedded in explicit contracts, even if they are necessarily incomplete. For example, Blumberg (1997) finds that network embedding is no substitute for contracts. Even if these contracts are never used, the very possibility that they could be used and tie up *both* parties in costly litigation, serves to reduce myopic opportunism on the level of the sharing group. The dyadic nature of these contracts should not distract from the fact that long-term relations are in all likelihood part of a larger sharing group(s) and the contracts are likely to refer explicitly or implicitly to practices and standards of that sharing group or collection of sharing groups.

The point I am trying to make is that, even if we concentrate on long-term relations, it seems wrong to assume that the various means for the reduction of myopic opportunism must be substitutes. Often, they are complements. Either, the stakes are low enough to allow a narrow range of protection against breach temptations. Then weak solidarity (with its own informal means) will be sufficient and the alternative use of non-solidary means would be counter-productive because of their lower flexibility *post hoc*. Or the stakes are too high for weak solidarity to handle alone, then non-solidary means are used to reduce the myopic opportunism enough for solidarity to do the rest. There is then nothing that can replace weak solidarity as a means of making long-term cooperative relationships possible, both in *ex ante* arrangements and in *ex post* adaptations. However, when stakes are high, other means must flank weak solidarity, the weaker the solidarity, the more help from other means there must be, and only in this sense is there substitutability. For example, Blumberg (1997) found for interfirm R&D cooperations that good experience with the same partner in the past led to fewer formal flanking of the cooperation.[34]

The fact that the flanking of solidarity is often not used is no sign that it is not necessary. As I elaborated above, social control is itself restricted by relational signaling. For this reason, escalation is stepwise and there is always the danger that it rips the relational fabric as it approaches litigation. Hostages and the courts thus are actually invoked only when the relationship has already failed.

7.2. Strong Solidarity

The higher the value to the individual of what is jointly produced (or used) and the fewer the non-solidaristic means of reducing opportunism, the stronger the hold of the group over the individual member. Imagine that a group of farmers do not just share a piece of equipment, but also neighborhood space, defense against destructive wild animals, ditches against flooding, construction of houses and barns, the risks of bad harvest and of bad health, child socialization, and a way of life. Such a group is strongly solidary. In such groups, it likely that one of the goods that is being jointly produced is shared risk (such as risk of bad health). This risk sharing will greatly increase the legitimate sacrifice in times of need which will *look like* strongly altruistic behavior. However, there is no need to make an assumption about altruistic behavior here. In fact, the theory proposed would definitely argue against the interpretation of helping behavior in terms of altruism because that would imply a stable preference changes in individuals rather than the influence of situational factors (i.e. sharing arrangements).

Since by assumption there are no superior alternative ways of production for any of these goods, it is very important for the group members that there is no deviation from the sharing rules. Frame stability is thus itself an important joint product and the tolerance for individual variance will be low.

In comparison to weak solidarity, strong solidarity differs both quantitatively and qualitatively. The quantitative difference lies mainly in the solidarity costs. The amount of money, time and effort people are expected to sacrifice for helping others in need, for reaching the common good, etc. are considerably higher than in weak solidarity. The qualitative difference is that there is no duality of frames (gain and solidarity) toward group members, but only solidarity, so that a number of expectations are thoroughly different. From a normative point of view, the importance of the individual will be small in comparison to the importance of the group; this is so because the individual's non-conformist wishes would be so loss-producing for the others that the wishes themselves are deemed illegitimate. For this very reason, the basic expectation in strong solidarity is *equality* rather than equity. Difference between group members will be played down and all behavior that increases these differences is discouraged. Need is only legitimate if it is related to the joint responsibility to keep things going. Differences in investment in the joint production or use refer to the ability to contribute, but they are decoupled from the size of the share of the joint result. Authority differences in strongly solidary groups clash with the claim to equality even though they may be functionally necessary for the achievement of the common goal and even though people contribute differently. For this reason, authority differences in such groups can only be legitimated in two ways: symbol of the group or need. Thus there are two such roles: the representation of the whole group and somebody who is able to recognize need (and maybe help) better than others. Legitimate differences in the share of the joint results can only come from differences in legitimate need, and these differences may in turn arise from members' different ability to contribute to the joint production or use (say children versus adults, men versus women, etc.). Because of the strength of the group, the range within which solidarity can deal with myopic opportunism without flanking arrangements is much larger than with weak solidarity. Indeed, the very wish for flanking arrangements (other than selection) for the reduction of opportunism can only be seen as a negative relational signal in a strongly solidary group. The downside of this strength is that its requirements for the purity of relational signals is very high. Relations to other groups and possibly conflicting loyalties are potential negative relational signals. For this reason, group boundaries will be strict.[35] Strong solidarity will thus automatically imply a possibility for unbridled opportunism between groups without the ability to engage in mutually advantageous exchanges within the group. Weber (1961, p. 261f) saw this clearly when he described the contrast of the moral code towards the ingroup ("Binnenmoral") and lack of any moral code towards the outgroup ("Aussenmoral"). Profitable economic relationships could not grow on the basis of strong solidarity and all the talk about embedding and the importance of trust, cooperation and solidarity for capitalism would do well make a clear distinction between strong and weak solidarity and pay attention to the different conditions under which they occur (see Lindenberg, 1988).

When the flanking arrangements for weak solidarity become endangered, say because the state apparatus is falling apart, as it happened
toward the end of the former Soviet Union or Yugoslavia, then the
range that could be handled by weak solidarity without the flanking
is too narrow to support the existing arrangements. If there is no quick
flanking alternative, individuals will gravitate to stronger sharing
groups, attempting to concentrate joint production and use of as many
goods as possible in one strong sharing group. Given the importance
of clear group boundaries for strong solidarity, the dimensions that
offer themselves for forming the nucleus of strong sharing groups in
such situations of weakening flaking arrangements, have to answer
three criteria: (a) it should be possible to say with a high certainty who
belongs and who does not, (b) it should be a criterion that cannot
easily be manipulated; (c) it should be a criterion that has worked for
strong solidarity in the past.

The first criterion puts an extra premium on selection and symbols
of identity. Ethnicity and practiced religion are often the criteria that
answer all three requirement, helped by sharing group entrepreneurs
who have their own goals in the process (see Hardin, 1995). In fact,
these entrepreneurs are likely to use the frame stabilizing techniques
discussed above, except that becoming part of a larger sharing group
is less likely when the strong solidarity comes about by failing supports
outside the group. In addition, a group that has many joint goals
would gain frame stability if the goals were seen as interdependent.
For these two reasons, a strongly solidary group is likely to turn to
abstract unifying goals embedded in *ideology* and stress more strongly
its own superiority to other groups. Because the ideological embedding
and because of the importance of conformity (and therefore of metarules), a strongly solidary group seemingly (re)turns to fundamental
values and clear norms. This is not without consequence for the size
of a strongly solidary group. Whereas the importance of strong group
boundaries favor a small size, the ideological support and also the
talents needed inside the group to jointly produce many goods, favor
a large group. Although there might be a size that optimizes both (see
Lindenberg, 1982), it is likely that such a group is subject to conflicting
"policies", expanding in order to increase ideological support and
internal diversity of talents and then contracting again as the expansion endangers the purity of the group boundaries.

Thus, like weakly solidary groups, strongly solidary groups are
likely to be locked onto other groups. However the reasons for and the
way of interlock are very different.

7.3. From Strong to Weak Solidarity

On the basis of the arguments just given, strong solidarity is the result
of the breakdown of weak solidarity when stakes are high and flanking
arrangements fail. Then solidarity muffles distinctions within groups,
and between groups unbridled opportunism reins high. Of course, the
development can also go the other way around, and that is closer
to the traditional story told by sociologists. From *Gemeinschaft* to
Gesellschaft, from mechanical to organic solidarity, from status to
contract. However, the story told in the context of the arguments
above would look different from these traditional accounts in some
important aspects.

The major difference comes from the two pillars of the solidarity
theory: the precariousness of solidarity and the productive context in
which all solidarity arises. All forces that change production and use
patterns are likely to affect solidarity. When a good is offered *via* the
market or the state, sharing groups which formerly produced it for
themselves are likely to turn to the market or the state if the price is
lower for these new alternatives (which it often is). For example, when
health insurance comes up *via* market or state, health risks will soon no
longer be shared in community-like arrangements. In addition, when
individual or family income goes up on a wide scale (as it would in
consequence of the changes in production), sharing groups for joint
consumption will become smaller and smaller with fewer joint goods
per group. For example, as farmers who share a combine and health
risks become richer, they purchase health insurance and split into
smaller combine sharing groups, eventually owing each their own combine. The reason for this is that sharing creates negative externalities
which are mitigated more effectively by making the sharing group
smaller than by regulating the externalities in the larger group. At the
same time, some sharing groups will grow into large anonymous
associations with no face-to-face interaction and little or no solidarity.
For example, sharing group entrepreneurs sell shares in a sharing
group on the market, such as mutual insurance companies.[36] In short,
increasing production by market and state and increasing income will
create less sharing in production and use. What does this mean for
solidarity? Clearly, where there was strong solidarity, it will diminish
and individualism in the midst of large producing or sharing units will
develop. Coleman (1982) called this the asymmetric society. As conformity becomes less important to each group, the solidarity costs will
turn towards zero, social control will greatly diminish, and rules,

including social norms and values, will feel vague. Notice that there may have also been weak solidarity before and that even weak solidarity will be affected by this development. There is no movement from strong to weak solidarity here, but from solidarity strong or weak to (atomistic) individualism with arm's length relationships and opportunism. But the important point is that this is only half of the story. There are goods which cannot be produced by the market or the state and which are still vital for individuals. These goods prominently include a sense of purpose, of being important, of being appreciated, and a sense of stability in acting, thinking and expecting. These goods have been by-products of functioning sharing groups in which the jointness of production and use created the foil for purpose, and the frame-stabilizing mechanisms of group identity, symbols, rituals, comparisons and external flanking created a sense of cognitive and motivational stability. In fact the "sense of belonging" which makes group membership so attractive is likely to be not just the result of help in need but also of these by-products of functioning sharing groups.

In addition, during this phase of atomistic individualism it turns out that the more complex the production for the market and by the state, the less it can function adequately without solidarity in face-to-face groups. The reason for this has been already mentioned above: the need for networks of patterned long-term relationships which, in turn, necessitate *ex ante* and *ex post* solidary behavior for quick coordination and flexible adjustments. Technological changes strengthen this need for flexibility and thus the need for weak solidarity (see Piore and Sabel, 1984).

There are then two developments where the second is not simply the complement of the first. First there is a change in production and use. This brings individualism and large production and sharing units with arm's length relationships among them. The second development deals with the changes brought about by the first. Above all, what used to be by-products of sharing groups must now be purposefully produced. In part, this will lead to changes in the role of work and home (with pressure for work as a provider of meaningful activity and importance especially for women, and home *ownership* providing a sense of stability and meaningful activity) and an increase in purely social sharing groups (hobbies, vacations and sports with others). And what seemed like a new order with arm's length relations and individualism (*Gesellschaft*) in business, develops new forms of solidarity. It is in these two contexts that weak solidarity comes up on a grand scale in modern societies and where lapses of weak solidarity produce both episodes of strong solidarity (say in ethnic groups) and of atomistic individualism.

There is still an important addition to this story. We know by now that weak solidarity needs to be flanked when stakes are high. That means that there is a crucial role for the state to aid that flanking by offering instruments for credible commitments and legal arrangements with the right criteria for evidence in courts and arbitration. But this is not enough. The state must also stand for a policy that reduces the chance for the development of strong solidarity. This is to say that the state must help prevent a failure of weak solidarity. Weak solidarity will only function if strong solidarity is kept in check. For example, great social inequalities in income, political rights, labor market chances, etc. are likely to create subgroups of strong solidarity, first among the permanent minorities who have to fend for themselves by whatever means they have (including violence), and then among the better-off who have to fend for themselves against the permanent minorities.

Blatantly strategic behavior by the state *vis-à-vis* citizens will encourage atomistic individualism. It belongs to the standard wisdom in the social sciences that in order to function, the state and its laws should have legitimacy. In this context, gaining legitimacy means that the state has to see to it that society as a whole is also seen as a sharing group with weak solidarity (turning to strong solidarity in times of disaster and external threat). Although society is so large that as a group it does not allow face-to-face interaction, it is present in all public and official face-to-face interactions and it contains nested sharing groups such as provinces or and communities. Legitimacy of the state translates directly into the use of relational signals in public and official face-to-face interactions. For example, there are many breach temptations regarding taxes, public assistance, etc. Monitoring and legal measures by the state will reduce but not eliminate these breach temptations, so that some solidarity will always be needed to achieve conformity to the laws that concern common goods, sharing situations and help for the needy. Can Ralph brag to his friends about having cheated in getting payments from the state meant for the needy? Will Ralph be susceptible to the opinion expressed in a debate among his colleagues about the importance of going against the misuse of public assistance money? Will Ralph support an initiative to reduce public assistance to the needy in favor of an increase of unemployment benefits to his own occupational group?

The state clearly has to fight the view that society is a strongly solidary group (except in emergencies) because otherwise the solidarity costs would be too high, the breach temptations too great, or the ideological and selective needs for the suppression of afouristic individualism too severe. However, there is still a burden of relational signaling to be carried by the state. All signs of strategic action by the state *vis-à-vis* the citizen, and all signs of corruption involving public money will send negative relational signals from the state to the citizen, lowering the salience of the solidarity frame and increasing the citizen's willingness to cheat. There has been no cost accounting on this point so far, but it stands to reason that negative relational signals by the state are very costly in terms of reduced tax income, waste of public assistance money, costs of increased monitoring, etc. The important point for weak solidarity in general, however, is not the individual free ride on taxes and public programs, but the impact legitimacy has on the workings of flanking support for private sharing groups. This support consists of adequate legal instruments, of generating adequate political support for measures that keep strong solidarity at bay, and of providing planning stability for long-term relations, creating a general atmosphere of gain from cooperativeness. In short, solidarity and its forms have everything to do with the state because it needs the state's flanking support to enlarge the range within which myopic opportunism can be held at bay by solidarity on the lowest level.

8. SUMMARY AND CONCLUSION

There is no topic that has captured the sociological imagination more than solidarity. Society would fall apart without it. Despite this prominent position of solidarity, there has been surprisingly little attention to the question what kind of behavior constitutes solidarity. Maybe as a result of this lack of behavioral anchorage of theories of solidarity, it is also not clear at all under what conditions solidarity is supposed to arise and why. Worse, there is no theory of the precariousness of solidarity and consequently also no theory of the solutions to this precariousness. Rational choice theories of solidarity and the related social capital theories have not gotten much further on these points.

In this chapter, I attempted to show these gaps and then to close them as best as I can. Even though the story is complex, the most important points can be summarized quite succinctly. Solidarity comprises a definite set of behavior; it arises in situations when groups attempt to reach common goals; and it is always precarious but cannot be replaced by something else. Because it is precarious, it needs mechanisms that support it and they always involve other groups and, in modern societies, also the state. The study of solidarity of dyads and even of single groups is therefore only of very limited usefulness.

More specifically, the paper makes the following points. Solidarity is defined in terms of *behavior* that involves a certain sacrifice for the actor in five problematic situations: contribution to common good situations, sharing joint costs and benefits, help in need, resisting breach temptations, and making up in mishap situations.

Solidarity arises in sharing groups. These are face-to-face groups that jointly produce and/or use one or more goods and that have joint responsibility for the maintenance of the conditions of sharing. These *sharing groups* create positive and negative externalities from each member to all other members. Thus there is mutual dependency with good and bad consequences. This creates potential conflict between individual and group interests. Sharing groups will create rules about the joint production and/or use and rules about sharing of costs and benefits arising from production and/or use. It is the potential non-conformity to the (spirit) of these sharing rules and the potential non-acceptance of joint responsibility due to conflicting interests that creates the problem of cooperation.

There are three prominent solutions in sociology to this problem. Individual *preferences change* in the direction of cooperation (say through gifts or other investments, socialization or the mediary of interpersonal attraction). Or, transaction *partners bind themselves* (say, through hostages) in such a way that it would be against their own interest to defect from cooperation. Or, individuals will cooperate because they are dependent and at the same time *closely watched and sanctioned* if they free-ride on the efforts of others. All three positions are criticized. Neither preference change nor self-binding nor conformity due to dependency and control can explain solidary behavior across the five problem situations and/or are compatible with the evidence. Another microfoundation is needed.

The new microfoundation begins with the empirically well-supported claim that individuals are not farsighted maximizers but only bound-edly rational in the sense that their attention is selective; it is guided by their goals (i.e. they perceive a situation in terms of a goal of action); and it is most frequently guided by short-term goals. People are thus by and large myopic and therefore prone to be tempted by short-term advantages. This makes people *myopic opportunists* and it makes cooperation and sharing precarious, particularly behavior in breach temptation, mishap and need situations.

Because individuals frame, the opportunity costs (i.e. the alternative ways of spending their resources) are mostly outside the frame (i.e. outside the direct attention). They will influence behavior the less, the stronger the frame is. Therefore, if the goal is solidary behavior and it is strong, the sacrifices required for this kind of behavior are only vaguely perceived and do not discourage cooperative behavior. The question then for cooperation is how such a frame of action can be and factually is sustained.

There is an extra danger for the stability of a cooperative frame because the strength of a frame decays over time unless there is special effort to prevent such a *decay*. Myopic opportunism and decay of frames render the self-binding and other explanations based on far-sightedness untenable. Experiments about the sensitivity of cooperativeness to situational cues render the preference change explanations (such as the investment and by-product theories) untenable. Theories that explain cooperativeness by dependency and control (such as Hechter's theory of solidarity) neglect the fact that surveillance is always imperfect, especially surveillance of intentions, which leaves such theories without explanation for mishap situations and resistance to unobserved breach temptations.

Instead, it is argued that a solidarity frame is stabilized through mechanisms of building *group identity* including common symbols and rituals and – this is very important here – positive and negative comparisons with other groups. These points have often been stressed in sociology. But they have not been linked to precariousness and to the need for flanking arrangements. Unless the aggregate value of the goods being jointly produced or used is very high, solidarity frames will be also stabilized by an *embedding in external means* for the reduction of opportunism: reputation, credible commitments, and legal means. Such means factually reduce the payoff from giving in to breach temptations, thereby rendering the breach temptations small enough to be handled by framing effects (which reduce the perception of opportunity costs). In terms of the logic of the explanation, this is a very important point because it shows that solidarity and other means of reducing opportunism are in this important sense not substitutes but complements and it shows that solidarity should not be treated as a matter between dyads or even as a matter of single groups.

Solidary behavior will ultimately always depend on the stability of the frame and this stability is always precarious. For this reason, every behavior relating to the group in some way acquires a signaling function: is the other still in a solidarity frame or is he beginning to slip? Such *relational signals* latch on first and foremost to the recurring situations in which solidarity could go wrong: common good, sharing, need and mishap situation, as well as breach temptations. For this reason, solidary behavior cannot be compensated by much conformity in some situations and little in others. If you contribute to the common good but refuse to make up when you did something wrong, then your intentions are under suspicion and the cooperative behavior is reinterpreted as strategic rather than solidary. It is thus relational signaling that gives solidarity this broad range of behavior.

Framing also suggests an important difference between weak and strong solidarity. This difference is not always well appreciated. *Weak solidarity* allows for the importance of the individual member of the group, for individual gain. The distributional principle recognizes individual investments and is therefore equity. The amount of time, money and effort individuals are expected to sacrifice for the group is modest or low, except with regard breach temptations. Ideological requirements are medium or low. In *strong solidarity* (i.e. solidarity in sharing groups with a very high aggregate value of the goods being jointly produced or used), individual interests are negligible in comparison to group interests; *vis-à-vis* other group members only the solidarity frame is legitimate; and *vis-à-vis* members of outgroups there are no restraints. And the distributional principle is equality, rather than equity. The amount of time, money and effort individuals are expected to sacrifice for the group are high or very high. Group boundaries are sharp, to maintain clear identifiability and group identity, and ideological embedding of group goals is strong in order to create interdependence of goals and thereby stabilization of the frame (which may lead to conflicting direction in development: enlargement for ideological support, compacting for sharpness of group boundaries). When compared to weak solidarity, strong solidarity is bad for business within and between groups.

Lastly, the traditional idea is being rejected that the historical movement is from *strong to weak solidarity*. Rather, due to technological developments in production and to increasing wealth, strong and weak solidarities have been giving way to a stronger (atomized) individualism with a wide-spread incidence of arm's length relationships and opportunism. Only as a reaction against this kind of individualism did we get a wide-spread development of weak solidarity and its embedding in flanking measures in policies of the state (including income policies). At times, when the flanking measures fail, strong solidarity reappears with sharp group boundaries, intergroup conflict and declining social product, as does atomistic individualism.

All in all, solidarity turns out to be much more anchored in the macrostructures than often assumed *because* it is so precarious in its microfoundations.

NOTES

1. I would like to thank Henk Flap and Rafael Wittek for a critical reading of an earlier version and for useful suggestions. I am afraid that in some points I had to remain stubborn, especially with regard to the complexity needed to come to a full microfoundation of solidary behavior.
2. In that, I will draw on a variety of work I have done in this area. But the paper is meant to be more than a summary of my own previous thoughts on the matter.
3. Hechter talks about "group solidarity" in order to capture what sociologists have implied all along: that groups influence their member's behavior (more or less).
4. This point has also been made by Fararo and Doreian (in Chapter 1).
5. A prisoners' dilemma could be seen as either a common good situation or as a breach temptation, depending on the particular interpretation given to the story.
6. Observe that strength of solidarity is not defined by the factual "average proportion of a member's private resources contributed to collective ends" (as Hechter does) but by the (legitimately) *expected* sacrifice in trying situations. Whether these costs are factually incurred depends on the frequency with which trying situations occur.
7. My critique of Durkheim's approach also holds for Collins' elaboration of that approach.
8. This does not mean that they would exclude groups. Rather, for them groups are either just the aggregate result of concatenated ties or the locus in which the formation of solidarity ties takes place. Homans said: "Small groups are not what we study but where we study it" (*ibid.*, 1961, p. 7).
9. In this context, Hollis' (1992) article on honor among thieves is instructive. Hollis shows that within the framework of game theory there can be no such thing as honor among thieves.
10. See Hogg and Abrams (1988) and Lindenberg (1997) for a critique of the interpersonal attraction theories of social cohesion.
11. A variant of the by-product theory is the idea that there are cooperative personality types (Liebrand, 1983). Then cooperation would be a question of selective processes.
12. There is an interesting recent attempt to deal with group solidarity by Markovsky and Chaffee (1995). They work with the assumptions of preference change (interpersonal attraction, here tied to emotional reactions, see Markovsky and Lawler, 1994) but they add structural aspects (reachability) and cognitive aspects (the cognition of the group as group). While this seems an advance in many ways, it still contains no notion of solidary behavior, no theory of the importance of solidarity nor a theory of its precariousness.
13. It is, of course, progress to view solidarity as a phenomenon of groups rather than of dyads. But as we will see later, it is necessary to look at systems of groups and other kinds of embedding of solidarity.
14. Close supervision is even likely to crowd out the motivation to be cooperative, see Frey (1997).

15. The economist Buchanan (1965) had before me developed a theory of "clubs" on the basis of which I had built the sharing group theory which took a more sociological direction. It should also be mentioned that early on in group dynamics (Lewin, Deutsch), the group had also been defined in terms of the pursuit of a common goal. Only later did this view gave way to interpersonal attraction (see Lindenberg (1997) for an account of this development).

16. For an interesting description and analysis of such a process, see Ostrom (1995).

17. Raub and Weesie (1993) add legal or extra-legal *ex ante* commitments, a basis for "'precontractual solidarity' à la Durkheim". They also add conditions that make certain credible threats feasible, such as network effects that induce concern for one's reputation. Williamson (1993) himself mentions these things under the heading of "institutional trust" (see next footnote).

18. Williamson suggests to reserve the term "trust" for situations where calculativeness and monitoring are purposefully suppressed (as in very special relations) and for institutional environments that provide strong safeguards. How, from the perspective of a rational choice theory, it is possible to "suppress" calculativeness, is not answered by Williamson. Again, if one allows suppression of calculativeness one should have a theory that explains how this is possible and why it can be ignored.

19. The term "framing" is being used in different ways in the literature. Observe that framing here refers specifically to the definition of the situation and not to any subjective distortion of objective reality as Kahneman and Tversky (1984) often use the term. The framing theory presented here is based on the discrimination model of stochastic choice (see Lindenberg, 1980).

20. Of course, it is also possible that all interaction partners come into the situation with a preconceived goal in which case the definition of the situation will be negotiated (see Goffman, 1969).

21. I do not assume any general human desire to act appropriately. This assumptions is sometimes made by advocates of a "logic of appropriateness" (for example March and Olsen, 1995, p.30ff). Rather, the importance of "acting appropriately" comes from the importance of social (dis)approval [including self-(dis)approval]. The anticipated (dis)approval for acting (in)appropriately, rather than appropriateness itself is the relevant motivator in such a situation.

22. This point has been worked out in some more detail in Lindenberg (1994).

23. See Carr and Landa (1983).

24. Sherif (1966) had clearly identified the framing aspect of these processes by showing that individuals act differently toward members of other groups depending whether they act as members or as individuals.

25. The basis for such rules is again solidarity rather than the principle of welfare maximization of the group (see Ellickson, 1991). For example, the rule would have to follow sharing conventions and need considerations used in this group, and these differ in weak and strong solidarity (see below).

26. See Lindenberg (1993) and Wielers (1993) for more detailed information of the relational signaling theory.

27. In this context, Tannen's popular book on the power of meta-messages that accompany ordinary conversation is very much to the point (see Tannen, 1990).

28. For example, this has been empirically shown to be the case with long-term baby-sitters, where solidary behavior from both sides play an important role (see Wielers, 1993). Murnighan and Pillutla (1995) found in ultimatum games that unfair offers elicited negative emotional responses and rejection.

29. This is one reasons why solidarity plays an important role in networks of long-term business relations (see, for example, Uzzi, 1997).

30. It is quoted in Goffman (1974, p. 462).

31. Whereas clarity of relational signal can be interpreted as low transaction costs, this only shows that Williamson's theory (1985) can be related in some way to this theory

of solidarity. It does not indicate that Williamson's theory could have generated anything in this theory of solidarity.
32. This difference has been discussed in more detail in Lindenberg (1988; 1992).
33. A sharing group may also have a very loose organization, as in neighbors sharing common space and therefore also some risks without any conscious effort at rule formation. Another example of such a loose sharing group is what White (1993) has called an "interface" (as group of producers who produce the same good and share the creation of an intelligible front *vis-à-vis* the buyers). White however has not taken up the relational signaling within such an interface.
34. See also Raub (1996).
35. Contrary to balance theory, the claim here is that the group is not closed because strong individual ties create a pressure for transitivity. Rather, dyadic solidary ties are part of the sharing group and the latter is not the result of concatenation of dyads. If a friend of a friend is added to the group, then a larger group size is useful for the joint production or the cost-sharing. Beyond that size, if there is at all a friend of a friend outside the group, there will be no transitive closure (see Lindenberg, 1982).
36. For more detail on these arguments, see Lindenberg (1986).

REFERENCES

Abell, P., 1996. A model of the informal structure (culture) of organizations: help, trust, rivalry and team spirit. *Rationality and Society* **8**, 4: 433–452.
Andreoni, J., 1988. Why free ride?: Strategies and learning in public goods experiments. *Journal of Public Economics* **37**, 291–304.
Ben-Porath, Y., 1980. The F-connection: families, friends and firms in the organization of exchange. *Population and Development Review* **6**, 1: 1–30.
Binmore, K., 1994. *Game Theory and the Social Contract Volume I: Playing Fair.* Cambridge, MA: MIT Press.
Blumberg, B., 1997. *Das Management von Technologiekooperationen.* Amsterdam: Thesis Publishers.
Buchanan, J., 1965. An economic theory of clubs. *Econometrica (New Series)* **32**: 1–14.
Burt, R.S., 1992. *Structural Holes. The Social Structure of Competition.* Cambridge, MA: Harvard University Press.
Burt, R.S. and Knez, M., 1995. Kinds of third-party effects on trust. *Rationality and Society* **7**, 3: 255–292.
Carr, J.L. and Landa, Janet T., 1983. The economics of symbols, clan names and religion. *Journal of Legal Studies* **12**, 1: 135–156.
Casson, M., 1991. *The Economics of Business Culture.* Oxford: Clarendon Press.
Coase, R., 1960. The problem of social cost. *Journal of Law and Economics* **3**: 1–44.
Coleman, J.S., 1982. *The Asymmetric Society.* Syracuse, NY. Syracuse University Press.
Coleman, J.S., 1990. *Foundation of Social Theory.* Cambridge, MA: Harvard University Press.
Collins, R., 1985. *Three Sociological Traditions.* Oxford and New York: Oxford University Press.
De Graaf, N. D. and Flap, H., 1988. With a little help from my friends. Social resources as an explanation of occupational status and income in the Netherlands, the United States and West Germany. *Social Forces* **67**: 43–72.
De Vries, S., 1991. *Egoism, Altruism, and Social Justice.* Amsterdam: Thesis Publishers.
Durkheim, E., 1933. *The Division of Labor in Society.* [1893] New York: Macmillan.
Durkheim, E., 1965. *The Elementary Forms of Religious Life.* [1912] New York: Free Press.

Ellickson, R.C. 1991. *Order Without Law. How Neighbors Settle Disputes.* Cambridge, MA: Harvard University Press.

Feld, S., 1981. The focused organization of social ties. *American Journal of Sociology* **85**, 5: 1015–1035

Flap, H., 1988. *Conflict, Loyalty, and Violence.* Frankfurt: Peter Lang.

Frank, Robert H., 1988. *Passions within Reason. The Strategic Role of the Emotions.* New York: Norton.

Frey, Bruno S., 1997. *Not Just For the Money. An Economic Theory of Personal Motivation.* Brookfield: Edward Elgar Publishing.

Gál, R., 1997. *Unreliability: Contract Discipline and Contract Governance Under Economic Transition.* Amsterdam: Thesis Publishers.

Goffman, E., 1959. *The Presentation of Self in Everyday Life.* Garden City, NY: Doubleday Anchor Books.

Goffman, E., 1969. *Strategic Interaction.* Philadelphia: University of Philadelphia Press.

Goffman, E., 1974. *Frame Analysis. An Essay on the Organization of Experience.* Cambridge, MA: Harvard University Press.

Goleman, D., 1985. *Vital Lies, Simple Truths.* New York: Simon and Schuster.

Grieco, M., 1987. *Keeping it in the Family. Social Networks and Employment Chance.* London/New York: Tavistock Publications.

Hardin, R., 1995. *One for All: The Logic of Group Conflict.* Princeton, NJ: Princeton University Press.

Hechter, M., 1987. *Principles of Group Solidarity,* Berkeley: University of California Press.

Heimer, Carol, 1992. Doing your job *and* helping your friends: universalistic norms about obligations to particular others in networks, pp. 143–164, in: Nohria, N. and R. Eccles (eds), *Networks and Organization. Structure, Form, and Action.* Boston: Harvard Business School Press.

Hogg, M.A. and Abrams, D., 1988. *Social Identifications: A Psychology of Intergroup Relations and Group Processes.* London & New York: Routledge.

Hollis, M., 1992. Honour among thieves, pp. 115–130 in Hollis, M. und Vossenkuhl, W. (eds), *Moralische Entscheidung und Rationale Wahl.* Munich: Scientia Nova. Oldenbourg Verlag.

Homans, G.C., 1954. The cash posters. *American Sociological Review* **19**: 724–733.

Homans, G.C., 1958. Social behavior as exchange, *American Journal of Sociology* **63**, 6: 597–606.

Homans, G.C., 1961. *Social Behavior: Its Elementary Forms.* New York: Harcourt, Brace & World.

Kahneman, D., Knetsch, J.L. and Thaler, R.H., 1986. Fairness as Constraint on Profit Seeking: Entitlements in the Market. *American Economic Review* **76** (Sept.): 728–41.

Kahneman, D., Knetsch, J.L. and Thaler, R.H., 1991. Anomalies: the endowment effect, loss aversion, and status quo bias. *Journal of Economic Perspectives* **5**: 193–206.

Kahneman, D. and Tversky, A., 1984. Choices, values, and frames. *American Psychologist* **39**, 4: 341–350.

Kaplan, R.E., 1984. Trade routes: the manager's network of relationships. *Organizational Dynamics* (Spring): 37–52.

Kramer, R.M., Shah, P.P. and Woerner, S., 1995. Why ultimatums fail. Social identity and moralistic aggression in coercive bargaining. pp. 285–308, in Kramer, R.M. and Messick, D. (eds), *Negotiation as Social Process.* Thousand Oaks, London, New Delhi: Sage Publications.

Lawler, E. and Yoon, 1993. Power and the emergence of commitment behavior in negotiated exchange. *American Sociological Review* **58**: 465–481.

Lazega, E., 1995. Protecting the common good among equals: A lateral control regime of partners in a law firm. *LASMAS* Preprint Nr. 96/1.

Liebrand, W.B.G., 1983. A classification of social dilemma games. *Simulation & Games* **14**: 123–138.

Ligthart, P.A.M., 1995. *Solidarity in Economics Transactions: An Experimental Study of Framing Effects in Bargaining and Contracting*. Amsterdam: Thesis Publisher.
Lindenberg, S., 1975. 'Three psychological theories of a classical sociologist,' *Mens en Maatschappij* **50**, 2: 133–153.
Lindenberg, S., 1980. Marginal utility and restraints on gain maximization: the discrimination model of rational, repetitive choice. *Journal of Mathematical Sociology* **7**, 2: 289–316.
Lindenberg, S., 1982. Sharing groups: theory and suggested applications. *Journal of Mathematical Sociology* **9**: 33–62.
Lindenberg, S., 1986. The paradox of privatization in consumption, pp. 297–310, in Diekmann A. and Mitter P. (eds), *Paradoxical Effects of Social Behavior. Essays in Honor of Anatol Rapoport*. Heidelberg/Wien: Physica-Verlag.
Lindenberg, S., 1988. Contractual relations and weak solidarity: the behavioral basis of restraints on gain-maximization. *Journal of Institutional and Theoretical Economics* **144**, 39–58.
Lindenberg, S., 1992. An extended theory of institutions and contractual discipline. *Journal of Institutional and Theoretical Economics* **148**, 2: 125–154.
Lindenberg, S., 1993. Framing, empirical evidence, and applications, pp. 11–38, *Jahrbuch für Neue Politische Ökonomie*. Tübingen: Mohr (Siebeck).
Lindenberg, S., 1994. Norms and the power of loss: Ellickson's theory and beyond, in Furubotn, E.G. and Richter, R. (eds), *The New Institutional Economics. Bounded Rationality and the Analysis of State and Society. Journal of Institutional and Theoretical Economics* (Special Issue) **150**, 1: 101–113.
Lindenberg, S., 1997. Grounding groups n theory: functional, cognitive, and structural interdependencies, pp. 281–331, in *Advances in Group Processes*, Vol. 14. Greenwich CT: JAI Press.
Loewenstein, G.F., 1992. The fall and rise of psychological explanations in the economics of intertemporal choice, pp. 3–34, in Loewenstein, G.F. and Elster, J. (eds), *Choice over Time*. New York: Russell.
Loewenstein, G.F. and Elster, J. (eds) 1992. *Choice over Time*. New York: Russell Sage.
March, J.G. and Olsen, J.P., 1995. *Democratic Governance*. New York: Free Press.
Margolis, H., 1982. *Selfishness, Altruism, and Rationality: A Theory of Social Choice*. Cambridge: Cambridge University Press.
Markovsky, B. and Chaffee, M., 1995. Social identification and solidarity. *Advances in Group Processes* **12**: 249–270.
Markovsky, B. and Lawler, E.J., 1994. A new theory of group solidarity. *Advances in Group Processes* **11**: 113–137.
Melucci, A., 1989. *Nomads of the Present: Social Movements and Individual Needs in Contemporary Society*. Keane, J. and Mier, P. (eds) Philadelphia: Temple University Press.
Murnighan, J.K. and Pillutla, M.M., 1995. Fairness versus self-interest, pp. 240–267, in Kramer, R.M. and Messick, D. (eds), *Negotiation as Social Process*. Thousand Oaks, London, New Delhi: Sage Publications.
Olson, M., 1965. *The Logic of Collective Action*. Cambridge, MA: Harvard University Press.
Ostrom, E., 1990. *Governing the Commons: The Evolution of Institutions for Collective Action*. Cambridge: Cambridge University Press.
Ostrom, E., 1995. Constituting social capital and collective action, pp. 125–160, in Keohane, R.O. and Ostrom, E. (eds), *Local Commons and Global Interdependence*. London: Sage.
Piore, M. and Sabel, C., 1984. *The Second Industrial Divide*. New York: Basic Books.
Pizzorno, A., 1978. Political exchange and collective identity in industrial conflict, pp. 277–298, in Crouch, C. and Pizzorno, A. (eds), *The Resurgence of Class Conflict in Western Europe since 1968*. London: Macmillan.

112   LINDENBERG

Raub, W., 1996. Effects of temporal embeddedness on *ex ante* planning under incomplete information. Iscore-Paper Nr. 87, Utrecht: University of Utrecht, *mimeo*.
Raub, W. and Weesie, J., 1990. Reputation and efficiency in social interactions: an example of network effects. *American Journal of Sociology* **96**: 626–654.
Raub, W. and Weesie, J., 1993. Symbiotic arrangements: a sociological perspective. *Journal of Institutional and Theoretical Economics* **149**, 4: 1716–1724.
Raub, W. and Weesie, J., 1996. The Management of Matches. Decentralized Mechanisms for Cooperative Relations with Applications to Organizations and Households. Progress Report 1993–1995. Iscore-Paper Nr. 62, Utrecht: University of Utrecht, *mimeo*.
Ridgeway, C.L. and Walker, H.A., 1995. Status structures, pp. 281–310, in K. S. Kook, Fine, G.A. and House, J.S. (eds), *Sociological Perspectives on Social Psychology*. Boston: Allen and Bacon.
Sherif, M., 1966. *In Common Predicament: Social Psychology of Intergroup Conflict and Cooperation*. Boston: Houghton-Mifflin.
Spence, M., 1994. *Market Signaling*. Cambridge, MA: Harvard University Press.
Tajfel., H., 1970. Experiments in intergroup discrimination. *Scientific American*, **223**: 96–102.
Tajfel, H., Flament, C., Billig, M.G. and Bundy, R.P., 1971. Social categorization and intergroup behavior. *European Journal of Social Psychology* **1**: 1459–1478.
Tannen, D., 1990. *You Just Don't Understand: Women and Men in Conversation*. New York: William Morrow.
Turner, J.C. and Giles, H. (eds), 1981. *Intergroup Behaviour*. Oxford: Blackwell.
Uzzi, B., 1997. Social structure and competition in interfirm networks: the paradox of embeddedness. *Administrative Science Quarterly* **42**, 1: 35–67.
Vaill, P.B., 1986. The purposing of high-performance systems, pp. 85–104, in Sergiovanni, T.J. and Corbally, J.E. (eds), *Leadership and Organizational Culture*. Urbana and Chicago: University of Illinois Press.
Weber, M., 1961. *General Economic History*. New York: Collier Books.
White, H. C., 1993. Markets, networks and control, in Lindenberg, S. and Schreuder, H. (eds), *Interdisciplinary Perspectives on Organization Studies*. Oxford: Pergamon Press.
Wielers, R., 1993. On trust in employment relationships: the case of child-minders. *Netherlands' Journal of Social Sciences* **29**: 43–63.
Williamson, O.E., 1993. Calculativeness, trust, and economic organization. *Journal of Law and Economics* **XXXVI**: 453–486.

4 THE MANAGEMENT OF TRUST RELATIONS VIA INSTITUTIONAL AND STRUCTURAL EMBEDDEDNESS

JEROEN WEESIE, VINCENT BUSKENS and
WERNER RAUB

Utrecht University[1]

1. INTRODUCTION

The governance of exchange is a core topic of sociological theory and 'economic sociology'. Durkheim (1893, Book I, Chapter 7) highlighted the limits of explicit contractual agreements as a basis for efficient transactions. He addressed unforeseen or unforeseeable future contingencies that arise in the course of contract execution. He also stressed bargaining costs associated with the negotiation and re-negotiation of detailed contractual agreements. Weber (1921, p. 409) presented similar arguments in his sociology of law. According to Durkheim, efficient transactions presuppose appropriate legal and extra-legal institutions, e.g., moral norms of reciprocity and solidarity, that complement bilateral contracts. In an influential contribution to the sociology of law, Macaulay (1963) presented empirical evidence for the widespread use of non-contractual modes of arranging transactions. Granovetter (1985) has argued from a network perspective that the embeddedness of transactions in ongoing relations and in a network of relations with third parties has crucial implications for efficient governance via non-contractual means.

More recently, the social organization of transactions became a topic of a sizable literature in law and economics including, e.g., research on relational contracts (Macneil, 1980; Lindenberg, 1988), hybrid forms of organization (Williamson, 1985), and symbiotic arrangements (Schanze, 1991). This literature is strikingly similar to sociological approaches in stressing that transactions frequently differ in two related ways from the standard 'spot exchange transactions on anonymous markets' that are usually studied in neoclassical economics. First, transactions are often beset with incentives for 'opportunistic' behavior. These incentives may result from the lapse of time between the moments at which the partners have to deliver their part of the transaction and from asymmetric information that leads to imperfect determination whether or not the partner behaved appropriately (monitoring and agency problems). Second, given these incentive problems, markets cannot be anonymous and almost institution-free social structures as conceived in neoclassical economics. Rather, markets have to be embedded in a variety of spontaneous and constructed social institutions that reduce the imperfections that result from incentive problems (North, 1990).

Incentive problems in social and economic exchange can take a variety of forms. Of particular interest to solidarity theory are one-sided *trust problems* (see, e.g., Coleman, 1990, Chapters 5 and 8). A trust problem due to a *time lag* between the actions of trustor and trustee is associated with social exchange of help and support (Blau, 1964; Hechter, 1987). If Ego provides help or support for Alter today, Alter has to choose tomorrow between reciprocating or not reciprocating, i.e., helping or not helping Ego. Compared to the outcome where no one provides help, Ego and Alter may benefit if Ego trusts and helps Alter today while Alter reciprocates tomorrow. Likewise, however, it may be the worst outcome for Ego but the most attractive one for Alter if Ego provides help today while Alter exhibits opportunism and does not reciprocate tomorrow. Used cars are a standard illustration for *product quality problems* in economic exchange relations. The quality of a used car is usually known to the potential buyer but not to the potential seller. The buyer has to decide whether or not to trust the seller. If he decides to trust the seller, the seller has to choose between keeping trust by selling a good car and abusing trust by behaving opportunistically and selling a lemon. In such cases of transactions involving products that are either high or low quality and where quality is only known to the seller, the buyer is usually best off if trust is placed and a high quality product is sold, but worst off if trust is placed and a low quality product is sold. On the other hand, the seller frequently has an incentive to sell a low quality product. A trust problem also arises in the case of *sequential exchange*. Consider a lender and a borrower. The lender has to make the first decision and has to choose between trusting and not trusting the borrower. If he trusts and lends, the borrower has to decide later on between keeping trust by repaying and abusing trust by defaulting on the debt. Again, the lend–repay outcome may be optimal and the lend–default outcome worst for the potential lender while the borrower faces an incentive to default.

In this paper, we study the management of trust relations. While many studies analyze specific (contractual or non-contractual) elements of governance structures 'in isolation', we try to contribute to a more realistic analysis by considering governance structures that involve a *'mix' of mechanisms*. Such an integrated analysis will allow us to address conditions under which the mechanisms under consideration are substitutes or complements.[2] The set of mechanisms available to the actors reflect that transactions are embeddedness in a social context (Raub and Weesie, 1995).

First, transactions are *institutionally embedded*, i.e., they occur in an institutional environment that is, at least to a considerable extent, the result of intended social construction (Coleman, 1990). The institutional context is a set of rules and procedures, formal as well as informal, that influences the behavior of economic actors (North, 1990). The institutional context may offer economic actors opportunities to affect themselves the *short-term* consequences of given behavioral alternatives (see also Weesie and Raub, 1996). Main examples are short-term *contractual agreements* that detail the obligations of both partners of the transactions and the sanctions for any breach of the contract. Here, the institutional context is assumed to enforce the contract, e.g., via the judicial system. In addition, the institutional context may provide opportunities for ways to modify the incentives for opportunistic behavior in a *long-term* way via legal or extra-legal *ex ante* commitments (see Snijders (1986) for a theoretical and experimental analysis of the use of commitments for the solution of trust problems). Examples are long-term contracts, investments in excess capacity (Dixit, 1982), and formal and informal relationship-specific investments.

Second, transactions may be *structurally embedded* (Granovetter, 1985). We distinguish two types. Transactions may be *temporally embedded*: to some extent future transactions may occur between the same partners. This allows for *reciprocity* as a mechanism for the management of exchange: credible promises and threats that are feasible through long-term interactions induce concern for one's reputation towards the partner. Transactions may also be structurally embedded in another way, namely in *social networks*, that operate as information channels and link streams of transactions between overlapping sets of actors. Thus, actors may condition their behavior in a given transaction not only on their own experience with this partner, but also on the partner's behavior towards third parties. Consequently, networks of relations may induce concern for one's *reputation* towards partners and third parties (Raub and Weesie, 1990).

2. A MODEL FOR TRUST RELATIONS

2.1. A Model for Trust

We use a variant of the Trust Game (Dasgupta, 1988; Kreps, 1990) for modeling a simple transaction that is beset with incentive problems. In the Trust Game Γ_θ, actors move sequentially. This induces asymmetry and one-sided dependency. There are two actors. Actor 1 is the trustor. We refer to actor 1 as the 'buyer'. Actor 2 is the trustee to whom we refer as the 'seller'. While these labels suggest an economic exchange relation, it should be kept in mind that trust problems are a typical feature of social relations in general. The buyer moves first and has two options for organizing transactions with the seller. First, the buyer can refuse to trust his partner, denoted by D_1. An obvious interpretation would be that the buyer refuses to transact with the seller. However, we prefer another interpretation of the 'don't trust' – alternative for the buyer, namely, that he proposes an elaborate and externally enforceable but costly contract for the management of transactions. If D_1 is chosen, the actors receive payoffs P_i from their transactions. Alternatively, the buyer may trust his partner, denoted by C_1. This means that transactions are managed by an incomplete contract that saves (transaction) costs but leaves options for the seller to behave opportunistically. After C_1 has been chosen, the seller can decide to exhibit loyalty through honoring trust, denoted by C_2; e.g., he sticks to unwritten, tacit, and not formally binding agreements. In this case, the actors receive payoffs $R_i > P_i$, $i = 1, 2$. However, the seller can also decide to behave opportunistically and misuse trust, denoted by D_2; e.g., he violates agreements that are not externally enforceable. In this case, the buyer receives payoff $S_1 < P_1$ and the seller $R_2 + \theta$.[3] Here, $\theta > 0$ models the incentive for the seller to behave opportunistically. Consider now the Trust Game Γ_θ, played as a noncooperative game with complete information and assume that the structure of the game is common knowledge. Obviously, if $\theta > 0$ there is a unique and Pareto inefficient subgame perfect equilibrium (spe) such that the

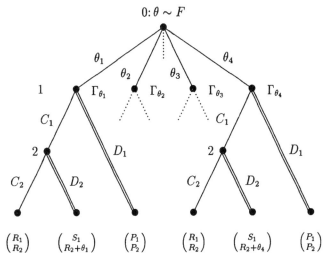

FIGURE 4.1.   Extensive form of the Heterogeneous Trust Game Γ_F, where $R_i > P_i$ $(i = 1, 2)$, $P_1 > S_1$, $\theta > 0$, and $\theta \sim F$.

buyer chooses D_1 while the seller would choose D_2 had the buyer chosen C_1. Hence, the outcomes of transactions are socially inefficient because they are managed by (too) costly contracts. Notice that our notation for moves and payoffs reflects that the Trust Game can be viewed as a one-sided Prisoner's Dilemma.

Up to now, we assumed that θ is fixed and known prior to playing the game. It is easily verified that the conclusions remain valid if prior to playing the trust game θ is generated at random from some probability distribution F that reflects the distribution of incentives for opportunistic behavior for the seller. Such a game is called a *Heterogeneous Trust Game* (HTG) Γ_F (Raub and Weesie, 1993). The extensive form of Γ_F is displayed in Figure 4.1.

For technical reasons that will become clear below we impose a regularity constraint on the distribution F,

F is an atomless probability distribution with support $(0, \infty)$.   (1)

2.2. Two Types of Social Embeddedness

In the introduction we argued that transactions typically do not occur in isolation ('atomized transactions') but are embedded in a social context. In this context, players have ongoing relations with each other. Moreover, actors are socially linked so that the behavior of actors in one transaction may affect the behavior of actors in other transactions because of, e.g., information impactedness. These forms of social embeddedness will be modeled as follows. First, transactions are *temporally embedded* to the extent that transacting actors share a common future. This is modeled by the assumption that one buyer and one seller play an *Iterated Heterogeneous Trust Game* in discrete time $t = 0, 1, 2, \ldots$ At time t, they play a HTG. The number T of iterations of the constituent HTG is a random variable with a *geometric distribution* $\text{Geo}(\delta_1)$ for $0 \leqslant \delta_1 \leqslant 1$. We can interpret δ_1 as the death rate of the buyer. The realized T is unknown to the players. Thus, if the iterated game has continued until time t, another game is played with probability $1 - \delta_1$, independent of the history of the game so far. (Below we will discuss what happens if a buyer dies.) It follows that the expected duration of the interaction between the buyer and the seller is $1/\delta_1$. Mainly for reasons of symmetry, the seller dies at time t with probability δ_2 and then the game is over. The sequence $\theta_1, \theta_2, \ldots$ of the consecutive HTGs are generated *independently* from the distribution F. Moreover, the θ_t's do not depend in any way on the history of the game. At time t, both players are informed about the past and present $\theta_{t'} (t' = 1, \ldots, t)$ but not about the future $\theta_{t'} (t' > t)$.

Second, transactions are *network embedded*. Here we restrict attention to social ties between buyers that operate as information channels about the behavior of the seller.[4] Since the joint analysis of four types of management of trust relations is a demanding task, we have to specify a relatively stylized scenario for network effects. In this scenario, the seller interacts for a random duration with only one buyer. When this buyer dies, a new buyer takes her place. If there exists a social tie between the 'old' and 'new' buyers, the new buyer acquires information from the old buyer: the full history of the game as far as the old buyer is informed about this. We make the strong *homogeneity assumption* that the probability that a social tie exists is independent of the history of the game and the identity of the old and new buyer. Now we can describe network embeddedness by a single parameter $\alpha \in [0, 1]$, which can be interpreted as the *density* (in terms of direct ties only) of the network between the buyers. Note that in our model ties among sellers and ties between buyers and sellers do not affect behavior of players.

2.3. Institutional Embeddedness: *Ex Ante* Commitments

Next, we assume opportunities for establishing some amount of precontractual solidarity. Durkheim stressed general legal rules, e.g., contract law, and moral norms as bases of pre-contractual solida-rity. We prefer a broad interpretation and, moreover, focus on pre-contractual solidarity as an endogenous variable. Hence, we assume that the seller can voluntarily incur *ex ante commitments* in a preplay period. Commitment or 'hostage posting' techniques (see Weesie and Raub (1996) for a game-theoretic analysis of 'hostage games') include the provision of formal and explicit warranties made feasible by, e.g., general legal rules. They also include more informal and implicit ways of bonding, e.g., through relationship-specific investments in specialized production technologies or delivery arrangements. Provid-ing independent professional experts as mediators and arbitrators in the case of conflict is another example. Finally, commitment purposes are served by feelings of moral obligation, assuming that these are, at least to some degree, objects of choice (see Frank, 1988; Raub and Voss, 1990).[5]

Technically, we model the choice of *ex ante* commitments by assum-ing that the seller chooses $h \in [0,1]$ in period 0 such that for Trust Game played with some buyer in period t the seller's payoff associated with abused trust is $R_2 + (1-h)\theta_t$ instead of $R_2 + \theta_t$, while all other payoffs in period t are unaffected by the *commitment h*. Hence, *ex ante* commitments moderate ex-post incentives for opportunism. Each buyer is informed on the seller's commitment choice h before period 1. The *commitment costs c(h)* are assumed to be fully paid by the seller. One could easily imagine and analyze other cost-sharing devices, e.g., the buyer pays part of the commitments costs via the price of the goods delivered by the seller. However, we wish to stress the counter-intuitive feature that it can be rational for the seller to incur commit-ments against own opportunism even if he has to bear the full costs. We assume that it is free not to enter commitments and assume increas-ing total as well as marginal commitment costs, while commitments that reduce incentives for opportunism to zero are infinitely costly,

$$c(0)=0, \quad c'>0, \quad c''>0, \quad \text{and} \quad \lim_{h \to 1} c(h) = \infty. \qquad (2)$$

2.4. Integration of the Elements of the Model

We have now introduced the main elements of the Iterated Hetero-geneous Trust Game IHTG($\Gamma_F, \omega_1, \omega_2, \delta_1, \delta_2, \alpha, F, c$). First, as a model of transactions we introduced the constituent Heterogeneous Trust Game Γ_F in which F describes the 'size' of the seller's temptation to behave opportunistically, and $R_i - P_i$ measures player i's costs if a buyer insists on using a complete short-term contract rather than trusting that the buyer will honor trust. Second, we modeled temporal embeddedness of transactions by assuming that the seller interacts with one buyer for an 'indefinite' number of period: After each period the buyer dies with probability δ_1 and the seller dies with probability δ_2. Thus temporal embeddedness increases with decreasing death rates δ_1 and δ_2. Third, network embeddedness is incorporated via the scenario that if the interaction between the seller and one buyer is over, a new buyer takes her place who is informed on possible opportunistic behavior of the seller with probability α. Thus, transactions are more network embedded the higher the α. Finally, we introduced a possibility for the seller to incur a credible commitment h in the preplay period that reduces his incentives for opportunistic behavior at costs $c(h)$.

Before we can turn to an analysis, two final elements of the model have to be defined. First, we have to define payoffs of players in the IHTG in terms of the costs of commitments in the preplay period and the payoffs u_{it} obtained in the constituent game at time $t = 0, 1, 2, \ldots$. We define an actors's payoff $u_{it} = 0$ for all time periods at which he/she does not play. We use standard exponential discounting with parameter $\omega_i \in (0, 1)$,

$$u_i = \sum_{t=0}^{\infty} \omega_i^t u_{it} - c_i,$$

where $c_2 = c(h)$ and $c_1 = 0$. Here ω_i denotes the pure time preferences or patience of player i that reflects the extent to which actors depreciate the value of a delayed reward with the delay (Ainsley, 1992).[6] Note that we assume that all buyers discount future payoffs at the same rate. Below we will sometimes consider *standardized utility*,

$$U_i = \frac{(1 - \omega_i)u_i - P_i}{R_i - P_i}.$$

We will see that in our solution of the IHTG, players receive only R_i's and P_i's. Thus $U_1^* \in [0, 1]$ for the solution payoff of the buyers. Moreover, we will see that a rational seller will choose his commitment level so that $U_2^* \in [0, 1]$. Now, U_i^* close to 1 means that player i received a payoff stream of mostly R_i's, while U_i^* close to 0 means that i he received mostly P_i's. Thus we can use standardized utility, in particular that of the seller, as a measure for the extent to which cooperation problem have been overcome by the efficient governance of trust relations. Second, we have to make assumptions regarding the information that the players have regarding the game that they play. We use the relatively standard assumption that the full description of the game, i.e., the order of moves, the payoffs of all players etc., are *common knowledge*. This implies that players are assumed to know the payoffs of each other, the discount rates ω_i, the distribution F, etc.

3. ANALYSIS OF THE MODEL

We now analyze how a rational seller (player 2) and rational buyers (players 1) behave in the IHTG game. In the noncooperative game-theoretic approach that we use in this paper, predictions are derived from a (Nash) *equilibrium* of the game, i.e., a collection of strategies of the players that form a 'self-enforcing agreement'. In our application, it will be necessary to find a pragmatic solution to one of the central problems in rational choice theory: in many games, multiple equilibria exist. In fact, in the dynamic game IHTG, the number of equilibria and the number of payoffs that are supported by equilibria, may well be uncountably infinite. From a strictly formal point of view, it is not directly clear which of these equilibria should be considered as the 'solution' from which we derive our predictions. While many equilibrium selection theories have been proposed in a rapidly expanding literature (e.g., Harsanyi and Selten, 1988; Harsanyi, 1995), none of these general theories selects a unique equilibrium in the IHTG, and so we have to define a solution in a more *ad hoc* fashion.

Our pragmatic 'solution' to the equilibrium selection problem comprises several elements. *First*, we use the standard refinement of the Nash equilibrium for dynamic games: subgame perfection. *Second*, mainly for reasons of analytical tractability, we consider special types of *trigger strategies* (Friedman, 1971). The seller's trigger strategy $\sigma_2(h, \vartheta_2)$ prescribes that (1) he places a commitment h in the preplay period and (2) he honors the trust of a buyer (cooperates) at all times t in the game Γ_F if and only if the temptation for dishonoring trust is sufficiently low, $\theta_t \leqslant \vartheta_2$. Similarly, a buyer's trigger strategy $\sigma_1(\vartheta_1)$ prescribes that a buyer places trust at time t if and only if (1) the seller's temptation is sufficiently low, $\theta_t \leqslant \vartheta_1$, and (2) the buyer has no information that the seller has dishonored trust in the past. Note that in scenarios with $\alpha > 0$, the buyer's information may be due to own experience but also to experiences of earlier buyers, provided that the information has been conveyed to her. The parameter ϑ_1 can be interpreted as the extent to which the buyer (player 1) trusts the seller (player 2). Thus, the higher ϑ_1, the less the buyer replies on complete contracts to manage her transactions with the seller. We want to stress that our assumption that the buyers use trigger strategies of the prescribed type precludes the possibility that the buyers 'force' the seller to commit himself to a high degree, by insisting to use complete contracts otherwise. Rather, the buyers adapt to the commitment decision of the seller. Thus, in principle the seller has a strong 'first mover advantage' in deciding his commitment level. We assume homogeneity among the buyers in the sense that the buyers use trigger strategies with the same trust-thresholds ϑ_2 (cf. the symmetry condition in Harsanyi and Selten, 1988, p. 72). *Third*, we will see below that there are often multiple subgame perfect equilibria in trigger strategies one of which is Pareto-optimal. We will select this equilibrium as the tentative 'solution' of the game ('payoff-dominance').

We are now ready to present formal results on the efficient governance of trust relation as modeled by the IHTG. Our results are presented in the following order. First, we derive as a Lemma that in a subgame perfect equilibrium in trigger strategies, the seller and the buyer(s) use the same trust-threshold. Thus, a self-enforcing governance structure for the IHTG can be described by a single trust-threshold that describes the extent to which complete short-term contracts are used. Second, we consider efficient governance structures that comprise structural mechanisms based on temporal and network embeddedness and the possibility to use complete contracts as an institution based mechanism, but exclude the use of *ex ante* commitments. Given our assumption of complete information and that players use trigger strategies, the mechanisms based on structural embeddedness are used 'fully', and so the only 'choice' parameter is the extent to which complete short-term contracts are used. Finally, we consider efficient governance with both *ex ante* commitment and complete short-term contracts as choice parameters.

Lemma 1 *In the* IHTG$(\Gamma_F, \omega_1, \omega_2, \delta_1, \delta_2, \alpha, F, c)$ *there exist subgame perfect equilibria (spe) in trigger strategies* $(\sigma_1(\vartheta_1), \sigma_2(h, \vartheta_2))$. *In each spe, the trust-thresholds are identical,* $\vartheta_1 = \vartheta_2 = \vartheta$. *In particular,* $(0, (0, 0))$ *is a spe.*

Proof Note that trigger strategies with $\vartheta_1 = \vartheta_2 = 0$ are in subgame perfect equilibrium (spe). Thus, existence is ensured. To demonstrate that in equilibrium, players use the same thresholds, we first assume that $\vartheta_2 < \vartheta_1$ in a spe. Since F has full support (see (1)), there is a positive probability that $\vartheta_2 < \theta < \vartheta_1$. In that case, the seller will receive $R_2 + \theta$, while the buyer receives S_1 and in all the following games the buyer plays D_1 and receives a payoff P_1. However, if the buyer in this case had chosen $\vartheta_1 = \vartheta_2$, he would have received P_1 in the first game and R_1 or P_1 in all the following games, which is more than he receives now. Now assume that $\vartheta_1 < \vartheta_2$. Here, the buyer gains at every time at which $\vartheta_1 < \theta \leqslant \vartheta_2$ an amount equal to $R_1 - P_2$ from increasing his threshold ϑ_1 to ϑ_2. Thus, if $\vartheta_1 \neq \vartheta_2$, the buyer is not using a best reply strategy against the seller's trigger strategy. We conclude that in a subgame perfect equilibrium, the trust-thresholds are necessarily the same. $\square$

Lemma 1 implies that if trust is given ($\vartheta > 0$), trust will never be abused on the equilibrium path. Consequently, we do not need to distinguish between the buyer's threshold and the seller's threshold. Therefore, we will denote a strategy-vector by $\sigma(h, \vartheta)$, where h is the *ex ante* commitment placed by the seller and ϑ the mutual threshold.

In the following theorems we present some further results. We will see that there exists a unique Pareto-efficient equilibrium in trigger strategies with associated trust-threshold ϑ^*. We consider this equilibrium as the 'solution' of the game. The theorem states some results on the comparative statics of the solution. Due to the fact that we have chosen a Heterogeneous Trust Game as the constituent game, we have the possibility to study comparative statics of the mechanisms in the model rather than follow the traditional approach to analyze comparative statics of the condition under which a cooperative equilibrium exists. We are especially interested in the *comparative statics* of the trust-threshold ϑ^*, the proportion of incomplete contracts ($F(\vartheta^*)$), and the standardized utilities U_i^*. The parameters we want to use for comparative statics are the costs of complete contracts $R_i - P_i$, the buyer's damage $P_1 - S_1$ if the seller behaves opportunistically, the time preferences ω_i, the death rates δ_i, the network density α of the buyers, the probability distribution F of incentives for opportunistic behavior, and, in later theorems, the cost function c for *ex ante* commitments. For the scalar parameters, comparative statics are determined via partial differentiation. For the distribution parameter F we will discuss comparative statics in terms of *stochastic ordering*, which is defined as $F^{(1)} > F^{(2)}$ if and only if $F^{(1)}(x) < F^{(2)}(x)$ for all $x > 0$. This implies that $E_{F^{(1)}}T(x) > E_{F^{(2)}}T(x)$ for all $x > 0$ for any increasing functional T, i.e., the incentives for opportunism are 'on average' higher under $F^{(1)}$ than under $F^{(2)}$ for any suitable definition of average. To derive comparative statics in the cost function c, we say that $c^{(1)} > c^{(2)}$ if $c^{(1)}(h) > c^{(2)}(h)$ and $c^{(1)\prime}(h) > c^{(2)\prime}(h)$ for all $h > 0$. We note that these definitions imply only partial orderings of the distributions F and the cost functions c.

In our first theorem, we suspend the seller's possibility for *ex ante* commitments, and derive the efficient governance structure of trust relations via short-term complete contracts (the buyer plays D_1) and the two mechanisms based on structural embeddedness. To present our results, we define two additional functions,

$$G(\theta) = \theta/F(\theta), \tag{3}$$

$$\Phi(x) = \max\{\theta | G(\theta) \leqslant x\}. \tag{4}$$

Note that Φ is increasing in x.

Theorem 1 *The solution of the* IHTG($\Gamma_F, \omega_1, \omega_2, \delta_1, \delta_2, \alpha, F, c$) *in which the seller does not commit himself,* $h^* = 0$, *has the following properties.*

(i) *The trigger strategy* $\sigma(\vartheta)$ *is a spe if and only if*

$$G(\vartheta) \leqslant \frac{w_2 q_1}{1 - w_2 q_1}(R_2 - P_2) =: \gamma. \tag{5}$$

Here $q_1 = 1 - \delta_1(1 - \alpha)$, *and* $w_i = \omega_i(1 - \delta_i)$. *We call* γ *the 'game index'.*

(ii) *The unique Pareto-efficient trust-threshold* ϑ^* *that is supported by spe's in trigger strategies statisfies*

$$\vartheta^* = \Phi(\gamma). \tag{6}$$

Thus, ϑ^* *increases in the game index* γ: *it increases in* $R_2 - P_2$, ω_2, *and* α, *and decreases in* δ_1, δ_2, *and* F. ϑ^* *does not depend on* $R_1 - P_1$, $P_1 - S_1$, *and* ω_1. *Moreover, the proportion* $F(\vartheta^*)$ *of incomplete contracts follows the same comparative statics as* ϑ^*.

(iii) *If* F *is concave, the collection* Θ *of* ϑ's *for which* $\sigma(\vartheta)$ *is a spe in trigger strategies is convex. Thus,* Θ *is an interval* $[0, \vartheta^*]$.

Proof According to Bellman's optimality criterion, a strategy cannot be improved upon if and only if *one-step deviations* from the strategy are not rewarding. Without loss of generality, consider the case $\theta < \vartheta$ in the first period. If the seller does not deviate now, his expected discounted payoff from the current period and all subsequent periods satisfies

$$Eu_2(C_2, \theta) = R_2 + \sum_{t=1}^{\infty} w_2^t(F(\vartheta)R_2 + (1 - F(\vartheta))P_2)$$

$$= R_2 + \frac{w_2}{1 - w_2}(F(\vartheta)R_2 + (1 - F(\vartheta))P_2). \qquad (7)$$

Next we have to analyze the seller's expected payoff from the current and all future periods if he dishonors trust now, but sticks to the trigger strategy in all future rounds. As time t, the seller still plays with a buyer who is informed about the seller's deviation in the past if and only if in *all* periods $1, \dots, t-1$, either the buyer survived or information has always been conveyed to the next buyer. Clearly this happens with probability q_1^{t-1}, with q_1 as defined in (5). It follows that

$$Eu_2(D_2, \theta) = R_2 + \theta + \sum_{t=1}^{\infty} w_2^t(q_1^t P_2 + (1 - q_1^t)(F(\vartheta)R_2 + (1 - F(\vartheta))P_2))$$

$$= R_2 + \theta + \frac{w_2}{1 - w_2}(F(\vartheta)R_2 + (1 - F(\vartheta))P_2)$$

$$- \frac{w_2 q_1}{1 - w_2 q_1} F(\vartheta)(R_2 - P_2)$$

and so $Eu_2(C_2, \theta) \geqslant Eu_2(D_2, \theta)$ if and only if

$$\frac{\theta}{F(\vartheta)} \leqslant \frac{w_2 q_1}{1 - w_2 q_1}(R_2 - P_2). \qquad (8)$$

The trigger strategies are in spe if and only if (8) holds for all $\theta \leqslant \vartheta$. Clearly(8) is most restrictive for $\theta = \vartheta$. It is easily seen that the buyer does never have an incentive to deviate from her trigger strategy. We conclude that a necessary and sufficient condition that trigger strategies are in subgame perfect equilibrium is $G(\vartheta) \leqslant \gamma$. This finishes the proof of (i).

   To prove (ii), note that higher thresholds ϑ result in utility improvements for both the buyers and the seller. Thus, the maximal threshold ϑ^* subject to the incentive constraint (5) is Pareto-efficient among the payoffs supported by a spe in trigger strategies. Note that ϑ^* is well-defined. Since $w_2 q_1/(1 - w_2 q_1)$ increases in ω_2 and q_1, ϑ^* increases in w_2, α, and $R_2 - P_2$ and decreases in δ_1 and δ_2. Note that ϑ^* depends continuously on γ if F is concave (cf. (iii)) but ϑ^* may be discontinuous in γ for general F. If $F^{(1)} > F^{(2)}$ in the sense of stochastic ordering, we have

$$\gamma = \frac{\vartheta^*_{F^{(1)}}}{F^{(1)}(\vartheta^*_{F^{(1)}})} \geqslant \frac{\vartheta^*_{F^{(1)}}}{F^{(2)}(\vartheta^*_{F^{(1)}})}. \tag{9}$$

Therefore, $\vartheta^*_{F^{(2)}} \geqslant \vartheta^*_{F^{(1)}}$. Except for the comparative statics in F, $F(\vartheta^*)$ follows the (directions of the) comparative statics of ϑ^*. Moreover, $F^{(2)}(\vartheta^*_{F^{(2)}}) = \vartheta^*_{F^{(2)}}/\gamma \geqslant \vartheta^*_{F^{(1)}}/\gamma = F^{(1)}(\vartheta^*_{F^{(1)}})$.

To prove (iii) we need to show that if ϑ^*_1 and ϑ^*_2 are two equilibrium thresholds for a ρ between zero and one $\rho\vartheta^*_1 + (1-\rho)\vartheta^*_2$ is an equilibrium threshold. This follows immediately from the following inequalities:

$$\rho\vartheta^*_1 + (1-\rho)\vartheta^*_2 \leqslant \rho\gamma F(\vartheta^*_1) + (1-\rho)\gamma F(\vartheta^*_2) \leqslant \gamma F(\rho\vartheta^*_1 + (1-\rho)\vartheta^*_2) \tag{10}$$

because F is concave.   □

We like to stress that our solution of the IHTG is a Pareto-improvement over the continued play of the one-shot equilibrium of the HTG, but since $\vartheta^* < \infty$, and $F(\vartheta^*) < 1$, it is *not* fully Pareto-efficient. This distinguishes our solution from and, we believe, makes it more realistic than many approaches in the repeated games literature. Clearly, all players would be better of if the buyer(s) always place trust and the seller never abuses trust. This, however, is *not* an equilibrium in the IHTG as a consequence of the assumption (1) that the support of F is unbounded. Thus, occasionally the seller faces incentives for opportunistic behavior that exceed the buyer's capacity for deterrence by the joint effects of conditional cooperation via reciprocity and of inflicting damage to the seller's reputation among future buyers. Due to the assumption that the buyer(s) have complete information about the seller's incentive for opportunistic behavior, the buyer will in such a case insist on using a complete contract rather than face exploitation by the seller. Thus, similar to many other repeated game models, trust is never abused on the equilibrium path, and so, essentially, the buyer can threaten without any costs that she will stop trusting the seller after his first defection. Consequently, the trust-threshold ϑ^* does not depend on the contract costs $R_1 - P_1$ and the discount rate ω_1 of the buyers. We will elaborate on this unrealistic feature of our model in the concluding section.

In the efficient governance structure for the IHTG in which the seller does not use the possibility to commit himself *ex ante*, the extent $1 - F(\vartheta^*)$ to which transactions are managed via institutional embeddedness via writing complete contracts (D_1) decreases with temporal (δ_1, w_i) as well as and with structural (α) embeddedness. Thus, the institutional mechanism relates to the structural mechanisms as a *substitute* (see again footnote 2). Below we will see that this strong result no longer holds if the seller rationally uses *ex ante* commitments.

Two interesting special cases can directly be derived from this theorem. First, let network embeddedness be absent, $\alpha = 0$, and so $q_1 = 1 - \delta_1$. This can be interpreted in two ways. As a statement about social structure it refers to the absence of social ties between buyers. Alternatively, the predictions about the governance structure for $\alpha = 0$ are valid if the buyers are informed about the behavior of the seller but use strategies that ignore such information. Theorem 1 implies, however, that rational buyers would use such information whenever available. Second, consider the case that network embeddedness is perfect and so information is transmitted indefinitely, $\alpha = 1$, and so $q_1 = 1$. In that case, δ_1 plays no role anymore: It does not matter whether a buyer dies or not, since information about the seller is automatically conveyed to the next buyer. Other comparative statics are again not affected.

We now enlarge the set of governance structures that the players may use to include both short-term complete contracts and long-term *ex ante* commitments. In the next theorem, we characterize the efficient governance structure and derive some comparative statics.

Theorem 2 *The* IHTG$(\Gamma_F, \omega_1, \omega_2, \delta_1, \delta_2, \alpha, F, c)$ *has the following properties.*

(i) *The trigger-strategy vector $\sigma(h, \vartheta)$ is a spe if and only if*

$$G(\vartheta) \leqslant \frac{\gamma}{1-h}. \tag{11}$$

(ii) *The unique Pareto-efficient strategies $\sigma(h^*, \vartheta^*)$ that is supported by the spe's strategies satisfies*

$$\vartheta^* = \Phi\left(\frac{\gamma}{1-h^*}\right), \tag{12}$$

where h^* is the maximizer of the expected utility function Eu_2^*:

$$Eu_2^* = \frac{1}{1-w_2}(F(\vartheta^*)(R_2 - P_2) + P_2) - c(h^*) \quad \text{for } 0 \leqslant h^* \leqslant 1. \tag{13}$$

(iii) *Standardized utility* U_2^* *increases in* $R_2 - P_2, \omega_2,$ *and* α *and decreases in* $\delta_1, \delta_2, F,$ *and* c.

(iv) *The Pareto-efficient equilibrium values for* $h^*, \vartheta^*,$ *and* U_1^* *decrease in* c.

Proof The proofs of (i) and (ii) are similar to analogous assertions in Theorem 1 if we substitute $(1 - h)\theta$ for θ. For the utility function, we need four arguments. First, in equilibrium trust will never be abused. Second, the expected payoff for the seller of the constituent game is $P_2 + F(\vartheta^*)(R_2 - P_2)$. Third, the seller has to pay $c(h^*)$ for his commitment in the preplay period. Fourth, there exists a maximum of Eu_2^* for $0 \leqslant h^* \leqslant 1$ because for $h^* = 0$ the expected utility equals $P_2/(1 - w_2)$, the expected utility is continuous and bounded above, and decreases to minus infinity for $h^* \to 1$. Proposition (iii) can be derived as follows. Increasing γ means that the original Pareto-efficient equilibrium is still an equilibrium, with the same utility or higher (increase in w_2). The original ϑ^* can now be increased by a small amount and we would have still an equilibrium, but now with a higher associated utility. Thus, in the new situation the Pareto-efficient utility level is higher than in the original situation. Similarly, in the case that we change to a smaller F or a smaller c, we are still in an equilibrium and the utility can be increased. If we change to a smaller c, in the original equilibrium dEu/dh becomes positive. Consequently, there exists a new equilibrium with a higher h^* and ϑ^* because Φ and γ do not depend on the commitment costs c.   □

We have seen before that standardized utility $U_2^* \in [0, 1]$ can be interpreted as an overall measure for the extent to which incentive problems in trust relations are 'solved' by efficient governance. Comparing Theorem 1 and Theorem 2 (iii), we see that this measure depends on the parameters $R_2 - P_2, \delta_i, \omega_i$ and on F in a similar and plausible way. Moreover, this measure is decreasing with increasing costs c for *ex ante* commitments.

The comparative statics of the components h^* and ϑ^* of the efficient governance structure of the IHTG appear to be much more complicated. Only for the costs c, general results are available: With increasing costs, *ex ante* commitments decrease and the use of short-term contracting increases. Thus, the institutional mechanism are substitutes in terms of c. To derive additional comparative statics, we will first present a specific example in which all analyses can be conducted by straightforward computation.

Corollary 1 *Consider the* $\text{IHTG}(\Gamma_F, \omega_1, \omega_2, \delta_1, \delta_2, \alpha, F, c)$ *with a specific distribution of temptations,*

$$F(\theta) = \theta/(a+\theta) \quad \text{for } a > 0,$$

and with a specific form of the costs for ex ante commitments,

$$c(h) = \lambda h/(1-h) \quad \text{for } \lambda > 0.$$

Then, the solution of the IHTG *has the following properties.*

(i) *The solution prescribes that* $h^* > 0$ *and* $\mathcal{G}^* > 0$ *if and only if*

$$\frac{\lambda(1-w_2)}{a} < \frac{1-w_2q_1}{w_2q_1} < \frac{(R_2 - p_2 + \lambda(1-w_2))^2}{4a\lambda(1-w_2)}. \tag{14}$$

Note that this implies that $R_2 - P_2 \geqslant \lambda(1-w_2)$. *Then*

$$h^* = 1 - \sqrt{\frac{\lambda w_2 q_1 (1-w_2)}{a(1-w_2q_1)}}, \tag{15}$$

$$\mathcal{G}^* = \sqrt{\frac{aw_2q_1}{\lambda(1-w_2q_1)(1-w_2)}} (R_2 - P_2) - a. \tag{16}$$

Thus, h^* *increases in* δ_1 *and* a, *and decreases in* α *and* λ. *Moreover,* h^* *increases in* w_2 *(and so increases in* ω_2 *and decreases in* δ_2) *if and only if* $w_2(2 - w_2q_1) > 1$.
$\mathcal{G}^*$ *increases in* $R_2 - P_2$, ω_2, *and* α *but decreases in* δ_1, δ_2, *and* λ. *Furthermore,* $\mathcal{G}^*$ *increases in* a *if and only if*

$$\frac{w_2q_1}{(1-w_2)(1-w_2q_1)} \geqslant \frac{4a\lambda}{(R_2 - P_2)^2}.$$

(ii) *The solution prescribes* $h^* = 0$ *and* $\mathcal{G}^* > 0$ *if and only if*

$$\frac{1-w_2q_1}{w_2q_1} < \frac{1}{a}\min(R_2 - P_2, \lambda(1-w_2)). \tag{17}$$

Here, $\mathcal{G}^* = ((w_2q_1)/(1-w_2q_1))(R_2 - P_2) - a$ *increases in* $R_2 - P_2$, ω_2, *and* α, *and decreases in* δ_1, δ_2, *and* a.

(iii) *If* $\mathcal{G}^* > 0$ *we have the following comparative statics for the proportion of complete contracts and the expected utilities:* $F(\mathcal{G}^*)$ *and* U_i^* *increase in* $R_2 - P_2$, ω_2, *and* α, *and decreases in* δ_1, δ_2, a, *and* λ.

(iv) *The solution prescribes* $\mathcal{G}^* = 0$, *and hence also* $h^* = 0$, *if and only if neither* (14) *nor* (17) *hold true.*

In our final theorem, we state some comparative statics using the same specific distribution F of temptations as in the example in Corollary 1, but with a general cost function c for *ex ante* commitments.

Theorem 3   *Consider   the   IHTG*$(\Gamma_F, \omega_1, \omega_2, \delta_1, \delta_2, \alpha, F, c)$ *with   a specific distribution of temptations*

$$F(\theta) = \theta/(a+\theta) \quad for \; a > 0,$$

but with a general cost function c for ex ante commitments. The solution has the following properties.

(i) *The trust-threshold ϑ and ex ante commitment h satisfy*

$$\vartheta \leqslant \frac{w_2 q_1 (R_2 - P_2)}{(1 - w_2 q_1)(1 - h)} - a. \tag{18}$$

(ii) *The unique Pareto-efficient trust-threshold ϑ^* satisfies*

$$\vartheta^* = \max\left(0, \frac{w_2 q_1 (R_2 - P_2)}{(1 - w_2 q_1)(1 - h^*)} - a\right) \tag{19}$$

where $h^* > 0$ if and only if there exists a solution to the following two conditions:

$$c'(h^*) = \frac{a(1 - w_2 q_1)}{(1 - w_2) w_2 q_1},$$

$$\frac{c'(0)(1 - w_2)}{a} \leqslant \frac{(1 - w_2 q_1)}{w_2 q_1} \leqslant \frac{R_2 - P_2 - c(h^*)(1 - w_2)}{(1 - h^*)a}.$$

(iii) *Let $h^* = 0$ and $\vartheta^* > 0$. Then ϑ^* and $F(\vartheta^*)$ increases in $R_2 - P_2$, ω_2, and α, and decreases in δ_1, δ_2 and a.*

(iv) *Let $h^* > 0$. Then the following comparative statics hold.*

   (a) *h^* increases in δ_1 and a, and decreases in α. Moreover, h^* increases in w_2 (i.e., increases in ω_2 and decrease in δ_2) if and only if $w_2(2 - w_2 q_1) > 1$.*
   (b) *ϑ^* increases in $R_2 - P_2$. ϑ^* increases in α and decreases in δ_1 if and only if*

$$(1 - h^*) c''(h^*) > \frac{(1 - w_2 q_1)a}{(1 - w_2) w_2 q_1},$$

which is implied by $(1 - h)c'(h)$ is increasing.

ϑ^* *increases in* w_2 *if and only if*

$$(1-h^*)c''(h^*) > \frac{(2-w_2q_1)(1-w_2q_1)a}{(1-w_2)w_2q_1},$$

which is implied by $(1-h)c''(h) \geqslant 2c'(h)$.
Finally, ϑ^* *decreases in* a *if and only if*

$$(1-h^*)^2c''(h^*) > \frac{R_2-P_2}{1-w_2}.$$

(c) $F(\vartheta^*)$ *follows the same comparative statics as* ϑ^* *for* R_2-P_2, ω_2, δ_1, δ_2, *and* α. *Furthermore,* $F(\vartheta^*)$ *decreases in* a *if and only if*

$$(1-h^*)c''(h^*) > \frac{(1-w_2q_1)a}{(1-w_2)w_2q_1},$$

which is again implied by $(1-h)c'(h)$ *is increasing.*

Proof   Tedious but straightforward.

4. CONCLUSION

In this paper, we studied the efficient individually rational governance of trust relations via mechanisms based on the institutional and structural embedding of transactions. The IHTG model that we presented, like any other tractable model, makes many assumptions that are not very realistic. An example is the assumption that players have complete information on the payoffs and the discount parameters of the other players. The theoretical costs of making unrealistic assumptions can only be justified by sufficient benefits in the form of predictions that can be derived from them. In fact, we would argue that the (formal or informal) derivation of implications from models, somewhat loosely defined as a consistent set of assumptions, is the main reason for constructing mathematical models. While *defining* models with an amazingly wide array of interreleated complex components if often surprisingly simple, our drive to propose such complicated models should be constrained by a modest recognition that we will be unable to derive substantively interesting *implications* from them, either by analytical reasoning or by computer simulation ("poor man's mathematics"). This emphasis on the derivation of implications, often in the form of comparative statics ('partial derivatives'), poses some contrast with the research agenda proposed by Fararo and

Doreian (1998; FD from now on) in this volume. In Section 4 of their agenda, FD describe a complicated set of interrelated differential equations that formalize theories by Homans, Lewin, and others. The proposal to model solidarity of a group in terms of sentiments between individual actors seems a fruitful one indeed. However, unfortunately, FD stop once the elaborate model has been *defined*. If a main goal of solidarity theory is the understanding how the levels of solidarity in a group depend on the possibilities for control, groups size, interdependency, etc., we have to be disappointed. Moreover, we are worried that the complexity of the model makes disappointment almost inevitable: non-linear models with so many parameters are usually intractable via formal mathematics as well as systematic simulation.[7]

In developing our game-theoretic model of trust relations, rather than designing the 'grand' model at once, we have moved gradually from a simple model with only one or two management mechanisms, to incorporate more of these behavioral alternatives. A focus on 'implications', of a kind that can ultimately can be tested empirically, is what should drive formal modelling – and informal (verbal) theorizing for that matter. Thus, we like to summarize the conclusions that our game-theoretic analysis of the dynamic IHTG model have yielded.

(1) The 'overall' degree to which incentive problems in trust relations are solved by the players' rational choice for a governance structure can be measured by the standardized utility $U_2^* \in [0, 1]$ of the seller.

   (a) U_2^* *decreases* with the 'problem potential' of the transactions, i.e., the distribution F of the size of the incentives for opportunism. Note that other factors of 'problem potential', in particular the buyer's damage that arises from opportunism by the seller, have *no* effect on U_2^*.

   (b) U_2^* *increases* with structural embeddedness of transactions. Here, structural embeddedness increases in the density α of the network between the buyers, increases in the expected duration of the transaction stream between a buyer and the seller (i.e., decreases in the death rates δ_i of the buyers and the seller), and increases in the discount parameter (patience) ω_2 of the seller.

   (c) U_2^* increases with the effectiveness of the management mechanisms, namely, with increasing costs $R_2 - P_2$ to the seller in the case that the buyers insist on using complete short-term contracts as a sanction to past opportunism by the seller, and with decreasing costs c to the seller for making *ex ante* commitments that reduce that seller's future incentives for opportunistic behavior.

Thus, in terms of the extent to which trust problems are solved by optimal cost-effective management, we conclude that the two classes of mechanisms that operate via structural and institutional embeddedness of transactions respectively, appear to be *substitutes*: Better prospects for 'spontaneous' management via structural embeddedness lead to less 'constructed' management via institutional mechanisms (Coleman, 1990), and vice versa.

(2) Studying the conditions under which substitution effects occur between the institutional mechanisms proved to be more complicated. For the costs c of *ex ante* commitments, we predict that with increasing costs c, management of transactions occurs less via *ex ante* commitments and more via short-term complete contracts. Thus, both institutional mechanisms are substitutes in term of commitment costs. Thus, the extent to which trust relations are managed via 'structural' mechanisms such as the threat to damage the reputation of a partner who breaches agreements is expected to increase with the costs of *ex ante* commitments. A similar result does *not* hold for the costs of contracting $R_2 - P_2$ (See the example outlined in Corollary 1).

For the other parameters of the model, the analyses yielded mostly ambiguous conclusions under the most general assumptions on the distribution F and the cost function c. Non-monotonous, and sometimes even irregular, relationships can occur between the parameters of the model (the 'independent variables') and the efficient use of institutional mechanisms (the 'dependent variables'). Moreover, the two institutional mechanisms can be both substitutes and complements, depending on the parameter values in a rather incomprehensible way.

However, if we are willing to make very specific assumptions on the distribution F and the cost function c, we arrive at clearer predictions. (cmp Coleman's arguments (1990: 674–680) for studying the competitive price equilibrium of a perfect market, subject to Cobb-Douglas utility functions.) With the specific assumptions of Corollary 1, we found that the two kinds of institution-based mechanisms are *complements* in terms of network density α, the death rates of the buyers δ_1, the incentives for opportunism F, and *substitutes* in the costs c. The effectiveness $R_2 - P_2$ of the buyer's threat to insist on complete short-term contracts does affect the extent to which short-term contracts are used but does not affect the level of commitments. Finally, the effect of w_2 is non-monotonic. The institution-based mechanisms are *complements* if and only if the seller's shadow of the future w_2 is sufficiently small, i.e., ω_2 is small and/or δ_2 is large. Thus, if the shadow of the future is large and hence threats of retaliation and damage to one's reputation are real, increasing the shadow of the future even further may actually lead to an *increase* in the extent to which actors incur *ex ante* commitments. The reason is that *ex ante* commitments serve as a form of relationship-specific investments that also become more valuable with an increasing shadow of the future.

Recently, Hechter (1992) criticized the application of game theory, especially repeated games models, for the construction of theories of collective action, a class of problems that are closely related to the topic of solidarity theory. Hechter makes two main critical points. First, the assumptions of these models are especially unrealistic when applied to collective action problems that involve large numbers of players (e.g., the frequently made assumption that players have full information on the payoffs and behaviors of all players). Second, Hechter criticizes the lack of predictive power of game theoretical analyses of repeated games, because they predict 'almost everything' for sufficiently high discount rates (cf. the 'folk-theorem' in Fudenberg and Maskin, 1986). Elsewhere, we have commented extensively on Hechter (Raub, Voss, and Weesie, 1992). Here, we will only provide some arguments why Hechter's critical assessment only partially apply to our analysis. First, our model actually addresses one of Hechter's central criticisms on the 'real-world' applications of n-person games, namely that actors tend to know only a limited fraction of the other actors, and hence cannot be expected to know everybody's behavior in the past (cf., the network parameter α in our model). In this way, we believe that our analysis is more realistic that earlier related work by, e.g., Taylor (1978) and Axelrod (1982). With respect to Hechter's second argument, we have shown (Theorem 1) that the indeterminacy of predictions for repeated games models can be eliminated within the class of behaviorally simple trigger strategies that we used as one of the central criteria of equilibria selection ('payoff-dominance').

5. FURTHER RESEARCH

The model presented in this paper was restrictive in numerous respects that could be elaborated upon in future research which would fit in nicely within the general agenda of problems for mathematical modeling in solidarity theory as advanced by Fararo and Doreian. Out of the many possibilities, we want to indicate two directions that are of particular interest to ourselves.

One important limitation of our analysis is that the costs to the buyer for the punishment that she can inflict on the seller by insisting on the use of complete contracts does not have any influence on the solution of the game. Similarly, the buyer's discount parameter does not affect the solution. We consider these properties unrealistic and, hence, undesirable artifacts of our game-theoretic specifications of the model and our proposed solution. This limitation is caused by our assumption that all players have complete information on the payoffs (including the θ's) and on the behavior of all players, and, in addition, that the players are able to execute their intended behavior (strategies) without any errors. Consequently, in the equilibria considered, the punishment threat never has to be executed. By including monitoring problems or unintended defective behavior by the seller (he sells a lemon but is not aware of it), punishment strategies have to be more subtle. Namely, in this case defective behavior occurs every now and then. In such a scenario, trigger-like punishment is too extreme since the buyer's threat 'to blow up the world' – which *is* a credible threat in our model in the sense of subgame perfection – will have to applied. Therefore, more subtle punishment strategies, which will be dependent on the costs for the buyers of punishment, are necessary. In future papers we will investigate this problem more extensively.

Another limitation of our analysis is that network effects have been modeled in a very restricted way. First, strictly homogeneous networks were assumed. Thus, only the effects of *density* of networks on the governance of transactions could be addressed. Structural properties of networks between buyers such as the degree of centrality, the degree of transitivity, and redundancy of ties could be expected to affect governance as well. In a model similar to the one studied here, Buskens (1998) demonstrates that the effects of such structural properties are indeed tractable with the game-theoretic approach. Second, informal networks between buyers and sellers have been ignored. In fact, given the assumption about the kinds of actions open to the players and the trigger strategies used by the players, networks between players at different sides of the market would have no impact. The theory of relational signaling (Lindenberg, 1988) suggests, however, that such informal networks may be very important for stabilizing trust once problems in the relationship occur. Thirdly, in our interpretation of networks as information channels that are used by the actors without any costs, we ignored individual incentives for making contributions to the reputations of actors in the social system. Reputations definitely have a public good character. Hence, one would expect under-production of information. However, given the low time budget required for spreading such information, often as a by-product of other social interactions, and ample opportunities to reciprocate against actors who fail to contribute, we feel that the free rider problems are probably insubstantial. Still, we do expect other and possibly stronger disincentives. For instance, it is at least intuitively plausible that when actor A talks about a problematic transaction with a partner B to a third party C, A not only gives a signal about the reliability of B, but unintendedly also about A's own possible incompetence in the management of transactions that may deter C from entering or continuing a relationship with A.

NOTES

1. Useful suggestions and comments by Chris Snijders are gratefully acknowledged. Financial support was provided by the Netherlands Organization for Scientific Research (NWO) under Grant PGS 50-370. Our address is: Department of Sociology/ ICS, Utrecht University, Heidelberglaan 1, 3584 CS Utrecht, Netherlands. E-mail: weesie@fsw.ruu.nl.
2. We say that two mechanisms are substitutes with respect to some parameter if they co-vary in opposite directions if the parameter is changed. Similarly, they are complements if they co-vary in the same direction.
3. Our results also hold if we assume that the 'sucker's' payoff S_1 varies with θ, in particular if S_1 decreases in θ.
4. Clearly there exist many other features of social networks that affect the behavior, such as the 'social definition' of the alternatives between which actors choose, the definition of a social reference point for a Simon-type behavioral theory of satisficing instead of optimizing, equilibrium selection ('conventions') etc. Incorporating these additional features of social networks would be a challenging research agenda for sociologists who analyze the effects of social embeddedness of transactions vis-à-vis the much more atomistic approaches of neo-classical economists.
5. Exogenous commitment, i.e., commitments that are not chosen, are assumed to be incorporated in the HTG via the payoffs and the distribution F of temptations for opportunistic behavior. Thus, in contexts of high normative pressure that cause strong feelings of moral obligation to honor trust, the distribution F will take low values relative to a context with less pressure. In principle, it is possible that such morals may actually yield a negative temptation for opportunism in some situations, $\theta < 0$.
6. The majority of the repeated games literature, including social science applications such as Taylor (1978) and Axelrod (1982), similarly assume that players exponentially discount the future. Axelrod labels the discount parameter the 'shadow of the future' and discusses both pure time preferences and uncertainty about the duration of the interactions as reasons for discounting the future. In our model, separate parameters are included for both these interpretations. The defined parameter $w_i = \omega_i(1 - \delta_i)$ (see our Theorem 1) is our equivalent to Axelrod's shadow of the future.

7. We like to contrast the Fararo and Doreian model with a partially game-theoretic model of sentiments ('social ties') proposed by van Dijk (1995). In this dynamic model, the voluntary contributions to a public good of actors depend on the sentiments between actors in a way similar to suggestions of Kelley and Thibaut (1978), while the sentiments are modified as a function of relative contributions. Van Dijk's model is definitely is simpler and less realistic in many respects than FD's. However, Van Dijk is able to derive a fair amount of predictions on, e.g., how the rate of mobility in a group affects the level of production of the public good and the sentiments (solidarity) between the actors.

REFERENCES

Axelrod, Robert 1984. *The Evolution of Cooperation*. New York: Basic Books.
Blau, Peter M. 1964. *Exchange and Power in Social Life*. New York: Wiley.
Buskens, Vincent 1998. Social Networks and Trust Amsterdam: Thesis Publishers (forthcoming).
Coleman, James S. 1990. *Foundations of Social Theory*. Cambridge, Mass.: Belknap Press.
Dixit, Avinash K. 1982. "Recent developments in oligopoly theory." *American Economic Review* (Papers and Proceedings) **76**: 48–52.
Dasgupta, Patha 1988. "Trust as a commodity," pp. 49–72, in Diego Gambetta (ed.) *Trust: Making and Breaking Cooperative Relations*. Oxford: Blackwell.
Durkheim, Emile 1893. *De la division du travail social*, 9th ed., Paris: PUF 1973.
Dijk, Frans van 1995. *Social ties, economic performance, and public intervention*. Ph.D. Thesis, University of Amsterdam.
Fararo, Thomas J. and Patrick Doreian 1998. "The theory of solidarity: An agenda of problems." Chapter 1 in P. Doreian and T.J. Faroro (eds.), *The Problem of Solidarity: Theories and Models.* (this volume).
Frank, Robert 1988. *Passions within Reason. The Strategic Role of the Emotions*. New York: Norton.
Friedman, James W. 1971. "A non-cooperative equilibrium for supergames." *Review of Economic Studies* **38**: 1–12.
Fudenberg, David and Eric Maskin 1986. "The folk theorem in repeated games with discounting or with incomplete information." *Econometrica* **54**: 533–554.
Granovetter, Mark S. 1985. "Economic action and social structure: The problem of embeddedness." *American Journal of Sociology* **91**: 481–510.
Harsanyi, John C. and Reinhard Selten 1988. *A General Theory of Equilibrium Selection in Games*. Cambridge, Mass.: MIT Press.
Harsanyi, John C. 1995. "A new theory of equilibrium selection for games with complete information." *Games and Economic Behavior* **8**: 91–122.
Hechter, Michael 1987. *Principles of Group Solidarity*. Berkeley, CA: University of California Press.
Hechter, Michael 1992. "The insufficiency of game theory for the resolution of real-world collective action problems." *Rationality and Society* **4**: 33–40.
Kelley, H.H., and Thibaut, J.W. 1978. *Interpersonal Relations*. New York: Wiley.
Kreps, David 1990. "Corporate culture and economic theory," pp. 90–143, in James E. Alt and Kenneth A. Shepsle (eds.) *Perspectives on Positive Political Economy*. Cambridge, Mass.: Cambridge University Press.
Lindenberg, Siegwart 1988. "Contractual relations and weak solidarity: The behavioral basis of restraints on gain-maximization." *Journal of Institutional and Theoretical Economics* **144**: 39–58.
Macaulay, Stewart 1963. "Non-contractual relations in business: A preliminary study." *American Sociological Review* **28**: 55–67.

Macneil, Ian R. 1980. *The New Social Contract.* New Haven: Yale University Press.

North, Douglas C. 1990. *Institutions, Institutional Change and Economic Performance.* Cambridge, Mass.: Harvard University Press.

Raub, Werner, and Thomas Voss 1990. "Individual interests and moral institutions: An endogenous approach to the modification of preferences," pp. 81–117, in Michael Hechter, Karl-Dieter Opp, and Reinhard Wippler (eds.), *Social Institutions: Their Emergence, Maintenance, and Effects.* New York: Aldine.

Raub, Werner, Thomas Voss, and Jeroen Weesie 1992. "On the usefulness of game theory for the resolution of real-world collective action problems." (Comment on Hechter 1992). *Rationality and Society* **4**: 95–102.

Raub, Werner and Jeroen Weesie 1990. "Reputation and efficiency in social interactions: An example of network effects." *American Journal of Sociology* **96**: 626–654.

Raub, Werner and Jeroen Weesie 1993. "Symbiotic arrangements: A sociological perspective." *Journal of Institutional and Theoretical Economics* **149**: 716–724.

Raub, Werner and Jeroen Weesie 1995. "The management of matches. Decentralized mechanisms for cooperative relations with applications to households and organizations," pp. 69–81, in Ulf Bernitz and Pär Hallström (eds.) *Principles of Justice and the European Union.* Stockholm: Juristförlaget.

Schanze, E. 1991. "Symbiotic contracts: Exploring long-term agency structures between contract and corporation," pp. 67–103, in Ch. Joerges (ed.) *Franchising and the Law: Theoretical and Comparative Approaches in Europe and the United States.* Baden-Baden: Nomos.

Snijders, Chris 1996. Trust and commitments. Ph.D. Thesis, Utrecht University.

Taylor, Michael 1987. *The Possibility of Cooperation.* Cambridge, Mass.: Cambridge University Press. (Rev. edition of *Anarchy and Cooperation.* London: Wiley 1976.)

Weber, Max 1921. *Wirtschaft und Gesellschaft,* 5. rev. Aufl. Tübingen: Mohr 1976.

Weesie, Jeroen and Werner Raub 1996. "Private ordering: A comparative institutional analysis of hostage games." *Journal of Mathematical Sociology* **21**: 201–240.

Williamson, Oliver E. 1985. *The Economic Institutions of Capitalism.* New York: Free Press.

5 A MATHEMATICAL MODEL OF GROUP DYNAMICS INCLUDING THE EFFECTS OF SOLIDARITY

WOLFGANG WEIDLICH and DIRK HELBING

Institut für Theoretische Physik, Universität Stuttgart

1. INTRODUCTION

The dynamics of groups under inclusion of the aspect of solidarity can be considered to be one of the most general and fundamental problems of sociology. Society, being one of the main subjects of sociology, is constituted by interacting human individuals. However, they are not an amorphous crowd. The interaction "forces" between the individuals generated by material, emotional, and mental needs and desires with respect to different aspects of life lead to a *selforganization of structures* within society. These structures take the form of *groups* (i.e. ensembles of individuals with certain common objectives). Each individual will in general *simultaneously* belong to *several groups* taking the role of a nominal or leading member in each of them.

It turns out that an indispensable element of the formation of groups is the *emerging solidarity* which provides a kind of glue between their members. The *theory of group dynamics*, in which the element of *solidarity* therefore should play the role of a *central concept*, intends to understand and to formally describe not only the *stationary structure*, but also the *rise, evolution*, and *decay* of social groups.

The authors Fararo and Doreian (1995) of the introductory chapter to this book have given a comprehensive overview of the extensive literature already devoted to this problem.

Three main, of course intertwined, kinds of problems can be distinguished in this chapter:

1. the *problems on the micro-level concerning individuals*, including their motivations, emotions, beliefs, activities, and forces,

2. the *problems on the macro-level concerning structures*, i.e. which part-whole relations, common interests and objectives, sanction mechanisms effecting compliance with obligations, feelings of loyalty, and identifications with a collectivity, etc. finally produce the *tie of solidarity* leading to the formation of groups, and

3. *problems referring to the operationalization* of these *qualitatively* formulated concepts in a *quantitative* framework capable of capturing structural as well as dynamic aspects in a *mathematical form*.

Our contribution focusses on the third problem, i.e. how to set up a sufficiently general mathematical model of group formation and evolution for a system of interacting and competing groups under inclusion of a quantitative concept of *solidarity*. It was our intention to explicitly incorporate as many ideas about group formation as possible from the literature analyzed in the above-mentioned chapter. This was much simplified by the fact that these ideas seem not to have a mutually exclusive but rather a complementary character.

Before proceeding to the details of our model design we shall now discuss some general problems of model construction implied in the present context.

(a) *The wholeness of model construction*. Because of the strong interrelatedness of all concepts in the context of group formation it seems impossible to construct a model part by part, in a piecemeal way. Instead, theoretical coherence corresponding to the correlation of all factors involved can only be reached by constructing the whole mathematical framework *at once*. Therefore also the *empirical validation* cannot take place piece by piece but by verifying the outcomes of the whole model in as many independent cases as possible where empirical measurements are feasible.

(b) *Operational and hidden variables*. Any mathematical model must obviously contain a set of *"operational variables"* which by definition are *directly measurable*, i.e. accessible for empirical validation. But *not all* relevant variables *need* to be operational. In order to obtain a coherent theoretical and interpretational conceptualization it may turn out to be necessary to introduce *"hidden variables"* whose values cannot be measured directly but which are *indirectly* measurable by observing their effects on the operational variables in the dynamic process.

(c) *The problem of interpretational ambiguity*. The mathematical model for a self-contained set of (operational and/or hidden) key-variables may have two or more possible *qualitative* interpretations. That means, more than one behavioral motivation may lead to the same group dynamics. Therefore the full wealth of qualitatively different descriptions of attitudes can in general *not* be depicted *one to one* in the mathematical framework. Instead, the mathematical model provides a *projection* (in the sense of a *homomorphism* rather than an *isomorphism*) of the full reality into a restricted representation by few key-variables (see Helbing, 1995, p. 14, 127f).

(d) *Fictitious and real scenarios and their relation to the verification process.* Every sufficiently comprehensive mathematical model contains a set of *"trend parameters"* which denote the parameters in the evolution equations of the relevant variables. Even if the *meaning* of the trend parameters is clear, their numerical *value* remains *open* for the first. Each set of trend parameters within the admissible domain and the corresponding simulation of the dynamics leads to a scenario which is *theoretically possible* within the frame of the model. However, most of these scenarios are *fictitious*, whereas the few *actually observable scenarios* should be seen as embedded into the vast manifold of theoretically possible but *fictitious scenarios*. The selection of *realistic* scenarios from all possible scenarios simultaneously leads to a *validation* of the model (if realistic scenarios are contained in the manifold of the theoretically possible ones) and to an appropriate *calibration* of the trend parameters. But also fictitious scenarios belonging to extreme choices of trend parameters and correspondingly biased motivation structures can be of high importance: They can serve for a study of the effect of artificially exaggerated motivations on the dynamics of the system.

The sections of this chapter are organized as follows: In Section 2 the design principles of the model will be explained in *qualitative terms.* Section 3 will then contain the explicit mathematical formulation of the model, beginning with the definition, explanation, and interpretation of the relevant key-variables, trend-functions, and trend-parameters. Further we will set up coupled differential equations for the evolution of these variables. In Section 4 selected scenarios will be simulated as special solutions of the model equations. Each scenario will be accompanied by a sociological interpretation. The simulations can of course not exhaust the content of the model and should be considered as a first step towards its numerical investigation. Finally, Section 5 is an attempt to establish a relation between our model and selected literature in this field.

2. THE DESIGN PRINCIPLES OF THE MODEL

In this section we shall exhibit the problems and develop the design principles of our model in a verbal non-mathematical form but with the intention to prepare its mathematical formulation in the next section.

The purpose of the model is to give an insight into the dynamics of the evolution of groups and their competitive interaction on the macroscopic level. The dynamics will imply stages of rise, evolution, stationarity, and decay.

Studying the literature (see also the discussion in Section 5) it becomes apparent that group structure and dynamics is considered on different scales and from different perspectives.

Some approaches focus on the more microscopic level of individual activities and interactions which represent the daily routine of group life and reproduction. We denote the fast and fluctuating variables belonging to this scale as *micro-variables*. These include the *network-variables* which describe the activities within the social network (*network activities*).

Other approaches focus on the slowly varying collective variables on the macro-level which characterize and dominate the global structure and evolution of a system of interacting groups. We denote these slow macro-variables as *key-variables* or *order-parameters*.

Evidently all variables are interconnected. In particular, the key-variables are somehow composed of the network-variables. Therefore a full theoretical description of group dynamics should comprise both the microscopic network-variables and the key-variables, however, at the cost of immense complexity and tangledness.

Instead we shall restrict ourselves to a formal description of the *macro-level* taking into account a set of relatively few *key-variables* only.

This procedure must be *justified* because it implicitly assumes that the key-variables exhibit a *quasi-autonomous self-contained sub-dynamics of their own*, without explicitly taking into account their connection with the microscopic network-variables.

In cases where a complete set of equations for both micro- and macro-variables is available, as it happens for many physico-chemical systems, such a justification can be given. It follows from the so-called *"slaving principle"* discovered by Haken (1977). Its qualitative meaning can be easily understood: The fast-moving micro-variables nearly instantaneously adapt to their momentary equilibrium values, which gradually vary with the slow temporal changes of the macroscopic order-parameters. By this, the dynamics of the micro-variables is *already determined* by the slowly changing order-parameters. Consequently, the micro-variables can be mathematically *eliminated* by expressing them in dependence on the macro-variables. There remains a reduced *set of autonomous dynamic evolution equations for the order-parameters only* into which the micro-variables enter merely implicitly via the elimination procedure.

Can this procedure be transferred to sociodynamics, in particular to our present problem?

On the one hand, it can be well substantiated that the relation between the fast network-variables of daily routine and the slow key-variables of global group structure is analogous to the one between the fast micro-variables and the slow macro-variables in physico-chemical systems. Indeed, the dynamics of the fast network-variables is constrained, guided, and dominated by the (slowly evolving) structure of the group. Presuming that the momentary global structure of the group is a reflection of the daily network activities, which, however, do not appear explicitly, the main remaining problem is the dynamics of the slowly evolving key-variables characterizing the macro-structure of the group.

On the other hand, there is no system of equations available at all for which an elimination procedure via the "slaving principle" could be applied. Therefore the search for a sufficiently comprehensive and self-contained set of key-variables and the introduction of their dynamics will base on a combination of observation and intuition.

In our modelling procedure we restrict ourselves to a deterministic (not stochastic) descriptive level, which is equivalent to a consideration of the mean-values of the key-variables neglecting their probabilistic fluctuations. This is done in order to avoid a too high complexity which could not be exhausted anyway. Our approximation can be justified if the probabilistic fluctuations of the considered variables are small. This holds if the considered groups are large enough so that the deviations from the mean-values are small. The approximation may however become problematic for groups in which the number of members is small.

An extension to stochastic equations which take into account fluctuations is possible. The equations for the key-variables then appear as the approximate mean-value equations of the corresponding stochastic equations; Weidlich and Haag (1983), Weidlich (1991, 1994) and Helbing (1995).

Let us now go over to the details of model design.

The Key-Variables of the Model

We have now to search for a set of adequate key-variables dominating the structure and evolution of groups on the macro-level. Our conclusion is that two kinds of variables are indispensable. The first kind are the.

Collective Personal Variables

The members of a group do not form a homogeneous crowd. A group rather develops a *hierarchy of subgroups* the members of which possess *different degrees of influence, responsibility, and obligation*. The hierarchy may comprise few or many organizational levels reaching from nominal membership to leadership. In any case, an essential structural feature of a group is the number of levels of influence and obligation and the distribution of its members over these hierarchical subgroups. The numbers of group members on the different hierarchical levels can be combined in a vector that is denoted as *group configuration*. Here, the group configuration summarizes a set of *slow time-dependent collective personal variables* that partially characterize the group structure and its dynamics at the macro-level.

If the activities, responsibilities and obligations as well as the attitudes and the mentality belonging to each organizational level were described in detail, we would have a description of the *micro-level of network-activities* of the group down to the behavior of a single individual member. These micro-activities however *do not explicitly appear* in the macro-variables of the group configuration which are nevertheless a *resultant* of the daily network activities.

Transpersonal Variables

The *"groupness of a group"* is only partially captured by variables like those comprised by the group configuration. A group is led by ideas and visions which sometimes even form a *coherent ideology* with respect to the common purposes and objectives of the group. These ideas and visions provide a kind of *glue* keeping the group together and establishing a feeling of *identification* with the group among its members. The *intensity* of this sentiment may reach from "feeling at home in the group" up to enthusiasm and fanaticism.

The togetherness and common bond of group members coming about in this way creates an *indirect* relation between them because each member is indirectly tied to the others by adhering to the same group ideology. This relation *differs* from the one coming about by *direct* interaction (e.g. by imitation, persuasion, urging to activities) between each pair of members of the group.

In general, *direct* as well as *indirect* relations will contribute to the formation of the groupness of a group but the relative weight of both may vary considerably. In groups of political extremists or religious sects the fanatic belief in the group ideology will prevail, whereas in clubs or associations devoted to sports or arts the interindividual partnership will prevail.

The aspects of group ideology are, on the one hand, established and sustained by all individual members. On the other hand, these ideas act back on the members by inspiring them and urging them to become active supporters of the group. But just by being supported by *all* and, vice versa, by inspiring *all* members of the group, the aspects of group ideology take on a *transpersonal quality* since they *cannot* be attributed and allocated to any particular person. Therefore it is adequate to treat them as *entities on their own*, i.e. as conceptual realities of separate and distinct existence, and to endow them with their *own dynamics*.

Our conclusion is that consequently one should attribute to each group a *set of transpersonal variables* satisfying their own dynamic equations (which are coupled to the variables of the group configuration) and describing substantial aspects of the group ideology and its interaction with the members. In a *minimal model* one should focus on one transpersonal variable which *abstracts* from the contents and colors of a specific ideology and simply provides a measure for the *intensity* of the *emotional affection and adherence* produced by the group ideology among the members of the group. *This central transpersonal variable is denoted as the group solidarity.*

At this stage we will postpone the question whether the group solidarity should be considered as an *operational* or a *hidden* variable (see Section 1), i.e. whether it can be measured directly or only indirectly.

The *full set* of key-variables of a minimal model of interacting groups thus will consist of the *group configuration* and the *group solidarity* for each group.

The Elementary "Driving Forces" of the Dynamics

The main problem now consists in finding the elementary driving forces responsible for changes of the key-variables in order to insert these in a consistent, self-contained system of evolution equations.

First we note that a stationary state of a system of groups will consist of the stationary numbers of non-members and members of all groups on the different levels of hierarchy and of the stationary values of the variables of group solidarity. However, the knowledge of the stationary state itself does not contain much information about the causes of its generation; in other words, there lacks a process conceptualization. In order to learn more about these causes we must try to understand how the *changes of the key-variables*, i.e. the changes of the numbers of the group configuration and the increases or decreases of the solidarity variables come about.

The change of the group configuration, i.e. the change of the numbers of members of a group occupying certain roles and levels in the hierarchy is evidently due to the *transition of individuals* from one role to another (for instance the transition from non-membership to the status of a nominal member of a group, or the transition from the status of a nominal member to that of a leading member).

At this point the dynamics of those key-variables which describe the group configuration is influenced by the decision-making of individuals who occupy a role which they want to change. The crucial *"driving force"* behind the decision to make such a transition is a *conditional motivation* to adopt – *ceteris paribus* – a certain new role in the group configuration, depending on the respective role one has occupied before.

The *mathematical formulation* of this matter, which is the subject of Section 3, will therefore consist in introducing *transition rates* (per unit of time) for individuals to move from old to new roles within the group configuration. These transition rates will depend on *conditional motivations*. And, since these motivations arise under the given situation, they will thus have to be appropriately chosen *functions* of all *key-variables* which characterize that situation. The so-defined transition-rates then immediately lead to the formulation of the *equations of motion for the collective personal variables of the group configuration*. They have the form of *generalized migratory equations*, Weidlich and Haag (1988) and Weidlich (1991), where of course the migration does not take place between locations as in conventional population dynamics but between status roles within the group configuration.

Finally we have to consider the *dynamics of the solidarity variable* of each group. It is clear that the evolution of this variable is coupled to collective activities and attitudes of all members of the own group and perhaps also of the competing ones. Since the solidarity is a transpersonal variable, only the *superposition* of individual activities and attitudes, i.e. only *collective efforts and moods* will lead to an increase or decrease of the quantified measure of solidarity.

Two main kinds of influences on the dynamics of the solidarity variable are conceivable:

Firstly, within a group constructive collective efforts of its group members towards *consolidation* of the group identity will lead to an *enhancement* of the amount of solidarity in that group whereas, on the other hand, members of other groups might make destructive efforts in order to disintegrate the identity of the competing group and thus possibly cause a diminution of solidarity. Of course, a superposition of the *constructive* and the *destructive* efforts will take place.

Secondly, there will exist a *saturation effect* prohibiting an unlimited increase of solidarity even in the absence of interfering competing groups. This saturation is due to a *limited total capacity* of every individual to engage in the pursuit of ideals such as the identification with a group. If the individual is simultaneously a member of several groups (belonging to different "dimensions of life"), he/she will have to divide his/her *receptivity* for group ideology and solidarity between these groups. The disappointment-creating factors like the free-rider phenomenon depend on the size of the group and so does the saturation level. Hence a *limit of group size* is connected with a *limited capacity for solidarity*.

Taking into account these two main influences one is led to setting up an equation of motion for the dynamics of solidarity in each group, containing a *growth term* and a *saturation term* in the form of a generalized logistic equation. However, the growth term and the saturation term will have to be appropriately chosen functions of the group configuration. Hence the dynamics of solidarity is coupled to the values of the other (collective personal) key-variables. We have seen above that the inverse is also true: The dynamics of the group configuration is coupled to the values of the solidarity variable because the conditional motivations depend on this variable, too.

In total there arises a system of *coupled autonomous differential equations of motion* for the components of the group configuration describing the evolution of the *size* and *composition* of a group, together with equations of motion for the evolution of *solidarity* within each group.

Concluding this section we stress once more that the quantitative model now to be set up in mathematical detail in the following section refers to macro-variables and not to micro-variables. The detailed behavior of the latter is therefore not explicitly reflected in this model. It is, however, presumed implicitly (and could be substantiated by a micro-theoretical approach) that the basic dynamics of the microscopic variables carries, supports, and sustains the macro-structure and macro-dynamics captured in this model.

3. THE MATHEMATICAL FORM OF THE MODEL

The design principles of Section 2 have now to be cast in concrete mathematical form.

In Section 3.1 we begin with some preliminary remarks which will prove useful in the course of the construction. Thereupon we follow the procedure indicated in Section 2.

The key-variables as such and some derivative variables are introduced in Section 3.2. In Section 3.3 the construction elements of the dynamics are introduced and interpreted. At the end of this chapter all key-variables, trend functions, and trend parameters together with their names, brief interpretations, and defining equations are summarized in tables. The pre-requisites built up in Sections 3.2 and 3.3 are then used in Section 3.4 to set up the system of evolution equations for the key-variables. In Section 3.5 problems connected with the solution of these equations are discussed. In particular we will see that the equations may possess one or more stationary solutions which are approached for $t \to \infty$.

3.1. Preliminary Remarks

At first we treat the question of the *range of interpretations*, which was already discussed in the introduction pointing at the possible ambiguity of interpretations of one and the same formal model. In Section 2 we have preferred a "psycho-social" vocabulary and have avoided interpretations with an economic touch. Now we shall *simultaneously* make use of both *psycho-social* and *economic* interpretations, i.e. of more value-oriented idealistic and more cost-oriented materialistic argumentations. For instance, in speaking about the positive and negative aspects of a certain status level we shall use *psycho-social terms* like advantage, gratification, satisfaction and frustration, burden of obligations, disappointment, etc. as well as *economic terms* like utility, benefit, payoff and costs, charges, fees, etc. Although some sociologists may refuse to compare economic matters of "filthy lucre" with psycho-social matters like values and idealistic commitment we think that it is not only *possible* but even *inevitable* in any quantitative sociodynamic theory to compare and to relate both interpretational aspects. If, for instance, in a decision process to change from one status level to another the immaterial and the material aspects play a simultaneous role, in any quantitative theory suppositions must be made about the quantitative amounts and the ratio of intensities of both motivations.

Secondly, we will now make a simplification by *restricting our group dynamic formulation to one "dimension of life"*. By "dimension" we mean one sector of social life belonging either to the religious, cultural, political, economic, or leisure sphere. Each individual may simultaneously be a member of a group in each of these sectors. But in *one* sector it can be assumed that the groups are *non-overlapping* (see Figure 5.1) because individuals will normally be members of at most *one group* in each sector. For instance, memberships in political parties are mutually exclusive. Neglecting interactions between the different sectors (and of memberships in groups belonging to different sectors) we consider one arbitrary sector only and assume that only non-overlapping groups exist in that sector.

Thirdly, we will make use of the following *notation of variables*, which is also summarized at the end of Section 3.3: *Key-variables* are denoted by *capitals; trend-functions* (depending on key-variables) and *trend-parameters* (constant coefficients) are denoted by *small italics*. All these quantities are dimensionless plain numbers. *Rates*, however, which have the dimension 1/(unit of time) are denoted by *greek letters*: their value determines the speed, i.e. the time scale on which the evolution takes place. This time scale will range from months to years or even decades since we consider the evolution of slowly varying macroscopic key-variables.

3.2. The Key-Variables

Let us consider G non-overlapping groups $G_i, G_j, \ldots, i, j = 1, 2, \ldots, G$ belonging to one sector of social life. As already indicated in Section 2, there exists a hierarchy of status levels $h, k = 0, 1, 2, \ldots, H_i$ in each group G_i from nominal membership $h = 0$ over staff levels up to the leading level $h = H_i$, where each level has benefits and advantages but also charges and obligations of its own. In each group G_i the *total*

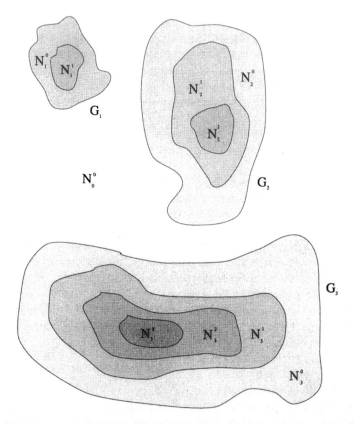

FIGURE 5.1.   The picture illustrates one social sector (dimension) with three nonover-lapping groups G_1, G_2, G_3. The points of the plane represent the individuals of the total population. Their position in this abstract space has nothing to do with their location in real space. The space between the groups represents the crowd of N_0^0 non-members. G_1 has two, G_2 three, and G_3 four hierarchical subgroups corresponding to nominal up to leading members of the groups. The components $\{N_1^0, N_1^1; N_2^0, N_2^1, N_2^2; N_3^0, N_3^1, N_3^2, N_3^3\}$ of the group configuration are assigned to these subgroups. The grade of obligations and influence of the subgroups are indicated by hatchings of different densities.

number of its members N_i is distributed over the status levels h in a characteristic way. If N_i^h denotes the *number of members of G_i occupying the status level h*, one obtains the obvious relation

$$N_i = \sum_{h=0}^{H_i} N_i^h. \tag{1}$$

A member of group G_i with status h will be said to be in state (ih). Furthermore we introduce the number N_0^0 of individuals being involved in none of the groups and refer to these as to the crowd of individuals. For these individuals we do not distinguish any status levels, i.e. $N_0^0 = N_0$.

Since double memberships in one and the same social sector are excluded by assumption, we have the relation

$$N_0^0 + \sum_{i=1}^{G} N_i = N_0^0 + \sum_{i=1}^{G} \sum_{h=0}^{H_i} N_i^h = N, \qquad (2)$$

where N is the total number of individuals in the social system considered. The set of (time-dependent) numbers

$$\mathbf{N} = \{N_0^0; N_1^0 \ldots N_1^{H_1}; \ldots; N_i^0 \ldots N_i^h \ldots N_i^{H_i}; \ldots; N_G^0 \ldots N_G^{H_G}\}$$

$$= \{N_0^0; \mathbf{N}_1; \ldots; \mathbf{N}_i; \ldots; \mathbf{N}_G\} \qquad (3)$$

is denoted as (total) *group configuration*, where $\mathbf{N}_i$ is the *partial group configuration of* G_i.

Furthermore we introduce the *shifted group configuration*

$$\mathbf{N}_{ji}^{kh} = \{N_0^0; N_1^0 \ldots N_1^{H_1}; \ldots; N_j^0 \ldots (N_j^k + 1) \ldots N_j^{H_j};$$

$$\ldots; N_i^0 \ldots (N_i^h - 1) \ldots N_i^{H_i}; \ldots; N_G^0 \ldots N_G^{H_G}\} \qquad (4)$$

arising from N after the transition of one individual from state (ih) into state (jk).

From the group configuration further variables can be directly derived. Evidently,

$$\sum_{k=0}^{h-1} N_i^k = \text{personnel below status } h \qquad (5)$$

is the number of all subordinates of the status level h, and the *average number of subordinates of* one *member with status* h is given by

$$n_i^h = \sum_{k=0}^{h-1} \frac{N_i^k}{N_i^h}. \qquad (6)$$

It is plausible to assume that the potential *influence and power* of a staff member of G_i with status h is more or less proportional to the number of members subordinate to him plus himself. Therefore we introduce the *potential influence in state* (i,h) as

$$i_i^h(\mathbf{N}_i) = n_i^h + 1 = \sum_{k=0}^{h} \frac{N_i^k}{N_i^h}. \tag{7}$$

An indicator of the *total* (internal as well as external) *potential influence* and power of group G_i can be defined as the sum of the influences i_i^h of all its members:

$$i_i(\mathbf{N}_i) = \sum_{h=0}^{H_i} N_i^h i_i^h = \sum_{h=0}^{H_i} \sum_{k=0}^{h} N_i^k. \tag{8}$$

However, a more detailed consideration leads to taking into account *saturation effects*: For instance, in large groups the potential influence i_i^h will not really grow proportionally to the number of subordinates because the intensity of direct personal interactions with these subordinates cannot be maintained if their number increases. Therefore, instead of N_i^h, we introduce saturated numbers $\tilde{N}_i^h$.

$$N_i^h \rightarrow \tilde{N}_i^h = N_{\max} \frac{N_i^h}{(N_{\max}-1)+N_i^h} = N_{\max} y_i^h. \tag{9}$$

with

$$N_{\max} > 1 \quad \text{and} \quad 0 \leqslant y_i^h = \frac{x_i^h}{1+x_i^h} \leqslant 1, \text{ for } x_i = \frac{N_i^h}{(N_{\max}-1)} = \frac{y_i^h}{1-y_i^h}. \tag{10}$$

Evidently, the *saturated numbers* $\tilde{N}_i^h$ have the following properties:

$$\tilde{N}_i^h = N_{\max} y_i^h = \begin{cases} 0 & \text{for } N_i^h = 0, \\ 1 & \text{for } N_i^h = 1, \\ \tilde{N}_i^h \lesssim N_i^h & \text{for small } N_i^h, \\ \tilde{N}_i^h \Rightarrow N_{\max} & \text{for } N_i^h \Rightarrow \infty, \\ \tilde{N}_i^h \Rightarrow N_i^h & \text{for } N_{\max} \Rightarrow \infty. \end{cases} \tag{11}$$

It is now easy to take into account the saturation effects in (6)–(8) by going over to the *saturated potential influence in state* (ih):

$$\tilde{i}_i^h(\mathbf{N}_i) = \sum_{k=0}^{h} \frac{\tilde{N}_i^k}{\tilde{N}_i^h} \leqslant (h+1) \frac{N_{\max}}{N_i^h} \tag{12}$$

and the *total (saturated) potential influence*:

$$\tilde{I}_i(\mathbf{N}_i) = \sum_{h=0}^{H_i} N_i^h \tilde{\imath}_i^h = \sum_{h=0}^{H_i} \sum_{k=0}^{h} \tilde{N}_i^k \leqslant \frac{(H_i+1)(H_i+2)}{2} N_{\max}. \qquad (13)$$

The number $N_{\max}$ appearing in $\tilde{N}_i^h$ has to be calibrated carefully because it limits the range of influence of higher status levels. It may be different in different social sectors or contexts, e.g. different for political parties and for sport clubs.

Finally, we assign a *solidarity variable* S_i to each group G_i. This variable is (see Section 2) to be interpreted as a transpersonal measure for the intensity of the emotional affection and adherence evoked in all members of the group by the common group ideology and by the group objectives.

Direct measurements of S_i are certainly difficult but not impossible. They could consist in measuring a composite indicator of reactions of members of the group (taking into account, e.g. the frequency of voluntary compliance with obligations). But independently of the question whether S_i is a directly measurable operational or a hidden variable it will play an explicit and definite role in the evolution equations as we will see in Section 3.4.

Anyway we are free to choose the domain of variation of S_i by an appropriate scaling and by confining $S_i(t)$ to a domain which it must not leave in the course of time. We choose

$$0 \leqslant S_i(t) \leqslant 1, \quad i = 1, 2, \ldots, G. \qquad (14)$$

All key-variables can now be comprised in the *total key-variable configuration*

$$\mathbf{C} = \{N_0^0; S_1, \mathbf{N}_1; \ldots; S_i, \mathbf{N}_i; \ldots; S_G; \mathbf{N}_G\} = \{\mathbf{S}, \mathbf{N}\}$$
$$= \{N_0^0; \mathbf{C}_1; \ldots; \mathbf{C}_i; \ldots; \mathbf{G}_G\}, \qquad (15)$$

where $\mathbf{C}_i = \{S_i, \mathbf{N}_i\}$ is the *key-variable configuration of G_i* and $\mathbf{S} = \{\mathbf{S}_1, \ldots \mathbf{S}_i \ldots \mathbf{S}_G\}$. Corresponding to (4) we also introduce the *shifted key-variable configuration* $\mathbf{C}_{ji}^{kh} = \{\mathbf{S}, \mathbf{N}_{ji}^{kh}\}$.

We conclude this section with Figure 5.1 illustrating a sytem of non-overlapping groups belonging to one social dimension and possessing internal hierarchical structures. All social dimensions together could be visualized by superposing figures of all dimensions of life. Then the groups of different figures would in general overlap because individuals can simultaneously be members of different groups belonging to different social dimensions.

3.3. Construction Elements of the Dynamics

On the way towards the construction of dynamic equations for the key-variables C we need an *intermediate* but very important step: the introduction of certain mathematical concepts providing the *elementary components of the dynamic process*. These elementary *dynamic components* must finally be connected with the *motivations* for those decisions of individuals which lead to changes of the key-variables.

With respect to the collective personal variables N we proceed in three steps. First we introduce *transition rates* which describe the elementary changes of the group configuration. Second we introduce *conditional motivation potentials* which are measures of the readiness of the individuals to perform transitions. Third we establish the relation between the transition rates and the motivation potentials.

(a) Transition Rates between States of Individuals

The elementary step leading to a change of the group configuration is the transition of a member of group G_i with status h, i.e. of an individual in state (ih), into state (jk) by becoming a member of group G_j with status k. Such elementary steps take place stochastically, i.e. the sequence of such steps is a random process. However, going over to *mean-values*, i.e. considering an ensemble of individuals doing such steps in the same environmental situation characterized by the key-variables C, one can introduce the well-defined quantity

$$v(jk; C_{ji}^{kh}|ih; C) = \text{total transition rate}, \qquad (16)$$

which is by definition, the fraction of individuals originally in state (ih) who per unit of time go over into the new state (jk).

The total transition rate is not only a function of the initial state (ih) and final state (jk) but also of the whole situation (expressed by the key-configuration C) *before* the transition and the whole situation (expressed by the shifted key configuration C_{ji}^{kh}) *after* the transition.

We now anticipate that two different processes contribute to the total transition rate: On the one hand, there exist transitions from (ih) to (jk) which are *indirectly* motivated by the general mood of the individuals in state (ih) originating from the global situation. On the other hand, there exist transitions from (ih) to (jk) which are *directly* induced by persuasive activities of the members of group G_j.

Hence it is plain to decompose the total transition rate into contributions arising from indirect and direct interactions:

$$v(jk; \mathbf{C}_{ji}^{kh}|ih; \mathbf{C}) = v_I(jk; \mathbf{C}_{ji}^{kh}|ih; \mathbf{C}) + v_D(jk; \mathbf{C}_{ji}^{kh}|ih; \mathbf{C}). \qquad (17)$$

(b) Conditional Motivation Potentials

Up to now the transition rate (16) is a *purely mathematical concept* and must in the following be specified in a sociological way. This leads us to the question how the *motivations* of the transition-making individuals can be cast into a mathematical form and how this form depends on the key-variables characterizing the situation within the system of competing groups.

We tackle this problem by introducing a quantitative measure for the readiness of the individual to change into state (jk) given that he/she is in state (ih) before the transition. This measure shall be called the *conditional motivation potential*:

$$m(jk; \mathbf{C}_{ji}^{kh}|ih; \mathbf{C}) = \text{conditional motivation potential.} \qquad (18)$$

For the time being we *postulate* only some general properties for the conditional motivation potential: It is a real function of the initial and final state and of the key-variables characterizing the situation. It can vary in the range from $-\infty$ to $+\infty$:

$$-\infty < m(jk; \mathbf{C}_{ji}^{kh}|ih; \mathbf{C}) < +\infty. \qquad (19)$$

If the final state (jk) is more attractive than the initial state (ih), $m(\ldots|\ldots)$ will be positive. In the opposite case $m(\ldots|\ldots)$ will be negative. Furthermore, $m(\ldots|\ldots)$ will increase monotonously with the attractiveness of the final state (jk) and decrease monotonously with the attractiveness of the initial state (ih). So far we have neglected transaction costs.

For a given attractiveness of the initial and final state $m(\ldots|\ldots)$ should decrease with growing (economic) *transaction costs* and with a growing (psychological) *resistance* against a transition from state (ih) to state (jk).

These requirements for the conditional motivation potential suggest the following functional form:

$$m(jk; \mathbf{C}_{ji}^{kh}|ih; \mathbf{C}) = u_j^k(\mathbf{C}_{ji}^{kh}) - u_i^h(\mathbf{C}) - t_{ji}^{kh}, \qquad (20)$$

where $u_j^k(\mathbf{C}_{ji}^{kh})$ and $u_i^h(\mathbf{C})$ are the *net utilities* of the state (jk) after the transition and of the state (ih) before it, respectively, and t_{ji}^{kh} is a term comprising the *transaction costs* (economic costs as well as the effect of psychological resistance) related to the transition from (ih) to (jk).

The net utility of a state (ih) – and analogously of any other state (jk) – measures the attractiveness of this state (ih) and varies within the same range as the conditional motivation potential, namely from $-\infty$ to $+\infty$. It describes the relative weight of *benefits* b_i^h (satisfactory, gratifying aspects) and *costs* c_i^h (frustrating, disappointing aspects) of state (ih). Therefore the following form of u_i^h (and analogously of any other utility u_j^k) is proposed:

$$u_i^h = b_i^h - c_i^h. \tag{21}$$

Benefits and costs can again be decomposed into sub-terms of different motivational origin:

$$b_i^h = p_i^h + f_i, \tag{22}$$

$$c_i^h = o_i^h + q_i. \tag{23}$$

For the subterms we choose the following terminology:

$p_i^h =$ payoff, $f_i =$ faith confirmation,

$o_i^h =$ obligations, $q_i =$ contributions.

The meaning of these four terms will now be shortly explained.

We begin with the *cost terms*: The *obligations* o_i^h comprise the burdens of duties and responsibilities as well as the work related to members of group G_i with status h. The obligations have a predominantly immaterial character. Compliance with these obligations can be partially enforced (by sanctions) and partially voluntary altruistic.

The *contributions* q_i have a material as well as immaterial character and consist of regular payments (e.g. membership fees and grants providing the financial support of the group) but also of personal initiatives.

Turning now to the *benefit terms*, the *payoff* term p_i^h consists of partially material, partially immaterial contributions. It comprises material rewards (status-dependent remunerations) as well as status-, influence- and solidarity-dependent advantages, honors, and satisfactions.

The *faith confirmation* term f_i describes the immaterial satisfaction by receiving a reconfirmation of the own ideas and beliefs due to being a member of group G_i. However, faith confirmation may turn into *opinion pressure*, and voluntary consent into an enforced one if the entrainment forces into the group ideology become too strong and penetrant. (In political parties this would mean the mutation from a liberal to a totalitarian structure (see also Weidlich and Haag, 1983; Weidlich, 1994)).

Finally, the *transaction costs* can also be decomposed in a plausible manner:

$$t_{ji}^{kh} = a_j^k + l_i^h, \tag{24}$$

where l_i^h are the "*leaving costs*" and a_j^k the "*admission costs*".

The *leaving costs* are often primarily immaterial losses and consist of losing and breaking off old contacts when withdrawing from a previously joined group G_i.

The *admission costs* consist of an entrance fee and of the efforts necessary to be accepted in a new group G_j. Both terms together diminish the motivation to change from the previous state (ih) to a new state (jk) even if the utility of (jk) is higher than the utility of (ih).

Inserting Eq. (21) together with (22)–(24) into (20) one obtains a *decomposed form of the conditional motivation potential* in which each term has a definite meaning and interpretation.

The next task is to calibrate the trend-parameters l_i^h, a_j^k and, even more important, to propose plausible forms for $o_i^h(\mathbf{C})$, $q_i(\mathbf{C})$, $p_i^h(\mathbf{C})$ and $f_i(\mathbf{C})$ as *functions of the key-variables*. We begin with the contributions q_i which are assumed to be independent of status h. They could also be considered as function of $\mathbf{C}_i$, e.g. as function of the group size $(\sim N_i)$ and of the solidarity S_i. But for the first we assume that this dependence is relatively weak and treat q_i as a *trend parameter* which only has to be appropriately calibrated.

Continuing with the *obligations* o_i^h the following form seems persuasive:

$$o_i^h = o_i h^{d_i}. \tag{25}$$

The meaning of this formula is the following: For members without any functions $(h=0)$ the costs (23) correspond to the contributions q_i only, i.e. $o_i^0 = 0$. Obligations for members with higher status $h > 0$ grow with a certain power $d_i \geqslant 0$ of the status level h, denoted as *exponent of obligations*.

The payoff p_i^h seems to be more complicated. We arrive at the following formula:

$$p_i^h(\mathbf{C}) = N_i q_i S_i (g_0 + g_1 \tilde{l}_i S_i) \frac{r_i^h}{\sum_{k=0}^{H_i} r_i^k N_i^k} \tag{26}$$

with

$$r_i^h = q_i + r_i o_i^h = q_i + r_i o_i h^{d_i}, \tag{27}$$

which has the following interpretation: $N_i q_i$ is the sum of all (material and immaterial) contributions available for group G_i. The solidarity factor $S_i \leqslant 1$ provides a measure for the reliability with which the members make their contributions. The next factor $(g_0 + g_1 \tilde{i}_i S_i)$ contains modifications of a pure redistribution of contributions q_i. The first term $g_0 < 1$ expresses the *diminution of the payoff by administration costs*. The second term represents an immaterial or material increase of the payoff by group activities. This term is proportional to the potential (saturated) total influence $\tilde{i}_i$ and to the solidarity S_i putting this influence into effect; the coefficient g_1 calibrates the *effective total influence* $\tilde{i}_i S_i$. The last factor, namely the fraction containing the *share coefficients* r_i^h, r_i^k is denoted as the *payoff distribution* and it determines the share received by a member of group G_i with status h. The *share coefficient* r_i^h itself consists of the status-independent term q_i and a term proportional to the obligations, $r_i o_i^h$, where r_i is a *reward coefficient*.

The payoff equation (26) has the following obvious implication:

$$p_i^h / p_i^k = r_i^h / r_i^k. \tag{28}$$

Furthermore, the total payoff for all members of G_i is

$$\sum_{k=0}^{H_i} N_i^k p_i^k = N_i q_i S_i (g_0 + g_1 \tilde{i}_i S_i). \tag{29}$$

Finally, the *faith confirmation* term is assumed to have the form

$$f_i(\mathbf{C}) = \sum_{j=1}^{G} w_{ij} \tilde{i}_j S_j, \tag{30}$$

which can be validated as follows: The *faith feedback coefficients* w_{ij} represent the strength of the effective total influence $\tilde{i}_j S_j$ of group G_j on the faith in the values of group G_i. The term $w_{ij} \tilde{i}_j S_j$ with $j = i$ and $w_{ii} > 0$ describes a positive feedback effect of the total effective (saturated) influence $\tilde{i}_i$ of group G_i on the firm belief into the values of the own group G_i. This reconfirmed belief is considered as a positive part of the utility u_i^h of state (ih). The influence of competing groups on the attitudes within G_i can be constructive $(w_{ij} > 0)$ but also destructive $(w_{ij} < 0)$ and thus diminish f_i. In this way a competing group can have a positive or a negative influence on the utilities of another group.

Inserting Eqs. (25), (26) and (30) into formula (21) and making use of Eqs. (22) and (23), one obtains the explicit expression

$$u_i^h(\mathbf{C}) = (p_i^h(\mathbf{C}) + f_i(\mathbf{C})) - (o_i^h + q_i) \qquad (31)$$

for the net utility as a function of the key-variables. Therefore also the conditional motivation potential (20) has now become an explicit function of the key-variables.

(c) Representation of Transition Rates in Terms of
   Motivation Potentials

Our last step consists in establishing a connection between the conditional motivation potential and the (indirect and direct) transition rates. In this way also the transition rates become explicit functions of the key-variables.

According to their definition, the indirect and direct transition rates $v_I(jk; \mathbf{C}_{ji}^{kh}|ih; \mathbf{C})$ and $v_D(jk; \mathbf{C}_{ji}^{kh}|ih; \mathbf{C})$, respectively, are positive definite quantities describing the frequency of transitions of individuals from an initial state (ih) to a state (jk) in dependence on these states and on the global situation $\mathbf{C}$ among the competing groups.

It is natural that these transition rates are higher the more attractive is the final state (jk) compared to the initial state (ih), and that they are smaller the higher are the transaction costs or the psychological resistance for a transition from (ih) to (jk).

In the same manner, the values of the conditional motivation potential (which, however, ranges from $-\infty$ to $+\infty$) *increase* with growing difference between the attractiveness of the final and initial state, and *decrease* with growing transaction costs.

Therefore it is *clear* that there must exist a monotonous functional relation between the (indirect and direct) transition rates and the conditional motivation potential. The simplest (and, as it will turn out, the most plausible) monotonous function transforming the domain $-\infty < m(\ldots|\ldots) < +\infty$ of the conditional motivation potential into the positive domain $v_I, v_D > 0$ of the transition rates is the exponential function. Therefore we postulate the proportionality relations:

$$v_I(jk; \mathbf{C}_{ji}^{kh}|ih; \mathbf{C}) \sim \exp[m(jk; \mathbf{C}_{ji}^{kh}|ih; \mathbf{C})],$$
$$v_D(jk; \mathbf{C}_{ji}^{kh}|ih; \mathbf{C}) \sim \exp[m(jk; \mathbf{C}_{ji}^{kh}|ih; \mathbf{C})]. \qquad (32)$$

Whereas the bias in favor of either the final state (jk) or the initial state (ih) is already sufficiently taken into account by $m(jk; \mathbf{C}_{ji}^{kh}|ih, \mathbf{C})$, the special effects of persuasion activities of members of the envisaged group G_j favoring the transition to state (jk) must be described by an additional factor regarding the direct transition rate v_D. This *persuasion activity* is assumed to have the form

$$e_j \sum_{k=0}^{H_j} N_j^k \tilde{i}_j^k = e_j \tilde{i}_j = \text{persuasion activity of } G_j, \tag{33}$$

where e_j is a global factor describing the *strength of individual persuasion activities* and $\tilde{i}_j$ takes into account the different persuasive power of members with different status.

Therefore we arrive at the following form for the transition rates:

$$v_I(jk; \mathbf{C}_{ji}^{kh}|ih; \mathbf{C}) = v_0 \exp[m(jk; \mathbf{C}_{ji}^{kh}|ih; \mathbf{C})],$$
$$v_D(jk; \mathbf{C}_{ji}^{kh}|ih; \mathbf{C}) = v_0 e_j \tilde{i}_j \exp[m(jk; \mathbf{C}_{ji}^{kh}|ih; \mathbf{C})], \tag{34}$$

which are combined in the formula for the total transition rate (see Eq. (17)):

$$v(jk; \mathbf{C}_{ji}^{kh}|ih; \mathbf{C}) = v_0(1 + e_j \tilde{i}_j) \exp[m(jk; \mathbf{C}_{ji}^{kh}|ih; \mathbf{C})]$$

$$= v_0 \exp[m'(jk; \mathbf{C}_{ji}^{kh}|ih; \mathbf{C})] \tag{35}$$

with the *effective conditional motivation potential*:

$$m'(jk; \mathbf{C}_{ji}^{kh}|ih; \mathbf{C}) = m(jk; \mathbf{C}_{ji}^{kh}|ih; \mathbf{C}) + \ln(1 + e_j \tilde{i}_j)$$

$$= u_j^k(\mathbf{C}_{ji}^{kh}) - u_i^h(\mathbf{C}) - t_{ji}^{kh} + \ln(1 + e_j \tilde{i}_j). \tag{36}$$

The *global rate* v_0 calibrates the transition speed, i.e. the time scale on which the whole transition process will take place.

The following transformations are of purely mathematical nature. They lead to equivalent forms of the total transition rate. However, owing to the postulated exponential form of the transition rate in terms of the effective conditional motivation potential, this transformation leads to additional interpretations which appeal to the intuition and give a further justification of the postulated form of $v(\ldots|\ldots)$. In these formal considerations we omit for simplicity the arguments $\mathbf{C}_{ji}^{kh}$ and $\mathbf{C}$ of $m'(jk; \mathbf{C}_{ji}^{kh}|ih; \mathbf{C})$.

At first we decompose the effective conditional motivation potential into a *symmetrical part* m_s' and an *antisymmetrical part* m_a':

$$m'(jk|ih) = m_s'(jk|ih) + m_a'(jk|ih) \tag{37}$$

with

$$m'_s(jk|ih) = m'_s(ih|jk) = \tfrac{1}{2}\{m'(jk|ih) + m'(ih|jk)\}, \qquad (38)$$
$$m'_a(jk|ih) = -m'_a(ih|jk) = \tfrac{1}{2}\{m'(jk|ih) - m'(ih|jk)\}.$$

Inserting Eq. (36) and the explicit form of t_{ji}^{kh}, Eq. (24), one obtains more detailed expressions:

$$m'_s(jk|ih) = -\tfrac{1}{2}(a_j^k + a_i^h + l_j^k + l_i^h) + \tfrac{1}{2}\ln[1 + e_j\tilde{\iota}_j)(1 + e_i\tilde{\iota}_i)] = -\ln d_{ji}^{kh} \quad (39)$$

with

$$d_{ji}^{kh} = d_{ij}^{hk} = \frac{\exp\{\tfrac{1}{2}(a_j^k + a_i^h + l_j^k + l_i^h)\}}{\sqrt{(1 + e_j\tilde{\iota}_j)(1 + e_i\tilde{\iota}_i)}} \qquad (40)$$

and

$$m'_a(jk|ih) = u_j^k - u_i^h - \tfrac{1}{2}[(a_j^k - l_j^k) - (a_i^h - l_i^h)]$$
$$+ \tfrac{1}{2}\ln(1 + e_j\tilde{\iota}_j) - \tfrac{1}{2}\ln(1 + e_i\tilde{\iota}_i)$$
$$= v(jk) - v(ih) \qquad (41)$$

with

$$v(jk) = u_j^k - \tfrac{1}{2}(a_j^k - l_j^k) + \tfrac{1}{2}\ln(1 + e_j\tilde{\iota}_j),$$
$$v(ih) = u_i^h - \tfrac{1}{2}(a_i^h - l_i^h) + \tfrac{1}{2}\ln(1 + e_i\tilde{\iota}_i). \qquad (42)$$

If Eq. (37) together with Eqs. (39) and (41) are inserted into (35), one will obtain an alternative though equivalent form of the transition rate:

$$v(jk|ih) = v_0 \exp[m'(jk|ih)] = v_0 \frac{\exp[v(jk) - v(ih)]}{d_{ji}^{kh}}, \qquad (43)$$

which suggests the interpretation of d_{ji}^{kh} as an *effective sociological distance* between states (ih) and (jk), and of $v(jk)$, $v(ih)$ as *effective attractivenesses* of the states (jk) and (ih), respectively.

The effective attractiveness $v(ih)$, and correspondingly $v(jk)$, can be further decomposed into positive and negative terms by splitting up u_i^h according to Eq. (21):

$$v(ih) = v_+(ih) - v_-(ih),$$

with

$$v_+(ih) = b_i^h + \tfrac{1}{2}l_i^h + \tfrac{1}{2}\ln(1 + e_i\tilde{\iota}_i),$$

$$v_-(ih) = c_i^h + \tfrac{1}{2}a_i^h, \tag{44}$$

where $v_+(ih)$ and $v_-(ih)$ are denoted as *effective pull towards* (ih) and *effective push away from* (ih), respectively. Inserting (44) in (43) yields another equivalent form of the transition rate:

$$v(jk|ih) = \frac{v_0}{d_{ji}^{kh}} \frac{\exp[v_+(jk)]}{\exp[v_-(jk)]} \frac{\exp[v_-(ih)]}{\exp[v_+(ih)]}, \tag{45}$$

which allows an interpretation of the transition rate in terms of "distance", "pulling", and "pushing" factors. Indeed, according to formula (45), the transition rate from the origin state (ih) to the destination state (jk) is large (small)

- for large (small) terms $v_+(jk)$ pulling towards (jk)
- for small (large) terms $v_-(jk)$ pushing away from (jk)
- for large (small) terms $v_-(ih)$ pushing away from (ih)
- for small (large) terms $v_+(ih)$ pulling towards (ih)
- for small (large) effective distances d_{ji}^{kh} between (ih) and (jk).

(d) Growth Rate and Saturation Rate of the Solidarity

Having discussed the elementary "dynamics-generating" quantities of the personal variables, namely the transition rates, we must now also consider the elementary quantities which produce the dynamics of the solidarity variables.

In Section 2 we have already indicated that two counteractive "forces" are at work producing the dynamics of S_i, namely a *growth rate* which is mainly due to the collective activities of the members of G_i to enhance their solidarity, and a *saturation rate* limiting the unrestricted growth due to frustration effects and a limited receptivity for group ideology and objectives among the members.

To formulate these effects in a quantitative form we first introduce an *activity rate* for the growth of solidarity:

$$\alpha_i' = \alpha_i'(\mathbf{C}_i) = (\alpha_{0i} + \alpha_{1i}N_i)(1 - S_i) = \alpha_i(N_i)(1 - S_i). \tag{46}$$

The activity rate contains an "absolute" term α_{0i} comprising solidarity creating (perhaps ideological) processes which enhance the sentiments of identity within G_i *independently* of the size of the group, and a term $\alpha_{1i}N_i$ *proportional to the number* of members of G_i. The latter includes all activities of members enhancing the feelings of commonness within G_i. However, as solidarity S_i approaches its maximum value 1 the activity rate is reduced. This is accounted for by the factor $(1-S_i)$. Secondly, we introduce a *saturation rate* which is *counteractive* to the activity rate (and which therefore enters the equation for $S_i(t)$ with a negative sign). The following form seems highly plausible:

$$\sigma_i' = \sigma_i'(\mathbf{C}_i) = \sigma_{0i}S_i + \sigma_{1i}N_i^2 S_i = \sigma_i(N_i)S_i. \tag{47}$$

The term $\sigma_{0i}S_i$ takes into account those saturation effects of S_i which are independent of the size of G_i (for instance the limited receptivity of each member of the group for too much ideology in G_i). The term $\sigma_{1i}S_iN_i^2$ takes into account the saturation of S_i caused by the free-rider effect.

A single individual is stronger tempted to behave in an un-cooperative way, the less apparent it will be (i.e. the easier he/she can hide in the crowd of members) and the less necessary it is to cooperate (i.e. the higher the level of solidarity S_i already is). That means the temptation is proportional to N_iS_i. Since this temptation affects every member, the total free-rider effect must be proportional to $N_i \cdot N_iS_i = N_i^2 S_i$.

Undoubtedly, one could think of more detailed formulas for $\alpha_i(\mathbf{C})$ and $\sigma_i(\mathbf{C})$ but we consider Eqs. (46) and (47) as the simplest form of these quantities which will lead to a reasonable dynamics of the solidarity variable.

At the end of this chapter we summarize all key-variables, trend functions and trend parameters, their names, brief interpretations, and their defining equations in tables (Tables 5.1–5.3).

3.4. The Dynamic Equations of the Key-Variables

Having supplied the construction elements of the dynamics, namely the transition rates for the collective personal variables and the rates for the solidarity variables, we are equipped with all requisites for setting up the equations of motion for the key-variables.

Indeed, the *equations for the collective personal variables* are nothing but generalized migratory equations (Weidlich and Haag, 1988;

TABLE 5.1
Key-variables

Variables	Name and interpretation	Defining equation
N_0^0	Number of the crowd of individuals belonging to no group	(2)
N_i^h	Number of members of group G_i with status level h	(1)
N_i	Total number of members of group G_i	(1)
N	Total number of individuals in the social system	(2)
$\hat{N}_i^h$	$rnd(N_i^h) = N_i^h$ rounded up to the next higher integer	(49)
$\tilde{N}_i^h$	Saturated number of members of group G_i in status level h	(9)–(11)
N_{max}	Limit of saturated numbers $\tilde{N}_i^h$	(9)–(11)
$\bar{N}_i^h$	Stationary value of the number of members of group G_i in status level h	(57)
n_i^h	Number of personnel (subordinates) per member of status h in group G_i	(6)
S_i	Solidarity variable of group G_i	(14)
$\bar{S}_i$	Stationary value of the solidarity variable of G_i	(57)
$i_i^h = n_i^h + 1$	Potential influence in state (ih)	(7)
i_i	Total potential influence of group G_i	(8)
$\tilde{i}_i^h$	Saturated potential influence in state (ih)	(12)
$\tilde{i}_i$	Total saturated potential influence of group G_i	(13)
$\tilde{i}_i S_i$	Effective total influence of group G_i	(26), (30)
$e_i \tilde{i}_i$	Persuasion activity of group G_i	(33)
N	Total group configuration = set of numbers $\{N_0^0, \dots N_i^h \dots N_G^{H_G}\}$	(3)
$\mathbf{N}_i$	Partial group configuration of G_i = set of numbers $\{N_i^0, \dots N_i^{H_i}\}$	(3)
$\mathbf{N}_{ji}^{kh}$	Shifted total group configuration after transition of one individual from state (ih) to state (jk)	(4)
C	Total key-variable configuration $\{N_0^0; \mathbf{C}_1 \dots \mathbf{C}_G\}$	(15)
$\mathbf{C}_i$	Partial key-variable configuration of G_i:$\{S_i; \mathbf{N}_i\}$	(15)
$\mathbf{C}_{ji}^{kh}$	Shifted total key-variable configuration = $\{\mathbf{S}, \mathbf{N}_{ji}^{kh}\}$	(15)

Weidlich, 1991). They take the form

$$\frac{dN_j^k}{dt} = \sum_{i,h} \nu(jk; \hat{\mathbf{C}}_{ji}^{kh}|ih; \hat{\mathbf{C}})\hat{N}_i^h - \sum_{i,h} \nu(ih; \hat{\mathbf{C}}_{ij}^{hk}|jk; \hat{\mathbf{C}})\hat{N}_j^k,$$

$$\text{for } j = 1, \dots, G; \ k = 0, \dots, H_j \tag{48}$$

and

$$\frac{dN_0^0}{dt} = \sum_{i,h} \nu(00; \hat{\mathbf{C}}_{0i}^{0h}|ih; \hat{\mathbf{C}})\hat{N}_i^h - \sum_{i,h} \nu(ih; \hat{\mathbf{C}}_{i0}^{h0}|00; \hat{\mathbf{C}})\hat{N}_0^0$$

with

$$\hat{\mathbf{C}} = (\hat{N}_0^0; S_1, \hat{N}_1^1, \dots \hat{N}_1^{H_1}; \dots; S_G, \hat{N}_G^1 \dots \hat{N}_G^{H_G}). \tag{49}$$

TABLE 5.2
Trend-functions

Trend-functions	Name and interpretation	Defining equation
$v(jk; C_{ji}^{kh}\|ih; C)$	Total transition rate from $(ih; C)$ to $(jk; C_{ij}^{kh})$	(16), (17), (35), (43), (45)
$v_D(jk; C_{ji}^{kh}\|ih; C)$	Partial transition rate induced by *direct* pair interactions	(17), (34)
$v_I(jk; C_{ji}^{kh}\|ih; C)$	Partial transition rate induced by *indirect* interactions	(17), (34)
$m(jk; C_{ji}^{kh}\|ih; C)$	Conditional motivation potential for transition from $(ih; C)$ to $(jk; C_{ji}^{kh})$.	(18)–(20)
$m'(jk; C_{ji}^{kh}\|ih; C)$	Effective conditional motivation potential	(35)–(37)
$m_s'(jk; C_{ji}^{kh}\|ih; C)$	Symmetrical part of $m'(jk; C_{ji}^{kh})$	(37)–(39)
$m_a'(jk; C_{ji}^{kh}\|ih; C)$	Antisymmetrical part of $m'(jk; C_{ji}^{kh})$	(37), (38), (41)
$d_{ji}^{kh}(C_{ji}^{kh}; C)$	Effective sociological distance between states (ih) and (jk)	(40)
$v(ih; C)$	Effective attractiveness of state (ih)	(41), (42)
$v_+(ih; C)$	Effective pull towards state (ih)	(44)
$v_-(ih; C)$	Effective push away from state (ih)	(44)
$u_i^h(C)$	Net utility of state (ih)	(20), (21), (31)
$b_i^h(C)$	Benefits of state (ih)	(21), (22)
$p_i^h(C)$	Payoff of state (ih)	(22), (26)
$f_i(C)$	Faith confirmation for members of G_i	(22), (30)
$c_i^h(C)$	Costs of state (ih)	(21), (23)
$o_i^h(C)$	Obligations in state (ih)	(23), (25)
$q_i(C)$	Contributions of members of group G_i	(23)
$t_{ji}^{kh}(C)$	Transaction costs of transition from state (ih) to state (jk)	(20), (24)
$l_i^h(C)$	Leaving costs when leaving state (ih)	(24)
$a_j^k(C)$	Admission costs when entering state (jk)	(24)
$\alpha_j'(C)$	Activity rate for growth of solidarity S_i	(46)
$\sigma_i'(C)$	Saturation rate for saturation of solidarity S_i	(47)

The values $\hat{N}_i^h = rnd(N_i^h)$ are N_i^h, rounded to the nearest integer. The sums on the right-hand side (r.h.s.) extend over the states $(ih) = (00)$ and (ih) with $i = 1, \ldots, G$ and $h = 0, 1, \ldots, H_i$.

The mathematical meaning of Eq. (48) is easily comprehensible: The *first term on the r.h.s.* describes the number of individuals arriving per unit of time in state (jk) and coming from one of the states (ih) by performing the transition $(ih) \rightarrow (jk)$. (Note that the states (ih) include also the state (00) of people not involved in any group, i.e. of the crowd

TABLE 5.3
Trend-parameters

Trend-parameters	Name and interpretation	Defining equation
v_0	Global rate calibrating the transition speed	(34)
e_j	Strength of individual persuasion activity	(33)
d_i	Exponent of obligations in group G_i	(25)
r_i^h	Share coefficient in the payoff expression	(26), (27)
r_i	reward coefficient	(27)
g_0, g_1	Coefficients calibrating the absolute and influence dependent part of the payoff	(26)
o_i	Global factor calibrating the obligations in G_i	(25)
w_{ij}	Faith feedback coefficients calibrating the faith confirmation	(30)
α_{0i}, α_{1i}	Rate coefficients determining the absolute and member dependent part of the activity rate $\alpha_i'(\mathbf{C})$	(46)
σ_{0i}, σ_{1i}	Rate coefficients determining the natural and member dependent part of the saturation rate $\sigma_i'(\mathbf{C})$	(47)

of individuals.) This term leads to an increase of N_j^k with time. The *second term* on the r.h.s. describes the number of individuals leaving state (jk) and performing transitions into any of the states (ih) (including (00)). This term leads to a decrease of N_j^k with time. Hence the change of N_j^k with time comes about by the counter-active effects of transitions into (jk) and transitions out of (jk). The analogous holds for Eq. (49), the evolution equation for the non-members. From (48) and (49) there follows

$$\frac{d}{dt}\left(N_0^0 + \sum_{j=1}^{G}\sum_{k=0}^{H_j} N_j^k\right) = \sum_{jk}\sum_{ih} v(jk; \hat{\mathbf{C}}_{ji}^{kh}|ih; \hat{\mathbf{C}})\hat{N}_i^h$$

$$- \sum_{jk}\sum_{ih} v(ih; \hat{\mathbf{C}}_{ij}^{kh}|jk; \hat{\mathbf{C}})\hat{N}_j^k = 0, \qquad (50)$$

i.e. the total number N of individuals remains constant in time. Therefore the "conservation law" expressed in Eq. (2) is compatible with Eqs. (48) and (49).

The quantities $N_0^0(t)$, $N_j^k(t)$ take on continuous values since they are mean-values for an ensemble of comparable systems of groups. However, for small groups some of their values can become very small (even between 0 and 1) so that $\mathbf{N}_{kh}^{ji}$ could formally contain non-allowed negative values. Therefore it is reasonable to insert (at evaluating dN_j^k/dt and dS_i/dt) the values $\hat{N}_i^h = rnd(N_i^h)$ (and $\hat{N}_j^k = rnd(N_j^k)$) which are rounded to the nearest integers. This accounts for the discreteness of the number of individuals. For sufficiently large numbers $N_i^h, N_j^k \gg 1$ the rounding procedure plays no significant role. The equations for the solidarity variables can also be obtained in straight manner: On the one hand, the relative rate of change of a variable $S_i(t)$ is defined by

$$\frac{dS_i/dt}{S_i(t)} = \text{relative rate of change of } S_i(t). \tag{51}$$

On the other hand, it is our proposition that this relative rate of change is composed of two counteractive terms, namely the activity rate $\alpha_i'(\hat{C})$ and the saturation rate $\sigma_i'(\hat{C})$.

$$\frac{dS_i/dt}{S_i(t)} = \alpha_i'(\hat{C}) - \sigma_i'(\hat{C}). \tag{52}$$

Rewriting (52) and inserting Eqs. (46) and (47) one obtains:

$$\frac{dS_i}{dt} = \alpha_i(\hat{N}_i)S_i - (\alpha_i(\hat{N}_i) + \sigma_i(\hat{N}_i))S_i^2 \quad \text{for } i = 1, 2, \ldots, G. \tag{53}$$

This dynamic equation for the solidarity variable S_i is a kind of logistic equation (see Pearl, 1924; Verhulst, 1845). However, the difference to the original logistic equation is that the coefficients $\alpha_i(\hat{N}_i)$ and $(\alpha_i(\hat{N}_i) + \sigma_i(\hat{N}_i))$ are not constants but functions of $\hat{N}_i$, the number of members of group G_i, which is a variable itself.

The $\sum_{i=1}^{G}(H_i+1) + 1 + G = (\sum_{i=1}^{G}H_i + 2G + 1)$ Eqs. (48), (49), and (53) for the G interacting groups G_i, each of them consisting of (H_i+1) status levels, and the crowd of non-members establish *the mathematical form of our group-dynamic model*. They become fully explicit by inserting the form (35) or (43) of the transition rates and by expressing them via (36) with (31) in terms of the key-variables. It is obvious that this set of equations is a coupled non-linear autonomous system of first-order differential equations in time.

3.5. Initial Conditions and Stationary Solutions

In this section we will first make a general remark about the *problem of the initial state* of the evolution of groups in view of our equations; secondly we will search for the structure of the *stationary solutions* of the model equations in important special cases where the generalized migratory equations fulfil the condition of "detailed balance".

The "natural" initial state for a system of emerging groups is the state where groups do not yet exist. This state can be characterized in our system by

$$N_0^0 = N, \qquad N_i^h = 0, \qquad S_i = 0, \quad i = 1, \ldots, G, \quad h = 0, \ldots, H_i \quad (54)$$

and it will turn out to be a metastable state (i.e. not a fully stable state) if our mean-value equations are formally applied to that extreme case. In fact, we obtain for this initial state

$$v(00) = 0 \quad \text{and} \quad v(jk) < 0 \quad \text{for} \quad (jk) \neq (00) \quad (55)$$

because for the state (54) we have (putting $a_j^k = l_j^k$)

$$v(jk) = u_j^k \quad \text{with} \quad u_j^k = (p_j^k + f_j) - (o_j^k + q_j) < 0 \quad (56)$$

since the payoff and faith confirmation are equal to 0 for the not yet existing groups but obligations and contributions do already exist for anyone wanting to initiate a group. Therefore the transition rate from the non-member state (00) to any state $(jk) \neq (00)$ is, according to (43), very small since it is more attractive to stay in the non-member state than to take the burden of obligations and contributions connected with the foundation of a group.

However, mean-value equations like those of our proposed model are not really applicable to a state like (54) with vanishing or extremely small numbers of members in all groups. In such cases statistical fluctuations play a dominant role so that a fully probabilistic formulation (e.g. in terms of the master equation (see Weidlich and Haag, 1983; Weidlich, 1991; 1994; Helbing, 1995)) for a theory of very small emerging groups is indispensable. Such a stochastic theory of the emergence of new groups would be a highly interesting topic but it is beyond the scope of the approach presented here.

A quite different situation is given if we investigate the structure of possibly existing *stationary solutions* of the system equations with time-independent key-variables:

$$\bar{C} = \{\bar{N}_0^0; \bar{S}_1, \bar{N}_1^0 \ldots \bar{N}_1^{H_1}; \ldots; \bar{S}_i, \bar{N}_i^0 \ldots \bar{N}_i^{H_i}; \ldots; \bar{S}_G, \bar{N}_G^0 \ldots \bar{N}_G^{H_G}\}. \quad (57)$$

We can expect that in such states for one or more groups the numbers of members $\bar{N}_i^h$ will be large compared to 1 so that the mean-value equations can safely be applied.

The stationary values (57) of the key-variables must evidently fulfil the stationary equations derived from Eqs. (48), (49) and (53) by putting the time derivatives equal to zero. This yields:

$$0 = \sum_{ih} \frac{v_0}{d_{ji}^{kh}(\bar{C})} \{\exp[v(jk,\bar{C}) - v(ih,\bar{C})]\bar{N}_i^h$$

$$- \exp[v(ih,\bar{C}) - v(jk,\bar{C})]\bar{N}_j^k\} \qquad (58)$$

and

$$0 = \sum_{ih} \frac{v_0}{d_{0i}^{0h}(\bar{C})} \{\exp[v(00,\bar{C}) - v(ih,\bar{C})]\bar{N}_i^h$$

$$- \exp[v(ih,\bar{C}) - v(00,\bar{C})]\bar{N}_0^0\}, \qquad (59)$$

where the sums extend over (ih) with $i = 1,\ldots,G$, $h = 0,\ldots,H_i$ and $(ih) = (00)$, as well as

$$0 = \alpha_i(\bar{N}_i)\bar{S}_i - (\alpha_i(\bar{N}_i) + \sigma_i(\bar{N}_i))\bar{S}_i^2. \qquad (60)$$

Here we have already used the explicit form (43) of the transition rates, and have neglected the shift $\bar{C} \to \bar{C}_{ji}^{kh}$ because the $\bar{N}_j^k$, $\bar{N}_i^h$ were assumed large compared to 1.

The stationary solidarity equations (60) can easily be solved with the result

$$\bar{S}_i = \frac{\alpha_i(\bar{N}_i)}{\alpha_i(\bar{N}_i) + \sigma_i(\bar{N}_i)} < 1, \qquad (61)$$

which shows that $\bar{S}_i$ is a function of $\bar{N}_i$ and is always in the required domain (14) between 0 and 1 (see Figure 5.2).

The result (61) can be inserted in (58) and (59) to obtain a set of equations depending on the single components $\{\bar{N}_0^0, \bar{N}_1^0, \ldots, \bar{N}_G^{H_G}\}$ of the stationary group configuration $\bar{N} = \{N_0^0, \bar{N}_1 \ldots \bar{N}_G\}$ only (instead of depending on both $\bar{N}$ and $\bar{S}$). We formulate this by substituting the following terms in (58), (59):

$$v(jk,\bar{C}) \to v(jk,\bar{N}), \quad v(ih,\bar{C}) \to v(ih,\bar{N}) \quad \text{and} \quad d_{ji}^{kh}(\bar{C}) \to d_{ji}^{kh}(\bar{N}). \quad (62)$$

Before turning to the solution of Eqs. (58) and (59) we have to specify the value of the effective attraction $v(00,\bar{N})$ of the set of non-members which has special properties. According to the general formula (42),

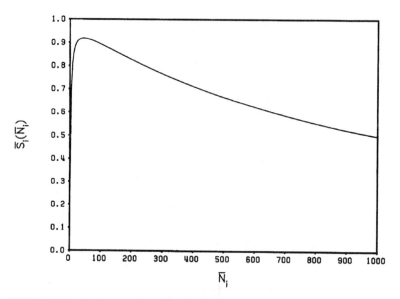

FIGURE 5.2. Stationary values $\bar{S}_i$ of solidarity in a group G_i as function of the stationary total number $\bar{N}_i$ of members of G_i according to eq. (60). The trend-parameters are chosen as $\alpha_{0i}=0.1$, $\alpha_{1i}=0.5$, $\sigma_{0i}=1.0$, $\sigma_{1i}=0.0005$.

$v(00,\bar{\mathbf{N}})$ should have the form

$$v(00,\bar{\mathbf{N}})=u_0^0(\bar{\mathbf{N}})-\frac{1}{2}(a_0^0-l_0^0)+\frac{1}{2}\ln(1+e_0\tilde{l}_0)$$

with

$$u_0^0(\bar{\mathbf{N}})=(p_0^0+f_0)-(o_0^0+q_0). \tag{63}$$

Since in the crowd of non-members there exist neither obligations ($o_0^0=0$) and contributions ($q_0=0$) nor payoff ($p_0^0=0$) and faith confirmation ($f_0=0$) (at least in the special case $w_{0j}=0$), we obtain $u_0^0(\bar{\mathbf{N}})=0$. Furthermore, no admission and leaving costs exist ($a_0^0=l_0^0=0$) and no persuasion activities to enter the crowd of non-members are developed ($e_0=0$). Therefore one comes to the conclusion that

$$v(00,\bar{\mathbf{N}})=0. \tag{64}$$

For solving Eqs. (58) and (59) let us consider the much simpler set of equations

$$\bar{N}_i^h=C\exp[2v(ih,\bar{\mathbf{N}})] \tag{65}$$

where $i=1,\ldots,G$, $h=0,\ldots,H_i$, or $(ih)=(00)$.

If the system of transcendental equations (65) for $\bar{\mathbf{N}} = \{\bar{N}_0^0, \bar{\mathbf{N}}_1, \ldots \bar{\mathbf{N}}_G\}$ has one or more than one solution at all, these solutions are simultaneously solutions of Eqs. (58) and (59), i.e. they are stationary group configurations! Indeed, inserting (65) in (58) and (59) one obtains:

$$\{\exp[v(jk, \bar{\mathbf{N}}) - v(ih, \bar{\mathbf{N}})]\bar{N}_i^h - \exp[v(ih, \bar{\mathbf{N}}) - v(jk, \bar{\mathbf{N}})]\bar{N}_j^k\}$$

$$= C\{\exp[v(jk, \bar{\mathbf{N}}) + v(ih, \bar{\mathbf{N}})] - \exp[v(ih, \bar{\mathbf{N}}) + v(jk, \bar{\mathbf{N}})]\} = 0.$$

$$\text{(66)}$$

This means that the brackets in the sums of (58) and (59) vanish individually so that (58) and (59) are fulfilled.

The meaning of Eq. (66) will become clear if one multiplies (66) by $v_0/d_{ji}^{kh}(\bar{\mathbf{N}})$ and re-inserts the expression (43) of the transition rate. Then (66) reads

$$v(jk \,|\, ih; \bar{\mathbf{N}})\bar{N}_i^h = v(ih \,|\, jk; \bar{\mathbf{N}})\bar{N}_j^k. \qquad \text{(67)}$$

This relation is called *detailed balance*. It means that the stationary flow of individuals (per unit of time) from state (ih) to state (jk) is the same as the stationary flow from state (jk) to state (ih) *for each pair of states* $(ih),(jk)$. If (65) has no solutions, there may still exist solutions of (58) and (59) because, for satisfying the latter equations, detailed balance is only a *sufficient* but not a *necessary* condition. Equations (58) and (59) require only that for each state (jk) the *total* inflow is equal to the *total* outflow.

Trying to solve Equations (65) one obtains with (64) in any case:

$$N_0^0 = C\exp[0] = C, \qquad \text{(68)}$$

where the constant C has to be determined by the normalization condition (see (1)):

$$N_0^0 + \sum_{i=1}^{G} \sum_{h=0}^{H_i} N_i^h = C\left(1 + \sum_{i=1}^{G} \sum_{h=0}^{H_i} \exp[2v(ih, \bar{\mathbf{N}})]\right) = N. \qquad \text{(69)}$$

Apart from this simple constraint the complexity of the set of equations (65) depends on the form of $v(ih, \bar{\mathbf{N}})$ as a function of the stationary group configuration $\bar{\mathbf{N}}$.

The solution of (65) is considerably simplified if $v(ih, \bar{\mathbf{N}})$ depends only on $\bar{\mathbf{N}}_i$, i.e. on the configuration of group G_i. The meaning of this simplification is that the effective attraction $v(ih, \bar{\mathbf{N}}_i)$ depends only on the size and compositionof G_i but not on interfering activities of other groups. Under this condition $v(ih, \bar{\mathbf{N}}) = v(ih, \bar{\mathbf{N}}_i)$ Equations (65) split up in G independent sets, one for each configuration $\bar{\mathbf{N}}_i = \{\bar{N}_i^0, \ldots, \bar{N}_i^G\}$, which are connected only by the normalization condition (69).

4. SIMULATION OF SELECTED SCENARIOS

In the previous section we have seen that the *stationary solutions* of the dynamic equations (48), (49) and (53) still have a relatively simple structure if the condition of detailed balance (67) holds. In this case the stationary solutions fulfil Eqs (65).

However, the *time-dependent solutions* of the dynamic equations do not have a simple, analytically tractable solution. They can only be obtained numerically by computer calculations.

These solutions represent an *immense manifold of possible evolutionary scenarios*: To each choice of initial conditions for the key-variables together with the calibrated trend-parameters from Table 5.3 there belongs exactly one out of an infinite number of possible scenarios.

Even if we exclude cases describing the rise of new groups (because of the problem of initial fluctuations for small numbers N_i^h), several characteristic scenarios are expected already in the simple case of two initial groups. For instance:

(a) a stable stationary state of co-existence of both groups could evolve,
(b) one group could score off or push out the other, for instance, by providing a better benefits–costs ratio,
(c) one group could wear down the other by destroying its internal faith with negative interference.

At investigating the structure of such cases one can make use of one advantage of the scenario technique: Whereas empirical situations always contain a *complex superposition* of (too) many factors of influence, the construction of fictitious scenarios can take place by *selectively* and *successively* "switching on" one trend parameter after another. Then, by studying the corresponding solutions of the equations, the effect of each of these trend parameters on the dynamic process can be distinguished and isolated more easily.

Using this circumstance, our procedure will consist in making a small excursion into the "vast forest of possible scenarios". (Of course the stations on this route do not at all exhaust the manifold of possible evolutions included in the model equations.) In detail this means

1. choosing the *same structure of the group configuration* in all simulations; it consists of two groups G_1 and G_2, each with three status
   levels $h = 0, 1, 2$, and the crowd of non-members,
2. choosing in all simulations the *same initial conditions* for the key
   variables $N_0^0; N_1^0, N_1^1, N_1^2, S_1; N_2^0, N_2^1, N_2^2, S_2$,
3. keeping the *same constant values* for *most* of the trend parameters
   in all simulations,
4. selecting just a *small group* of trend-parameters the values of which
   are *subject to changes* when passing from one scenario to another,
   but
5. changing the value of only one *trend-parameter* (which will be
   underlined) when passing on the "route of scenarios" from *one*
   scenario to the next.

For each of the seven "stations" on this route, we will present one
corresponding figure including four illustrations which depict, as
functions of time,

(a) the total numbers of individuals of the crowd and of the two
    groups: $N_0(t) = N_0^0(t)$ (—); $N_1(t) = \sum_{h=0}^{2} N_1^h(t)$ (- - -); $N_2(t) = \sum_{h=0}^{2} N_2^h(t)$ (- - - -),
(b) the solidarity variables $S_1(t)$ (- - -) and $S_2(t)$ (- - - - -),
(c) the occupation numbers of the hierarchy levels of group G_1:
    $N_1^0(t)$ (—), $N_1^1(t)$ (- - -), $N_1^2(t)$ (- - - - -),
(d) the occupation numbers of the hierarchy levels of group G_2:
    $N_2^0(t)$ (—), $N_2^1(t)$ (- - -), $N_2^2(t)$ (- - - - -).

Each scenario will be accompanied by a short interpretation stressing
particularly the parameter changes in comparison to the respective
previous scenario.

The initial conditions for the key-variables are chosen as follows:

$$N_0^0(0) = N_0(0) = 500, \quad N_1(0) = 160, \quad N_2(0) = 90,$$

$$S_1(0) = 0.8, \quad S_2(0) = 0.9,$$

$$N_1^0(0) = 125, \quad N_1^1(0) = 30, \quad N_1^2(0) = 5, \tag{70}$$

$$N_2^0(0) = 75, \quad N_2^1(0) = 15, \quad N_2^2(0) = 0.$$

At $t = 0$ we begin with already sufficiently large groups in order to
avoid the problems connected with emerging groups discussed in
Section 3.5 which are beyond the scope of the present article.

TABLE 5.4

$\alpha_{0i} = 0.1$; $\alpha_{1i} = 0.5$	Partial rates of the activity rate
$\sigma_{0i} = 1.0$; $\sigma_{li} = 0.0005$	Partial rates of the saturation rate
$q_i = 6.0$	Contributions
$r_1 = 0.7$	Reward coefficient of group G_1
$d_i = 1.0$	Exponents of obligations of groups G_i
$v_0 = 1.0$	Global scaling factor of transition rates
$e_0 = 0.0$; $e_1 = 0,0$	Persuasion coefficients of crowd and group G_1
$a_1^h = 0.0$	Admission costs of group G_1
$l_i^h = 0.0$	Leaving costs
$g_0 = 0.7$	Coefficients of influence-independent payoff
$w_{01} = w_{11} = w_{21} = w_{22} = 0.0$	Faith feedback coefficients
$o_i = 3.0$	Calibration factor of obligations
$N_{max} = 100$	Saturation level

Table 5.4 lists the values of all those trend parameters which are kept constant throughout all scenario simulations. The index $i = 1, 2$ refers to both groups G_1 and G_2.

The values of all trend parameters not listed above may change from one scenario to another. The variable trend parameters are: $g_1 =$ coefficient of influence-dependent payoff, $e_2 =$ persuasion coefficient of group G_2, $a_2^h =$ admission costs of group G_2, w_{12}, $w_{02} =$ faith feedback coefficients, $r_2 =$ reward coefficient of group G_2. The values of these trend parameters are defined separately for each scenario.

We begin with

Scenario 1

Choice of the variable trend parameters:

$$g_1 = 0.0, \quad e_2 = 0.0, \quad a_2^h = 0.0, \quad w_{12} = 0.0, \quad w_{02} = 0.0, \quad r_2 = 0.7.$$

Interpretation. In this case all trend parameters referring to groups G_1 and G_2 are equal. No group exerts influence on the internal faith of the other group (because all faith influence coefficients are zero). The influence-independent payoff coefficient is small ($g_0 = 0.7$, corresponding to 30% administrative losses) and the influence-dependent payoff coefficient is zero ($g_1 = 0.0$). Therefore membership in one of the groups is not really (materially or immaterially) profitable and remunerative. As expected, the result is (see Figure 5.3): The total number of members of both groups decreases; the groups decay and their members join the crowd of non-members. The originally rather high solidarity levels (given by the initial conditions) increase as long as there are still enough members to pursue their activities. Afterwards,

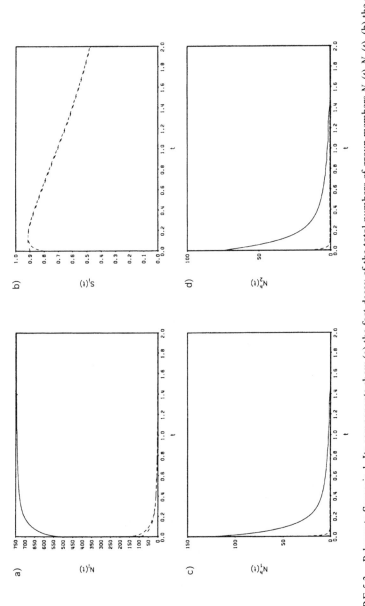

FIGURE 5.3.   Belongs to Scenario 1. Its components show (a) the fast decay of the total numbers of group members $N_1(t), N_2(t)$, (b) the slow decay of solidarities $S_1(t), S_2(t)$, (c) and (d) the fast decay of the occupation numbers $N_1^h(t), N_2^h(t)$ of the status levels of both groups G_1 and G_2 since group membership is not profitable.

with the decay setting in, the solidarity level decreases, too. The number of leading members (with status $h = 1, 2$) decreases even faster than the number of nominal members because there is no sufficient reward for their higher obligations. Consequently the higher obligations induce an earlier leaving of the group.

We proceed to

Scenario 2

with the following choice of the variable trend parameters:

$$\underline{g_1} = 0.004, \quad e_2 = 0.0, \quad a_2^h = 0.0, \quad w_{12} = 0.0, \quad w_{02} = 0.0, \quad r_2 = 0.7.$$

Interpretation. The payoff situation has now changed: For both groups a positive coefficient of the influence-dependent payoff was introduced. Both influences ("power") $\bar{\imath}_i(\mathbf{N}_i)$ and solidarity S_i now play a positive role leading to a higher (material and immaterial) payoff. As a consequence the positive term p_i^h in u_i^h now prevails, i.e. membership in groups G_1 and G_2 is now profitable and more individuals of the crowd enter the groups. This can be seen in Figure 5.4. It is also evident that stationary occupation numbers are approached independently of the initial values. Also, for both groups, the solidarity levels approach the same high stationary values, and the distribution of members over the status levels reaches the same stationary ratios. This scenario therefore represents the typical case of two co-existing groups without asymmetry and without interference between them.

We now pass on our route to

Scenario 3

with the following choice of the variable trend parameters:

$$g_1 = 0.004, \quad \underline{e_2} = 0.01, \quad a_2^h = 0.0, \quad w_{12} = 0.0, \quad w_{02} = 0.0, \quad r_2 = 0.7.$$

Interpretation. This provides an asymmetric behavior of groups G_1 and G_2 since the members of G_2 (and only of G_2) now canvass new members for their group via direct (pair-)interactions, in particular with the individuals of the crowd. The result can be seen in Figure 5.5 which shows that group G_2 reaches a much higher number of members due to its persuasion activity than group G_1 – at the cost of group G_1 and the crowd. From Figure 5.5 it can also be concluded that this result was *not* due to the indirect influence of solidarity because the higher stationary number of members in G_2 leads even to a lower saturation level of the solidarity in G_2 as compared to the solidarity

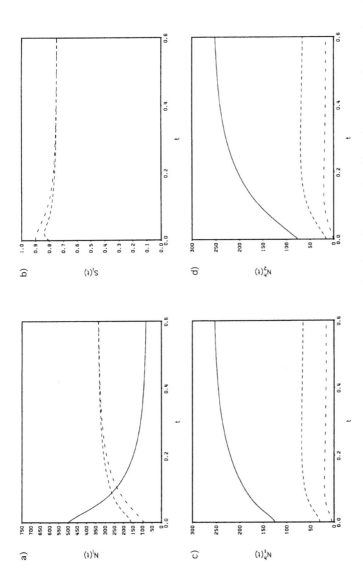

FIGURE 5.4.   Belongs to Scenario 2. Its components show (a) the stabilization of $N_1(t)$ and $N_2(t)$ at the same stationary values, (b) the stabilization of $S_1(t)$ and $S_2(t)$ at the same stationary values, (c) and (d) the evolution of the same occupation structure of status levels in groups G_1 and G_2 because the groups apply the same strategy and do not influence each other.

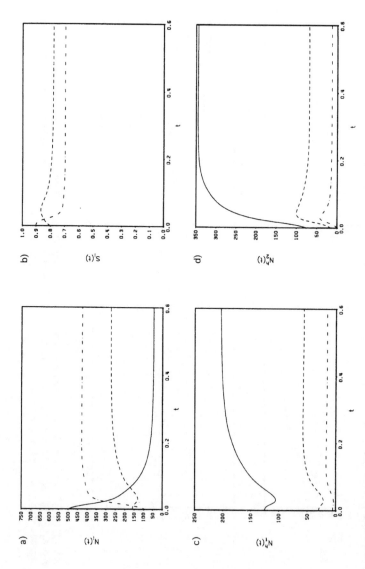

FIGURE 5.5.   Belongs to Scenario 3. Its components show (a) the stabilization of $N_1(t)$ and $N_2(t)$ at different stationary values, (b) the stabilization of $S_1(t)$ at different stationary values, (c) and (d) the evolution of different occupation numbers of status levels as a consequence of different total numbers of members in G_1 and G_2. The differences of the stationary levels are due to the canvassing activities of group G_2.

level in G_1. Now the distribution ratio between nominal members and leading members of group G_2 has changed. One observes a relative increase of the number of nominal members due to the increase of the total number of members whereas nothing has changed in this respect in group G_1.

Continuing our journey we arrive at

Scenario 4

with the following choice of the variable trend parameters:

$$g_1 = 0.004, \quad e_2 = 0.01, \quad \underline{a_2^h = 2.0}, \quad w_{12} = 0.0, \quad w_{02} = 0.0, \quad r_2 = 0.7.$$

Interpretation. Once more group G_2 is assumed to change its behavior, whereas group G_1 keeps its trend parameters constant. Group G_2 now demands admission fees from all new members. These fees are of course additional costs for the potential new members so that the relative attractiveness of group G_1 has grown. In other words: the greed of group G_2 to make profit of new members was a mistake. This can be seen in Figure 5.6. Group G_1 now keeps a permanent superiority over group G_2 in terms of the approached total number of members. However, the stationary solidarity level in G_2 is slightly higher than in G_1 because the number of members in G_2 is closer to that yielding an optimal stationary solidarity than the corresponding number in G_1 (confer also Figure 5.2). The distribution of members over the status levels in G_1 and G_2 reflects the dependence of their ratio on the respective total number of members.

Proceeding to the next station on the scenario route we arrive at

Scenario 5

with the following choice of the variable trend parameters:

$$g_1 = 0.004, \quad e_2 = 0.01, \quad a_2^h = 2.0, \quad \underline{w_{12} = -0.003}, \quad w_{02} = 0.0, \quad r_2 = 0.7.$$

Interpretation. Again group G_2 is assumed to change its behavior, while G_1 sticks to its trend parameters. Group G_2 is now trying to undermine the faith of group G_1 in its values. This is expressed by the negative faith influence coefficient w_{12}. The strategy is successful because Figure 5.7 shows that now (in spite of the admission fee) group G_2 gains an advantage over G_1 with respect to the total numbers of members. The distributions over status levels in G_1 and G_2 vary depending on the total numbers of members, and also the values of solidarity S_1, S_2 take values corresponding to N_1 and N_2.

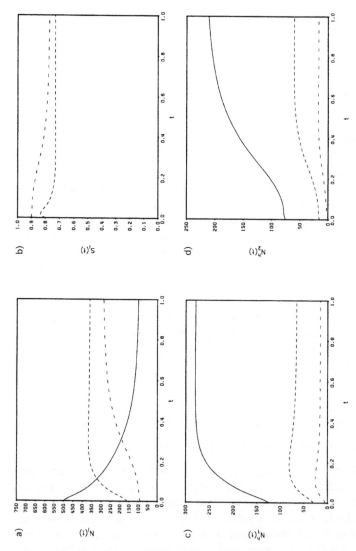

FIGURE 5.6. Belongs to Scenario 4. Its components show (a) that $N_1(t)$ stabilizes at a higher value than $N_2(t)$, (b) that $S_1(t)$ stabilizes at a lower value than $S_2(t)$, (c) and (d) that the occupation numbers in G_1 and G_2 result as a consequence of different total numbers of members in G_1 and G_2. The new stationary levels are due to admission fees demanded by group G_2.

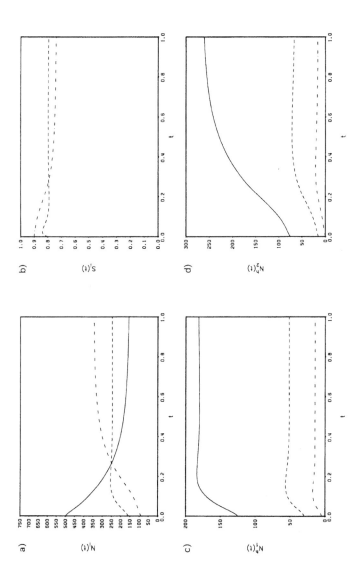

FIGURE 5.7. Belongs to Scenario 5. Its components show (a) that $N_2(t)$ gets ahead of $N_1(t)$, (b) that $S_1(t)$ stabilizes at a higher level than $S_2(t)$, (c) and (d) that the occupation numbers in G_1 and G_2 evolve accordingly. The new dynamics results from the activities of group G_2 undermining the faith in G_1.

Passing to the next station we reach

Scenario 6

with the following choice of the variable trend parameters:

$g_1 = 0.004$, $e_2 = 0.01$, $a_2^h = 2.0$, $w_{12} = -0.003$, $\underline{w_{02} = 0.003}$, $r_2 = 0.7$.

Interpretation. Group G_2 is now assumed to try out an additional trick to disturb group G_1 whereas this group G_1 sticks to its old behavior. G_2 supports and stabilizes the mood of the crowd of individuals (by the positive faith influence coefficient w_{02}) thus prohibiting transitions to G_1 in addition to weaken the faith within G_1. Both influence factors w_{12} and w_{02} have a dramatic effect on the evolution of G_1. One can see in Figure 5.8 that, in spite of an initial advantage and of initial growth of group G_1, the cunning group G_2 catches up and gets ahead of group G_1 which finally breaks down completely. The solidarity within G_1 which exceeds that of G_2 for a long time cannot prevent this breakdown. Finally only G_2 survives having a stabilized status level structure whereas G_1 has decayed completely.

Our journey on the scenario route ends at

Scenario 7

with the following choice of the variable trend parameters:

$g_1 = 0.004$, $e_2 = 0.01$. $a_2^h = 2.0$, $w_{12} = -0.003$, $w_{02} = 0.003$, $\underline{r_2 = 1.0}$.

Interpretation. Group G_2 which has defeated group G_1 under the trend parameter conditions of the previous scenario is now assumed to introduce another "innovation", namely a benefit for its leading members by increasing the reward coefficient r_2. However, this "benefit" proves to be lethal for group G_2 and advantageous for group G_1. As one can see in Figure 5.9, the ratio of the numbers of members in the leading hierarchy levels compared to the number of nominal members in G_2 increases substantially after a short time. However, this means that G_2 is quickly becoming "hydrocephalic" and that not much payoff is left for the nominal members. Thus there is no incentive to enter this group G_2 as a simple member. Therefore the fast decline of G_2 is inevitable. The disappearance of the disturbing influences of G_2 on G_1 thereupon leads to a straight evolution of G_1 to a high total number of members and a regular distribution of the members over status levels. The same holds for the solidarity in group G_1 which approaches its stationary value whereas, as expected, the solidarity of G_2 slowly decays.

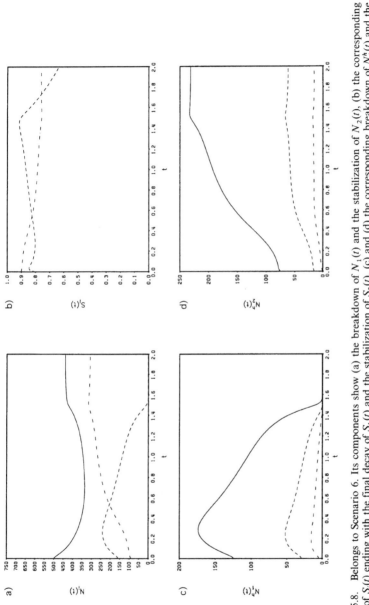

FIGURE 5.8. Belongs to Scenario 6. Its components show (a) the breakdown of $N_1(t)$ and the stabilization of $N_2(t)$, (b) the corresponding evolutions of $S_1(t)$ ending with the final decay of $S_1(t)$ and the stabilization of $S_2(t)$, (c) and (d) the corresponding breakdown of $N_1^h(t)$ and the stabilization of $N_2^h(t)$. The new dynamics results from stabilizing the crowd and from preventing transitions to G_1 by interfering activities of G_2.

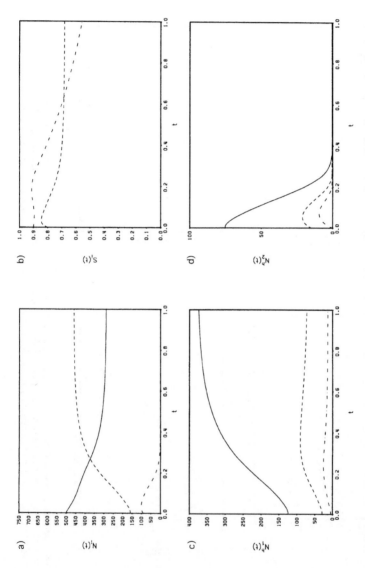

FIGURE 5.9. Belongs to Scenario 7. Its components show (a) the breakdown of $N_1(t)$ and the stabilization of $N_2(t)$ and (b) the corresponding evolutions of $S_i(t)$ ending with the final decay of $S_2(t)$ and the stabilization of $S_1(t)$, (c) and (d) the corresponding stabilization of $N_1^h(t)$ and the breakdown of $N_2^h(t)$. The new dynamics results from the introduction of exaggerated rewards for staff members of G_2.

On the way from one scenario to another, passing some possible choices of trend parameters, we have seen that rather different outcomes arise according to the "strategies" (expressed by the trend parameters) chosen by the interacting groups. Taking into account that all trend parameters could in principle also slowly vary with time one becomes aware of the immense complexity of group dynamics even if captured by such simple macroscopic models like ours.

For better understanding of Figures 5.3–5.9 we repeat our drawing conventions. Each figure consists of four illustrations representing

(a) the numbers of individuals $N_0(t)$ of the crowd (—),
   the total number $N_1(t)$ of members of G_1(- - -), and
   the total number $N_2(t)$ of members of G_2(·-·-·),
(b) the solidarity level $S_1(t)$ of G_1(- - -),
   the solidarity level $S_2(t)$ of G(·-·-·),
(c) the occupation numbers N_1^h of the status levels h in G_1: $N_1^0(t)$(—),
   $N_1^1(t)$(- - -), $N_1^2(t)$(·-·-·),
(d) the occupation numbers N_2^h of the status levels h in G_2:
   $N_2^0(t)$(—), $N_2^1(t)$(- - -), $N_2^2(t)$(·-·-·).

5. THE MODEL IN THE LIGHT OF SELECTED APPROACHES TO GROUP FORMATION IN THE LITERATURE

We will now consider a small part of the comprehensive literature about group formation under the very restrictive point of view of elucidating the accomplishments and limitations of our model. Even so we need some ordering principles serving as guidelines on our way of evaluating the literature. These guidelines will facilitate the positioning of the achievements of some authors in view of their meaning for our modelling procedure. Some of the ordering principles have already been indicated in the introduction and are repeated here.

(a) Reality is stratified in several relatively self-contained layers which are still connected by "bottom up" and "top down" relations. Social systems are also embedded in this general layer structure. Here we may at least distinguish the following three strata:

• the *personality layer* consisting of partially genetically inherited individual constitutions and predispositions which are of potential sociological relevance but exist already *before* the entrainment into social systems like groups.

- the *micro-sociological layer* which refers to the inter individual interactions and relations which provide the necessary inner lining and background of any cooperative "synergetic" effect leading to the formation of groups. Effects making individuals ready for cooperation also consist in their conditioning by internalization of ideas like traditions and ideologies. In particular network-variables belong to this layer.
- the *macro-sociological layer* consisting of the collective macro-structures and macro-dynamics of social systems. *The formation of groups is a generic example of the emergence of such macro-patterns.* Collective personal variables and transpersonal variables like solidarity belong to this layer.

Between the micro- and macro-sociological layer there exists a *cyclical relationship, i.e. a feedback loop*, because individuals generate collective structure and dynamics (bottom–up relation), and collective structures act back on individual attitudes and decision-making (top–down relation).

Since our model belongs to the macro-sociological layer, all qualitative conceptualizations and explanations of the emergence of macro-patterns are of relevance for this model and it should be possible to relate them to the dynamics of key-variables. However, also micro-sociological theories are relevant in so far as the structure of the model (e. g. the existence of status-levels), the form of trend-functions, and the values of trend-parameters must in principle be related to the micro-sociological layer.

(b) At appropriate junctions we will have to explain some of the implications of non-linear versus linear modelling of dynamic processes since earlier quantitative approaches in sociology (as well as in economics) have used *linear models*.

(c) In discussing *different* qualitative explanatory and interpretational schemes we must take into account – as already mentioned – that they may lead to *equivalent* or at least complementary results with respect to the dynamics of a restricted set of macro-sociological key-variables like those of our model. Fararo and Doreian (1995) state that "experience with formal theories teaches that apparently very different "approaches" turn out to be complementary and, in fact, possible to coordinate and subordinate within a more comprehensive framework".

(d) Furthermore, *cyclic relationships* may appear between different explanatory schemes of group formation (e.g. between the rational choice approach, the structuralistic, and the functionalistic approach). This seems also to be the case in view of our model. However, cyclic relationships simultaneously interconnect the causation principles and relativate their absoluteness. It seems that cyclic relationships exist not only in the objective world of sociological layers but also on the "metalevel" of the theoretical understanding of causation principles.

We begin our discussion of work related to group formation with a book of Burt (1982) in which he gives a survey about *network models* as a powerful framework for social differentiation in terms of relational patterns among actors in a system. He distinguishes between *relational approaches* focussing on the relationship between pairs of actors and *positional approaches* focussing on the pattern of relations which defines the position (status) of an actor in a system of actors. That means, "all statuses are network positions in the sense of being defined by patterns of relations linking status occupants with other actors in the system".

Evidently, in particular the *positional approaches* are of potential importance for our model because they yield the micro-sociological foundation for the *status level* structure of the group configuration. Furthermore they can give justifications – or, if necessary, modifications – for the form of trend functions like payoff and obligations in state (ih) appearing as mathematical terms in the conditional motivation potential which in turn determines the dynamics of the status occupants. Also the relational approaches have potential importance for our model because they provide the background for direct pair interactions like persuasion activities and faith confirmation strength.

Also the work of Cook, Emerson and Gillmore (1983) belongs to the *micro-sociological* context of *network theories*. They consider theories of centrality and power distribution for small groups and validate them by computer simulations. This could also be of relevance with respect to the number and power distribution of the status levels assumed in our group configuration.

The fact criticized by Fararo and Doreian in the introductory chapter that these authors take the structural form as *given* and derive the implied distribution of power *within* the structure *without considering the dynamics* of that structure is perhaps of minor importance here because of the following reasons: The *structure* belongs to the *slowly varying macro-variables*, whereas the *power distribution* between occupants of this structure is a *micro-variable quickly adapting* to the momentary state of the structure. Because of this difference in the time scale of changes the micro-variables can be considered in each moment "to have already gone into equilibrium" with respect to the given structure.

The next author interesting for us is Homans (1950, 1958, 1974) whose work is devoted to the analysis of small groups with preferentially direct interaction between their members. Hence, his work also belongs primarily to the category of network theories although he goes beyond that. He structures the inter-individual relations by a few main *micro-sociological* variables, namely *sentiments, activities,* and *interactions*, however, already including *emergent group customs, norms,* and *practices*. He investigates the mechanisms explaining the *maintenance* of the equilibrium structure of a group as well as the elements of dynamics which he thinks to arise from a *social behavior of exchange*.

It seems, however, that in his qualitative formulations the micro-level is not clearly separated from the macro-level (which has its own quasi-autonomous dynamics). Emerging norms, customs, the ideology of a group, solidarity, etc. are still considered as directly coupled to inter-individual interactions and not as entities of their own. Nevertheless, Homans already realizes the problems of the *emergence* and not only of the stationary structure of groups.

Some of his qualitative considerations, e.g. how customs, norms, and other "transpersonal variables" (using our terminology) emerge from inter-individual interactions, could perhaps be made fruitful by translating them into equations for the evolution of transpersonal variables on the basis of the activities of individuals.

Let us now come to the influential and important work of Coleman (1964, 1990) who is one of the pioneers of mathematical sociology. Already very early he has freely used mathematical formulations. Among the mathematical formalisms used by him are stochastic equations and integrations of social choice theory with economic concepts. Thus he has demonstrated that conceptual integration instead of building barriers between sociology and economics is reasonable.

Moreover, Coleman (1990) has for instance used economic terminology in setting up a "dynamics of the linear system of action" for social exchange processes. The mathematics of his model consists in adaptation processes, namely in an *adjustment process of values* (prices) of certain goods and an *exchange process of goods* between agents. A generalization of Coleman's approach, namely a "socially embedded exchange" has recently been thoroughly discussed by Braun (1993).

Comparing Coleman's theory with our model one can find several parallels: We also make use of utility functions comprising economical as well as immaterial terms. However, his equations are *linear exchange equations* for values and goods the solution of which approach one unique equilibrium state independently of the initial state.

Our model can also be seen as a generalized exchange model – at least with respect to the collective personal variables – but our utility functions appear in a dynamic context and lead to *non-linear migratory equations* of a rather complex character.

Admittedly also a nonlinear model like ours must start from a *pre-supposed frame* of a maximum number of potentially arising groups with a pre-assumed maximum number of internal structures (e.g. status levels).

However, the non-linear dynamics is able to describe the emergence (the coming into existence) of a group from zero membership towards a finite size and also the complete decay (the disappearance) of a group. These are events of structural change!

Furthermore, it does not only depend on the chosen calibration of trend parameters but also on the chosen initial conditions which scenario will be realized. This implies that the finally approached attractor state – which could be a stable stationary state or a limit cycle or even a so-called chaotic "strange attractor" – is path-dependent and not uniquely determined independently of initial conditions as in linear theories.

We continue our consideration of related work with the discussion of authors who have, in different ways, stressed the importance of the *concept of solidarity* in sociological theory.

Let us begin with Durkheim (1964, 1973, 1915), the early thinker about the arisal and the role of solidarity in modern society. Summarizing briefly his earlier and later work, he distinguishes several ways how solidarity comes about.

In undifferentiated societies the *similarity* and *uniformity* of its members leads to a solidarity bond of common thoughts, common behavior and common culture. In differentiated and industrialized societies the *division of labor* leads to an interdependence of all members thus creating an integrative force. And even in a modern society of individualists the looming decay of integrations is halted if individualism itself is *institutionalized* to a *"cult of the individual"* which may unify the participants around common beliefs and practices.

We see that Durkheim invokes *rational necessities* (division of labor) as well as *emotional bonds* (cults, a kind of religion) to explain the emergence of solidarity. Once more it turns out that *different* rational or emotional reasons may give rise to the *same* evolution process of solidarity.

After Durkheim, research for understanding the general role of solidarity proceeds on different lines.

Parsons (1937, 1951, 1967), generalizing the ideas of Durkheim, sees solidarity as the basis of any social system and stresses the *normative character* of the sources of solidarity. He distinguishes between the two levels of common and of differentiated normative culture, where the common level is shared by all members of the society, while the differentiated level consists of *values* and *specifying norms* belonging to *functions* and *structures* of subunits of society. According to Parsons, any social structure is defined by *roles* and *collectivities, norms* and *values*.

In view of our model one could say that roles and collectivities are captured by the collective personal variables, whereas norms and values belong to the realm of transpersonal variables.

Collins (1967, 1981, 1988), also starting from Durkheim, does not follow a structuralistic–functionalistic line but in his search for the sources of solidarity he focusses on the *emotional* and *ideological* causes, e.g. when speaking of *ritual solidarity*. The elements of his "ritual model", namely co-presence, focus of attention, common emotions, membership symbols, reactions to violations and attitudes toward non-members include also (speaking in the terminology of our model) collective personal components (co-presence, reactions, attitudes) and transpersonal components (common attentions, common emotions, and membership symbols). Even more important, his concepts do already imply the *process character* of the emergence of solidarity, e.g. when speaking about the *mutual amplification* of different elements like common focus of attention and common emotional mood. In essence these arguments already amount to explaining the emergence of solidarity as a self-organization process via a feedback loop of mutually enhancing components. It seems appropriate to distinguish in the formal description of this complicated process between the *initial stage* and the *fully developed stage* of group formation.

At the initial stage of *emerging solidarity* the group is still borne and carried by a few intensely interacting individuals who *initiate solidarity*. But this emerging solidarity is still bound more or less directly to the fluctuating individual activities and interactions. However, solidarity soars up along with the growth and development of the group and there consolidates more and more its transpersonal character as an entity of its own.

In the fully developed stage of a group we have an *established solidarity* instead of an *emerging solidarity*. In this stage solidarity has become a smoothly evolving transpersonal variable representing the "groupness of the group". The *indirect coupling effects* of established solidarity can then be clearly distinguished from the *direct interactions* between the members.

Before we finish our discussion of authors' approaches to solidarity we must make a remark about a problem which lurks behind solidarity like an ever present antagonist: the *free-rider problem*, i.e. the problem why cooperation and solidarity is not destroyed or frustrated by those who abuse it. This variant of the well-known *prisoners dilemma* has been intensely treated (see for instance Axelrod, 1984; Schuessler, 1989; 1990). An advanced and more recent formal treatment of this problem relevant for group formation is that of Glance and Huberman (1993). These authors introduce the new and plausible aspect that people who cooperate have the expectation that their decision will positively influence other agents to do the same in future. However, this effect depends on the *size of the group*; it becomes effective for smaller groups only, where "outbreaks of cooperation" can occur as detailed computer simulations show. The conclusion derivable from their article is that under appropriate conditions (not too large groups) cooperation (e.g. voluntary compliance with obligations) is maintainable against abuse even without coercion.

In a macro-sociological model like ours the free-rider effect can only be taken into account in a lump manner. It is included in the saturation term of the evolution equation for solidarity. This term depends on the size of the group and reduces the attainable level of solidarity for larger groups. Therefore all trend functions which depend on the solidarity variable depend also on the solidarity-reducing influence of free-riders.

We conclude our discussion of approaches to solidarity with considerations about the book "Principles of Group Solidarity" of Hechter (1987), which is relevant for our formal modelling approach in several respects:

Hechter's approach is primarily formulated in terms of collective behavior, i.e. in terms of macro-sociological concepts. He uses concepts of rational choice theory after a concise comparative consideration of normativistic, functionalistic, and structuralistic approaches. It is of interest whether and where these concepts of causal relations in group formation can find their place in formal approaches. In his rational choice approach the question of how compliance with obligations can be attained plays a central role. We will ask how and to which degree this behavioral question can enter the macro-dynamics. Furthermore, in Hechter's approach there reappears the question of operationality of concepts and variables and the question whether or not his approach already contains a process theory, i.e. a "true dynamics" or only concepts of "comparative statics". These questions are important for any formal description of group dynamics including our model.

Hechter is satisfied neither by normativistic and functionalistic nor by structuralistic explanations of solidarity. Therefore he prefers a *rational choice approach* to group solidarity. However, then he has to cope with the problem of how solidarity and cooperation arises in a group of egoists because "rational members will seek membership in a group only if the benefit derived from access to the joint good exceeds the costs of the obligations". This problem is even sharpened because he argues against concepts of solidarity deriving from affection, fearing the lack of operationality of such concepts.

The remaining possibility of introducing a pure rationalist's operational concept of solidarity (dropping internalization of norms, emotional satisfaction, voluntary insight in group functions) is to define solidarity as a function of the extensiveness of corporate obligations and of the probability of compliance with these obligations. Here, according to Hechter, the first factor is a function of the dependence of members on the group: "the more dependent a member, the more extensive will be its obligations", and the second factor is (because of rational egoists' temptation to become a free-rider) a function of control (i.e. monitoring and sanctioning): "the greater the control the greater the compliance to obligations".

We have already mentioned how the free-rider problem is treated in our model. However, a macro-model like ours cannot reflect all psychological details, even if they are important from a micro-sociological standpoint. For instance: If *voluntary* or *coerced* compliance with obligations should lead to the *same dynamics* of the variables considered in our model, this difference could not show up anywhere in that restricted model. However, an extended model containing also micro-variables could then reveal a different fine-structure of the groups in both cases.

Hechter stresses the operationality (possibility of direct measurement) of his definition of solidarity. However, this operationality concept neglects the not easily measurable but nevertheless important solidarity creating factors and is also at the cost of the transpersonal character of solidarity. Common internalized norms, common feelings of group identity, and beliefs in group ideology establish the transpersonal character of solidarity, whereas for instance the estimations of rational egoists, in terms of how much compliance to obligations is necessary to evade sanctions, are detrimental to the formation of solidarity. For such reasons we have in our definition of the solidarity variable not insisted on its full operationality by *direct* measurements. It seems sufficient to us that the solidarity variable plays an important role in the coupled dynamic equations and thus has an *indirect* influence on the evolution of the directly measurable variables.

On the other hand it is certainly a positive aspect of Hechter's conceptualization to give the *rational choice of individuals* a central place because the decisions and actions of individual agents are the basis of group formation even if transpersonal entities eventually emerge in this process.

However, the concept of "rationality" in the decision-making of individuals should be generalized: It seems to be a fact of social psychology that norms and ideologies of a group *are* to some extent internalized by its members. This corresponds to a change of the psychological state of the individuals which implies that the estimation of benefits and costs also takes place from a new perspective. Under this perspective the realization of group purposes can become a matter of personal satisfaction, and the corresponding satisfaction terms compete – e.g. in utility functions – with terms describing personal obligations, costs, and sacrifices. *Generalized rational choice* then means that the material and immaterial benefit and cost terms of the utility of the individual member of a group depend not only on the satisfaction of immediate egoistic interests but also on the welfare of the group which is also perceived as a factor of personal satisfaction.

In our formalization of group dynamics via introduction of a conditional motivation potential we have implicitly used such a *generalized concept of rational choice*. The formal expression for this is the dependence of the motivation potential on the key-variables of the groups. That means the personal motivations depend not only on individual gains and losses in a narrow sense but on personal satisfactions or frustrations depending on the global state of the groups including their solidarity.

Finally we come back to the fundamental question which causation schemes are relevant in the formation process of groups. Our view differs from that of Hechter in so far as we do not see the decision-making individuals as the only centres of causation. Instead, we see a *cyclical relationship* between different causative factors which comprise the elements of (generalized) rational choice, structure, functions, and norms. All elements are embedded into a feedback loop which makes it impossible to isolate one element and to construct a "linear" causal nexus.

Being aware of the high complexity of cyclic causality we can only suggest a stylized cyclic causation scheme which is probably not complete:

1. Individuals coalesce in nascent groups by virtue of sharing common (material or immaterial) interests.
2. Simple collective structures are built up under individual rational aspects of construction.
3. The simple group structures bring along and carry simple functions facilitating the pursuit of the common interests.
4. Compliance with obligations is still fully voluntary and needs no norms because of the close direct interaction between the few members of the small group.
5. It is observed by the members of the growing group that the stabilizing structure can carry extended functions leading to power and influence of the group as a whole and of the individual members, but also to obligations going beyond and transforming the original interests.
6. Feelings of group identity and manifest formulations of group objectives begin to develop and rules consolidating to norms begin to be practised and entrained.
7. A transition takes place from inter-individual cooperation and rationality to transpersonal solidarity and formulations of group ideology. This facilitates further growth and efficiency of the group because direct interactions are no longer indispensable but partially substitutable by the indirect bond of group-solidarity and -ideology.
8. The loss of direct inter-individuality also favors free-riders but simultaneously stabilizes norms which, if necessary, can justify sanctions and enforce the compliance with obligations.
9. The now fully stabilizing structures, including hierarchical levels, lead to an efficient performance of functions secured by fully consolidated norms.
10. The stabilized structural, functional, and normative system of the group acts back on the members of the group by psychological

internalization processes. The identification with the transpersonal superego of the group leads to a transformation of the perspectives of estimation of benefits and costs, of satisfaction and frustration in the sense that group ideals are now partially taken over as personal desires.

11. Equipped with this transformed mentality the "modified rationalists" begin a new round of organizing a new level of structure in the now fully developed group.

12. The modified mentality of the members and the reformed structures lead to the emergence of new functions and new influences of the group, etc. In total, the cyclic coupling of the causation elements of the group which simultaneously involves a "bottom up" and "top down" interaction between the micro-sociological and macro-sociological layer leads also to a slow transformation of the shape and the objective of the group.

ACKNOWLEDGEMENTS

The authors want to thank Dipl.-Phys. Richard Čalek for thoroughly revising the English text and Mrs Anja Steinhauser for her tireless care in typing the different versions of the manuscript.

REFERENCES

Axelrod, R., 1984. *The Evolution of Cooperation*. Basic Books, New York.

Braun, N., 1993. *Socially Embedded Exchange*. Verlag Peter Lang, Frankfurt.

Burt, R.S., 1982. *Toward a Structural Theory of Action*. Academic Press, New York, London.

Coleman, J.S., 1984. *Introduction to Mathematical Sociology*. MacMillan, The Free Press, New York.

Coleman, J.S., 1990. *Foundations of Social Theory*. The Belknap Press of Harvard University Press, Cambridge, MA.

Collins, R., 1981. On the micro-foundations of macrosociology. *American Journal of Sociology*, **86**, 984–1014.

Collins, R., 1985. *Three Sociological Traditions*. Oxford University Press, New York.

Collins, R., 1988. *Theoretical Sociology*. Harcourt Brace Jovanovich, San Diego.

Durkheim, E., 1915. *The Elementary Forms of Religious Life*. Free Press, New York.

Durkheim, E., 1964. *The Division of Labor in Society*. MacMillan, New York.

Durkheim, E., 1973. Individualism and the intellectuals. In R.N. Bellatz, Ed., *Emile Durkheim on Morality and Society*. University of Chicago Press, Chicago.

Emerson, R.M., K.S. Cook and M.R. Gillmore. 1983. The distribution of power in exchange networks: Theory and experimental results. *American Journal of Sociology*, **89**, 275–305.

Fararo, T.J. and P. Doreian, 1995. The theory of solidarity: an agenda of problems for mathematical sociology.

Glance, N.S. and B.A. Huberman, 1993. The outbreak of cooperation. *Journal of Mathematical Sociology*, **17**, 281–302.

Haken, H., 1977. *Synergetics – An Introduction*. Springer, Berlin, Heidelberg, New York.

Hechter, M., 1987. *Principles of Group Solidarity*. University of California Press, Berkeley.

Helbing, D., 1995. *Quantitative Sociodynamics. Stochastic Methods and Models of Social Interaction Processes*. Kluwer Academic Publishers, Dordrecht.

Homans, G.C., 1950. *The Human Group*. Harcourt Brace, New York.

Homans, G.C., 1958. Social behavior as exchange. *American Journal of Sociology*, **65**, 597–606.

Homans, G.C., 1974. *Social Behavior: Its Elementary Forms*. Harcourt Brace Jovanovich, New York.

Emerson, R.M., K.S. Cook and M.R. Gillmore. 1983. The distribution of power in exchange networks: Theory and experimental results. *American Journal of Sociology*, **89**, 275–305.

Parsons, T., 1937. *The Structure of Social Action*. Free Press, New York.

Parsons, T., 1951. *The Social System*. Free Press, New York.

Parsons, T., 1967. *Sociological Theory and Modern Society*. Free Press, New York.

Pearl, R., 1924. *Studies in Human Biology*. Williams and Wilkins, Baltimore.

Schuessler, R., 1989. Exit threats and cooperation under anonymity. *Journal of Conflict Resolution*, **33**, 728–749.

Schuessler, R., 1990. Threshold effects and the decline of cooperation. *Journal of Conflict Resolution*, **34**, 476–494.

Verhulst, P.-F., 1845. Recherches mathématiques sur la loi d'accroissement de la population. *Nouveaux Mémoires de l'Académie Royale des Sciences et Belles-Lettres de Bruxelles*, **18**, 1–41.

Weidlich, W., 1991. Physics and social science – the approach of synergetics. *Physics Reports*, **204**, 1–163.

Weidlich, W., 1994. Synergetic modelling concepts for sociodynamics with application to collective political opinion formation. *Journal of Mathematical Sociology*, **18**(4), 267–291.

Weidlich, W. and G. Haag (eds.). 1988. *Interregional Migration – Dynamic Theory and Comparative Analysis*. Springer, Berlin, Heidelberg, New York.

Weidlich, W. and G. Haag. 1983. *Concepts and Models of a Quantitative Sociology*. Springer, Berlin, Heidelberg, New York.

Part III

Affect and Solidarity

6 CONDITIONS FOR EMPATHIC SOLIDARITY[1]

DAVID R. HEISE

Indiana University

Fararo and Doreian's essay (Chapter 1) presents solidarity as a construct that relates a number of different social phenomena, including empathic alignment of individuals, emergence of shared identity, and containment of members by a group that serves their needs. This note focusing just on the first of these phenomena extends some of their ideas in the context of the sociology of emotions. I will attempt to specify how specific events induce emergence of what I call "empathic solidarity." This term is intended to combine the meaning of *empathy* – "Identification with and understanding of another's situation, feelings, and motives; the attribution of one's own feelings to an object" – and *solidarity* – "A union of interests, purposes, or sympathies among members of a group; fellowship of responsibilities and interests" (definitions from the *American Heritage Dictionary*).

Fararo and Doreian (Chapter 1) proposed that solidarity among individuals is engendered by the individuals' common relation to a central figure. This seems a useful insight, but the Fararo–Doreian proposal that individuals infer their relation with each other from the common relation to the central figure seems oriented around "cold cognition," and a model of empathic solidarity needs to bring back some of their expressed concern with affect (as in their discussion of Collins' model, their critique of Hechter for eliminating sentiments, and their attention to sentiment in discussing Homans). I will sketch a provisional description of the key features of empathic solidarity wherein emotional and motivational phenomena are central. My speculative formulation might be wrong, but it at least can suggest empirical studies to start assembling useful data on empathic solidarity.

To begin I first reproduce the Fararo–Doreian formulation of a solidarity relation, with adjustments to facilitate my own discussion. The focus is on individuals a and b. According to Fararo and Doreian (Chapter 1), solidarity can arise when a and b each has a relation S with a central figure outside the a–b dyad. I will refer to the central figure as a pivot, symbolized by p. Then if aSp and bSp, a may infer solidarity with b by virtue of their mutual allegiance to p. The inferred relation, SS^{-1}, is the solidarity relation.

Fararo and Doreian characterize the pivotal figure, p, through the example of a and b being subjects of a king. However, p need not be an individual and in fact p could be different individuals who are "regularly equivalent".[2] For example, husbands can feel solidary by virtue of discussing some common aspect in their relations to their respective wives. In this case, the pivot, p, is the spousal identity to which both a and b relate. Moreover, it seems that a solidarity pivot can exist in any emotionally laden symbol or stimulus that becomes an object of mutual relation. For example, on July 4 disparate Americans gain solidarity from their allegiance to a flag passing in an Independence Day parade.

REFORMULATION

In the Fararo–Doreian formulation, solidarity arises as an inference about the SS^{-1} relation, and as such it is a cognitive product of reasoning. However, it is arguable whether such a cognition is sufficient for empathic solidarity, even when it emerges. For example, diners a and b have the same relation to their waiter and they may become aware of that when competing for his attention, but diners rarely develop empathic solidarity unless the scene becomes emotional somehow.

Restricting S to a relation of allegiance makes it easier to imagine empathic solidarity arising from SS^{-1} inferences. Yet under some conditions the inference still seems insufficient for the development of empathic solidarity. For example, a newcomer to a group of devotees may report her own record of allegiance to the pivot, yet she does not gain solidarity ties immediately. Intellectually everyone understands the mutual allegiance, but the sense of empathic solidarity awaits joint experiences with others in the group. Moreover, empathic solidarity can arise from a relation other than allegiance. Indeed, Marx supposed that solidarity of the Working Class would arise from the antagonistic relations of workers with capitalists. Though that has yet to happen on a wide scale, there are numerous instances of solidarity arising from a shared antagonism. For example, newsletters of an Indiana environmental group, *Protect Our Woods*, describe the group's emergence as "a landowner uprising" against National Forest administrators.

I propose the following. An empathic bond arises when *a* observes his own emotional response to *p* mirrored in the emotional response of *b* to *p*. Seeing one's own emotions resonating in another person creates a unification in which self and other seem to be experiencing events with the same consciousness. Moreover, when *a* and *b* experience resonating emotions in response to *p*, they may experience consonant impulses to action with regard to *p*. Then *a* may act toward *p* in a way that fulfills *b*'s motives, paralleling *b*'s own actions toward *p* with either identical or equivalent behaviors. Collateral action by *a* offers observable evidence to *b* that *a* and *b* are allies.

Empathic solidarity is established for *a* when *a* unifies consciousness with *b* through emotional resonance, and *a* also infers from *b*'s collateral actions that the two of them are allied. In general, this happens when both *a* and *b* have the same relationship with the pivot, and they are experiencing the same emotional event involving the pivot. Then *a* and *b* merely have to observe each other for emotional resonance, and their personally motivated acts toward the pivot are collateral, each thereby providing evidence to the other of alliance. The solidarity bond is established for both. Non-emotional events with a pivotal figure would not induce solidarity, according to this formulation.

This formulation depends on the existence of two interpersonal phenomena – empathic consciousness from emotional resonance with another, and induction of alliance from observing collateral action. I will offer some justification for believing that such phenomena are plausible and then examine some aspects of this formulation of empathic solidarity in more detail.

The work of Paul Ekman and his associates (Ekman, 1972; Ekman and Friesen, 1975) lends credibility to the notion of emotional resonance as a basis for empathy. Their research program demonstrated that the human face is a refined emotion display system, and different emotions are reflected in specific facial expressions that have cross-cultural currency in terms of recognizability. Everyone is empathic about others' emotions in the sense of being able to "infer the specific content of another interactant's ... feelings" (Ickes et al., 1990, p. 731), as long as the other is not masking her or his emotions, and in general an observer can determine when another shares the same emotions as the observer is feeling. The emergence of a unified consciousness as a result of emotional resonance corresponds to the dictionary meaning of empathy as "identification with and understanding of another's situation, feelings, and motives."

Another program of research by Tajfel (1981) and others (see Brown, 1986, Chapter 15) offers some credibility for the notion that alliance can emerge from collateral action. They found that any basis of collective segmentation, even a form so trivial as random assignment to different aggregates by coin toss, produces group identification to the extent that members give each other preferential treatment. Parallel action is a powerful stimulus for aligning characters into differentiated sets (Heider, 1967). Thus it is possible and indeed likely that a person will partition out those who are acting collaterally with the self and consider them allies.

ELABORATION

This formulation of empathic solidarity between a and b requires that they share a relationship with a pivotal figure whereby they experience parallel emotions and motives with regard to p, that they are situated so that they can observe each others' emotions and actions, and that their experiences with p are synchronized so that they can resonate emotionally and ally through observation of collateral action. Thus empathic solidarity has relational aspects, location aspects, and temporal aspects.

Relational Aspects

Computer analyses based on affect control theory (Heise, 1979; Smith-Lovin and Heise, 1988; MacKinnon, 1994) suggest that emotional asymmetry is common in social interactions; for example, a judge sentencing a thief might feel relieved while the thief feels apprehensive. Specifically, it seems that dyads where participants differ in power will not resonate emotionally but rather will have distinct emotions from their joint interaction. Since people's emotions so often are different in ordinary dyadic encounters, the interactants do not get the chance to resonate emotionally, and dyadic encounters typically do not generate empathic solidarity. That is why solidarity generally involves two people relating to a pivotal external figure. In that particular interactional structure the two people can be emoting similarly to each other even though they are emoting differently than the pivot.

Affect control theory posits that emotion is a function of a person's interactional identity and of the event involving that person at the moment (Smith-Lovin, 1990). The identity carries a fundamental sentiment that defines how good, potent, and lively the person should be. The event creates a transient impression of how good, potent, and lively the person actually is in the circumstances. The person's emotion is an internal and interpersonal signal that registers the transient impression and how it compares to the identity sentiment. Consequently, if two people feel the same emotion with regard to a pivotal figure, then most likely the two people have the same identity with respect to the pivot and they are experiencing the same event with the pivot. In fact, parallel emotions are so unlikely under any other conditions, that sharing relational identities and events with respect to the pivot are virtual prerequisites for empathic solidarity. Thus, the Fararo–Doreian formulation of solidarity in terms of an unspecified relation, S, can be interpreted more specifically in terms of identities. Persons a and b both have an identity I that is foregrounded in an event with the pivot, and experiencing the same event with the pivot from the viewpoint of that common identity provides the empathy and alliance that lead to empathic solidarity.

People might experience the same event with a pivotal figure either as objects or actors. A pivotal character sometimes acts on a set of people collectively and thereby creates a solidarity opportunity for the joint objects of action – for example, a judge could collectively sentence political mavericks, a president could collectively honor a unit of warriors, or "regularly equivalent" police officers could attack the members of a crowd. People also can orchestrate their behavior so all are equivalent actors engaging in equivalent actions toward a pivot. That is the essence of ritual (e.g., a congregation worshipping God), and ritual is an especially effective opportunity for empathic solidarity because orchestrated action demonstrates collaterality of purpose at the same time as it generates emotional resonance.

Although emotional responses in dyadic interaction ordinarily are asymmetric so that an external pivot figure is needed to achieve empathic solidarity, analyses with affect control theory indicate that relationships do exist in which emotional resonance can arise as participants enact their roles with one another. For example, two people enacting the role of sweetheart might laugh with, caress, and make love to each other, and as these acts happen both might feel affectionate and appreciative. If additionally the other's behaviors are understood as fulfilling one's own motives, then the two parties are engaging in collateral action, and they fulfill the conditions for empathic solidarity with each other. In essence, two people in a passionate relationship serve as regularly equivalent pivots for each other, allowing them to develop emotional resonance and alliance without a third party.

The relational identity, I, that people share with respect to the pivot is a cognitive self classification that remains in the background of the self even when the participants are not involved in an event with p, and I could be foregrounded apart from an engagement with a pivot. Humphreys and Berger (1981) suggested that people encountering each other for the first time (e.g., people conversing on a plane) search for related identities that offer a basis of discrimination between them. Doing so provides distinctive roles for each during the encounter. However, because we organize identities in abstraction hierarchies, finding a basis of discrimination also offers an awareness of some similarity. For example, one person on a plane may be a tourist on vacation and the other a businesswoman flying between offices, but both of these are kinds of travelers. "Having found their difference, people also have their basis of identification with each other – the next higher category of identity where they are the same" (Heise, 1987, p. 4). That raises the question of whether identification in terms of a shared identity induces a sense of empathic solidarity.

When people discover a shared identity, they might imagine a solidarity-generating scene and then presume they are solidary on the basis of this imaginative production until evidence indicates otherwise. To illustrate, suppose that the vacationing traveler and the business traveler are talking and one of them gets a flash of herself and the other coping together at the baggage claim, with the two of them sharing the same emotions and helping one another. Thereby she gets a provisional sense of empathic solidarity. This provisional solidarity is fragile in the sense that there is no real event with remembered emotions and collateral activity to recall if a chasm begins opening between the two, so the grounds for solidarity are easily undermined by future events indicating disparity. Nevertheless, the provisional solidarity could be a basis for preferential treatment of the other in the manner described by Tajfel (1981).

Another way that assignment of a single identity to self and other could lead to empathic solidarity is through an interaction in which each helps the other within the role defined by their mutual identity. The travelers, for example, might help each other as travelers by exchanging information about ground transportation and hotels. If this collateral action led to shared emotions, the two would experience empathic solidarity in the same way that two sweethearts do. The crucial elements in this case are that they act collaterally to evidence alliance and that their interaction generates emotions that are the same for both parties in order to support the sense of merged consciousness.

The range of identities for which both of these conditions are liable to be fulfilled in $I-I$ interactions could be examined mathematically through analyses of affect control theory's mathematical model (Heise, 1987; 1992). Studies with a computer simulation program that implements the model suggest, for example, that if both parties have the same good, potent, lively identity (like sweetheart) then they will engage in collateral activity and experience intense similar emotions. If both parties have a good, impotent, and passive identity (perhaps like traveler) then they will engage in collateral activity but may not experience enough emotion to induce a sense of merged consciousness. If both parties have a bad, potent, lively identity (like gangster) then their interaction together yields similar intense emotions but no collateral activity. Thus the fundamental sentiment attached to an identity acts as a parameter setting the likelihood that empathic solidarity will emerge from interactions of people enacting that identity with each other.

The simulations suggest that solidarity achieved through mutual identification apart from engagement with a pivot occurs only with identities that are attached to certain kinds of sentiments. Maintaining such solidarity requires maintaining the sentiments. That would be accomplished in rituals, which not only produce solidarity directly through shared experience with a pivot, but also produce immediate situational feelings that conform to the ideal identity sentiment, thereby strengthening the sentiment and counteracting any decay in the sentiment. Thereby ritualists maintain a sentiment resource that can be used to produce solidarity with each other through identification later on.

Location Aspects

Empathic solidarity emerges as people observe others' emotions and behavior, so it quintessentially is a small group phenomenon. Accordingly solidary groups mainly should be localized and scattered, spotting a population rather than stratifying it. However, there are several factors that can increase the expansiveness of solidarity bonding.

Rituals not only are an effective means for producing empathic solidarity, they also can increase the size of the bonded group by arraying individuals so that each person observes the emotions and actions of many more people than ordinarily is possible. For example, rituals sometimes organize people in a circle where each person can see everyone else, and rituals also may march and mill people around in a way that increases the number of observed others. Rituals held in coliseum-like structures with raised, circular tiers of seats can increase the number of people who are experiencing solidarity conditions. Choreic vocalizations and choreographed activities can create legions of participatory clones, and an individual might emotionally resonate and ally with all in the uniform multitude, even though observing only a fraction of the total participants. Leni Riefenstahl's 1934 propaganda film, *Triumph of the Will*, documents how such factors were used to achieve vast solidarity rituals in Nazi Germany.

An examination of the social psychology of staged dramas refines our understanding of solidarity. Dramas frequently are effective at establishing the viewer in a relationship with a pivotal figure which parallels the relationship of a character in the drama; pivotal characters in dramas typically epitomize some communal virtue or repugnance. Then the viewer experiences emotional resonance as that dramatic character encounters the pivotal figure – for example, members of the audience sob and cheer as they watch the misfortunes and triumphs of the hero. A sense of alliance or identification arises as the dramatic character's actions fulfill the observer's motives. Yet a drama does not produce empathic solidarity between the audience and a stage hero. Most likely this is because the audience understands that stage actors are unauthentic in their emotions and uncommitted to their actions, so the actors are neither empathic nor allied with the audience. This suggests an additional condition for empathic solidarity beyond those defined above: a achieving empathic solidarity with b requires that a finds emotional resonance and alliance in the $a–b$ relationship, and additionally a believes that b also finds emotional resonance and alliance in the $b–a$ relationship.

Even though members of an audience do not achieve solidarity with the actors, it seems like their sustained emotional resonance while watching a drama could create an opportunity for empathic solidarity with each other. Interestingly, audiences usually are kept in the dark (literally) concerning each other's emotional responses, as if to discourage emotional resonance. Moreover, each member of the audience has to suppress whatever motivations that arise toward the pivotal figure on stage in order to sustain the observer role, and the collective passivity keeps members of audiences from acting collaterality with each other. Thus the physical environment of theaters and the nature of the observer role prevent dramas from becoming solidarity rituals.

Electronic media mainly vary some of the elements that are involved in classical staged dramas with audiences. However, electronic media can allow people to have audio-visual experiences with others at a distance, and in principle the expansiveness of solidarity rites could be magnified through multimedia displays of collective behavior at multiple sites. For example, New York protestors could emotionally resonate with Los Angeles protestors whom they see imaged on a wall and hear through loudspeakers, and they might gain a sense of alliance by interpreting the pivotal authorities in Los Angeles as regularly equivalent to authorities in New York. Such situations would overcome the usual distance constraints on empathic solidarity.

Temporal Aspects

People must assemble at the same time in order to emotionally resonate and display collateral purpose with each other, and societal schedules can preclude or foster the required synchronicity. The business day, for example, effectively keeps workers from assembling at sites where they could relate jointly to legislating politicians as pivotal figures, thereby preempting one potential basis for worker solidarity. Meanwhile, the work day forces workers to congregate in small groups where either they achieve solidarity through their mutual relation to objects of production or else they have their individuality emphasized in divided labor without a shared pivotal figure. The disjunctive scheduling in Western societies of students, members of the work force, and retirees suggests that solidarity groups mostly will not intermingle the three age grades of youths, adults, and the elderly, except in family, leisure, and religious groups that are constituted on evenings and weekends.

Empathic solidarity diminishes with time. For example, soldiers who have achieved solidarity in a combat zone lose it after the war is ended; and a community's solidarity in the wake of a natural disaster dissipates within weeks. Also, the periodic scheduling of church services, athletic contests, conventions, etc. suggests that the effects of solidarity rituals decay and require regular renewal. Dissipation of empathic solidarity must be rooted in the loss of emotional resonance or in the breakdown of alliance, according to the formulation presented here.

At first thought, the emotional basis of solidarity seems to be the most likely locus of solidarity dissipation since emotions are such transitory phenomena. However, emotions redintegrate in conversations and daydreams, and emotional resonance can be reproduced over and over through such imagery. For example, redintegration of emotion seems to be what is involved when grief over loss of a loved one continues for a year or two. Thus, inability to reconstitute emotional resonance through reminiscences might only set an outer time limit on the order of months or years for maintenance of solidarity.

The other basis of solidarity – the inference of alliance from perceiving collateral action – seems more vulnerable to rapid disruption. Once the joint relationship with a pivot is gone, members of a solidarity group must return to other relationships, and those relationships can give evidence of competition and conflict that undermines a sense of alliance. Indeed, the frequency of solidarity rituals may be an indicator of how often members of a solidarity group interact with each other in competitive or conflictual ways.

RECAPITULATION

I have proposed that a solidarity bond is established for a when a unifies consciousness with b through emotional resonance, and a also infers from b's collateral actions that the two of them are allied. To explain why solidarity does not arise between dramatic actors and an audience, I further proposed that a additionally has to believe that b finds emotional resonance and alliance in the b–a relationship. The latter proposition requires some elaboration.

Let us assume that emotional resonance is an automatic process, so that observing another person emoting the same as oneself invariably produces a sense of unified consciousness with the other. It follows that if a is emotionally resonating with b, then a can infer that b also is emotionally resonating with a, providing that a knows that b is perceiving a's emotions. If a sees b looking at a's face, that would be reason enough for a to believe b is emotionally resonating with a. Clear transmission of a's emotions through other senses also would work; e.g., a could believe that b is experiencing reciprocal emotional resonance if b is in earshot of a's cheers or sobs or angry growls. Moreover, a can force reciprocal emotional resonance by projecting expressions of emotion into b's perceptual field – say, by facing b, or by vocalizing so b hears.

The sense of alliance arises from collateral action in which a observes b acting toward the pivotal figure in a way that fulfills a's goals. Again, assume that the process is automatic, at least when a has a sense of unified consciousness with b. (Emotional resonance may be a prerequisite of automatic allying, in which case empathic solidarity is attained through a "value added" collective process, as described by Smelser, 1963, p. 14). In other words, when a sees b acting toward the pivot in a way that fulfills a's desires, then a invariably feels allied with b. Accordingly, a will know that b also feels a sense of alliance if a sees that b has observed a acting in accord with the motives of their unified consciousness. Checking to assure that b has seen or heard a's action toward the pivot provides a with all the evidence required to believe that b feels allied with a. Moreover, a can jockey so as to make sure that b perceives a acting toward the pivot.

Overall, then, a typical emergence of empathic solidarity occurs as follows:

- a and b invest identities that put them in the same relationship with a pivotal figure, p;
- a and b experience the same event with p, resulting in the same emotions and the same impulses to action with regard to p;
- a and b observe each other's emotions, whereby each obtains a sense of unified consciousness with the other, and they observe each other's behavioral reactions to p, whereby each obtains a sense of alliance with the other;
- a and b each assures that the other perceives the self's emotions and actions, whereby each believes the other is reciprocating a sense of unified consciousness and a sense of alliance.

An interesting aspect of this formulation is that it helps in understanding some kinds of social interaction that do not produce solidarity.

Panics ordinarily do not induce solidarity but rather are a condition "arising out of and expressing collective demoralization" (Lang and Lang, 1961, p. 97). Open flight from a pivotal figure produces emotional resonance and perhaps even a sense of collateral purpose, as long as the escapees can see and hear each other. However, the centrifugal movements of fleeing individuals may cause successful escapees to move beyond each other's perceptual fields, whereupon they no longer can observe each other's emotional displays or actions, and they lose the bases for experiencing either a unified consciousness or a sense of alliance. Additionally, flight through passages with limited capacity leads to clear indications of competition instead of alliance. Thus panics initially fulfill the conditions for empathic solidarity, but then they interfere with mutual observation, and may induce competition, so solidarity fails to emerge. On the other hand, groups of intimates typically flee together from a threatening situation (Feinberg and Johnson, 1995), staying within each other's perceptual fields and providing continuing evidence of collateral action. Thus we can expect panicked flight to increase the solidarity of pre-existing primary groups within a collectivity even though solidarity fails to emerge in the collectivity as a whole.

The formulation also helps to account for non-occurrence of solidarity in romantic triangles. In a romantic triangle, two admirers each give allegiance to the same pivotal third party, and the outcome generally is antagonism between the two admirers. This is problematic for the Fararo and Doreian proposal that solidarity corresponds to the relation, SS^{-1}, since that proposal leads to the conclusion that the two admirers would be in a state of solidarity rather than antagonism. (Antagonism in a romantic triangle also is problematic for balance theory in social psychology, which Fararo and Doreian review.) The formulation presented here includes a non-intuitive hypothesis – that the two admirers would emotionally resonate and attain a unified consciousness, if their feelings of affection for the pivotal third party are synchronized and mutually observable. However, the formulation additionally proposes that solidarity arises only when a sense of alliance is achieved as well as unified consciousness. Alliance will not arise from the admirers seeing each other's actions toward the third party. The situation is zero-sum in the sense that romantic actions by one admirer pre-empt fulfillment of the other's motives, and therefore the actions of the two admirer's are not collateral. The two admirers are in a state of conflict rather than solidarity. (Perhaps the conflict is especially profound when the admirers have attained unified consciousness with one another.)

CONCLUSION

The idea of merged consciousness in collective behavior was presumed by Le Bon (1893), and by McDougall (1920) in his book *The Group Mind*. Later, though, Floyd Allport (1924) critiqued the notion of group mind, and recently McPhail (1991) argued from empirical evidence that most crowds lack behavioral alignment, let alone mental alignment. Despite the later work, I suggest that Le Bon and McDougall discerned something useful. However, the unified consciousness that I introduce above is not group mind. It is a mental state close to what Lang and Lang (1961, p. 221) call *rapport*: "a focusing and narrowing of attention, a mutual sensitivity to feelings and behavior of others, and the exclusion of other stimuli that interfere." The causal sequence that I propose also is different from early formulations, which proposed that mere massing caused a unified consciousness and that emotionality spread by contagion. The formulation presented here proposes that the (sometimes fortuitous) occurrence of resonating emotions is the source of unified consciousness.

Influenced by McPhail's empirical work (reviewed in his 1991 book), I have tried to offer a formulation of empathic solidarity in which the lack of polarization of most crowds is beside the point. Unified consciousness and collateral action are presumed to occur only in the relatively few collectivities that achieve solidarity. In fact, the formulation presented here leads us away from crowds and towards rituals as the hotbed of solidarity and other collective phenomena. Many rituals are meant to produce resonating emotions, unified consciousness, collateral action, and alliance – they are intended to be regenerators of empathic solidarity. Thus ritualistic scenes are where we are most likely to find these processes, either the grand rituals of major social institutions or the petite rituals of everyday interaction to which Collins (1981) drew attention.

The affect control theory perspective on solidarity leads to the view that emotional resonance arises out of culturally given forms of relationship implemented in definitions of situations. This means that people must define their situation with the pivot in the same way if they are to achieve emotional resonance. Moreover, the same meanings must be attributed by all to the pivot, to the self identity in relation to the pivot, and to the actions involving the pivot, or else emotional convergence will not occur. The overall implication is that people must share culture in order to achieve emotional resonance, and the eddies of empathic solidarity in a society are culturally grounded, arising as a product of various kinds of culturally given relationships. Whenever emotional resonance and solidarity occurs across cultures, it must be because some meanings are cross-culturally invariant. (Fararo and Doreian propose that solidarity can be a basis for new group identifications that expand culture; I suspect that this occurs only rarely, and when it does occur, it involves event-driven identifications like victim, victors, or vanquished being transmuted to labels that reference an ethnicity or other shared feature of the collectivity that attained solidarity.)

The formulation of empathic solidarity that is presented here could be examined in laboratory studies that team subjects in an encounter with an outside pivotal figure – e.g., another team. The amount of collateral activity that arises within a team is manipulatable through explicit instructions or through reward structures that make it more, or less, sensible to favor one's partners in exchanges. The intensity and kind of shared emotion that is experienced within a team can be influenced by controlling the character and results of interaction with the pivot. For example, inter-team relations could be defined as cooperative or competitive and the researcher could provide success or failure outcomes. The observability of emotions and actions can be varied by controlling what passes over real-time multimedia linkages between group members. The general hypothesis to be tested is that teammates who observe more collateral action and more shared emotion end up with more empathic solidarity.

Empirical studies will require a measure of empathic solidarity. Such a measure would assess the sense of unified consciousness (e.g., "How well do you know what your partner's thinking?"), alliance (e.g., readiness to distribute resources preferentially to the partner), and faith in the other's commitment to common interests and purposes (e.g., conviction that the other is a useful, meaningful person). These three aspects of empathic solidarity do not fit a latent trait model with the components being intercorrelated. Rather, the three aspects together are an induced variable in which the combination of unified consciousness, alliance, and faith in other constitutes the essence of empathic solidarity.

NOTES

1. Ron Wright was a sounding board for many of the ideas in this paper and the originator of some. I deeply appreciate the suggestions and helpful criticism that he offered while he was a post-doctoral fellow in Indiana University's Department of Sociology. I also am indebted to Tom Fararo and Patrick Doreian for providing me with a pre-publication rejoinder to this paper, which allowed me to correct some of the shortcomings they found in my presentation.
2. Quoting from Fararo and Doreian in Chapter 1: "actors are regularly equivalent if they are equivalently connected to equivalent others. (Two jurors on the same jury are structurally equivalent; two jurors on different juries are regularly equivalent.)"

REFERENCES

Allport, F.W. (1924). *Social Psychology*. Boston: Houghton Mifflin.
Brown, R. (1986). *Social Psychology: The Second Edition*. New York: Free Press.
Collins, R. (1981). On the microfoundations of macrosociology. *American Journal of Sociology*, **86**: 984–1014.
Ekman, Paul. (1972). Universal and cultural differences in facial expressions of emotions. In J.K. Cole (ed.), *Nebraska Symposium on Motivation, 1971*. Lincon: University of Nebraska Press, pp. 207–283.
Ekman, Paul and Friesen, W.V. (1975). *Unmasking the Face: A Guide to Recognizing Emotions from Facial Clues*. Englewood Cliffs, NJ: Prentice-Hall.
Fararo, Thomas and Doreian, Patrick (1996). The theory of solidarity: An agenda of problems for mathematical sociology. *Journal of Mathematical Sociology* _____.
Feinberg, William E. and Johnson, Norris R. (1995). FIRESCAP: A computer simulation model of reaction to a fire alarm. *Journal of Mathematical Sociology*, **20**: 247–269.

Heider, F. (1967). On social cognition. *American Psychologist*, **22**: 25–31.

Heise, D.R. (1979). *Understanding Events: Affect and the Construction of Social Action.* New York: Cambridge University Press.

Heise, D.R. (1987). Affect control theory: Concepts and model. *Journal of Mathematical Sociology*, **13**: 1–33.

Heise, D.R. (1992). Affect control theory's mathematical model, with a list of testable hypotheses: A working paper for ACT researchers. Bloomington: Department of Sociology, Indiana University.

Humphreys, Paul and Berger, Joseph (1981). Theoretical consequences of the status characteristics formulation. *American Journal of Sociology*, **86**: 953–983.

Ickes, W., Stinson, L., Bissonnette, V. and Garcia, S. (1990). Naturalistic social cognition: Empathic accuracy in mixed-sex dyads. *Journal of Personality and Social Psychology*, **59**: 730–742.

Lang, K. and Lang, G.E. (1961). *Collective Dynamics*. New York: Thomas Y. Crowell.

Le Bon, G. (1893). *The Crowd: A Study of the Popular Mind*. London: T.F. Unwin.

McDougall, W. (1920). *The Group Mind*. New York: G. P. Putnam's Sons.

MacKinnon, Neil J. (1994). *Symbolic Interactionism as Affect Control*. Albany: State University of New York Press.

McPhail, Clark (1991). *The Myth of the Madding Crowd*. New York: Aldine de Gruyter.

Smelser, Neil J. (1963). *Theory of Collective Behavior*. New York: Free Press.

Smith-Lovin, Lynn (1990). Emotion as the confirmation and disconfirmation of identity: An affect control model. Chapter 9 in T.D. Kemper (ed.), *Research Agendas in the Sociology of Emotions*. Albany: State University of New York Press.

Smith-Lovin, Lynn and Heise, D.R. (1988). *Analyzing Social Interaction: Advances in Affect Control Theory*. New York: Gordon and Breach.

Tajfel, H. (1981). *Human Groups and Social Categories*. Cambridge, England: Cambridge University Press.

7 MODELLING THE INTERACTION RITUAL THEORY OF SOLIDARITY

RANDALL COLLINS

University of Pennsylvania

ROBERT HANNEMAN

University of California, Riverside

1. DEVELOPMENT OF INTERACTION RITUAL THEORY

The Interaction Ritual chain model originated in an effort to systematize the theory of social stratification on the basis of new research in micro-sociology. By 1970 a great deal of research had accumulated from traditional methods of surveys and community studies, on cultural and attitudinal differences among social classes. Collins (1975) proposed that much of the evidence falls under Durkheim's dimension of organic and mechanical solidarity. On the one hand, the culture of the higher social classes is cosmopolitan, abstract, relativistic, tolerant, features corresponding to the Durkheimian ethos of highly differentiated social structures; on the other hand, the culture of working classes and rural and isolated communities is localistic, tradition-oriented, symbolically reified, emphasizing close ties and distrust of outsiders, features corresponding to Durkheimian low social differentiation. Collins also concluded that these patterns could be derived from the patterns of micro-interaction in everyday life recently explored by Goffman under the rubric of "interaction rituals"; and proposed that Goffman's "frontstage" performance in the formal rituals of everyday life generates the self-presentation and cultural attitudes of higher classes, whereas "backstage" informality is characteristic of lower classes subordinated or excluded by formal rituals.

Over the years, this general model has been tightened theoretically, and integrated with evidence on the details of interaction that has accumulated as micro-sociological research expanded into ethnomethodology, conversation analysis, and sociology of emotions. The next step (Collins, 1981) was to propose that all macro-sociological phenomena (class structures, formal organizations, etc.) can be translated into chains of interaction rituals (IRs). In each encounter, individuals negotiate an IR, which varies in the degree of solidarity and dominance among its participants. These outcomes raise or lower the accumulation of cultural capital (CC) and emotional energy (EE) which these individuals carry away with them;[1] in turn, the match-up of CC and EE in their next encounters determines the success or failure of the next IR, and so on. Translated into micro-empirical detail, social structures are the shape of just such Interaction Ritual chains.

A detailed mechanism was needed for what takes place within the interaction ritual. Goffman had only vaguely designated certain kinds of interaction as ritualistic, because of their Durkheimian solidarity-producing outcomes. Collins' early formulations were verbal lists of the ingredients of a successful ritual:

(1) the face-to-face assembly of a group of at least two persons;
(2) their common focus of attention and mutual awareness of it;
(3) a shared emotional mood.

If these conditions are high enough, the result is

(4) enhanced emotional energy and confidence for individuals who participate in the ritual;
(5) a sense of membership in the group;
(6) a feeling of emotional respect for cultural symbols (those focussed upon in #2) which are now taken to represent membership in the group – i.e. what Durkheim called "sacred objects";
(7) feelings of righteous anger against persons who disrespect these sacred objects.

This listing already involved some transformation of the concept of ritual. In ordinary parlance, "ritual" means highly stereotyped actions following an explicit tradition (e.g. a church ceremony, flag salute, etc.). These do not appear in the list of ingredients because it turns out upon analysis that stereotyping *per se* is not necessary; stereotyped actions are one way in which ingredient #2 (mutual focus of attention) occurs, but stereotyped tradition is superfluous if the group spontaneously or through the nature of the situation, engages in an activity (such as cheering together at a game, or chatting together in a sociable conversation) which has the same effect of focussing attention. The

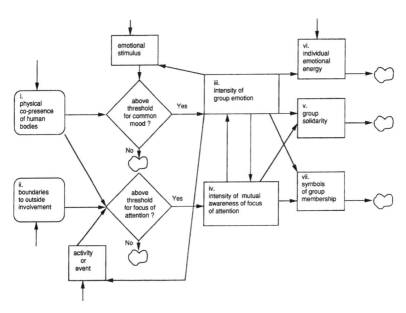

FIGURE 7.1. Omits some weaker feedback links: from v. and vi. to i. (as solidarity and emotional energy keep the group assembled); from iv. to ii (as high focus of attention increases boundaries). Also omitted are long-term feedbacks (as vi. and vii. facilitate renewed IRS on later occasions). Source: Collins, 1983, p. 207, 1933: 207.

slightly greater degree of verbal formalization shifts our attention to the theoretically more central elements.[2]

The next step was to connect these variables into a flow chart. Each step in formalization brings to the surface ambiguities and blank spots in the earlier verbal statements. The flow chart (Figure 7.1) brings into the open that there are feedback loops among the list of ritual ingredients. A heightened mutual focus of attention increases the strength of the shared mood (thus one grows increasingly more solemn in church, more humorous at a party, more aroused in an argument); conversely the growth of shared mood locks participants into closer focus upon each other. These are short-term feedbacks. There are also long-term feedback loops; the former unfold over a matter of seconds and minutes, the latter over a period of days or weeks. The Interaction Ritual chain is a long-term feedback, determining the distribution of EE and CC over periods of time which in principle are as long as participants' lives or even longer. Analytically, we cut into the chain at the point of a particular encounter to examine the dynamics which change the direction of EE and CC flows.

One point which becomes more explicit as we consider the repetition of IRs in a chain is that the effects of any one encounter are transitory. Individuals do not remain permanently at the level of EE and CC which they reach at the end of one IR; if this were so, they would soon lose motivation for further encounters. Durkheim saw the point, noting that rituals take place recurrently in order to remind individuals of social norms that would otherwise be forgotten. To put it another way: emotional energy runs down and dissipates over time. Without renewed contact with the group, individuals lose their emotional identifications, and the membership significance of symbols fades away. We need to model this explicitly as a time-decay or sink for the major outcome variables (hence the sinks at the far right-hand side of Figure 7.1). The tempo of this decay in strength remains to be precisely measured by research, but we can make some estimates from the patterns of everyday rituals: most strong solidarity groups such as churches or political movements meet at least weekly, and highly intense groups meet daily.

Another time pattern applies to the very short run; although we tend to overlook it in simple formal models of IR theory until we move to the level of dynamic simulation. Then we see there must be a short-run satiation in some key processes, so that the interaction is terminated and does not run on forever. Thus we need to specify limits on how intense the situational common mood can become, and how long individuals can sustain high levels of attention; these satiation levels need to be set at empirically realistic levels if the model is to produce a social interaction which approximates the length of a normal conversation or meeting.

The effort to incorporate empirical findings into the IR model led to a further set of modifications. The most common type of everyday interaction is the ordinary conversation. This has been studied since the 1970s with great precision by conversation analysis using tape recordings. Here we find a very high degree of social coordination, indeed at the level of tenths of seconds. Sacks, Schegloff and Jefferson (1974) specified a set of turn-taking "rules" by which conversation appears to be governed. These may be recast as a Durkheimian process, once we note that the "rules" are not always followed, but that interactions break down to particular ways when particular patterns are violated.

The key turn-taking rules are: one person speaks at a time; when the turn is finished, another person speaks. The full force of this is not apparent until we see the minute coordination of tempos with which this is carried out. In a successful conversation, the gap between one person ending their turn and the next person starting is typically less than 0.1 s; alternatively there are very slight overlaps (ca. 0.1 s) between speakers. (See data in Heritage, 1984, Chapter 8; Schegloff, 1992). We may characterize conversations which follow this pattern as high-solidarity conversations: friendly chatting or animated discussions among friends. But solidarity is a variable; not all conversations are of this sort. The turn-taking rules can be violated in two directions. Two (or more) persons can all speak at the same time; this is the pattern which we find in angry arguments. (See example in Schegloff, 1992, p. 1335). Or turn-taking can fail because one person stops talking and the other person does not pick up immediately. In fact the gaps need not be very large in order to signal that there is a breakdown in solidarity; what is colloquially known as an "embarassing pause" is often on the order of 1.5 s or less (examples in Heritage, 1984, p. 248). The baseline of normal solidarity conversation is that turns are coordinated at tempos of tenths of seconds; anything as long as 0.5 s is already missing several beats, and longer periods are experienced subjectively as huge gaps. These patterns are important not only in small interpersonal interactions such as private conversations. The large-scale political rituals of public speeches reach their emotional high points of group solidarity when the speaker is supported by bursts of applause (or interrupted by boos); application of conversation analysis to such recordings shows that fine-grained temporal rhythms are the key by which speaker and audience can anticipate and coordinate with one another (Clayman, 1993).

Another line of research pushes even further our growing theoretical awareness that solidarity is a matter of rhythmic synchronization. By applying instrumentation for Fast Fourier Transform (FFT) analysis to conversation recordings, Gregory et al. (1993, 1994) show that acoustical voice frequencies become attuned as conversations become more engrossing. This is rhythmic synchronization at a level much more fine-grained than the 0.1–2 s segments of which humans can be consciously aware. Again we need to stress that this is a variable; according to the hypothesis of IR theory, it is a channel by which solidarity is generated as a shared emotional mood.

The ultimate aim is a theoretical model which predicts observed empirical patterns within social interactions. It should be recognized that measurement of the relevant variables for the most part remains to be carried out. Development of the model however has not been entirely theory driven. The ethnographic observations upon which Durkheim relied, and which Goffman added from his extensive research in natural settings, were crudely qualitative, but they were empirical. Research on conversational rhythms has become increasingly precise, although it has not yet been adapted for the purposes of testing the IR model. Other key variables, degree of commonness of mood, focus of attention, and level of emotional energy, have not been measured with any precision. Techniques for examining such matters are becoming available, for example in studies of facial expression and nonverbal gesturing (e.g. Ekman and Friesen, 1975). Although the model as presented here is essentially theoretical, its recent versions have been developed in an effort to narrow the gap with empirical studies.

2. A MODEL OF MICRO-INTERACTIONAL DYNAMICS

The most recent model of IR puts rhythmic coordination into the center of micro-interactional dynamics. What is it that is taking place during a conversational ritual (or any other kind of ritual), by means of which common emotional mood and focus of attention are enhanced, and also by means of which the outcomes (emotional energy, cultural capital, feelings of solidarity) are generated? This is depicted in Figure 7.2. When human bodies are present in the same place, a common mood and a focus of attention set them off orienting towards each other. Their gestures and sounds (which may take the

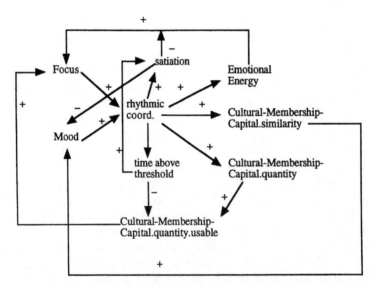

FIGURE 7.2.   Interaction ritual: Basic micro-model.

form of articulate speech, as well as non-verbal behavior) become in some degree coordinated. It is because these gestures and sounds have a rhythmic structure that coordination can build up; what is monitored, and what becomes socially contagious, is the rhythm, more than the overt contents.

We specify a threshold for rhythmic coordination to take off into self-sustaining action. This threshold is to take account of the empirically frequent event that persons present in the same place do not interact, or that small beginnings towards interaction do not pan out. The initial levels of common mood and focus of attention must be strong enough for the rest of the sequence to take place. Once this point is passed, short-term feedbacks kick in. In the earlier flow-chart (Figure 7.1), mood and focus of attention somehow enhance one another. How precisely does this happen? For parsimony, we may derive these short-term feedbacks from the main outcome variables of the IR. That is to say, emotional energy is not merely a quantity which enters into the long-term chain of situations; it also builds up directly in this immediate encounter. Increased emotional energy raises the common focus of attention (for instance, as cheering at a game grows more animated, participants become more caught up in it to the exclusion of other actions). Of course this cannot go on escalating forever; hence we have to put in a satiation process, driven by the length of time that rhythmic coordination is above the threshold.

There are two other significant short-term feedback loops. Again we parsimoniously make use of outcome variables which figure in the long-term Interaction Ritual chain. In Figure 7.1 above, a successful ritual produces both cultural capital, and feelings of group membership. How are these stored? On the verbal level, cultural capital consists in things that people have to talk about, items which they can invest in future conversations. We have renamed this store of talk, previously called cultural capital, as Cultural-Membership-Capital (CMC), to emphasize that feelings of membership are directly embodied in feelings about verbal (and visual, gestural, etc.) symbols. Membership is not a separate process; if two persons do not share any CMC, they cannot enact membership because they have nothing to fill the contents of their interaction. In Figure 7.2, rhythmic coordination increases CMC. That is to say, as mutually engrossing talk takes place, the individuals gain shared verbal culture.

We separate this into two streams for purposes of the short-term feedback loops. One is the extent to which the participants in the conversation have similar CMCs (this is marked as CMC.similarity).

CMC.similarity is already set at a given level before the conversation starts, because of past histories of the participants in Interaction Ritual chains; CMC.similarity also changes in the course of the current conversation. The short-term loop is from CMC.similarity to common mood; i.e. having similar things to talk about (complaining about the same political enemy; laughing at the same kinds of jokes) enhances the immediate mood and keeps the conversational loop going. The other stream is the sheer quantity of CMC that the individuals have available at any one moment: the sheer amount of things which (because they have the requisite level of similarity) can be talked about. This quantity governs the short-term duration of the conversation. As time above threshold grows, some proportion of the CMC.quantity is used up (certain topics are already talked out). This is modelled by a loop from the CMC.quantity which remains usable (not yet used up), to focus of attention. The latter is the aspect of the interaction situation which brings individuals to pay attention to one another; as CMC.quantity is used up, there are fewer things to pay attention to, and eventually the conversation dissipates and breaks off.

Figure 7.2 is analytically simplified to display only the links among the endogenous IR variables. In real life, conversations do not exist in a vacuum. We provide a elaborated, more realistic model in Figure 7.3. Here focus of attention is determined not only by emotional energy and by CMC.similarity, but also by the local situation (being seated next to another person in an airplane, or being separated by a partition); in other words, the sheer physical ecology of social life is an important variable affecting whether IRs can get started. We list a second external condition, event: this is the activity which is occuring at that location, which can by itself give rise to at least the initiation of an interaction (people passing on the street are drawn into inter-action if an airplane crashes near by; less dramatically, working at the same task in the same place gives persons something to talk about).[3] We link this external variable to common mood, in order to model the emotional effects of events, rather than leaving mood purely to the infinite regress of past conversational experiences. This is a realistic way of depicting how intense public rituals actually get started; in the vein of Malinowskian and Durkheimian theory of ritual (and also Weber's analogous conception of the rise of charisma), we may say that emotionally disruptive public events cause groups to form and to institute ritual to deal with those emotions.

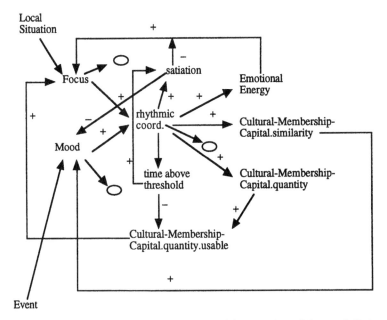

FIGURE 7.3. Interaction ritual: Micro-model with external conditions and dissipation sinks.

Figure 7.3 also adds sinks to the short-run variables; focus of attention, common mood, and rhythmic coordination dissipate over time if they are not sustained by inflows.

What is modelled here are the aggregate characteristics of interaction within a generic undifferentiated group. There is no specification as to whether this is a dyad, a cocktail party, or a crowd, or some subcomponent thereof. More differentiated models could be built; what is presented here, we suggest, is a common framework.

3. FORMALIZING THE MODEL

The theory diagrammed in Figure 7.3 contains nine endogenous quantities and two exogenous quantities (Local Situation and Event). Like any causal diagram, Figure 7.3 can be translated into a system of simultaneous difference or differential equations by writing functions that describe how each endogenous quantity is hypothesized to change with those variables that cause it. Our formalization of the theory as relatively simple difference equations is shown below, along with a short verbal translation and description of the quantities.

$$F_{t+1} = F_t + (CU_t + L_t)(E_t - S_t) - aF_t. \tag{1}$$

The degree of shared focus in the group is increased if the local situation and/or quantity of cultural-membership capital available for interaction is non-zero; and if the difference between the level of emotional energy and satiation is non-zero. In addition, shared focus dissipates at a rate proportional to its current level.

$$M_{t+1} = M_t + (b\,CS_t + V_t) - cM_t. \tag{2}$$

The degree of common mood in the group is increased as a constant function of the level of cultural-membership-capital similarity plus exogenous events that produce common mood. Common mood dissipates at a rate proportional to its current level.

If: $(M_t - H_m)$ and $(F_t - H_f)$ are each greater than or equal to zero,
then: $R_{t+1} = R_t + (M_t * F_t) - dR_t$,
else: $R_{t+1} = -dR_t$. $\tag{3}$

The level of rhythmic coordination among persons in the group increases as the product of the levels of common mood and common focus, when both exceed threshold values. Rhythmic coordination dissipates at a rate proportional to its current level.

If: R_t is greater than or equal to zero,
then: $T_{t+1} = T_t + 1$,
else: $T_{t+1} = 0$. $\tag{4}$

The length of time that sustained rhythmically coordinated activity has been occuring in the group accumulates at a constant rate when any such activity occurs.

$$S_{t+1} = S_t + T_t^{(e)}. \tag{5}$$

The degree of satiation increases at an exponentially increasing rate with the duration of sustained rhythmically coordinated activity.

$$CS_{t+1} = CS_t + fR_t. \tag{6}$$

The degree of similarity of the cultural-membership capital of members of the group increases at a rate proportional to the extent of rhythmically coordinated interaction occuring in the group.

$$CQ_{t+1} = CQ_t + gR_t. \tag{7}$$

The quantity of cultural-membership capital of members of the group increases at rates proportional to the extent of rhythmically coordinated interaction occuring in the group.

$$CU_{t+1} = CQ_t - hT_t. \qquad (8)$$

The quantity of cultural-membership-capital available to sustain interaction is used up at rates increasing with the duration of rhythmically coordinated interaction.

$$E_{t+1} = E_t + R_t. \qquad (9)$$

The emotional energy of the group increases directly with the extent of rhythmic coordination.

In Eqs. (1)–(9):

F_t is the level of common focus of attention at time t, ranging from random ($F_t = 0$) to singular ($F_t = 1$) focus of attention of group members.

M_t is the extent to which actors share a common mood at time t, ranging from $M_t = 0$ (member moods are randomly distributed) to $M_t = 1$ (member moods are identical).

R_t is the level of rhythmic coordination among persons in a conversation or other face-to-face interaction at time t, ranging from $R_t = 0$ (no coordination of interaction) to $R_t = 1$ (complete synchronization).

T_t is the length of time that rhythmically coordinated interaction has been occuring in the group up to the current time, ranging from 0 (no prior rhythmic interaction) to t (the current time).

S_t is the degree of satiation with interaction at time t, the extent to which persons interacting experience their fill of the emotional arousal and rhythmic coordination, ranging from 0 (no satiation) to 1 (complete satiation).

CS_t is the degree of similarity in the cultural-membership capital among the persons interacting at time t, ranging from 0 (complete dissimilarity of all group members) to 1 (complete similarity of all group members).

CQ_t is the average quantity of cultural-membership-capital stored in the memories of persons interacting at time t. In principle, this quantity could range from a value zero (no cultural membership capital), to an unspecified upper bound. We have fixed an upper bound of 1.0, indicating a situation in which all members of the group have high levels of cultural-membership-capital.

CU_t is the average quantity of cultural-membership-capital in the memories of persons interacting at time t that has not yet been used in the current interaction. It ranges from 0, indicating that all cultural-membership-capital has already been used in interaction, to an upper bound of CQ_t.

E_t is the level of emotional energy of the group, on a continuum ranging from depression (zero) to extreme enthusiasm (1.0), at time t.

L_t is the extent to which the local situation produces a shared focus of attention (by assembling persons, providing a common activity, and setting barriers to outside intrusions) at time t. It ranges from 0, indicating that the local situation contributes nothing to the production of shared focus, to 1.0, indicating that the local situation compels all members of the interacting group to share focus.

V_t is the extent to which an exogenous event produces a common mood among the persons interacting at time t. It ranges from 0, indicating no events contributing to a common mood to 1.0, events compel all members of the group to share a common mood.

H_m and H_f are constant threshold values of common mood and shared focus, respectively, which must be exceeded for each variable to contribute to rhythmic coordination.

a, b, c, d, e, f, g, h are positive constants.

4. ANALYZING THE MODEL BY SYSTEM DYNAMICS SIMULATION

Because the system described by the theory has been kept relatively simple (involving only nine variables, and mostly linear or other simple functions connecting them), it is possible to analyze the system, at least qualitatively, simply by logical deduction. That is, because of the simplicity of the system, it is not too difficult to discern which variables and combinations of variables may be "most important" by looking for variables that are "central" (i.e. have relatively high between-ness, or high in and out degree). It is somewhat more difficult, but hardly impossible, to work out logically which assumptions or hypotheses may be the most critical ones (i.e. be the most sensitive parameters). To understand the implications of the theory, we can also perform mental experiments of trying to work through what the patterns of interaction dynamics would look like in groups that began with different initial conditions (e.g. how do of high-similarity versus low-similarity groups differ, and why, according to the theory?).

Alternatively, since we have formalized the theory as a system of linearizable difference or differential equations, we could attempt to understand its full implications by direct solution (actually, multiple solutions to describe the dynamics under each of the "if-then-else" conditions in the formalization). Performing a bit of algebra on the difference equations, or calculus on the differential equations can tell us a number of useful things about the theory as we have stated it. Perhaps the most useful of these would be whether the system has equilibria, and the general relationships among the values of the variables that produce these situations, if they exist. By substituting equations for variables and simplification, it is also possible to derive full and general expressions for how the rate of change in one variable depends on each of the others.

Our preferred method of "understanding" the implications of the theory as formalized, and exploring its reasonableness and predictions, is to perform simulation experiments. In this approach, one selects a set of values that describe the state of the system at an inital point in time, and then calculates the subsequent values for all variables of the system by iterative calculation of the difference or differential equations. By comparing the results of multiple experiments that vary one or more initial conditions, parameters, or even functional forms, we can build up a qualitative understanding of the (usually limited number of) types of histories the model can produce, and the combinations of conditions associated with each qualitative type of behavior. The use of simulation experiments as a way of analyzing formal models lacks the rigor, precision, and elegance of direct mathematical solution. However, it may enable us to have a better, if qualitative, understanding of the range of characteristic or ideal-typical "histories" of events that the theory is capable of predicting, and the conditions under which they are predicted (Hanneman, 1988).

For our simulation experiments, we have translated the mathematical model stated above into the DYNAMO language (Pugh-Roberts Associates, 1984). The documented model, in the DYNAMO language, is appended. We have found this particular language useful for performing simulation experiments for two reasons. First, a small and relatively inexpensive application is available using the language, which makes model editing, compilation, calculation, and viewing very simple on a personal computer. Second, the language itself is a tool developed by the System Dynamics group following Forrester (1973), that embodies a way of thinking about simultaneous non-linear dynamics formally but qualitatively, rather than mathematically. The language has a substantial library of functions for describing qualitative and non-linear relations that we have found useful in theorizing about social dynamics. The resultant language resembles algebra, but is considerably less elegant than conventional mathematics because complex expressions are broken down into multiple but simpler component parts (which are labelled as to their function as integrating, rate calculation, auxillary calculation, initialization, etc.).

5. AN ANALYSIS OF THE MODEL

The model in Figure 7.3 places rhythmic coordination at the center of the process, resulting from the joint action of common mood and focus, and resulting in emotional energy and the creation of common cultural capital. In examining the formal model, it is useful to focus our attention on the conditions that give rise to the emergence of rhythmic coordination, and how such emergent patterns evolve over time.

As formalized, no initial level of any one variable is sufficient to produce rhythmic coordination when all other variables are at zero (this could be deduced logically from studying the equations, or, as here, tested by performing a series of simulation experiments in which all initial level of variables, save one, are set to zero). Groups with high levels of cultural membership capital, in the absence of emotional energy or shared mood do not produce rhythmic coordination; groups with shared mood do not produce rhythmic coordination if focus is absent; groups may share a common focus, but unless they have the same mood, no rhythmic coordination will occur. Rhythmic coordination, then, is the result of sets of necessary conditions that are jointly sufficient; no single variable is sufficient to produce rhythmic coordination.

There are two sets of sufficient conditions for rhythmic coordination to occur in the model as stated. First, if both common mood and common focus simultaneously exceed their required thresholds, rhythmic coordination ensues. This condition, according to the model, is produced when local conditions are sufficient to produce the threshold value of focus and events occurring in the setting are sufficient to produce the threshold value of common mood. Second, rhythmic coordination can be produced in the absence of conducive local conditions and exogenous events if levels of cultural membership capital and emotional energy are sufficient to raise common focus and mood beyond their threshold levels.

The occurrence of rhythmic coordination in a group with low arousal and little common membership capital then, depends upon exogenous conditions. In order for events to occur, local conditions must give rise to shared focus at a rate sufficient to hold it above its threshold, while events must be sufficient to simultaneously push common mood beyond its threshold. Both common focus of attention and common mood have inherent tendencies to dissipate in the absence of other stimuli. One might deduce then that the onset of rhythmic coordination in placid settings with random actors is not very likely, and depends on exogenous conditions.

But, the necessary focus to produce rhythmic coordination can occur even in the absence of exogenous conditions if there is some degree of emotional arousal and members share high levels of cultural membership capital. High levels of cultural membership capital, interacting with at least some level of emotional arousal can, through uncoordinated activity, eventually give rise to sufficient group focus to result in rhythmic coordination.

These two alternative sets of sufficient conditions for the onset of rhythmic coordination are simple logical (or experimental) deductions from the formal model. They do, however, correspond to plausible scenarios of group interaction. We can play out these scenarios with simulation experiments.

First, imagine a group of children, perhaps at a day-care center, who share little cultural membership capital in common. As children, each actor's stock of cultural capital may be relatively small to begin with; we will assume that the children do not know each other initially, and hence have nothing in common from prior interaction. Let us also suppose that the children have low levels of emotional energy (perhaps being depressed by separation from parents), and that their moods, initially, are random (that is, shared mood is zero). The children, however, do share a local condition sufficient to raise their common focus above the threshold necessary for rhythmic coordination and solidarity to build, simply as a result of physical proximity in the environment. We can implement this scenario by setting the initial conditions of the cultural membership capital, rhythmic coordination, emotional energy, and common mood variables to zero. We initialize common focus at a level slightly above its threshold (0.25). Now, let us suppose that an actor (perhaps the care giver) creates an event by involving the children in a game that begins at the fifth time point of the simulation and continues for five time points. The game abruptly increases the commonality of mood among the children, and satisfies the conditions for rhythmic coordination to begin. The results of this scenario are shown in Figure 7.4.

The exogenous event results in the onset of rhythmic coordination among the members of the group, because common focus is sufficient.

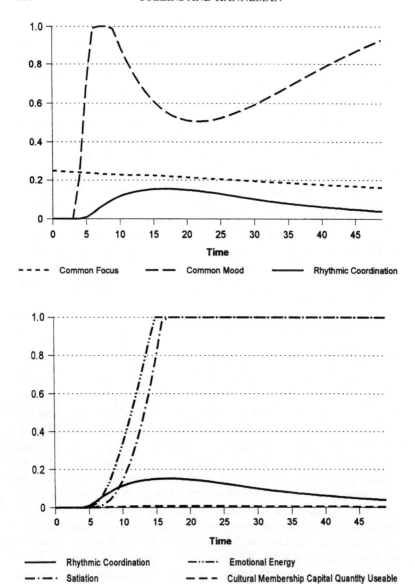

FIGURE 7.4.   External event scenario: Children's game.

If the care giver had not intervened until later (when common focus had dissipated below its threshold) no rhythmic coordination would have resulted. Rhythmic coordination builds in the group's interaction, generating emotional energy (which rises, then levels off). A small amount of usable cultural membership capital is built up,[4] contributing to the prolongation of the rhythmic coordination, but satiation also accumulates, gradually weakening the shared focus and mood of the group. If allowed to continue for a sufficient time, the group arrives at a new equilibrium of low levels of common mood and focus, a moderate degree of emotional energy, and satiation. Rhythmic coordination, after its initial peak, continues to decline toward zero.

A second simulation illustrates the alternative sufficient conditions for rhythmic coordination can occur. A group of faculty from a variety of departments, who do routinely interact, have been invited to a cocktail party and reception for an outside speaker at the Dean's spacious home and grounds. Local conditions for facilitating interaction are minimal (resulting in a focus initialized at zero). Members of the group have had their emotional energy levels raised somewhat by the speaker's lecture but share no common mood (mood is also initialized at zero). Thus, the conditions of both common mood and common focus, initially, are insufficient to produce rhythmically coordinated interaction. As adults with high levels of cultural capital and similar background, however, usable common membership capital is moderate (initialized at 0.25 in the results shown here), an interesting process occurs, as shown in Figure 7.5.

As the actors engage in conversation, their high levels of cultural membership capital similarity becomes apparent, and common mood and focus build. As the threshold is passed, rhythmic coordination of the interaction gradually builds to a peak, then begins to gradually dissipate as satiation with interaction builds, and the stock of topics of conversation are used up. Coordinated interaction persists for a lengthy period, and actors feel both enervated and satiated. (We do not introduce an additional time-line for the effects of injesting alcohol upon emotional energy; such additional specifications are easy in DYNAMO modelling.)

We do not propose these two scenarios as realistic empirical predictions, though many of the differences in the levels and time-shapes of the two cases could be tested. Rather, they serve as illustrations of the analytical point that the building of rhythmic coordination in interaction, and its solidaristic consequences, can be produced by a variety of empirical conditions. We can envision a research program,

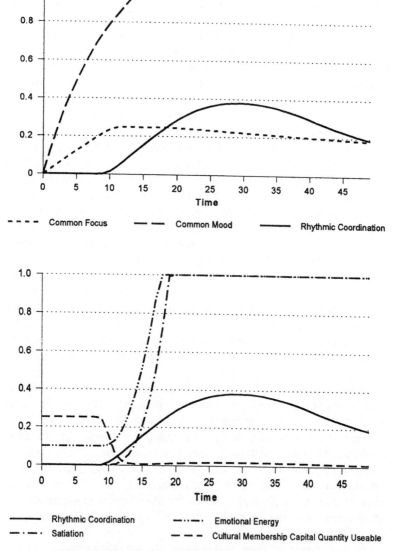

FIGURE 7.5.   Moderate similarity scenario: Cocktail party.

performing simulation experiments designed to model a variety of social situations, and comparing the time-profiles of the variables with empirical measurements from laboratory experiments or recordings of natural settings. In this way a more refined theoretical model could be progressively achieved.

6. APPENDIX: MICRO-INTERACTION DYNAMICS MODEL

6.1. Initial Conditions Block

Each of the model's variables is provided with a starting value for time zero. In most cases, this is done by setting the initial value to a variable name in an "N" equation, and then defining the variable as a constant in a "C" equation. This is done to facilitate re-runs, as DYNAMO allows constants to be changed on re-runs, but not initial values. The initial values of the two exogenous variables, LOCAL and EVENT are defined internally by functions.

N FOCUS = FOCUSI	FOCUSI is the initial level of group common.
C FOCUSI = 0.1	theoretical range from zero to unity.
N MOOD = MOODI	MOODI is the initial level of group common mood.
C MOODI = 0.1	theoretical range from zero to unity.
N RHYTH = RHYTHI	RHYTHI is the initial level of rhythmic coordination.
C RHYTHI = 0.0	theoretical range from zero to unity.
N DUR = 0.0	DUR is the number of time periods that rhythmic coordination has been in at non-zero levels. At the beginning of the simulation, it is set to zero.
N SAT = SATI	SATI is the initial level of satiation.
C SATI = 0.0	theoretical range from zero to unity.
N EE = EEI	EEI is the initial level of group emotional energy.
C EEI = 0.1	theoretical range from zero to unity.
N CMCSIM = CMCSIMI	CMCSIMI is the initial level of similarity in cultural capital among group members.
C CMCSIMI = 0.1	

N CMCQU = CMCQUI   CMCQUI is the initial level of the quantity
C CMCQUI = 0.1   of cultural membership capital useable.

6.2. Parameters Block

The magnitudes of effects of changes in variables on others in the model
are specified as variables, which are set as constants, to facilitate
experimentation.

C PARM1 = 0.01   Proportional rate of dissipation of group focus
C PARM2 = 0.50   Effect of CMCSIM on MOOD
C PARM3 = 0.10   Proportional rate of dissipation of common mood
C PARM4 = 0.05   Proportional rate of dissipation
                    of rhythmic coordination.
C PARM5 = 0.20   Threshold value that must be exceeded for the
                    common mood of the group to affect rhythmic
                    coordination.
C PARM6 = 0.20   Threshold value that must be exceeded for the
                    common focus of the group to affect rhythmic
                    coordination.
C PARM7 = 1.05   The exponential rate at which duration affects
                    the effect of rhythmic activity on satiation. In the
                    code, this is done by a table.
C PARM8 = 0.05   Rate at which rhythmic activity is converted into
                    similar cultural membership capital.
C PARM9 = 0.05   Rate at which rhythmic activity is converted into
                    cultural membership capital available for
                    producing common focus.
C PARM10 = 0.10   Rate at which prolonged rhythmic activity dissi-
                    pates cultural membership capital available for
                    producing common focus.

6.3. Main Model Equations

The model contains two exogenous conditions: LOCAL and EVENT,
which are described first. Then the equations for the endogenous
variables, from left to right in the text figure are presented. DYNAMO
uses L equations to describe integration, R equations to describe the
functions to be integrated, and A equations for supplementary calculations of non-integrating quantities.The code for each core equation
is often divided into several sequential steps in the DYNAMO code
for clarity.

6.4. Exogenous Variables

Events are exogenous shocks that stimulate the creation of shared mood among group members. For experimentation, an exogenous series of shocks is read by use of a table function that describes the value of EVENT (which ranges between zero and one) for each of the first 20 points of time.

A EVENT.K = TABHL(EVENTTAB,TIME.K,0,20,1)
T EVENTTAB = 0/0/0/0/.5/.5/.5/.5/.5/0/0/0/0/0/0/0/0/0/0/0

Local situation is an exogenous variable (ranging from zero to one) that contributes to increasing the focus of the members of the group on a common object. For experimentation, it is defined here as a series of exogenous shocks for each of the first 20 points of time.

A LOCAL.K = TABHL(LOCALTAB,TIME.K,0,20,1)
T LOCALTAB = 0/0/0/0/0/0/0/0/0/0/0/0/0/0/0/0/0/0/0/0

6.5. Endogenous Variables

6.5.1. Common Focus

The degree of common focus of the group ranges from zero to unity. The degree of common focus is the result of two factors, the first RIFOCUS is a complex function of other model conditions, the second RDFOCUS suggests that focus dissipates at a constant rate (PARM1) proportional to its current level.

L FOCUS.K = FOCUS.K + DT*(RIFOCUS.JK-RDFOCUS.JK)
R RIFOCUS.KL = MAX(CLIP(0,(CMCQU.K + LOCAL.K)*
                  (EE.K-SAT.K),FOCUS.K,1.00),0)
R RDFOCUS.KL = PARM1*FOCUS.K

6.5.2. Common Mood

The degree of common mood among group members ranges from zero to unity. The degree of common mood is the result of two factors, the first RIMOOD is a result of other model condition (governed, in part, by PARM2), the second RDMOOD suggests that common mood dissipates at a constant rate (PARM3) proportional to MOODs current level.

L MOOD.K = MOOD.J + DT*(RIMOOD.JK-RDMOOD.JK)
R RIMOOD.KL = MAX(CLIP(0,(PARM2*CMCSIM.K) +
                  EVENT.K,MOOD.K,1.00),0)
R RDMOOD.KL = PARM3*MOOD.K

6.5.3. Rhythmic Coordination

The degree of rhythmic coordination among group members ranges from zero (none) to unity. Rhythmic coordination dissipates at a rate (PARM4) proportional to its current level. The other causes of rhythmic coordination are more complex and are dealt with subsequently.

L RHYTH.K = RHYTH.J + DT*(RIRHYTH.JK-RDRHYTH.JK)
R RDRHYTH.KL = PARM4*RHYTH.K

Common mood in the group may contribute to increased rhythmic coordination to the degree that common mood exceeds a threshold value (PARM5)

A RMT.K = CLIP(MOOD.K-PARM5,0,MOOD.K-PARM5,.0001)

Common focus in the group may contribute to increased rhythmic coordination to the degree that common focus exceeds a threshold value (PARM6)

A RFT.K = CLIP(FOCUS.K-PARM6,0,FOCUS.K-PARM6,.0001)

The effects of common mood and common focus of attention on rhythmic coordination take the form of a multiplicative interaction.

R RIRHYTH.KL = CLIP(0,RMT.K*RFT.K,RHYTH.K,1.00)

6.5.4. Duration

The magnitudes of two feedback effects depend upon how long non-zero rhythmic activity has been occurring. This duration is calculated using integration of duration of one unit per unit time if rhythmic activity has been occurring, and emptying the level if there is no rhythmic activity.

L DUR.K = DUR.J + DT*(RIDUR.JK-RDDUR.JK)
R RIDUR.KL = CLIP(1.0,0,RHYTH.K,.0001)
R RDDUR.KL = CLIP(0,DUR.K,RHYTH.K,.0001)

6.5.5. Satiation

Satiation accumulates as a function of the current level of rhythmic coordination times an exponential function of the length of time that rhythmic activity has been continuously occurring; the magnitude of the exponent is specified as PARM7.

L SAT.K = SAT.J + DT*(RCSAT.JK)
R RCSAT.KL = CLIP(0,RHYTH.K*FDUR.K,SAT.K,1.00)

A FDUR.K = TABXT(FDURTAB,DUR.K,0,10,1)
T FDURTAB = 0/.1/.21/.32/.43/.54/.66/.77/.89/1.00/1.12

6.5.6. Emotional Energy

The emotional energy of the group ranges from zero (none) to a maximum of unity. Emotional energy accumulates at rates proportional to the level of rhythmic coordination occurring.

L EE.K = EE.J + DT*(RIEE.JK)
R RIEE.KL = CLIP(0,RHYTH.K,EE.K,1.00)

6.5.7. Cultural Membership Capital Similarity

The amount of cultural capital that is common to group members ranges from zero (none) to unity (all cultural capital in common). The similarity of capital accumulates at a rate (PARM8) proportional to the level of rhythmic coordination occurring.

L CMCSIM.K = CMCSIM.J + DT*(RICMCSIM.JK)
R RICMCSIM.KL = CLIP(0,PARM8*RHYTH.K,CMCSIM.K,1.00)

6.5.8. Cultural Membership Capital Quantity Usable

The amount of cultural membership capital that is available to serve as a resource for producing common focus accumulates at rates proportional (PARM9) to the level of rhythmic activity. It dissipates at rates proportional (PARM10) to the duration of that rhythmic activity, if the predicted decline is less than the amount available, else the amount available is taken.

L CMCQU.K = CMCQU.J + DT*(RICMC.JK-RDCMC.JK)
R RICMC.KL = MAX(CLIP(0,RHYTH.K*PARM9,CMCQU.K,
        1.00),0)
R RDCMC.KL = CLIP(DUR.K*PARM10,CMCQU.K,CMCQU.K,
        DUR.K*PARM10)

7. SAVED RESULTS

SAVE LOCAL,EVENT
SAVE FOCUS,RIFOCUS,RDFOCUS
SAVE MOOD,RIMOOD,RDMOOD
SAVE RHYTH,RIRHYTH,RDRHYTH,RMT,RFT

SAVE DUR,SAT,RCSAT,EE,RIEE
SAVE CMCSIM,RICMCSIM,CMCQU,RICMC,RDCMC
NOTE SIMULATION CONTROL
SPEC DT = .1,LENGTH = 50,SAVPER = 1

NOTES

1. Emotional energy is a distinctive concept in this theory. It is a continuum, ranging from enthusiasm at the high end, to depression at the low end; at normal levels it is typically unnoticed, although its behavioral (and psychological and hormonal manifestations) are in principle observable. EE is not a specific sentiment toward objects, nor it is a short-term emotion manifested in situational outbursts such as anger, joy, or fear. These distinctions are elaborated in Collins (1990).
2. Notice that we have unpacked the concept of "social solidarity". It involves a sense of membership in the group; this includes the feelings of individuals towards each other, which in some empirical studies (such as Homans' 1950 review of the small-group literature) is described as mutual liking. There is also the feeling of self as group member, manifested in emotional energy, and respect for group symbols as well as potential for anger against violaters of those symbols. To capture the full dynamics of the situation, it is useful to advance beyond a single dimension, and to tap aspects which do not come through in the folk concept of "liking another person". In the following discussion, the term "solidarity" will sometimes be used as a convenient summary of these outcome variables.
3. Homans (1950) formulated a set of principles, based on evidence of small group studies, that converges with the IR model. His basic principles, that common activity brings social interaction, and interaction increases mutual liking (solidarity) and conformity of belief (cultural membership capital), incorporate several of the IR variables, while leaving blank the micro-dynamic processes by which they are connected.
4. In the bottom panel of Figure 7.4 shows, Cultural Membership Capital Quantity Usable, which was initialized at zero, rises slightly after time point 5, reaches its maximum at time 15, and thereafter slowly subsides. Due to the scale of this parameter, the pattern is not clearly visible from the graph alone.

REFERENCES

Clayman, Stephen E. (1993) "Booing: the anatomy of a disaffiliative response." *American Sociological Review* **58**: 110–130.

Collins, R. (1975) *Conflict Sociology: Towards an Explanatory Science.* New York: Academic Press.

Collins, Randall (1981) "On the micro-foundations of macro-sociology." *American Journal of Sociology* **86**: 984–1014.

Collins, Randall (1990) "Stratification, emotional energy, and the transient emotions." in Theodore D. Kemper (ed.), *Research Agendas in the Sociology of Emotions.* Albany: SUNY Press, pp. 27–57.

Collins, Randall (1993) "Emotional energy as the common denominator of rational action." *Rationality and Society* **5**: 203–230.

Ekman, Paul, and Wallace V. Friesen (1975) *Unmasking the Face.* Englewood Cliffs NJ: Prentice-Hall.

Forrester, Jay W. (1973) *World Dynamics.* Cambridge, MA: Wright-Allen Press.

Gregory, Stanford W., Stephen Webster and Gang Huang (1993) "Voice pitch and amplitude convergence as a metric of quality in dyadic interviews. *Language and Communication* **13**: 195–217.

Gregory, Stanford W. (1994) "Sounds of power and deference: acoustic analysis of macro social constraints on micro interaction." *Sociological Perspectives* **37**: 497–526.

Hanneman, Robert (1988) *Computer-Assisted Theory Building. Modelling Dynamic Social Systems.* Beverly Hills: Sage.

Heritage, John (1984) *Garfinkel and Ethnomethodology.* Cambridge: Polity Press.

Homans, George C. (1950) *The Human Group.* New York: Harcourt, Brace.

Pugh-Roberts Associates (1984) *Micro-DYNAMO System Dynamics Modelling Language.* Reading, MA: Addison-Wesley.

Sacks, Harvey, Emanuel A. Schegloff and Gail Jefferson. (1974) "A simplest systematics for the organization of turn-taking for conversation." *Language* **50**: 696–735.

Schegloff, Emanuel (1992) "Repair after last turn: the last structurally provided defense of intersubjectivity in conversation." *American Journal of Sociology* **97**: 1295–1345.

Part IV

Social Networks and Solidarity

8 SOLIDARITY AND SOCIAL NETWORKS

RONALD L. BREIGER

Cornell University

JOHN M. ROBERTS, JR.

University of New Mexico

1. INTRODUCTION

"The study of solidarity thus grows out of sociology."
– Emile Durkheim (1893, p. 67)

In their agenda of problems with respect to the theory of solidarity, Fararo and Doreian (1998) have formulated a call and a challenge to mathematical sociology to situate itself at the core of the sociological enterprise. What is taken as problematic in the foundational paper of Fararo and Doreian is "the very 'groupiness' of the group itself" (1998, p. 6). These writers accord prominence, substantively and analytically, to networks of interaction. Moreover, they call for models that "lift" these networks to "what is, for the actors, a higher-order social entity" (p. 6). At least as one major component of their agenda, they call for models and analyses of the group as an entity that emerges from social flux to be characterized dually as a social network with a structural form and as a higher-order social entity that transcends its individual members (p. 6).

As theorists of solidarity often do, Fararo and Doreian introduce their review of sociological approaches by mentioning Durkheim. In this paper we spend more time with this progenitor of modern sociology, and in particular with his 1893 work, *The Division of Labor in Society*, aptly described by LaCapra (1985, p. 79) as now "referred to with the *pro forma* awe which scholars reserve for recognized classics, but to which little real reference is made in the analysis of problems." We aim to end such neglect of Durkheim's relevance for social network analysis, much as Alexander (1988) has championed his centrality for cultural studies (see also footnote 5). We agree with Collins (1994, p. 236) that the Durkheimian tradition "remains somewhat of a half-kept secret amidst the various empirical and theoretical proceedings of the field today," despite the fact that its potential for "pulling sociology together around a common core" remains "even more powerful today than ever before."

This paper begins, then, with a discussion of Durkheim's understanding of the problem of solidarity and its implications for formal modeling. We focus on four aspects: the morphology of social association, collective representation as an emergent property of groups, the analytical tension that Durkheim insists on bringing to bear in identifying both the opposition and the unity of individuals and groups, and the implications of types of solidarity for types of exchange.[1]

In Section 3 of the paper we bring these considerations to bear in the formulation of a new interpretive context for one family of log-linear models for networks of interaction frequency, namely: models of quasi-symmetry and of skew-symmetry. All the technical results that we need are already known (Caussinus, 1965; Goodman, 1985; Sobel, Hout and Duncan, 1985; Yamaguchi, 1990). Their application in the formulation of network-analytic models for square tables of interaction frequency is novel. In particular, our framework postulates, and therefore allows the test of, a unidimensional collective representation of group hierarchy as coexisting with a network of social relations, the reduced-form structure of which is itself subject to representation and testing within the same model. Moreover, the degree to which specific individuals take part in group life can be measured, and inferences can be tested.

The data context for Section 4 is interagreement among U.S. Supreme Court justices during the first four terms of the "Rehnquist Court" (Segal and Spaeth, 1993). Several features of this network are incorporated within a single modeling context: detailed patterns of agreement, reduced-form "block" structure, the emergence of person-specific "strengths" as a single dimension partially governing the detailed interactions, and a second dimension pertaining to the degree to which actors can stand apart from the ideological structuring and weave coalitions together. This modeling context for group solidarity thus allows incorporation of multiple principles of social order that should have wider applicability to analyses of square networks of counted data.

One limitation of the work reported here should be identified at the outset. Fararo and Doreian call for models that bridge structure and process; however, models in this paper, while relevant for process outcomes, are purely structural. We claim to make progress in articulating relations between social networks and emergent collective properties, but we have made no direct progress in combining process and structural models.

2. DURKHEIM ON SOLIDARITY

Is friendship based on resemblance or on dissimilarity among friends? This question is posed in the opening chapter of Durkheim's 1893 work, *The Division of Labor in Society*. After reviewing the various positions taken by classical thinkers (Aristotle, Euripides, Heraclitus) and by modern authors on this question, Durkheim concludes that "we seek in our friends the qualities we lack, since in joining with them, we participate in some measure in their nature and feel less incomplete" (1893, pp. 55–6). It is "this division of labor, which determines the relation of friendship." In fact, the "true function" of the division of labor is "to create in two or more persons a feeling of solidarity." It follows that, contrary to analysts who see the division of labor in rational, economic terms, it is necessary to consider the division of labor "in a new light," since "the economic services that it can render are picayune compared to the moral effect that it produces" (p. 56).

It seems as if Durkheim requires three actors in order to discuss two friends: the two individuals and the collective unit that they form with their interpersonal ties of exchange or sharing across several domains of activity. Indeed, Alpert (1941, p. 174) argued that the term *solidarité* as Durkheim used it in the 1890s in France referred, in an objective and even biological sense, to a type of relation between a whole and its parts, and he suggested "cohesion" as a possible synonym. Here in Durkheim's discussion of friendship we have the "membership relation linking two levels of structure" that is labeled a "solidary tie" by Fararo and Doreian (1998). For Durkheim an important quality of this tie is its variable expression in concrete social forms; "it is not the same in the family and in political societies; we are not attached to our country in the same fashion as the Roman was to his city or the German to his tribe" (p. 66).

It follows for Durkheim that "the study of solidarity thus grows out of sociology" (p. 67). Durkheim felt that the economists, along with the "moralists and psychologists," had made little progress in the

scientific study of solidarity owing to their common analytical focus on
what he referred to with evident scorn as "independent individuals, the
zero of social life" (1893, p. 179 n. 12), and on the possible motivations
of such imaginary individuals to seek to be part of a group. Such
analysts thereby eliminated from the phenomenon "all that is peculiarly
social in order to retain only the psychological germ whence it
developed" (p. 67).[2]

What Durkheim has to contribute to a discussion of the mathematical formalization of the concept of solidarity, we argue, is not so much
the contents of his theory of solidarity and the division of labor, but
rather the envelope of important analytical concerns that he brought
to bear in his analysis. In addition to his admonition (already discussed) to begin with the social rather than with the individual, we will
focus on four types of concern that Durkheim elaborated: social
morphology, collective representation of the group, the strain between
individualizing and collective group tendencies, and implications of
solidarity for social exchange.

The first constellation of concerns, social morphology, pertains to
what we might today call the reduced-form, or ideal-typical representation of complex networks. In his Latin thesis, Durkheim traced his
interest in morphology to that of Montesquieu, who distinguished
types of societies "differ[ing] in the number, arrangement, and cohesion of their component parts.... Moreover, the structures of these
societies are not the same, nor are their members united by the same
ties" (Durkheim, 1892, pp. 26–27). Montesquieu had identified various
types of society, such as monarchy, aristocracy, and republic.
Durkheim pointed out (p. 32) that Montesquieu had distinguished
them and named them "not on the basis of division of labor or the
nature of their social ties, but solely according to the nature of their
sovereign authority." Durkheim criticized this as a failure to see "that
the essential is not the number of persons subject to the same
authority, but the number bound by some form of relationship"
(p. 38).[3] As to reduced-form representation, Durkheim observed for
example that in a republic the city-state appears to be "a kind of block
made up of homogeneous components, none superior to the others"
(p. 27). "Block" is a translation of the Latin word *molis* that Durkheim
used; this molar or "block-like" character of elementary social units is
just what Durkheim went on to call, in his French-language thesis,
"mechanical solidarity." Structures characterized by mechanical solidarity "are coherent, not in spite of their homogeneity, but because of
their homogeneity" (1893, p. 179).

If earlier and simpler forms of social life were in Durkheim's mind characterized by the mechanical solidary of homogeneous "blocks," then more complex and contemporary social structure required for Durkheim a representation that perhaps comes closer to the "block-models" of White and collaborators (White, 1992; Breiger, 1991), Burt (1992), and Faust and Wasserman (1992), which models emphasize ideal-typical relations among the units.[4] Today according to Durkheim the direct bond is the one of interdependence among the units; direct subsumption of the individual within a social group is attenuated (Alpert, 1941, p. 177). In modern societies each individual draws "a profound distinction between himself and society," hence "social solidarity cannot be the same" as in earlier times; today solidarity "results from the division of labor, which makes the citizen and the social orders dependent upon each other" (Durkheim, 1892, pp. 33–34). The unity of the social organism is "as great as the individuation of the parts is more marked," and "because of this analogy, we... call solidarity which is due to the division of labor, organic" (1893, p. 131).

Seemingly in an anticipation of Granovetter's (1973) thesis on the strength of ties that is no less than startling to a contemporary network analyst, Durkheim's theory about the transition from mechanical to organic solidarity rests on the weakness of the strong ties characteristic of mechanical solidarity. "What truly measures the relative force of two social ties is the unequal facility with which they break down" (1893, p. 148). Where solidarity rests on resemblances, breaks are more frequent and easier to bring about; members of nomadic clans simply abandon their chief when they find his authority too oppressive. In such societies the individual "contains within himself all that social life consists of," and so "he can go and carry it elsewhere." Therefore, "it may appear astonishing that a tie which binds the individual to the community by absorbing him into it can be broken or made with such facility. But what makes a social tie rigid is not what gives it resistive force" (p. 151). Under a regime of mechanical solidarity, precisely because social work is very little divided, society can lose a certain number of its members "without the economy of its internal life being disturbed," and so does not strongly oppose these departures (p. 151). The evolutionary argument is thus based on the assumption that "all social links which result from likeness progressively slacken" (p. 173) to the extent that "there are more individuals sufficiently in contact to be able to act and react upon one another." The phrase Durkheim proposes for this development is "dynamic or moral density" (p. 257), one cause for example being the concentration in space of disparate groups; Durkheim recognized that "the union of groups is also accompanied by interstitial growth" and multiplication of relations (p. 257). Thus, although according to common sense "the ties which result from the division of labor, while being more numerous, would be weaker than the others, ... the contrary is the truth" (p. 148).

A second major set of issues of Durkheim's that we believe is pertinent to the formulation of models of solidarity concerns emergent properties of groups and, in particular, collective representations that both issue from and regulate interaction within groups. Much of *The Division of Labor* is taken up in expounding the argument that each type of solidarity, mechanical and organic, is associated with the emergence of distinctive systems of legal rules – repressive and restitutive, respectively, in rough analogy to primitive criminal law in comparison to the law of contracts – which "impose uniform beliefs and practices upon all" (1893, p. 226).

Mechanical solidarity can be consistent with a "unilateral" structuring of authority, such as that of a father of a Roman family with his children (p. 180). Indeed, one of the most astute readers of Durkheim draws a connection between ritualized interactions and the emergence of a hierarchical or power dimension based on location with respect to "sacred objects" (Collins, 1988, p. 114). In contrast, even under a complex division of labor, society "does not become a jumble of juxtaposed atoms;" rather, the members are united by "ties which extend deeper and far beyond the short moments during which the exchange is made." In fact, "from the nature of the chosen task permanent duties arise" (1893, p. 227).

In all of the above-mentioned cases, the specific structuring of the group is responsible for the quality of emergent law, morality, and regulation. The emergent representation that the group comes to hold of itself "must be sought chiefly in the way in which the associated individuals are grouped" (quoted by Lukes, 1973, p. 231). Rules, habits and daily routines do not "create the state of mutual dependence in which solidary organs find themselves, but only express in clear-cut fashion the result of a given situation" (1893, p. 366). In a manner that again recalls Montesquieu, as Lukes points out, Durkheim stipulates that society is comprised not only of a material side but a "spirit," a soul, which is "nothing other than a complex of ideas" which transcend the individual and "come into being and sustain themselves only through the interaction of a plurality of associated individuals" (quoted by Lukes, p. 131). Thus does morphology lead to an emergent property: collectively held conceptions of the group, its stratification system, and its morality, especially insofar as the last-mentioned term refers to "attachment to social groups" (quoted by Lukes, p. 113).[5]

The third set of problems on which Durkheim focused and which we believe are productive for insight with regard to the formulation of models of solidarity concern strains between individualizing and collective group tendencies. In particular, in his essay on the dualism of human nature and its social conditions, Durkheim defines "duality" as "the double existence that we lead concurrently: the one purely individual and rooted in our organisms, the other social and nothing but an extension of society" (1914, p. 162; see also Breiger, 1990 on relations between Durkheim's conception of duality and that of his contemporary, Georg Simmel). The imbalances that lead to suicide pertain to disproportions in the ratio of strengths of collective versus individual forces. Too much society leads to insufficient development of individualism and, thus, to pathologies of altruism (such as the suicide of women upon the death of their husbands; here suicide is not a right but a duty). On the contrary, too little society leads to a conditions of normlessness and egoism that also render the problem of solidarity insoluble, giving rise to a person who is "a mystery to himself, unable to escape the exasperating and agonizing question: to what purpose?" (quoted by Lukes, p. 209).

In *The Division of Labor*, Durkheim defined "negative solidarity" as relations that link mere things (such as personal property) to persons, rather than persons to each other (1893, p. 116). Positive solidarity binds the individual to society directly, without any intermediary. Under regimes of mechanical solidarity, characterized by positive solidarity, "this solidarity can grow only in inverse ratio to personality" (p. 129). Regimes of organic solidarity in contrast call for the development of individual personalities, as the person depends upon others "in the same measure that he is distinguished from them, and consequently upon the society which results from their union" (p. 226). At issue here is the extent with which individuals are constrained to accept a common group life, and the corollary extent to which they can exercise their own decisions about the degree of their participation in a common collective life.

The fourth set of concerns that motivate our interest in formalizing Durkheim's ideas on solidarity pertain to social exchange. While Durkheimian, this emphasis on exchange was not a primary focus of his. Although Durkheim was not by any means an "exchange theorist," one of his notable intellectual descendants was. Lévi–Strauss likened mechanical solidarity to restricted exchange and organic solidarity to generalized exchange (though he subsequently backed away a bit from this analogy; see Ekeh, 1974, p. 61). Restricted exchange for Lévi-Strauss refers to "mutual reciprocities limited to two partners" (Ekeh, p. 50). Generalized exchange refers to reciprocities involving at least three actors. The difference is that "in generalized exchange no party gives to the party from whom he receives" (p. 50); thus, the two types of exchange differ qualitatively, not quantitatively. With respect to three persons, generalized exchange might operate as follows: $A \rightarrow B \rightarrow C \rightarrow A$, where "$\rightarrow$" signifies "gives to" (Ekeh, p. 50). However, a large number of close variants is possible (Ekeh, pp. 52–55).

Restricted social exchange relationships are "brittle in nature" (Ekeh, p. 52). With respect to the analysis we sketched above of Durkheim as a theorist of the weakness of strong ties, we may agree with Ekeh (p. 52) that a system of restricted exchange "is marked by mechanical solidarity." As a corollary, Ekeh (p. 74) observes that under a regime of organic solidarity integrative mechanisms are increasingly required to the extent that differentiation increases; thus he suggests "that ideally the growth of this differentiation is within a cultural matrix infused with a morality of generalized exchange."

Having identified four sets of problems that concern us in Durkheim's theory of solidarity, we will now consider specific models.

3. MODELS OF SOLIDARITY

Maintaining our focus on types of social exchange, we now turn our attention from the influential corpus of a classical French sociologist to a seminal publication of a contemporary French statistician. In 1965 in Toulouse, Henri Caussinus published an article on contingency tables in which the loglinear model of quasi-symmetry was the centerpiece. As to notation, with respect to a $g \times g$ table of counts, we will refer to an observed count in cell (i, j) as f_{ij}, and we will use F_{ij} to refer to the frequency in the same cell that is expected under some model. Under the model of symmetry, for all i and j, $F_{ij} = F_{ji}$. Among the ways Caussinus represented the model of quasi-symmetry was (in our notation)

$$\frac{F_{ij}}{F_{ji}} \frac{F_{jk}}{F_{kj}} \frac{F_{ki}}{F_{ik}} = 1 \qquad (1)$$

(Caussinus, 1965, p. 147; see also Breiger and Ennis, 1997). For any i and j, defining F_{i+} as the sum of row i and F_{ij}/F_{i+} as the conditional probability $pr(j|i)$, then (1) implies

$$pr(j|i)\,pr(k|j)\,pr(i|k) = pr(i|j)\,pr(k|i)\,pr(j|k). \tag{2}$$

In the extensive subsequent literature on quasi-symmetry, it is rare to see the model represented in either of these ways (Bishop, Fienberg and Holland, 1975, p. 287 provide one exception; see also footnote 8).

Now Caussinus certainly did not appear to consider himself a contributor to social exchange theory. Nonetheless, the implications of quasi-symmetry for generalized exchange are startlingly straightforward. Consider the $g \times g$ contingency table as expressing counts of interactions among group members. Under the model, all exchanges of the form $i \rightarrow j \rightarrow k \rightarrow i$ are equal in magnitude to flows in the opposite direction: $i \rightarrow k \rightarrow j \rightarrow i$. From this perspective, pure symmetry is a model of strong connections that are "brittle" (as in Ekeh, 1974, p. 52), while quasi-symmetry signifies a more robust and far-reaching interlocking of relations in the sense that the relevant flows in each triple of actors are directed "to" different people than they come "from."[6]

A principal motivation for the following discussion is that it is useful to provide new interpretations for existing statistical models, where possible, in order to harness their power for social network analysis and, in particular, for the study of social solidarity. Following the pathbreaking work of Sobel, Hout and Duncan (1985), whose principal concern was to provide a new interpretation for the model of quasi-symmetry in a substantive context – social mobility analysis – that is fairly distinct from the one that concerns us here, it has become customary to parameterize the quasi-symmetry model as follows:

$$F_{ij} = \alpha_j \beta_i \beta_j \delta_{ij}, \tag{3}$$

where $\prod_j \alpha_j = 1$, $\beta_i = \beta_j$ if $i = j$, $\delta_{ij} = \delta_{ji}$ if $i \neq j$, and $\delta_{ij} = 1$ if $i = j$. Maximum likelihood procedures for estimation of the parameters and expected frequencies under this loglinear model are well-known (Bishop, Fienberg and Holland, 1975; Goodman, 1984; Agresti, 1990; Clogg and Shihadeh, 1994). Notice that Eq. (3) implies (1), so this parameterization allows us to maintain our focus on generalized exchange. An advantage of the Sobel–Hout–Duncan parameterization is that it distinguishes the symmetric components of the model (pairwise symmetry, the δ_{ij}, and marginal homogeneity, the β_j) from the asymmetric components, the α_j, which pertain in our context to the difference in volume between ties sent and ties received by any actor.

With respect to a pair of actors, say i and j, we may consider the extent to which each actor is oriented toward the other rather than toward herself. For actor i, the odds are F_{ij}/F_{ii} that i chooses j rather than herself, and for actor j the odds are F_{ji}/F_{jj}. For both actors in this dyad, the average (geometric mean) of these odds is just δ_{ij}, as may be verified by substitution of Eq. (3); see also Sobel et al. (1985, p. 364):

$$\sqrt{\frac{F_{ij}}{F_{ii}}\frac{F_{ji}}{F_{jj}}} = \delta_{ij}$$

Each δ_{ij} is thus the average odds, estimated under the model, that actors i and j exchange with each other, rather than being self-sufficient. In the model of quasi-symmetry a possibly unique, symmetric δ parameter is required to be estimated for each pair of actors.

Our discussion of Durkheim's social morphology suggests that a more parsimonious version of quasi-symmetry may be formulated by identifying structured regions in a group's interaction table within which these pair-specific symmetries are equated. Suppose for example that, on *a priori* grounds, we have partitioned the set of g actors into B sets or "blocks," and that we apply this partition to both the rows and columns of the group interaction table of counts, such that the set of cells representing the interaction from actors in block k to those in block l is denoted B_{kl} (where k and l might index the same set). Then we may define the model of quasi-symmetry for "blocked" tables of counts of social interaction as Eq. (3) with the additional constraint that the symmetric δ_{ij} are constant for all cells $(i, j) \in B_{kl}$.

Until this point, we have discussed quasi-symmetry as a model of generalized exchange, and we have defined a more parsimonious version of quasi-symmetry that allows reduced-form ("blockmodel") representation of the interactional densities among pairs of actors. We now point out that quasi-symmetry, in both its usual and "blockmodel" versions, also implies the existence of an overarching hierarchy of actors that exists simultaneously with the pairwise patterning of ties and the possible presence of structured blocks of actors. For any actors i and j we may define the "excess" or "net" exchange from i to j as $R_{ij} = F_{ij}/F_{ji}$. (If i gives less to j than she receives, then the "net" exchange R_{ij} is less than unity.) Then under the model of quasi-symmetry Eq. (1) above may be rewritten as,

$$R_{ij}R_{jk} = R_{ik}$$

for any triples of actors i, j, k. Across all the actors in the group, there is a one-dimensional ordering with respect to "net" exchanges of the relationship in question. By substitution of Eq. (3) into the definition of R_{ij}, it is seen that $R_{ij} = \alpha_j/\alpha_i$, and the matrix $\mathbf{R}$ of size $g \times g$ whose typical entry is R_{ij} can be understood as composed of one dimension: $\mathbf{R} = \mathbf{uv}$ where $\mathbf{u}$ is a $g \times 1$ vector of entries $\langle 1/\alpha_1, \ldots, 1/\alpha_g \rangle$ and $\mathbf{v}$ is a $1 \times g$ vector of entries $\langle \alpha_1, \ldots, \alpha_g \rangle$.[7]

We think of the set of R_{ij} as analogous to an emergent "collective representation" of the group's hierarchy, in the following sense. If the model of quasi-symmetry fits the data, then in spite of whatever patterning the symmetric association takes among all the pairs of actors (as measured by the δ_{ij} parameters), the "net" magnitudes of exchange (the R_{ij}) form a one-dimensional hierarchy: the "net" exchange is precisely the ratio of the relative "strengths" (measured by the α_j parameters) of the two actors.[8] In a world governed by quasi-symmetry, it is as if all actors know, and universally agree upon, everyone's strength, including their own, so that the "net" exchanges among all pairs of actors depend on just g parameters, the α_j.

Because this single dimension composes the matrix $\mathbf{R}$ of net exchanges, the α_j are somewhat analogous to the economists' "structure of relative prices" that one contemporary theorist finds "very congenial to the structuralist approach" (Lindenberg, 1995, p. 85). Moreover, because the choice axiom of Luce (1959) provides a theoretical model of pairwise comparison processes that generates the hierarchy that is parameterized by our loglinear models (see footnote 8), it is incorrect of Skvoretz (1998) to assert that none is proposed. Indeed, this bridging of individual-level axiomatics and group properties – within a framework for empirical falsifiability of our claims – is a major feature exploited by our approach. More generally, we do not see why "theory" should be identified with individual-level processes, and on this point we recommend Markovsky's (1998) discussion of the "anthropocentrist trap."

One strategy that Lindenberg expounds for building bridges between structuralist and rational choice approaches is to develop "a theory of framing" to provide context for these "relative prices." We now turn to the articulation of some parameters that could well be relevant to the formulation and testing of such a theory.

The above feature of a collective representation of the group's hierarchical image, universally agreed upon, seems unduly rigid for many applications. In a manner that is at least loosely analogous to the formal model of self-location in a class system developed by Kosaka and Fararo (1991), we would like to incorporate our third theme from Durkheim, pertaining to the extent to which individuals are capable of differentiating themselves from totalistic adherence to the collective representation of the group's hierarchy. For this purpose we consider a skew-symmetry model, which is (Yamaguchi, 1990, Eq. (21)) a natural generalization of quasi-symmetry:

$$F_{ij} = \alpha_j \beta_i \beta_j \delta_{ij} \epsilon_{ij},\qquad(4)$$

subject to the constraints of (3) and, in addition, for $i > j$, that $\epsilon_{ij} = \epsilon_j$ and $\epsilon_{ji} = 1/\epsilon_j$; $\epsilon_{ij} = 1$ if $i = j$; $\prod_j \epsilon_j = 1$. Estimation of the ϵ_j requires $g - 2$ nonredundant parameters beyond those estimated for quasi-symmetry; model (4) therefore leaves $(g-2)(g-3)/2$ degrees of freedom. Unlike quasi-symmetry, skew-symmetry requires the postulation of an ordering of the social actors.

For the skew-symmetry model (4), the quantity $(F_{ij} F_{ji} / F_{ii} F_{jj})^{1/2}$ is equal to δ_{ij}, just as it is in the quasi-symmetry model; this is the average odds that each member of a pair chooses the other, rather than oneself (other orientation vs. self-sufficiency). And as with quasi-symmetry, the analyst may modify (4) by stipulating that blocks of the δ_{ij} have identical magnitudes, thus obtaining a "blockmodel" version of skew-symmetry. The difference between (4) and (3) that becomes substantive in our discussion concerns the image of the group's hierarchy. Continuing to define R_{ij} as F_{ij}/F_{ji}, the "net" exchange between the actors, under model (4) we have, for $i > j$,

$$R_{ij} = \frac{\alpha_j}{\alpha_i} \epsilon_{ij}^2$$

thus introducing a person-specific ability to warp (i.e., to place greater or lesser emphasis upon) the one-dimensional, universally understood strengths. In other words, the network of "net" exchanges under skew-symmetry model (4) is conceptualized as two-dimensional, requiring strengths (α_j) and scores on a second dimension (ϵ_j) for each actor.

Characterization of this second dimension is of interest. Under the skew-symmetry model (4) we have

$$R_{ij} R_{jk} = R_{ik} \epsilon_j^2$$

for $i > j > k$. So for indirect relations which are monotone with respect to ordering, the middleman j has an actor-specific ability, constant across all appropriate i and k, to affect the magnitude of the exchange. In that this ability is a property of the actor "between" any two others (though not in all other respects), it is analogous to the "betweenness" centrality of Freeman (1979; Freeman, Borgatti and White, 1991). We think of this parameter as indexing each actor's ability to thwart the group's hierarchy. At one extreme, an actor may be so committed to one part of the group that existence of a one-dimensional hierarchy is of little relevance to her. At the other extreme, an actor may bridge multiple segments of the group's morphological subdivisions, thus helping to interweave a network that confounds the hierarchy.

Markovsky (1998) criticizes us for not presenting "a metric for solidarity" as a means of quantifying approaches to or departures from such a state, and Skvoretz (1998) raises a similar concern. Therefore we state explicitly that the fit of our models may be assessed using standard maximum-likelihood and chi-square techniques, which do allow us to postulate a large family of substantive and relatively parsimonious models the fit of which to observed data may be assessed quantitatively (see also Breiger and Ennis, 1997). Following Durkheim's elaboration of a "sociological" approach to the study of solidarity, we reject perspectives which impose an assumption that solidarity is a scalar quantity. Nonetheless, we do exploit the available metric for assessing the degree of conformity of an observed structure to any of our models.

4. APPLICATIONS

Scholars who study decision-making in the U.S. Supreme Court have often relied on what Segal and Spaeth (1993) refer to as the legal model, which holds that Supreme Court decisions are based on the "plain meaning" of the Constitution, the intent of the framers, and precedent. Segal and Spaeth are among the leading researchers who investigate Supreme Court decision-making by use of an alternative framework, one which emphasizes the attitudes and values of the justices. We seek to study interagreement among Supreme Court justices as a network phenomenon amenable to analysis by the family of models that we have discussed. Our application is to a network of frequencies appearing as a table in Segal and Spaeth (1993, p. 280).

The data concern "special opinions" during the first four terms of the Rehnquist Court, 1986–1989. We include the eight justices who served continuously throughout this period, omitting two others: L. Powell and A. Kennedy.[9] The assignment of opinions by the chief justice to his associates is clearly a non-random process. For this and related reasons, Segal and Spaeth confine themselves to "special opinions," defined as those which no justice can be forced to join or prevented from joining. (One example is the writing of an opinion notwithstanding membership in the majority or plurality opinion coalition; a more elaborate, technical definition is given in Segal and Spaeth, 1993, pp. 276–79.) Segal and Spaeth (p. 279) argue that writing and joining of special opinions "bespeak an ability to persuade or convince another of the correctness of one's position...without the use of coercion, authority, or political control."

The data in Table 8.1 are to be understood as in the following example. Justice Marshall joined Brennan in 92 special opinions that Brennan wrote (cell [1, 2] in the first panel of Table 8.1 is 92) and did not join him in 21 others (cell [1, 2] in the second panel). The total number of opinions Brennan wrote is $92 + 21 = 113$, reported as the second entry in the right-most column of Table 8.1. The proportion of times that Marshall joined Brennan is therefore $92/(92 + 21) = 0.814$.

As a baseline model, we consider the elementary loglinear model that fits all two-way marginals of the $8 \times 8 \times 2$ array in Table 8.1, letting i refer to citing justice, j to cited justice, and k to citations given vs. not given. (Segal and Spaeth did not consider this network as a three-dimensional array, and therefore they did not control for the total number of opinions written by each justice, nor indeed did they consider application of loglinear models to their analytical concerns.)[10] Notation for this model, as well as test statistics, are reported in the first line of Table 8.2. In Table 8.2 the notation γ_{ij} refers to parameters necessary in order to insure that the sum of expected frequencies across the third dimension (indexed by k) exactly equals the corresponding sum of the observed frequencies, thus fitting the total number of opinions written by each justice. In addition to the degrees of freedom left by the model, the likelihood ratio chi-square (G^2), and the associated p-value, we report an alternative measure of model fit, the *bic* statistic of Raftery (1986), which is an effort to compensate for the overfitting that commonly results from extensive model search; large negative values of the *bic* statistic are to be preferred.

We can radically improve the fit of the baseline model at the expense of just one additional degree of freedom. Let us consider a partition of the eight justices, formulated *a priori*, into two blocks according to their typically understood ideological leanings as liberals (Marshall, Brennan, Stevens, Blackmun) or conservatives (O'Connor, White, Rehnquist, Scalia); see Simon (1995, pp. 14–16). We add one parameter to the baseline model, defined as follows and shown below with its

TABLE 8.1

Interagreement in Special Opinions, 1986–1989 terms (from Segal and Spaeth, 1993, p. 280)

	Frequency of opinion joining								Frequency of not joining								Number of opinions
Marshall	0	92	38	39	5	5	0	7	0	21	111	55	72	70	31	109	58
Brennan	46	0	33	40	6	6	0	6	12	0	116	54	71	69	31	110	113
Stevens	16	27	0	12	8	4	3	5	42	86	0	82	69	71	28	111	149
Blackmun	18	43	27	0	7	5	3	5	40	70	122	0	70	70	28	111	94
O'Connor	1	2	9	7	0	16	12	21	57	111	140	87	0	59	19	95	77
White	0	2	9	0	2	0	9	11	58	111	140	94	75	0	22	105	75
Rehnquist	0	0	8	1	19	22	0	24	58	113	141	93	58	53	0	92	31
Scalia	0	0	7	1	18	9	10	0	58	113	142	93	59	66	21	0	116

Special opinions are those in which no justice can be forced to, or prevented from, concurring or dissenting. Justices Powell and Kennedy are omitted as they did not serve throughout this period.

TABLE 8.2
Models Applied to Supreme Court Data of Table 1

Model	Parameterization	df	G^2	bic	p
All two-way effects	$F_{ij}=\alpha_{jk}\beta_{ik}\beta_{jk}\gamma_{ij}$	41	693.6	344	<0.001
Blockmodel Quasi-Symmetry (2 blocks)	$F_{ij}=\alpha_{jk}\beta_{ik}\beta_{jk}\gamma_{ij}\delta_{ij}$, $\delta_{ji}=\delta_{ij}=\delta_{qr}$ for $(i,j)\epsilon B_{qr}$	40	203.4	−137	<0.001
Quasi-Symmetry for 3 dimensions	$F_{ij}=\alpha_{jk}\beta_{ik}\beta_{jk}\gamma_{ij}\delta_{ij}$, $\delta_{ji}=\delta_{ij}$	21	33.8	−145	0.038
Skew-Symmetry for 3 dimensions	$F_{ij}=\alpha_{jk}\beta_{ik}\beta_{jk}\gamma_{ij}\delta_{ij}\epsilon_{ij}$, $\delta_{ji}=\delta_{ij}$ and $\epsilon_{ij}=\epsilon_j; \epsilon_{ji}=1/\epsilon_j$	15	19.1	−109	0.21

Blocks are (Marshall, Brennan, Stevens, Blackmun) vs. (O'Connor, White, Rehnquist, Scalia).

estimated value under maximum likelihood:

$$
\begin{bmatrix} \delta_{ij} & \dfrac{1}{\delta_{ij}} \\ \dfrac{1}{\delta_{ij}} & \delta_{ij} \end{bmatrix} = \begin{bmatrix} 2.942 & .3399 \\ .3399 & 2.942 \end{bmatrix}.
$$

Thus, all choices among the liberals, and all choices among the conservatives, are estimated to be 2.942 times the value they would have under the parameters of the baseline model, while all choices between these two groups are estimated to be only 1/2.942 as strong. Clearly this is a parsimonious version of quasi-symmetry (extended to the three-dimensional case) in which all symmetric interaction parameters are represented by a two-block blockmodel. As seen from a comparison of the first two lines of Table 8.2, this expenditure of one degree of freedom reduces the lack of fit by 71%($=1-203.4/693.6$), and the *bic* criterion suggests no evidence of overfitting.

Moving from the blockmodel (line 2 of Table 8.2) to a natural three-dimensional representation of quasi-symmetry (line 3 of Table 8.2) involves estimating a unique δ_{ij} parameter for each pair of cells. The degrees of freedom left by this model is 20 less than that left by the baseline model (one df less than the number of pairs among 8–1 justices), but the lack of fit is also greatly reduced, leading to the most favorable *bic* value among models considered here and to a conventional level of fit ($p=0.038$) that is perhaps marginally acceptable.

In order to push the logic of this family of models, we consider in the fourth line of Table 8.2 a three-dimensional representation of our skew-symmetry model. This model requires postulation of an ordering of the actors, and the ordering we report is one of several that we explored.[11] The model fits very well by conventional standards ($p = 0.21$). Estimates of parameters corresponding in the three-dimensional case to the δ parameters are reported in Table 8.3; similarly, estimates of the α and ϵ parameters are reported in Table 8.4.

The fine-grained patterning of the δ parameters in Table 8.3 is compatible with those estimated for the blockmodel (line 2 of Table 8.2) in the following sense. If we partition the justices in Table 8.3 into liberal and conservative blocks (the first four listed there vs. the last four), then the lowest δ_{ij} in the two submatrices reporting "within-group" propensities to join in opinions is 0.113, whereas the highest "between-group" propensity is only 0.080. In addition to this crucial cleavage within the structure of interactions that was captured with simplicity in the blockmodel of Table 8.2, however, more fine-grained detail is conveyed by the δ_{ij} of Table 8.3. For example, the liberals have a higher propensity to interact with one another than do the conservatives; in particular, the Brennan-Marshall tie is of extraordinary strength. This inward orientation of the liberals was during a period of apparent increasing conservative ascendancy (footnote 13; compare the nuanced account of Simon, 1995). The δ_{ij} also indicate that each of the conservatives has a higher propensity to join with Rehnquist than with anyone else, and this in spite of the formidable effort of Segal and Spaeth to eliminate from the dataset any special advantage accruing to the role of the chief justice.

Each of the entries in the 8×8 table **R** of net flows in Table 8.4 can be understood as the odds that a choice is made (rather than avoided)

TABLE 8.3
Estimated δ Parameters for Model of Skew-Symmetry (3 Dimensions)

Justice	$\delta^* = \{[(F_{ij1}F_{ji1})/(F_{ii1}F_{jj1})]/[(F_{ij2}F_{ji2})/(F_{ii2}F_{jj2})^1\}^{1/2}$							
Brennan	1.000	4.098	0.676	0.298	0.020	0.039	0.000	0.042
Marshall	4.098	1.000	0.571	0.344	0.024	0.026	0.000	0.035
Blackmun	0.676	0.571	1.000	0.190	0.019	0.024	0.034	0.079
Stevens	0.298	0.344	0.190	1.000	0.048	0.064	0.081	0.080
Scalia	0.020	0.024	0.019	0.048	1.000	0.120	0.381	0.254
White	0.039	0.026	0.024	0.064	0.120	1.000	0.369	0.113
Rehnquist	0.000	0.000	0.034	0.081	0.381	0.369	1.000	0.455
O'Connor	0.042	0.035	0.079	0.080	0.254	0.113	0.455	1.000

TABLE 8.4
Net Flows R^*, and Estimated α and ϵ Parameters, for model of skew-symmetry (3 dimensions)

Justice	$R^* = (F_{ij1}/F_{ji1})/(F_{ij2}/F_{ji2})$								Justice	α^*_j	Justice	ϵ^2_j
Brennan	1.000	0.875	1.267	0.971	5.424	4.924	8.624	3.434	Rehnquist	3.136	Stevens	3.972
Marshall	1.143	1.000	1.462	1.120	6.258	5.682	9.950	3.962	Scalia	1.973	White	2.864
Blackmun	0.789	0.684	1.000	1.070	5.977	5.427	9.504	3.785	White	1.791	O'Connor	1.000
Stevens	1.030	0.893	0.934	1.000	1.406	1.277	2.236	0.890	Brennan	1.396	Marshall	0.991
Scalia	0.184	0.160	0.167	0.711	1.000	1.467	2.569	1.023	O'Connor	1.249	Rehnquist	0.768
White	0.203	0.176	0.184	0.783	0.682	1.000	0.611	0.243	Blackmun	0.461	Blackmun	0.716
Rehnquist	0.116	0.101	0.105	0.447	0.389	1.636	1.000	0.519	Stevens	0.353	Scalia	0.619
O'Connor	0.291	0.252	0.264	1.123	0.978	4.108	1.928	1.000	Marshall	0.318	Brennan	0.261

$\alpha^*_j = (\alpha_{j1}/\alpha_{i1})/(\alpha_{j2}/\alpha_{i2})$.

from actor i to j, in ratio to the odds that it is made (rather than avoided) in the opposite direction. This matrix of "net intensity" of flows is, according to the skew-symmetry model, capable of decomposition into two dimensions: an overall "strength" of each justice (the aj) and the extent to which each justice mediates flows among others in a sense roughly analogous to Freeman's "betweenness" (the ϵ_j parameters). Consider the "net intensity" of the tie from O'Connor (i) to Scalia (k). This value, 0.978 from matrix **R** in Table 8.4, is equal to $(1.973/1.249) (0.619) = (\alpha_k/\alpha_i)(\epsilon_k)$; see the right-hand side of Table 8.4. Consider also the extent to which the net exchange from O'Connor to Scalia is mediated through Byron White (j). This is the value of the net exchange from O'Connor to White ($R_{ij} = 4.108$) times that from White to Scalia ($R_{jk} = 0.682$) times the extent to which Byron White affects the flow ($1/2.864 = 1/\epsilon_j$), which is also equal to 0.978 ($= R_{ik}$). Moreover, according to the model Byron White affects the flow between any two actors to exactly the same extent, $1/\epsilon_j$.

We substantively interpret the dimensional parameters in Table 8.4 as follows. First, the "strengths" (α_j) make a good deal of sense. Rehnquist, the chief justice, emerges with the highest score, a finding which perhaps calls into question the ease with which even a dataset confined to "special opinions" can be successful in eliminating the influence of the "first among equals." The next four highest "strengths" include the other conservatives on the court plus Brennan, who is described as the leader of the liberal wing (Simon, 1995, p. 14).

The skew-symmetry parameters estimated in Table 8.4 are of particular interest. The two lowest ϵ_j scores are for the two most ideological justices: Brennan, the leader of the liberal wing, and Scalia, the Court's most aggressive conservative. At the other end of this pole, the highest ϵ_j are those of Stevens, White, and O'Connor, all of whom could well be argued to be "swing" voters. For example, Stevens is often characterized as a liberal but has "confounded a media eager to place the justices into neatly defined categories" (Simon, 1995, p. 15); Stevens joined the conservatives in opposing a right for protesters to burn the flag, and he was described by Blackmun as "a maverick, imaginative."[12] As to Byron White and O'Connor, one or more of these conservatives voted with the liberals in all three of the 22 cases in which the liberals voted as a block and prevailed during the term ending in June 1989.[13]

With reference to our third theme from Durkheim, we would say that departures from the one-dimensional set of strengths governing net exchanges under quasi-symmetry are due to two extremes that are identified by the "second" dimension that appears in the estimated parameters from skew symmetry: on the one hand extreme commitment to a subgroup (as in the cases of Scalia and Brennan), and on the other hand extreme commitment to individual courses of action (as in the case of the "swing" voters among the justices).

5. CONCLUSION

We have used social network thinking to create a family of models that build directly on the work of Durkheim. Our concern is focused on the morphology of social association and the collective representation of group hierarchy. We model solidarity as part of the emergence of morality through generalized exchange in social collectivities.

All four of the foci identified in Durkheim's treatment of solidarity were seen to be applicable to the modeling framework that was brought to bear in analyzing interagreement among Supreme Court justices. Detailed pairwise relationships were largely captured in a simplified macro-structure. These pair-specific symmetric exchanges were fully compatible with a hierarchical set of "strengths" that is universal in the quasi-symmetry model in the sense that "net" exchanges are functions of ratios of strengths of the actors (one dimension). In the skew-symmetry model, "net" exchanges are two-dimensional, the second dimension pertaining to ideological commitments to the group or to a segment of the group (at one extreme) and to the ability to weave coalitions together, making or breaking them (at the other extreme).

It seems remarkable that such different notions of structure – a detailed patterning of symmetric interpersonal interaction within the group, possibly represented by a much simpler blockmodel image, but also a rigid hierarchy of "net" exchange captured by one dimension (quasi-symmetry) or two (skew-symmetry) – can coexist within the same social group, and indeed within the same model of that group. And yet, it may be argued that a major result of network analysis is the recognition of a potential multiplicity of equivalences that can be mobilized so as to complement each other in analyzing social structure (Doreian, 1988). In the context of social mobility studies, analysts have recognized the different forms of structuring that are captured in quasi-symmetry ("exchange" and "structure," in the terminology of Sobel et al., 1985) and in skew-symmetry (Yamaguchi, 1990). In this paper we have developed a parallel interpretive framework for making feasible the application of these models to the study of solidarity in social networks that arise in the form of frequency data. It will continue to be important, in further work that brings together concerns of loglinear modelers and network analysts, to be aware of different organizing principles such as those identified here, and to capture various organizing principles within the same model or family of models.

NOTES

1. Skvoretz (1998) criticizes us for giving no indication of how "the group's level of solidarity shapes... patterns and structures" of group interaction, but he provides no justification for his implicit assumption that solidarity is a scalar quantity. In viewing solidarity as morphological, we follow the theoretical analysis of Durkheim. In that each of our models (Table 2) provides an ideal-type image of group structure, these models bear interesting relations to the "referent networks" sought by Markovsky (1998). We also provide a statistical context for relating observed network data to referent network imagery.

2. Lindenberg (1995, pp. 84–85) faults both the early Durkheim and contemporary structural analysts for "this innocence with regard to a theory of action." Similar epithets are hurled in the opposite direction (see the chapter on "Rhetoric and Theory" in White, 1992, pp. 287–316). Both camps are sites of important analytical insights and models, and the distance between them is occasionally exaggerated. Indeed, as we briefly mention in Section 3 of this paper, the modeling framework that we articulate can be developed as yet another bridge between rational choice and structuralist analyses.

3. More recently, Frey (1960) has advocated so-called "objective" definitions of democratic, autocratic, and laissez-faire structures, based on the mathematics of graph theory. Application of Frey's idealized models to real data of any size would prove impractical, however, due to the small likelihood that any actual group would conform precisely to any of them. See Breiger (1991, pp. 98–175) for a blockmodel approach to analysis of governance structures.

4. Just as a blockmodel presupposes homogeneous blocks and then describes their interrelations, so Ralph Turner has argued that organic solidarity does not replace, but "requires, in addition to the division of labor, an effective substratum of mechanical solidarity" (quoted in Ekeh, 1974, p. 66).

5. The points at issue in the on-going debate between culturalist interpreters of Durkheim (see the collection edited by Alexander, 1988) and structuralists (seemingly at times everyone else) are, first, the extent to which the emergent culture of representations becomes autonomous from the social structure, and, second, the extent to which there was a great divide between Durkheim's own early and later writings on this topic. We are persuaded, however, by Collins' argument that the ingredients of Durkheim's theory of solidarity are in all his major works, early and late, and that, in its entirety, Durkheim's corpus challenges us to elaborate "principles of how different degrees and conditions of structural density of interaction result in degrees of 'moral density' and hence in different kinds of symbolic and emotional consciousness of the group" (Collins, 1988, pp. 110–11).

6. Extensions of generalized exchange to models for exchanges among quartets (or more) of actors are implied by models of skew-symmetry such as the one discussed later in this section; see also Bishop et al. (1975, p. 291).

7. Moreover, with respect to inner-product matrix multiplication used to compute powers, the matrix $\mathbf{R}^k = \mathbf{u}g^{k-1}\mathbf{v}$.

8. This discussion of R_{ij} is somewhat analogous to related formulations. Luce (1959) brings concepts of strong and weak stochastic transitivity to bear in elucidating implications of the choice axiom for the scaling of preferences. Theorem 2 in Luce (1959, pp. 16–17) concerns symmetry of intransitivity among triples of choices and is similar to the focus of our Eqs. (1) and (2) on symmetry among triples of actors. The Luce model implies a linear preference model in the logit scale (Fienberg and Larntz, 1976, p. 248), and aspects of Luce's model, as well as the Bradley–Terry model for paired comparison experiments, have been formulated in terms of the quasi-symmetry model by Fienberg and Larntz (see also discussions in Agresti, 1990, pp. 370–74, and in Roberts, 1990, pp. 85–86). In a very different substantive context, in their discussion of "structural mobility" Sobel et al. (1985) also imply the one-dimensionality upon which we focus with respect to the network of the R_{ij}.

9. We have performed analyses similar to those reported below on data for all ten justices (including Powell and Kennedy); the results for the eight justices included here are very similar. We confine ourselves here to the eight justices present throughout the observation period in order to insure that all justices we include have the same chance to join one another in opinions.

10. Representation of a square, $g \times g$ network of counts by means of a three-dimensional, $g \times g \times 2$ array (where the third dimension indexes ties given versus ties withheld) is formally analogous to the problem of modeling blockmodel densities that was first considered with respect to loglinear models by Marsden (1989), whose model (9) is identical to our baseline. This topic is further considered in Breiger and Ennis (1997).

11. The ordering we imposed is {Brennan, Marshall, Blackmun, Stevens, Scalia, White, Rehnquist, O'Connor}. The first four would be conventionally labeled "liberal" and the second four as "conservative." In this sense the ordering is a more fine-grained version of the two-block model of line 2 of Table 8.2.

12. *New York Times* of June 22, 1989 and July 18, 1988, respectively.

13. Linda Greenhouse, "News analysis: The year the court turned right," *New York Times*, July 7, 1989.

REFERENCES

Agresti, A. 1990. *Categorical Data Analysis*. New York: John Wiley.

Alexander, J.C., ed. 1988. *Durkheimian Sociology: Cultural Studies*. Cambridge: Cambridge University Press.

Alpert, H. 1941. "Emile Durkheim and the Theory of Social Integration." *Journal of Philosophy* **6**: 172–184.

Bishop, Y.M.M., Fienberg, S.E. and Holland, P.W. 1975. *Discrete Multivariate Analysis: Theory and Practice*. Cambridge, MA: MIT Press.

Breiger, R.L. 1990. "Social control and social networks: a model from Georg Simmel" pp. 453–476 in C. Calhoun, M.W. Meyer and W.R. Scott (eds.), *Structures of Power and Constraint: Papers in Honor of Peter M. Blau*. Cambridge: Cambridge University Press.

Breiger, R.L. 1991. *Explorations in Structural Analysis: Dual and Multiple Networks of Social Interaction*. New York: Garland.

Breiger, R.L. and Ennis, J.G. 1997. "Generalized Exchange in Social Networks: Statistics and Structure." *L'Année sociologique* **47**(1): 73–88.

Burt, R.S. 1992. *Structural Holes: The Social Structure of Competition*. Cambridge, MA: Harvard University Press.

Caussinus, H. 1965. "Contribution à l'analyse statistique des tableaux de corrélation." *Anales de la Faculté des sciences de l'Université de Toulouse* **29**: 77–182.

Clogg, C.C. and Shihadeh, E.S. 1994. *Statistical Models for Ordinal Variables*. Thousand Oaks, CA: Sage.

Collins, R. 1988. "The Durkheimian tradition in conflict sociology." pp. 107–128 in J.C. Alexander, ed. (1988).

Collins, R. 1994. *Four Sociological Traditions*. New York: Oxford.

Doreian, P. 1988. "Equivalence in a Social Network." *Journal of Mathematical Sociology* 13: 243–282.

Durkheim, E. [1892] 1965. *Montesquieu and Rousseau: Forerunners of sociology*, tr. A. Cuvillier. Ann Arbor, MI: University of Michigan Press.

Durkheim, E. [1893] 1964. *The Division of Labor in Society*, tr. G. Simpson. New York: Free Press.

Durkheim, E. [1914] 1973. "The dualism of human nature and its social conditions," tr. C. Blend, pp. 149–163 in R.N. Bellah (ed.), *Emile Durkheim on Morality and Society*. Chicago: University of Chicago Press.

Ekeh, P. 1974. *Social Exchange Theory: The Two Traditions*. Cambridge, MA: Harvard University Press.

Fararo, T.J. and Doreian, P. 1998. "The theory of solidarity: An agenda of problems." Chapter 1 in P. Doreian and T.J. Fararo (eds.), *The Problem of Solidarity: Theories and Models*. (This volume)

Faust, K. and Wasserman, S. 1992. "Blockmodels: Interpretation and evaluation." *Social Networks* 14: 5–61.

Fienberg, S.E. and Larntz, K. 1976. "Loglinear representation for paired and multiple comparisons models." *Biometrika* 63: 245–254.

Freeman, L.C. 1979. "Centrality in social networks: I. Conceptual clarification." *Social Networks* 1: 215–239.

Freeman, L.C., Borgatti, S.P. and White, D.R. 1991. "Centrality in valued graphs: A measure of betweenness based on network flow." *Social Networks* 13: 141–154.

Frey, L. 1960. "La démocratie objectivement défini." *Revue française de science politique* 10: 66–82.

Goodman, L.A. 1984. *The Analysis of Cross-Classified Data Having Ordered Categories*. Cambridge, MA: Harvard University Press.

Goodman, L.A. 1985. "The analysis of cross-classified data having ordered and/or unordered categories: Association models, correlation models, and asymmetry models for contingency tables with or without missing entries." *Annals of Statistics* 13: 10–69.

Granovetter, M.S. 1973. "The strength of weak ties." *American Journal of Sociology* 78: 1360–1380.

Kosaka, K. and Fararo, T.J. 1991. "Self-location in a class system: A formal theoretical analysis." pp. 29–66 in E.J. Lawler, B. Markovsky, C. Ridgeway and H.A. Walker (eds.), *Advances in Group Processes: A Research Annual* 8, Greenwich, CT, JAI Press.

LaCapra, D. 1985. *Emile Durkheim: Sociologist and Philosopher*. Chicago: University of Chicago Press.

Lindenberg, S. 1995. "Comment: Complex constraint modeling (Ccm): a bridge between rational choice and structuralism." *Journal of Institutional and Theoretical Economics* 15: 80–88.

Luce, R.D. 1959. *Individual Choice Behavior: A Theoretical Analysis*. New York: Wiley.

Lukes, S. 1973. *Émile Durkheim, His Life and Work: A Historical and Critical Study*. Hammondsworth, England: Penguin Books.

Markovsky, B. 1998. "Social Network Conceptions of Group Solidarity." Chapter 11 in P. Doreian and T.J. Fararo (eds.), *The Problem of Solidarity: Theories and Models*. (This volume)

Marsden, P.M. 1989. "Methods for the Characterization of Role Structures in Network Analysis," pp. 489–530 in L.C. Freeman, D.R. White and A.K. Romney (eds.), *Research Methods in Social Network Analysis*. Fairfax, VA: George Mason University Press.

Raftery, A.E. 1986. "Choosing a model for cross-classifications." *American Sociological Review* 51: 139–141.

Roberts, Jr., J.M. 1990. "Modeling hierarchy: Transitivity and the linear ordering problem." *Journal of Mathematical Sociology* **16**: 77–87.

Segal, J.A. and Spaeth, H.J. 1993. *The Supreme Court and the Attitudinal Model*. New York: Cambridge University Press.

Simon, J.F. 1995. *The Center Holds: The Power Struggle Inside the Rehnquist Court*. New York: Simon and Schuster.

Skvoretz, J. 1998. "Solidarity, social structure, and social control." Chapter 12 in P. Doreian and T.J. Fararo (eds.), *The Problem of Solidarity: Theories and Models*. (This volume)

Sobel, M.E., Hout, M. and Duncan, O.D. 1985. "Exchange, structure, and symmetry in occupational mobility." *American Journal of Sociology* **91**: 359–372.

White, H.C. 1992. *Identity and Control: A Structural Theory of Social Action*. Princeton, NJ: Princeton University Press.

Yamaguchi, K. 1990. "Some models for the analysis of asymmetric association in square contingency tables with ordered categories," pp. 181–212 in C.C. Clogg (ed.), *Sociological Methodology* 1990. Washington, DC: American Sociological Association.

9 STRUCTURES AND PROCESSES OF SOLIDARITY: AN INITIAL FORMALIZATION

EUGENE C. JOHNSEN

University of California, Santa Barbara

1. SOLIDARITY AND ITS CHARACTERISTICS

In the study of social phenomena the idea of "solidarity" has been invoked or applied in a variety of situations and contexts. These include communes (Abrams and McCulloch, 1976), the welfare state (Baldwin, 1990), interaction ritual chains (Collins, 1981; 1994), clans and lineages (Fortes, 1945), group obligations and members' compliance with obligations (Hechter, 1987), communities (Loewy, 1993), governance and management of common-pool-resources (Ostrom, 1990), unity of the poor with the Church in Central America (Sobrino and Pico, 1985), positive and negative interpersonal involvement (Tamney, 1975), the opposite of estrangement (Torrance, 1977) and initiation ceremonies as dramatization of status transitions (Young, 1965). Probably the best known articulation of the idea of solidarity was given by Durkheim (1888), who classified this concept into the two types of "mechanical" and "organic" solidarity.

It is curious that in the social science reference literature the key words "solidarity", "group solidarity", "social solidarity" or "solidarism" are not always defined. For example, of the following ten reference works: Abercrombie et al. (1994), Bardis (1985), Borgatta and Borgatta (1992), Boudon and Bourricaud (1989), Jary and Jary (1991), Johnson (1995), Mann (1984), Marshall (1994), Mitchell (1979), and Stang and Wrightsman (1981), in which one would expect to find a definition of at least one of these key word combinations,

(i) four define at least one of these combinations,

(ii) two give no definition for any of these combinations, although they do refer to at least one combination in other definitions, and

(iii) four give no definition for any of these combinations, nor do they refer to any of them in other definitions.

However, various characteristics or properties of solidarity, well known to sociologists, can be gleaned from these references and placed into a reasonably coherent conceptual scheme:

(a) *common attitudes of individuals* – shared interests, purposes, norms, beliefs, values, experiences, needs, culture, feeling of support and identification with social system,

(b) *common attributes of individuals* – likeness, similarity, the inverse of independence and personality,

(c) *common relations between individuals* – cohesion, integration, direct mutual relations, kinship,

(d) *common prescribed behaviors of individuals* – cooperation, mutual aid and participation, exchange, shared responsibilities, integrative ritual,

(e) *common proscribed behaviors of individuals* – non-cooperation, behavior requiring restraint by external authority, repressive law and punishment,

(f) *collective attitudes of the group* – collective conscience,

(g) *collective attributes of the group* – strength and resistance, unity of the group,

(h) *collective behaviors of the group* – complementarities, division of labor, collectivism.

It should be mentioned that the concept of "cohesion" has sometimes been identified or confused with that of "solidarity". For example, Johnson (1995) identifies "solidarity" with "cohesion". In the process of restating a collection of sociological and social psychological propositions from the literature, Davis (1963) derives propositions which link mechanical solidarity with affective cohesion, and in the review of various investigations by Cartwright (1968) it is evident that cohesion has several salient properties and characteristics in common with solidarity. Here we shall distinguish these two concepts by positing cohesion as an important component of solidarity.

We begin by taking the above scheme as propaedeutical, subject to more precise formalization, axiomatization and theory development. Here we shall focus on the solidarity characteristics which fall under (a) and (c). Those which fall under (b) can be viewed as equivalence relations, each of which partitions the group into attribute classes. Whether they are taken as relations in their own right or whether combined with other relations in the group the result is a set of common relations between individuals of the group, which allows this category to be subsumed formally under (c). Although we will not be directly concerned here with (d) and (e) we will show toward the end of the paper how the small schema involving (a) and (c) (and (b)) may be embedded in a larger schema which also involves (d) and (e). Finally, what is developed here will encroach on the characteristics of solidarity under (f)–(h); however, the latter should be viewed as macrolevel characteristics emerging from those under (a)–(e), which very likely will require an expansion of the analysis.

Here, then, we shall take as a standard feature in our conceptualization of *(social) solidarity* or *solidarism*, the presence of a set $\mathscr{I}$ of one or more important issues, ideals, goals, beliefs, principles, interests, needs, values or special persons which are present in the thoughts and discourse of a group of persons G, to which some members G^+ adhere or are committed, certain others G^- are opposed, and all others G^0 are neutral or indifferent (cf. Marshall, 1994, p. 503; Stang and Wrightsman, 1981, p. 86; Fararo and Doreian, 1998). This is a rather simplified description. Examples include (i) G = world population, $\mathscr{I}$ = {Catholic beliefs and practices, the Pope}, G^+ = Catholics, G^- = anti-Catholics, G^0 = all others; (ii) G = U.S. adult population, $\mathscr{I}$ = {the right that a pregnant woman may choose an abortion in the case of incest, rape or threat to the life of the mother}, G^+, G^-, G^0 = U.S. adults who support, oppose, and are neutral or indifferent to this right, respectively; and (iii) G = California state residents, $\mathscr{I}$ = {policy of affirmative action in making admissions to the University of California}, G^+, G^-, G^0 = California state residents who favor, oppose, and are neutral or indifferent to this policy, respectively.

As discussed by Fararo and Doreian (1998) the commitments to $\mathscr{I}$ by the individual members of G^+ may serve as ties which indirectly bind the members of G^+ to each other. This subgroup's cohesiveness may be further increased by the interpersonal ties of liking, esteem, trust, etc., and decreased by the interpersonal ties of hate, disliking, distrust, etc., which develop between the members of G^+. Likewise, the opposition to $\mathscr{I}$ by the members of G^- and the interpersonal ties of liking, etc., and hate, etc., may have analogous structural effects within G^-. If members of G^- strongly and actively dislike $\mathscr{I}$ this is tantamount to hostility or opposition, which indirectly can bind the members of G^- to each other. If the members of G^0 are earnestly neutral a similar bonding might occur within G^0, but we would not expect such an effect if their orientation to $\mathscr{I}$ is indifference. This small schema, consisting of a set $\mathscr{I}$, a partitioned group or population $G = G^+ \cup G^- \cup G^0$, the adherence or commitment relation $S(G^+) = +$, which links the members of G^+ favorably to $\mathscr{I}$, the opposition relation $S(G^-) = -$, which links the members of G^- adversely to $\mathscr{I}$, and the neutral or indifference relation $S(G^0) = 0$, which links the members of G^0 neutrally or indifferently to $\mathscr{I}$, will be the focus of our study of solidarity here. This schema is, of course, an idealization and simplification. In a real-world situation the members of G may possess a variety of attitudes and attitude levels towards $\mathscr{I}$ so that membership in the set G^+ will depend on both the particular combinations of attitudes of support for $\mathscr{I}$ and the intensities of these attitudes.

As is readily apparent from the above, the concept of "solidarity" presents a complex of features. Those under (f)–(h) lead to the important sociological problem of integrating structure (form) and process (agency) at the microlevel so that empirically observed structural forms and processes emerge and change at the macrolevel (cf. discussion by Fararo and Doreian, 1998). For example, in discussing E-State Structuralism Fararo and Doreian sum up by stating

> "Thus, structural form is endogenous, dynamic, emergent. Process is stochastic, involves actors in interaction and the consequences of their encounters in terms of change of state of the system of interaction."

Later, and more generally, they state

> "Let us agree that whatever else a group is, some sort of social structure is involved... In a sense, what is problematic is the very 'groupness' of the group itself... There may be a generic process involved here, one that builds a sense of common membership and 'lifts' the network of interactions to what is, for the actors, a higher-order social entity... The network N of interactions generating a structural form of relations among the actors also generates a conception of N as an entity, this conception linked to some symbolization (cognitive element) and this entity is the object of some sort of sentiment (a moral-affective synthesis). The 'group' that emerges is *both* a social entity constituted by the cognitive-affective nexus focussed on it but, for the actors, transcending them as individuals. When actions are taken in the name of the collectivity... the group is an emergent actor in a wider system of action. Exactly how this generic process works is the theoretical problem."

To begin, we shall assume that the *solidarity* of a group G^+, which is always relative to a set $\mathscr{I}$, reflects what we would informally call the "robustness of existence" of the $[G^+, \mathscr{I}]$ combination and is functionally related to the survivability of G^+ and its capability for collective action. To say that G^+ has high or low solidarity is to say that it has high or low resistance, respectively, to the social forces internal and external to itself which threaten either the dissolution or fragmentation of the $[G^+, \mathscr{I}]$ combination or its capability for collective action. The internal forces may be the results of disagreements between individual members of G^+ over new values being proposed for inclusion in $\mathscr{I}$ or over old values being pressed for removal from $\mathscr{I}$. The external forces may be the results of disagreements between members of G^+ and G^- over issues in $\mathscr{I}$ or disagreements between members of G^+ and $G^- \cup G^0$ over new values, goals, etc., gaining inclusion in $\mathscr{I}$. The susceptibility of $[G^+, \mathscr{I}]$ to fragmentation or dissolution or to failure to preserve certain beliefs, values, goals, special persons, etc., may be due either to the inability of a weakly cohesive internal structure of G^+ to withstand these forces or to the ability of a strongly cohesive internal structure of G^- or a strongly hostile intergroup tie structure between G^+ and G^- to support these forces. Briefly, high solidarity of a group G^+ corresponds to a strong positive orientation of the members of G^+ towards $\mathscr{I}$ together with a highly cohesive set of positive interpersonal ties within G^+ with respect to which G^+ is highly invulnerable to the dissolution or fragmentation of the structure or the failure to preserve the beliefs, values, goals, special persons, etc. of G^+ by forces internal or external to G^+. Although they are clearly relevant to the existence (and hence solidarity) of G^+, G^0 and G^-, we shall not consider the effects of external physical forces such as natural or man-made disasters. The exclusion of such external forces from consideration will be a scope condition of our development here. Before proceeding further with this development we will need to introduce some formal background concerned with these issues.

2. PRELIMINARIES AND PREVIOUS WORK

Let the total group or population of individuals under consideration at a given time t be represented by $G = \{a_1, a_2, \ldots, a_k, \ldots, a_n\}$ and let G have a three-valued relation R, where each ordered pair (u, v) in $G \times G, u \neq v$, is labeled either $+$, $-$ or 0, written $R(u, v) = +, R(u, v) = -$ or $R(u, v) = 0$, and drawn as a $+$, $-$ or 0 labeled arrow from u to v, respectively. If $R(u, v) = +$ and $R(v, u) = +$ then u and v are *positively* or *mutually* related (connected, linked), which we denote by uMv. If $R(u, v) = -$ and $R(v, u) = -$ they are *negatively* related and we write uNv, and if $R(u, v) = 0$ and $R(v, u) = 0$ they are *null* related and we write uOv. If $R(u, v) = +$ and $R(v, u) = -$, $R(u, v) = +$ and $R(v, u) = 0$, or

$R(u, v) = -$ and $R(v, u) = 0$ then u is *asymmetrically* related to v in one of three different ways, written uAv, uPv and uQv, respectively. Note that if uMv then vMu, if uNv then vNu and if uOv then vOu, but if uAv, uPv or uQv then we do not have vAu, vPu or vQu, respectively. Thus M, N and O are symmetric relations (connections, links, ties) and A, P and Q are asymmetric relations between distinct members of G. We can extend M, N, O, A, P and Q to full relations on G by taking as a convention, for example, that uMu, uAu and uPu, but not uNu, uQu or uOu, for all u in G. This makes M, A and P, but not N, Q and O, reflexive on G as well.

Now, on a set of three different but unlabeled members from G there are 138 different (nonisomorphic) triadic combinations of M, A, N, P, Q and O dyads between the three pairs of members from the set. Each combination is a *triad type* expressed as an ordered sextuple of non-negative integers, $m:a:n:p:q:o$, where m, a, n, p, q, and o are, respectively, the numbers of M, A, N, P, Q and O dyads in the triad and $m + a + n + p + q + o = 3$, together with a special letter C^w, D^x, T^y or U^z denoting the various types of "cyclic", "down", "transitive", or "up" in the orientations of its dyads. The set Ψ of the 138 different triad types based on these six dyad types is not given here. With a different notation they are shown (with a few minor errors) in Kishida (1990, Figure 4.2.1).

If we collapse the two values $-$ and 0 to the single value $-$ then these 138 triad types reduce to the familiar set of 16 different triad types, Θ, based on the symmetric dyads M and N and asymmetric dyad A, of the form $m:a:n$, where $m + a + n = 3$, together with the special letters C, D, T or U, given in Figure 9.1 (Holland and Leinhardt, 1970; 1971; Johnsen, 1985; 1986; 1989a,b). By identifying $-$ and 0 we no longer distinguish negative and null relations; they are considered to be the same.

With repect to each of the sets Ψ and Θ a group macrostructure model X can be described either in terms of the subset P_X of all triad types which appear in the structure, or in terms of the complementary subset $P_{X^c} \equiv (P_X)^c = \Psi - P_X$ or $\Theta - P_X$ of all triads which do not. For an arbitrary subset P_X it may not be possible to exhibit all of the triads of P_X and none of those in P_{X^c} in a single general macrostructure. When it is possible, however, the macrostructure is called an *exact macrostructure* corresponding to P_X and P_{X^c} and to any corresponding microprocess which generates it, and we say that P_X or P_{X^c} is a *(triadic) micromodel*. For example, with respect to Θ, $P_X = \{300, 003\}$ cannot produce a macrostructure exhibiting both triads 300 and 003 but no others simultaneously, and is hence not a micromodel. The set

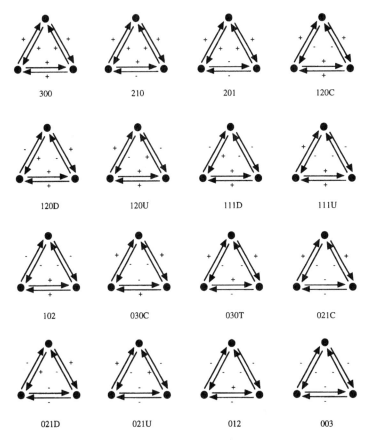

FIGURE 9.1   The sixteen triad types.

of all exact macrostructures corresponding to a micromodel P_X is called the *macromodel* for P_X.

The following examples present generic exact macrostructures for seven triadic micromodels from the set Θ. These will appear again in our examination of the agreement–friendship processes postulated for solidarity. The latter five are the principal micromodels for affect derived from the Davis–Leinhardt set of 742 empirical sociomatrices (Davis, 1970; Johnsen, 1985) and are expected to play a role in the interpersonal structuring of the groups of sufficiently small size involved in a solidarity structure. Diagrams of the corresponding macrostructures can be found in Johnsen (1985; 1986; 1989a,b).

Example 2.1 $P_{BA} = \{300, 102\}$. Here the A relation does not appear and the M and N connections can be viewed as single undirected signed links. The resulting macrostructure from the complete *balance* model BA of Cartwright and Harary (1956), who formalize sociologically most aspects of Heider's psychological model of balance (Heider, 1946), consists of two M-cliques (maximal subsets of members, pairwise connected by the M relation) which are related by N^* (i.e., completely interconnected by the N relation).

Example 2.2 $P_{CL} = \{300, 102, 003\}$. As in Example 2.1 we view the M and N connections as single undirected signed edges. The resulting macrostructure, from the complete *clustering* model CL of Davis (1967), consists of three or more M-cliques which are pairwise related by N^*.

Example 2.3 $P_{RC} = \{300, 102, 003, 120D, 120U, 030T, 021D, 021U\}$. The resulting macrostructure, from the *ranked clusters of M-cliques* model RC of Davis and Leinhardt (1972), consists of a single hierarchy of clique levels, with cliques at the same level pairwise related by N^* and cliques at different levels pairwise related by A^* (i.e., completely interconnected by the A relation, all A relations going in the same direction) from the lower clique to the higher one.

Example 2.4 $P_{R2C} = \{300, 102, 120D, 120U, 030T, 021D, 021U\}$. The resulting macrostructure, from the *ranked 2-clusters of M-cliques* model R2C (Johnsen, 1985), which is basically the same as that for the previous example except that there are at most two cliques at each level.

Example 2.5 $P_{TR} = \{300, 102, 003, 120D, 120U, 030T, 021D, 021U, 012\}$. The resulting macrostructure, from the *transitivity* model TR of Holland and Leinhardt (1971), consists of a collection of M-cliques partially ordered by the A^* relation (by convention, every M-clique is in relation A^* to itself) where incomparable M-cliques are pairwise related by N^*.

Example 2.6 $P_{HC} = \{300, 102, 003, 120D, 120U, 030T, 021D, 021U, 012, 210\}$. Here the macrostructure, from the *hierarchical cliques* model HC of Johnsen (1985), consists of a set of $\tilde{\ }M$-cliques (maximal M-chain-connected subsets of vertices pairwise linked by either M or A and partially ordered by A) which are partially ordered by the A^* relation (by convention, every $\tilde{\ }M$-clique is in relation A^* to itself), where incomparable $\tilde{\ }M$-cliques are pairwise related by N^*. Thus, within the group, M links form cliques which partition the group. Within the cliques and between members of different cliques a ranking relation A

forms which partially orders each clique and partially orders the set of cliques in a consistent manner so as to partially order the entire group.

Example 2.7 $P_{39+} = \{300, 102, 120D, 120U, 030T, 021D, 021U, 012, 210, 120C\}$. The macrostructure here corresponds to the Davis–Leinhardt data for group sizes 39–79 (Johnsen, 1985) and consists of either (a) two superclusters of $\tilde{}M$-cliques, i.e., sets of $\tilde{}M$-cliques which are pairwise chain-connected by the interclique $A^{\#}$ relation (where $\tilde{}M$-cliques related by $A^{\#}$ are completely interconnected by A relations with no restriction on their directions), where each supercluster is a complete graph on its $\tilde{}M$-cliques with respect to the $A^{\#}$ relation and the $\tilde{}M$-cliques of each supercluster are partially ordered with respect to the A^* relation, or else (b) one supercluster of $\tilde{}M$-cliques, of diameter at most 3 with respect to the $A^{\#}$-distance between $\tilde{}M$-cliques, in which the $\tilde{}M$-cliques are partially ordered with respect to the A^* relation. The internal microstructure of the $\tilde{}M$-cliques is like that for the HC model except that A need not be transitive within the $\tilde{}M$-cliques.

As a natural extension of Newcomb's study of *positive balance* (Newcomb, 1968), we investigated how various proposed agreement–friendship processes might account for the above empirically based macrostructures for affect, that is, how friendship and nonfriendship in a group G may be produced by agreement and disagreement between pairs of individuals in G as they become aware of each other's attitudes towards other members of the group (Johnsen, 1986; 1989a). These macrostructures exhibit various forms of social cohesion of the group. The processual contrapositives of these microprocesses can be stated as how agreement and disagreement between pairs of individuals in G on their attitudes towards others in G are influenced by their friendship or nonfriendship, respectively. Although at stasis the latter statements are logically equivalent to the former, they are not substantively the same with regard to the actual microprocesses occurring. It can be seen, however, that at stasis the triads which are unstable (forbidden) with regard to a microprocess are the same as those which are unstable with regard to its processual contrapositive, which means that at stasis the triads permitted by the two processes are the same. Thus, at stasis the triadic micromodels for a microprocess and its processual contrapositive are the same. Shortly thereafter (Johnsen, 1989b) we were able to derive microprocesses which generate these empirically based macrostructures exactly from the associated empirically based triadic microstructures.

Henceforth, unless stated to the contrary, we shall assume that the group G is *sufficiently small*, which means, from our analysis of the Davis–Leinhardt set of sociomatrices, that G has less than 80 members. Let R be an affect relation in G which at each time t can take either of the two values $+$ or $-$ on each ordered pair (a, b) in $G \times G$, $a \neq b$, where $R(a, b; t) = +$ means that a has positive affect towards b (b is a friend of a) and $R(a, b; t) = -$ means that a has a null or negative affect towards b (b is a nonfriend or enemy of a) at time t. We may interpret "$-$" in two ways: as non-liking (absence of liking) and disliking (presence of negative liking or hate). However, because our groups are sufficiently small, we can assume that in the typical case "$-$" will mean disliking. Now let c be another member of G. If $R(a, c; t) = R(b, c; t)$ then we say that a and b *agree on* c at time t; otherwise they *disagree on* c at time t. In Johnsen (1986, 1989a) we studied four elementary and eight compound microprocesses on G which specify how agreement on other group members affects friendship and vice versa. In each case the microprocess is expressed in terms of the relations which should hold at time $t+$ when certain initial relations are assumed to hold at time t a short time before.

3. A MICROSTRUCTURAL AND MICROPROCESSUAL APPROACH

An agreement–friendship microprocess in which agreement is with respect to a set $\mathscr{I}$ of important issues, ideals, goals, beliefs, principles, needs, values or special persons, rather than to the members of the group G, is substantively a different microphenomenon. One approach to this situation is to assume, when $\mathscr{I}$ is relevant to a group, that some members become identified with the "pro" ($+$) side and others with the "con" ($-$) side of the matter, and that members' attitudes towards $\mathscr{I}$ transfer reasonably faithfully to these members (Johnsen, 1986; 1989a). Then an agreement–friendship process with respect to persons (group members) may operate to govern the formation of the affect structure in the group. Such a shift, involving multiple issues and values, has been described by Newcomb (1961) for the rooming house groups in his study of the acquaintance process. In our approach, however, we will assume that $\mathscr{I}$ and G remain disjoint. One reason for doing so is to acknowledge that orientations towards persons and $\mathscr{I}$ are qualitatively different so we can allow for the possibility that a person A may hold different attitudes towards $\mathscr{I}$ and another person B when B has a favorable attitude towards $\mathscr{I}$, or to hold the same attitude towards $\mathscr{I}$ and B when B has an unfavorable attitude towards $\mathscr{I}$. A lesser reason, for our purposes here, is that the orientations of members of G towards $\mathscr{I}$ may take any of three values $+$, $-$ or 0, while the orientations of members of G towards themselves shall take only the two values $+$ and $-$. In any case, we develop another analytic approach here.

The relation between the members of G and $\mathscr{I}$ we denote by S, as per Fararo and Doreian (1998). Then, under the assumption that the members of G have complete information, we postulate the following agreement–friendship microprocesses with respect to $\mathscr{I}$, together with their processual contrapositives, operating at time t:

Proc $S1t$. Those who agree on $\mathscr{I}$ tend to become mutual friends:
$S(a, \mathscr{I}; t) = S(b, \mathscr{I}; t)$ induces $R(a, b; t+) = +$ and $R(b, a; t+) = +$.
Contra. Those who are not mutual friends tend to disagree on $\mathscr{I}$:
$R(a, b; t) = -$ or $R(b, a; t) = -$ induces $S(a, \mathscr{I}; t+) \neq S(b, \mathscr{I}; t+)$.

Proc $S2t$. Those who agree on $\mathscr{I}$ tend to have some friendship:
$S(a, \mathscr{I}; t) = S(b, \mathscr{I}; t)$ induces $R(a, b; t+) = +$ or $R(b, a; t+) = +$
or both.
Contra. Those who are mutual non-friends tend to disagree on $\mathscr{I}$:
$R(a, b; t) = -$ and $R(b, a; t) = -$ induce $S(a, \mathscr{I}; t+) \neq S(b, \mathscr{I}; t+)$.

Proc $S3t$. Those who have some friendship tend to agree on $\mathscr{I}$:
$R(a, b; t) = +$ or $R(b, a; t) = +$ induces $S(a, \mathscr{I}; t+) = S(b, \mathscr{I}; t+)$.
Contra. Those who disagree on $\mathscr{I}$ tend to become mutual non-friends:
$S(a, \mathscr{I}; t) \neq S(b, \mathscr{I}; t)$ induces $R(a, b; t+) = -$ and $R(b, a; t+) = -$.

Proc $S4t$. Mutual friends tend to agree on $\mathscr{I}$:
$R(a, b; t) = +$ and $R(b, a; t) = +$ induce $S(a, \mathscr{I}; t+) = S(b, \mathscr{I}; t+)$.
Contra. Those who disagree on $\mathscr{I}$ tend not to become mutual friends:
$S(a, \mathscr{I}; t) \neq S(b, \mathscr{I}; t)$ induces $R(a, b; t+) = -$ or $R(b, a; t+) = -$
or both.

As expressed by Procs $S1t$ and $S2t$, agreement on $\mathscr{I}$ with $S(a, \mathscr{I}; t) = S(b, \mathscr{I}; t) = -$ or $S(a, \mathscr{I}; t) = S(b, \mathscr{I}; t) = 0$ has the same effect on interpersonal relations within G^- and G^0, respectively, as agreement on $\mathscr{I}$ with $S(a, \mathscr{I}; t) = S(b, \mathscr{I}; t) = +$ has within G^+. The former can occur when the opposition to $\mathscr{I}$ is as strong as the support for $\mathscr{I}$, a realistic possibility when $\mathscr{I}$ is an issue or value, etc., having a highly polarizing effect in G. The latter might occur when taking the middle ground between support and opposition to $\mathscr{I}$ is as strong as taking either of the polarized positions, possibly a difficult position to maintain.

Here we shall investigate the special case where the relationships (tie structure) within G^0, between G^0 and G^+, and between G^0 and G^- are benign in their effect on the solidarity of G^+, that is, they do not support forces, internal or external to G^+, which could dissolve or fragment the structure or cause the failure of G^+ to preserve any of the beliefs, values, goals, special persons, etc., in $\mathscr{I}$. This could occur, for example, when there are no agreements, disagreements or other forces acting between the members of G^0 and G^+ or G^0 and G^-. With a stable internal structure for G^0 this seems reasonable, since a continuing zero orientation towards $\mathscr{I}$ does not support either the agreement, disagreement or other forces contesting the orientations of G^+ and G^- towards $\mathscr{I}$. This special case becomes problematical when there are processes over time which, for example, can induce the conversion of members of G^0 to the orientation of either G^+ or G^-. In our special case, however, we shall ignore the presence of G^0.

We shall allow for the possibility that the "agreement induces friendship microprocesses" occurring within G^+ and G^- may be different or that such a microprocess may not occur in one of them, e.g., Proc S1t occurs in G^+ and Proc S2t occurs in G^-, or Proc S2t occurs in G^+ and neither microprocess occurs in G^-. If neither Proc S1t nor Proc S2t occurs in G^x then the dyads in G^x are unrestricted and can be either M, A or N; in other words, the microprocesses operating within G^x are too general to constrain the dyads within it, $x = +$ or $-$. Now, the "friendship induces agreement microprocesses" Procs S3t and S4t (or their processual contrapositives) only determine the relations between G^+ and G^-, not the relations within them. If neither Proc S3t nor Proc S4t occurs between G^+ and G^- then the dyads linking them are unrestricted and can be either M, A, or N; in other words, the microprocesses operating between G^+ and G^- are too general to constrain the dyads between them. Whether within G^+ or G^- or between G^+ and G^-, we shall represent the absence of a constraining microprocess by the "non-process" Proc S$\emptyset$t.

Since we are assuming that G^0 is benign in its effect on G^+, we shall only consider the microprocessess within G^+, between G^+ and G^-, and within G^-, written in that order. Denoting a model by the Procs which generate it, the different models possible when G^- is present are denoted by the triple (Sxt, Syt, Szt), where $x, z = 1, 2$ or $\emptyset$ and $y = 3, 4$ or $\emptyset$, which we will abbreviate to $Sxyzt$. There are thus $3 \times 3 \times 3 = 27$ different triples of microprocesses, or models, involving both G^+ and G^-.

If G^- is absent, i.e., empty of members, we have a situation where $[G^+, \mathscr{I}]$ is not threatened, either actively or potentially, by any forces emanating from another subgroup. In this case we are dealing with what we call the *unthreatened* solidarity of G^+. Here we denote the model simply in terms of the microprocesses operating within G^+. These are $S1t$, $S2t$ and $S\emptyset t$, which, to avoid confusion, we shall henceforth denote by $+S1t$, $+S2t$ and $+S\emptyset t$. The first two are defined as follows:

Proc $+S1t$. Those who agree positively on $\mathscr{I}$ tend to become mutual friends:
$S(a, \mathscr{I}; t) = S(b, \mathscr{I}; t) = +$ induces $R(a, b; t+) = +$ and
$R(b, a; t+) = +$.
Contra. Those who are not mutual friends tend not to agree positively on $\mathscr{I}$:
$R(a, b; t) = -$ or $R(b, a; t) = -$ induces $S(a, \mathscr{I}; t+) \neq +$ or
$S(b, \mathscr{I}; t+) \neq +$ or both.

Proc $+S2t$. Those who agree positively on $\mathscr{I}$ tend to have some friendship:
$S(a, \mathscr{I}; t) = S(b, \mathscr{I}; t) = +$ induces $R(a, b; t+) = +$ or
$R(b, a; t+) = +$ or both.
Contra. Those who are mutual non-friends tend not to agree positively on $\mathscr{I}$:
$R(a, b; t) = -$ and $R(b, a; t) = -$ induce $S(a, \mathscr{I}; t+) \neq +$ or
$S(b, \mathscr{I}; t+) \neq +$ or both.

Here the Contra Procs do not occur if they imply the emergence of a non-empty subgroup G^-. Thus, the occurrence of either Contra Proc will further the growth of the benign subgroup G^0. Note that a model with a G^+ and no G^- is not the same as a model with a G^+ and G^- but no microprocess between G^+ and G^-. Although the solidarity of G^+ may have the same level in both cases, the presence of G^- in the latter case introduces the potential for the development of forces antagonistic to G^+ in case of a future disagreement between G^+ and G^-, i.e., the potential for a decrease in the solidarity of G^+ not present in the former case. As we shall see in the next section, each of these 30 microprocess combinations will induce the formation of a macrostructure at stasis in which each microprocess of the combination holds in its domain of relations in the structure. Each microprocess combination produces a class of macrostructures which we shall call the *protomodel* corresponding to the combination.

So far we have only been considering microprocesses and macrostructures which capture the effects on group cohesion due to the orientations of group members towards $\mathscr{I}$. We can also include microprocesses and macrostructures which capture the effects due to the orientations of the group members towards themselves, i.e., their affect relations with each other. We shall discuss this after developing the generic structure of these protomodels at stasis.

4. PROTOMODELS

At each time t the sufficiently small group $G = \{a_1, a_2, \ldots, a_k, \ldots, a_n\}$ partitions into three subsets

$$G \equiv G(t) = G^+(t) \cup G^-(t) \cup G^0(t), \tag{4.1}$$

where

$$G^+(t) = \{u \text{ in } G: S(u, \mathscr{I}; t) = +\}, \tag{4.2}$$

$$G^-(t) = \{v \text{ in } G: S(v, \mathscr{I}; t) = -\} \tag{4.3}$$

and

$$G^0(t) = \{w \text{ in } G: S(w, \mathscr{I}; t) = 0\}, \tag{4.4}$$

and where each of $G^+(t)$, $G^-(t)$ and $G^0(t)$ may be changing over time in both personal composition and interpersonal relations. We shall assume that as time proceeds the applicable microprocesses operate until the structure of $G(t)$ reaches stasis at $t = \varepsilon$ after which, in the absence of any other disturbances, these microprocesses maintain this structure dynamically. This means that at stasis the structures they yield satisfy the following structural versions of the above Procs and their contrapositives:

Struc $S1\varepsilon$. Those who agree on $\mathscr{I}$ are mutual friends:
$S(a, \mathscr{I}; \varepsilon) = S(b, \mathscr{I}; \varepsilon)$ implies $R(a, b; \varepsilon) = +$ and $R(b, a; \varepsilon) = +$.
Contra. Those who are not mutual friends disagree on $\mathscr{I}$:
$R(a, b; \varepsilon) = -$ or $R(b, a; \varepsilon) = -$ implies $S(a, \mathscr{I}; \varepsilon) \neq S(b, \mathscr{I}; \varepsilon)$.

Struc $S2\varepsilon$. Those who agree on $\mathscr{I}$ have attained some friendship:
$S(a, \mathscr{I}; \varepsilon) = S(b, \mathscr{I}; \varepsilon)$ implies $R(a, b; \varepsilon) = +$ or $R(b, a; \varepsilon) = +$ or both.
Contra. Those who are mutual non-friends have attained disagreement on $\mathscr{I}$:
$R(a, b; \varepsilon) = -$ and $R(b, a; \varepsilon) = -$ imply $S(a, \mathscr{I}; \varepsilon) \neq S(b, \mathscr{I}; \varepsilon)$.

Struc $S3\varepsilon$. Those who have some friendship have attained agreement on $\mathscr{I}$:

$R(a, b; \varepsilon) = +$ or $R(b, a; \varepsilon) = +$ implies $S(a, \mathscr{I}; \varepsilon) = S(b, \mathscr{I}; \varepsilon)$.

Contra. Those who disagree on $\mathscr{I}$ have become mutual non-friends:

$S(a, \mathscr{I}; \varepsilon) \neq S(b, \mathscr{I}; \varepsilon)$ implies $R(a, b; \varepsilon) = -$ and $R(b, a; \varepsilon) = -$.

Struc $S4\varepsilon$. Mutual friends have attained agreement on $\mathscr{I}$:

$R(a, b; \varepsilon) = +$ and $R(b, a; \varepsilon) = +$ imply $S(a, \mathscr{I}; \varepsilon) = S(b, \mathscr{I}; \varepsilon)$.

Contra. Those who disagree on $\mathscr{I}$ have not become mutual friends:

$S(a, \mathscr{I}; \varepsilon) \neq S(b, \mathscr{I}; \varepsilon)$ implies $R(a, b; \varepsilon) = -$ or $R(b, a; \varepsilon) = -$ or both.

Struc $+S1\varepsilon$. Those who agree positively on $\mathscr{I}$ have become mutual friends:

$S(a, \mathscr{I}; \varepsilon) = S(b, \mathscr{I}; \varepsilon) = +$ implies $R(a, b; \varepsilon) = +$ and $R(b, a; \varepsilon) = +$.

Contra. Those who are not mutual friends have not attained positive agreement on $\mathscr{I}$:

$R(a, b; \varepsilon) = -$ or $R(b, a; \varepsilon) = -$ implies $S(a, \mathscr{I}; \varepsilon) \neq +$ or $S(b, \mathscr{I}; \varepsilon) \neq +$ or both.

Struc $+S2\varepsilon$. Those who agree positively on $\mathscr{I}$ have attained some friendship:

$S(a, \mathscr{I}; \varepsilon) = S(b, \mathscr{I}; \varepsilon) = +$ implies $R(a, b; \varepsilon) = +$ or $R(b, a; \varepsilon) = +$ or both.

Contra. Those who are mutual non-friends have not attained positive agreement on $\mathscr{I}$:

$R(a, b; \varepsilon) = -$ and $R(b, a; \varepsilon) = -$ imply $S(a, \mathscr{I}, \varepsilon) \neq +$ or $S(b, \mathscr{I}; \varepsilon) \neq +$ or both.

Likewise, the structure of G arrives at stasis to the partition

$$G(\varepsilon) = G^+(\varepsilon) \cup G^-(\varepsilon) \cup G^0(\varepsilon), \qquad (4.5)$$

where

$$G^+(\varepsilon) = \{u \text{ in } G: S(u, \mathscr{I}; \varepsilon) = + \}, \qquad (4.6)$$

$$G^-(\varepsilon) = \{v \text{ in } G: S(v, \mathscr{I}; \varepsilon) = - \} \qquad (4.7)$$

and

$$G^0(\varepsilon) = \{w \text{ in } G: S(w, \mathscr{I}; \varepsilon) = 0\}. \qquad (4.8)$$

Since we are investigating the special case where $G^0(\varepsilon)$ is benign with respect to the solidarity of $G^+(\varepsilon)$ we will limit our analysis to macrostructures consisting of $G^+(\varepsilon)$ and $G^-(\varepsilon)$

$$G'(\varepsilon) = G^+(\varepsilon) \cup G^-(\varepsilon), \qquad (4.9)$$

and these macrostructures will be consistent with and maintained by the microprocesses which are operant. We first give some results which describe the effects of the action of individual Procs in G^x on the structure of G^x, $x = +, -$.

Lemma 4.1 *At stasis* Proc $S1\varepsilon$ *dynamically maintains* Struc $S1\varepsilon$ *within $G^x(\varepsilon)$, where $G^x(\varepsilon)$ is an M-clique in which every dyad is M, $x = +, -$. We call such an M-clique an M_1-group. The resulting macromodel consists of single M-cliques with micromodel $P_{S1\varepsilon} = \{300\}$.*

Proof If u and v are in $G^x(\varepsilon)$ then $S(u, \mathscr{I}; \varepsilon) = S(v, \mathscr{I}; \varepsilon) = x$ whence, by Struc $S1\varepsilon$, $R(u, v; \varepsilon) = + = R(v, u; \varepsilon)$, $x = +, -$. Since this is true for every u and v in $G^x(\varepsilon)$ we see that $G^x(\varepsilon)$ is an M-clique, where every dyad is M. The only triad in an M-clique is 300. This macromodel is the same as that for the positivity (friendship) bias model FR (Johnsen, 1986, p. 301; 1989a, p. 273).

Corollary 4.2 *At stasis* Proc $+S1\varepsilon$ *dynamically maintains the protomodel* Struc $+S1\varepsilon$ *for $G'(\varepsilon) = G^+(\varepsilon)$ where $G^+(\varepsilon)$ is an M-clique. The resulting macromodel consists of single M-cliques with micromodel $P_{+S1\varepsilon} = \{300\}$.*

Proof This is Lemma 4.1 with $x = +$.

Lemma 4.3 *At stasis* Proc $S2\varepsilon$ *dynamically maintains* Struc $S2\varepsilon$ *within $G^x(\varepsilon)$ where $G^x(\varepsilon)$ is an M/A-group, in which every dyad is either M or A, $x = +, -$. We call such an M/A-group an M_2-group. Each macrostructure in* Struc $S2\varepsilon$ *is an M/A-group having all its triads in the micromodel $P_{S2\varepsilon} = \{300, 210, 120C, 120D, 120U, 030C, 030T\}$.*

Proof If u and v are in $G^x(\varepsilon)$ then $S(u, \mathscr{I}; \varepsilon) = S(v, \mathscr{I}; \varepsilon) = x$ whence, by Struc $S2\varepsilon$, $R(u, v; \varepsilon) = +$ or $R(v, u; \varepsilon) = +$ or both, $x = +, -$. Since this is true for every u and v in $G^x(\varepsilon)$ we see that $G^x(\varepsilon)$ is an M/A-group, where every dyad is M or A. Here $P_{+S2\varepsilon}$ is defined as the set of all triads in Θ which can appear in a single M/A-group, i.e., all triads consisting of just M and A dyads. By completely joining the vertices of individual copies of all seven triads in $P_{+S2\varepsilon}$ by M and A dyads we can obtain an exact macrostructure corresponding to $P_{+S2\varepsilon}$, showing that $P_{+S2\varepsilon}$ is a micromodel.

Corollary 4.4 *At stasis* Proc $+S2\varepsilon$ *dynamically maintains the protomodel* Struc $+S2\varepsilon$ *for $G'(\varepsilon) = G^+(\varepsilon)$ where $G^+(\varepsilon)$ is an M/A-group. Each macrostructure in* Struc $+S2\varepsilon$ *is an M/A-group having all its triads in the micromodel $P_{+S2\varepsilon} = \{300, 210, 120C, 120D, 120U, 030C, 030T\}$.*

Proof   This is Lemma 4.3 with $x = +$.

Lemma 4.5   *At stasis* Proc $S\emptyset\varepsilon$ *dynamically maintains* Struc $S\emptyset\varepsilon$ *within* $G^x(\varepsilon)$ *where* $G^x(\varepsilon)$ *is an* $M/A/N$-*group, in which no dyad is restricted, i.e., each dyad is either* M, A *or* N, $x = +, -$. *We call such an* $M/A/N$-*group an* $M_\emptyset$-*group. The set of all triad types permitted in any macrostructure of this model is the micromodel* $P_{S\emptyset\varepsilon} = \Theta$.

Proof   If u and v are in $G^x(\varepsilon)$ then $S(u, \mathscr{I}; \varepsilon) = S(v, \mathscr{I}; \varepsilon) = x$ whence, by Struc $S\emptyset\varepsilon$, $R(u, v; \varepsilon) = +$ or $R(v, u; \varepsilon) = +$ or both or neither, $x = +, -$. Since this is true for every u and v in $G^x(\varepsilon)$ we see that $G^x(\varepsilon)$ is an $M/A/N$-group, where every dyad is M, A or N. Note that every macrostructure formed from M, A and N dyads is in Struc $S\emptyset\varepsilon$, i.e., Struc $S\emptyset\varepsilon$ is the set of all possible macrostructures. By completely joining the vertices of individual copies of all sixteen triads in Θ by M, A and N dyads we can obtain an exact macrostructure corresponding to $P_{S\emptyset\varepsilon}$, showing that $P_{S\emptyset\varepsilon}$ is a micromodel.

Corollary 4.6   *At stasis* Proc $+S\emptyset\varepsilon$ *dynamically maintains the protomodel* Struc $+S\emptyset\varepsilon$ *for* $G'(\varepsilon) = G^+(\varepsilon)$ *where* $G^+(\varepsilon)$ *is an* $M/A/N$-*group. Each macrostructure in* Struc $+S\emptyset\varepsilon$ *is an* $M/A/N$-*group having all its triads in the micromodel* $P_{+S\emptyset\varepsilon} = \Theta$.

Proof   This is Lemma 4.5 with $x = +$.

Lemma 4.7   *At stasis* Proc $S3\varepsilon$ *dynamically maintains* Struc $S3\varepsilon$ *between* $G^+(\varepsilon)$ *and* $G^-(\varepsilon)$ *where* $[G^+(\varepsilon)]N^*[G^-(\varepsilon)]$, *i.e., every dyad linking* $G^+(\varepsilon)$ *and* $G^-(\varepsilon)$ *is* N. *We call such an intergroup relation* N_3^*.

Proof   If u is in $G^+(\varepsilon)$, v is in $G^-(\varepsilon)$, and either $R(u, v; \varepsilon) = +$ or $R(v, u; \varepsilon) = +$ then, by Struc $S3\varepsilon$, $S(u, \mathscr{I}; \varepsilon) = S(v, \mathscr{I}; \varepsilon)$, a contradiction. Thus, $R(u, v; \varepsilon) = - = R(v, u; \varepsilon)$. Since this is true for every u in $G^+(\varepsilon)$ and v in $G^-(\varepsilon)$ we have $[G^+(\varepsilon)]N^*[G^-(\varepsilon)]$, where every dyad between $G^+(\varepsilon)$ and $G^-(\varepsilon)$ is N.

Lemma 4.8   *At stasis* Proc $S4\varepsilon$ *dynamically maintains* Struc $S4\varepsilon$ *between* $G^+(\varepsilon)$ *and* $G^-(\varepsilon)$ *where* $[G^+(\varepsilon)](A/N)^*[G^-(\varepsilon)]$, *i.e., every dyad linking* $G^+(\varepsilon)$ *and* $G^-(\varepsilon)$ *is either* A *or* N. *We call such an intergroup relation* N_4^*.

Proof   If u is in $G^+(\varepsilon)$, v is in $G^-(\varepsilon)$, and $R(u, v; \varepsilon) = + = R(v, u; \varepsilon)$ then, by Struc $S4\varepsilon$, $S(u, \mathscr{I}; \varepsilon) = S(v, \mathscr{I}; \varepsilon)$, a contradiction. Thus, $R(u, v; \varepsilon) = -$ or $R(v, u; \varepsilon) = -$, or both. Since this is true for every u in $G^+(\varepsilon)$ and v in $G^-(\varepsilon)$ we have $[G^+(\varepsilon)](A/N)^*[G^-(\varepsilon)]$, where every dyad between $G^+(\varepsilon)$ and $G^-(\varepsilon)$ is either A or N.

Lemma 4.9 *At stasis* Proc *SØε dynamically maintains* Struc *SØε between* $G^+(\varepsilon)$ *and* $G^-(\varepsilon)$ *where* $[G^+(\varepsilon)](M/A/N)^*[G^-(\varepsilon)]$, *i.e., every dyad linking* $G^+(\varepsilon)$ *and* $G^-(\varepsilon)$ *is either* M, A *or* N. *We call such an intergroup relation* $N_\emptyset^*$.

Proof If u is in $G^+(\varepsilon)$ and v is in $G^-(\varepsilon)$ then there is no restriction on the structure of the u–v dyad. Consequently, the u–v dyad may either be M, A or N. Since this is true for every u in $G^+(\varepsilon)$ and v in $G^-(\varepsilon)$ we have $[G^+(\varepsilon)](M/A/N)^*[G^-(\varepsilon)]$, where every dyad between $G^+(\varepsilon)$ and $G^-(\varepsilon)$ is either M, A or N.

The following general theorem describes the macrostructures corresponding to the 27 microprocess combination Procs *Sxyzε*, where $x, z = 1, 2, \emptyset$ and $y = 3, 4, \emptyset$.

Theorem 4.10 *At stasis* Proc *Sxyzε dynamically maintains the protomodel* Struc *Sxyzε for* $G'(\varepsilon) = G^+(\varepsilon) \cup G^-(\varepsilon)$ *where* $G^+(\varepsilon)$ *is an* M_x-*group,* $G^-(\varepsilon)$ *is a* M_z-*group and the intergroup relation is* N_y^*, *i.e.,* $[G^+(\varepsilon)]N_y^*[G^-(\varepsilon)]$, $x, z = 1, 2, \emptyset$, $y = 3, 4, \emptyset$. *The set* $P_{Sxyzε}$ *consists of all triads in* Θ *which appear in some macrostructure* $G'(\varepsilon)$.

Proof By Lemmas 4.1, 4.3, 4.5 and 4.7–4.9, if Proc *Sxyzε* dynamically maintains the protomodel Struc *Sxyzε* for $G'(\varepsilon) = G^+(\varepsilon) \cup G^-(\varepsilon)$ then Proc *Sxε* dynamically maintains Struc *Sxε* within $G^+(\varepsilon)$, Proc *Szε* dynamically maintains Struc *Szε* within $G^-(\varepsilon)$, and Proc *Syε* dynamically maintains Struc *Syε* between $G^+(\varepsilon)$ and $G^-(\varepsilon)$. Thus, $G^+(\varepsilon)$ is an M_x-group, $G^-(\varepsilon)$ is an M_z-group, the intergroup relation is N_y^* and $P_{Sxyzε}$ consists of all triads in Θ which appear in some $G'(\varepsilon)$.

Certain especially interesting cases of Theorem 4.10 can be stated as corollaries, for $x, z = 1, 2$ and $y = 3$ or 4. Note from Lemma 4.5 that if either $x = \emptyset$ or $z = \emptyset$ the set of possible triads in the protomodel is the universal micromodel $P_{SØyzε} = P_{SxyØε} = P_{SØyØε} = \Theta$.

Corollary 4.11 *At stasis* Proc *S131ε dynamically maintains the protomodel* Struc *S131ε for* $G'(\varepsilon) = G^+(\varepsilon) \cup G^-(\varepsilon)$ *where* $G^+(\varepsilon)$ *and* $G^-(\varepsilon)$ *are M-cliques and* $[G^+(\varepsilon)]N^*[G^-(\varepsilon)]$. *The resulting protomodel is* BA (*Balance*) *with micromodel* $P_{S131ε} = P_{BA} \equiv \{300, 102\}$.

A typical macrostructure in this protomodel is represented in Figure 9.2.

Corollary 4.12 *At stasis* Proc *S132ε dynamically maintains the proto-model* Struc *S132ε for* $G'(\varepsilon)=G^+(\varepsilon)\cup G^-(\varepsilon)$ *where* $G^+(\varepsilon)$ *is an M-clique,* $G^-(\varepsilon)$ *is an M/A-group and* $[G^+(\varepsilon)]N^*[G^-(\varepsilon)]$. *The resulting protomodel determines the triad set* $P_{S132\varepsilon}=\{300, 210, 120C, 120D, 120U, 030C, 030T, 102, 012\}$.

A typical macrostructure in this protomodel is represented in Figure 9.3.

Corollary 4.13. *At stasis* Proc *S141ε dynamically maintains the proto-model* Struc *S141ε for* $G'(\varepsilon)=G^+(\varepsilon)\cup G^-(\varepsilon)$ *where* $G^+(\varepsilon)$ *and* $G^-(\varepsilon)$ *are M-cliques and* $[G^+(\varepsilon)](A/N)^*[G^-(\varepsilon)]$. *The resulting protomodel determines the triad set* $P_{S141\varepsilon}\equiv\{300, 120C, 120D, 120U, 111D, 111U, 102\}$.

A typical macrostructure in this protomodel is represented in Figure 9.4.

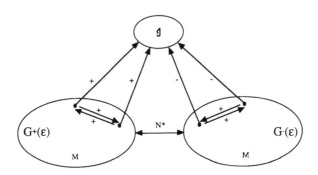

FIGURE 9.2. Macrostructure for model *S131ε*.

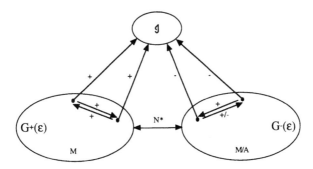

FIGURE 9.3. Macrostructure for model *S132ε*.

Corollary 4.14 *At stasis* Proc *S*142ε *dynamically maintains the proto-model* Struc *S*142ε *for* $G'(\varepsilon) = G^+(\varepsilon) \cup G^-(\varepsilon)$ *where* $G^+(\varepsilon)$ *is an M-clique,* $G^-(\varepsilon)$ *is an M/A-group and* $[G^+(\varepsilon)](A/N)^*[G^-(\varepsilon)]$. *The resulting proto-model determines the triad set* $P_{S142\varepsilon} = \{300, 210, 120C, 120D, 120U, 030C, 030T, 111D, 111U, 102, 012\}$.

A typical macrostructure in this protomodel is represented in Figure 9.5.

Corollary 4.15 *At stasis* Proc *S*231ε *dynamically maintains the proto-model* Struc *S*231ε *for* $G'(\varepsilon) = G^+(\varepsilon) \cup G^-(\varepsilon)$ *where* $G^+(\varepsilon)$ *is an M/A-group,* $G^-(\varepsilon)$ *is an M-clique and* $[G^+(\varepsilon)]N^*[G^-(\varepsilon)]$. *The resulting protomodel determines the triad set* $P_{S231\varepsilon} = \{300, 210, 120C, 120D, 120U, 030C, 030T, 102, 012\}$.

A typical macrostructure in this protomodel is represented in Figure 9.6.

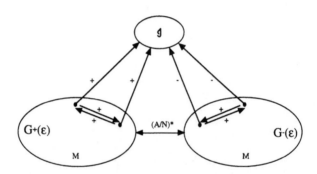

FIGURE 9.4. Macrostructure for model *S*141ε.

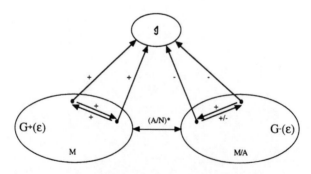

FIGURE 9.5. Macrostructure for model *S*142ε.

Corollary 4.16 *At stasis* Proc *S232ε dynamically maintains the proto-model* Struc *S232ε for G'(ε)=G⁺(ε)∪G⁻(ε) where G⁺(ε) and G⁻(ε) are M/A-groups and [G⁺(ε)]N*[G⁻(ε)]. The resulting protomodel determines the triad set* $P_{S232ε}=\{300, 210, 120C, 120D, 120U, 030C, 030T, 102, 012\}.$

A typical macrostructure in this protomodel is represented in Figure 9.7.

Corollary 4.17 *At stasis* Proc *S241ε dynamically maintains the proto-model* Struc *S241ε for G'(ε)=G⁺(ε)∪G⁻(ε) where G⁺(ε) is an M/A-group, G⁻(ε) is an M-clique and [G⁺(ε)](A/N)*[G⁻(ε)]. The resulting protomodel determines the triad set* $P_{S241ε}=\{300, 210, 120C, 120D, 120U, 030C, 030T, 111D, 111U, 102, 012\}.$

A typical macrostructure in this protomodel is represented in Figure 9.8.

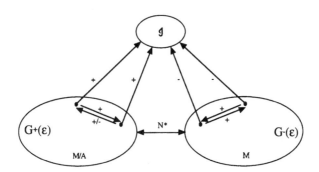

FIGURE 9.6.   Macrostructure for model *S231ε*.

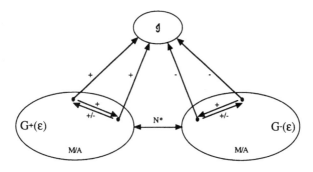

FIGURE 9.7   Macrostructure for model *S232ε*.

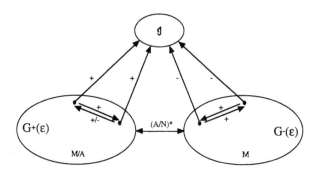

FIGURE 9.8.   Macrostructure for model $S241\varepsilon$.

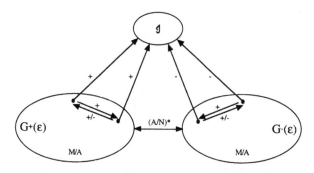

FIGURE 9.9.   Macrostructure for model $S242\varepsilon$.

Corollary 4.18. *At stasis* Proc $S242\varepsilon$ *dynamically maintains the protomodel* Struc $S242\varepsilon$ *for* $G'(\varepsilon)=G^+(\varepsilon)\cup G^-(\varepsilon)$ *where* $G^+(\varepsilon)$ *and* $G^-(\varepsilon)$ *are M/A-groups and* $[G^+(\varepsilon)](A/N)^*[G^-(\varepsilon)]$. *The resulting protomodel determines the triad set* $P_{S242\varepsilon}\equiv\{300, 210, 120C, 120D, 120U, 030C, 030T, 111D, 111U, 102, 012\}$.

A typical macrostructure in this protomodel is represented in Figure 9.9.

5. MACROSTRUCTURES AND SOLIDARITY

The protomodels developed in Section 4 only account for the effects of the agreement–friendship microprocesses occurring among two persons and $\mathscr{I}$. It is remarkable that some of these processes by themselves exactly define the resulting macrostructures. The macrostructures determined in Struc $+S1\varepsilon$ and Struc $S131\varepsilon$ are from the friendship bias and balance models FR and BA, respectively, two simple but special affect models encountered in social groups. Like those in Struc $S131\varepsilon$, those in Struc $S141\varepsilon$ also permit just two M-cliques, but with somewhat more variation in the interclique relations. Now, in a sufficiently small social group it is reasonable to expect some purely interpersonal influences on the structure of the group in addition to those resulting from group members' orientations towards $\mathscr{I}$. Thus, we revisit the protomodels of Section 4 to see whether all or part of any of the known empirically based interpersonal affect structures (Johnsen, 1985) can be embedded in them in a consistent manner, when there is room to do so.

The macrostructures in Struc $S141\varepsilon$ only allow variation in the intergroup relations between $G^+(\varepsilon)$ and $G^-(\varepsilon)$. Among the macrostructures for $G'(\varepsilon)=G^+(\varepsilon)\cup G^-(\varepsilon)$ here are those with the special intergroup relations $G^+(\varepsilon)N^*G^-(\varepsilon)$, $G^+(\varepsilon)A^*G^-(\varepsilon)$ or, more generally, $G^+(\varepsilon)A^{\ddagger}G^-(\varepsilon)$ and $G^-(\varepsilon)A^{\ddagger}G^+(\varepsilon)$, where $UA^{\ddagger}V$ means there is a partition of $V=Y\cup Z$ such that UA^*Y and UN^*Z. Note that A^* and N^* are the special cases of $A^{\ddagger}$ where Z, respectively Y, is the empty set. Here, in general, $G^-(\varepsilon)$ is more friendly to $G^-(\varepsilon)$ than it is in $S131\varepsilon$, hence less threatening to the solidarity of $G^+(\varepsilon)$.

For macrostructures in Struc $Sxyz\varepsilon$, where $x,z=1,2$ and $y=3,4$, the subgroups $G^+(\varepsilon)$ and $G^-(\varepsilon)$ can only be M-cliques and M/A-groups interconnected by N^* or $(A/N)^*$. These M/A-groups may in turn be collections of M/A-subgroups, such as $\tilde{M}$-cliques, pairwise interconnected by A^* or $A^{\#}$ relations, as occurs with a single branch hierarchy from the HC model discussed in Example 2.6 above. These interconnections $(A/N)^*$ may be of a special form such as $A^{\ddagger}$. Moreover, the structures $G^+(\varepsilon)\cup G^-(\varepsilon)$ may also be $A^{\#}$-interconnected collections of $\tilde{M}$-cliques coming from macrostructures of the agreement–friendship process models discussed in Johnsen (1986; 1989a).

Now, for a fixed or average $G^-(\varepsilon)$ the solidarity of $G^+(\varepsilon)$ is threatened less by $G^-(\varepsilon)$ when $y=4$ than when $y=3$, because in the former case $G^-(\varepsilon)$ is more friendly to $G^+(\varepsilon)$. Likewise, for a fixed or average relation between $G^+(\varepsilon)$ and $G^-(\varepsilon)$ the solidarity of $G^+(\varepsilon)$ is threatened less by $G^-(\varepsilon)$ when $z=4$ than when $z=3$, because on average $G^-(\varepsilon)$ is less cohesive in the former case than in the latter.

When either $x=\emptyset$ or $z=\emptyset$ these macrostructures allow $G^+(\varepsilon)$, respectively $G^-(\varepsilon)$, to be free of structural constraints, hence capable of evolving into a macrostructure from one of the empirical affect models R2C, RC, TR, HC, or 39+. If $x=\emptyset$ then $G^+(\varepsilon)$ is not shaped or organized by any orientation or commitment of its members to an $\mathscr{I}$, hence would not qualify as a solidary group. Nevertheless, its structure might be shaped or organized by the orientations of its members to each other, as occurs in the macrostructures from various theoretical and empirical affect models (cf. Johnsen, 1986; 1989a,b). Thus, the group may exhibit a measure of *cohesion* without exhibiting solidarity. If $z = \emptyset$ then the same can be said for $G^-(\varepsilon)$. Here, because of the lack of solidarity of $G^-(\varepsilon)$, the solidarity of $G^+(\varepsilon)$ is not threatened by $G^-(\varepsilon)$ *as a group*, although individual members of $G^-(\varepsilon)$, weakly reinforced by others in $G^-(\varepsilon)$, may pose local threats when $y = 3$ or 4 via their individual relations with the members of $G^+(\varepsilon)$. When $y = \emptyset$ then there are no "disagreement induces non-friendship" influence processes operating in $G'(\varepsilon)$, so as long as $y = \emptyset$ is in effect, $G^-(\varepsilon)$ does not systematically threaten the solidarity of $G^+(\varepsilon)$. We now consider $x \neq \emptyset \neq y$ and $z = \emptyset$ and examine some of the special cases which can occur here.

(a) *Struc S13Øε.* Here $G^+(\varepsilon)$ is an M-clique and $G^+(\varepsilon)N^*G^-(\varepsilon)$. If $G^-(\varepsilon)$ is a macrostructure from either model CL, TR or HC, then one can verify that the resulting total group G is also a macrostructure from that model (Johnsen, 1986; 1989; Lemma 3.3(a)). Thus, if the highly cohesive M-clique $G^+(\varepsilon)$ were to encounter the group $G^-(\varepsilon)$ from either CL, TR or HC, it could do so without generating violations of the triadic structure and process rules (collectively called the *social rules*) of the prevalent group $G^-(e)$ (Johnsen; 1986, pp. 275–277; 1989, pp. 255–256). Nevertheless, subgroups of $G^-(\varepsilon)$ could pose local threats to the solidarity of $G^+(\varepsilon)$.

The same can also be said for

(b) *Struc S14Øε,* when $G^-(\varepsilon)$ is from either R2C, RC, TR, HC, or 39+ and the intergroup relation is either $G^+(\varepsilon)A^*G^-(\varepsilon)$ or $G^-(\varepsilon)$ $A^*G^+(\varepsilon)$ (Johnsen, 1986; 1989, Lemma 3.3(b)). Here $G^-(\varepsilon)$ is friendlier to $G^+(\varepsilon)$, hence less threatening to the solidarity of $G^+(\varepsilon)$ than in (a).

(c) *Struc S23Øε,* when $G^-(\varepsilon)$ is from either TR or HC and $G^+(\varepsilon)$ is from an M/A submodel of the model for $G^-(\varepsilon)$ but is not an M-clique (Johnsen, 1986; 1989, Lemma 3.3(a)). Here $G^-(\varepsilon)$ is as threatening to the solidarity of $G^+(\varepsilon)$ as it is in (a), but $G^+(\varepsilon)$ is less cohesive, hence less solidary.

(d) *Struc S24Øε,* when $G^-(\varepsilon)$ is from either R2C, RC, TR, HC, or 39+, $G^+(\varepsilon)$ is from an M/A submodel of the model for $G^-(\varepsilon)$

but is not an M-clique, and the intergroup relation is either $G^+(\varepsilon)A^*G^-(\varepsilon)$ or $G^-(\varepsilon)A^*G^+(\varepsilon)$ (Johnsen, 1986; 1989, Lemma 3.3(b)). Here $G^-(\varepsilon)$ is as threatening to the solidarity of $G^+(\varepsilon)$ as it is in (b), but $G^+(\varepsilon)$ is less cohesive, hence less solidary.

We note that this type of compatible social joining of two groups $G^+(\varepsilon)$ and $G^-(\varepsilon)$ with different orientations towards a set $\mathscr{I}$ as in the above examples, cannot happen in Strucs $S131\varepsilon$, $S141\varepsilon$, and $S232\varepsilon$. In $S131\varepsilon$ and $S232\varepsilon$, the N^* intergroup relation between $G^+(\varepsilon)$ and $G^-(\varepsilon)$ results in the formation of triads 102 or 012, neither of which is in the micromodel for either group. In $S141\varepsilon$ a nontrivial A/N intergroup relation between $G^+(\varepsilon)$ and $G^-(\varepsilon)$ results in the formation of triads containing A dyads, none of which are in the micromodel $\{300\}$ of the two groups. Thus, in these cases the joining of the two groups results in new social rules different from those prevailing in the two groups involved. The migration of an M-clique or M/A-group $G^+(\varepsilon)$ into the environment occupied by $G^-(\varepsilon)$ in these three models will result in the formation of a macrostructure which is not a member of the macromodel for $G^-(\varepsilon)$. In $S242\varepsilon$ a compatible social joining is possible within the social rules of $G^-(\varepsilon)$ if the intergroup A/N relation is $A^\#$, which consists entirely of A dyads in either direction, provided the intergroup triads and the micromodel for $G^+(\varepsilon)$ are contained in the micromodel for $G^-(\varepsilon)$.

Thus we see that all the protomodels for solidarity, in which the orientations of all group members toward $\mathscr{I}$ are captured, can be completed to full models for solidarity which capture the interpersonal affect macrostructure of the total group in which the group structures $G^+(\varepsilon)$ and $G^-(\varepsilon)$ are taken from the set of empirical macromodels.

6. THE RELATIVE STRENGTH OF SOLIDARITY ACROSS MACROMODELS

At stasis the solidarity of $G^+(\varepsilon)$ in the social environment $G^-(\varepsilon)$ should depend directly on the strength of the commitment relation $S(G^+) = \Sigma^+$ of $G^+(\varepsilon)$ to $\mathscr{I}$ and directly on the internal cohesion Γ^+ of $G^+(\varepsilon)$. If we stop here we are dealing with the *unthreatened solidarity* or *u-solidarity* of G^+. If we assume, in addition, that the solidarity of $G^+(\varepsilon)$ should depend inversely on the absolute strength of the adverse relation $S(G^-) = \Sigma^-$ of $G^-(\varepsilon)$ against $\mathscr{I}$, inversely on the internal cohesion Γ^- of $G^-(\varepsilon)$, and directly on the level of amity or friendliness Φ^{+-} between $G^+(\varepsilon)$ and $G^-(\varepsilon)$ then we are dealing with the *threatened* or *vulnerable solidarity*, also called the v-solidarity, of $G^+(\varepsilon)$. It seems clear that if the group $G^+(\varepsilon)$ is insufficiently committed to $\mathscr{I}$, the group $G^-(\varepsilon)$ is sufficiently adverse to $\mathscr{I}$, the group $G^+(\varepsilon)$ is insufficiently cohesive, the external social environment $G^-(\varepsilon)$ is sufficiently cohesive, and the intergroup relations between G^+ and G^- are sufficiently hostile, i.e., the v-solidarity of $G^+(\varepsilon)$ is sufficiently weak, then the group $G^+(\varepsilon)$ may not survive intact or its beliefs, values, goals, special persons, etc., may not be preserved.

One measure of Σ^+ and Σ^- is the average strength of the values in $\{S(g)\,|\,g \text{ in } G^+\}$ and $\{|S(g)|\,|\,g \text{ in } G^-\}$, respectively, where $|S(g)|$ is the absolute value of $S(g)$. Another is the minimum strength of the values in $\{S(g)\,|\,g \text{ in } G^+\}$ and $\{|S(g)|\,|\,g \text{ in } G^-\}$, respectively. One measure of the cohesion of $G^+(\varepsilon)$ is the relative number of positive directed edges in $G^+(\varepsilon)$, $\delta^+ = (2M^+ + A^+)/g^+(g^+ - 1)$, where M^+, A^+, g^+ represent the total numbers of M and A dyads and total number of members in $G^+(\varepsilon)$, respectively. Another measure is the $+$ directed edge connectivity of $G^+(\varepsilon)$, $\kappa^+ = $ the minimum number of $+$ directed edges whose signs need to be changed to $-$ in order to disconnect $G^+(\varepsilon)$ on its $+$ directed edges. Similarly for $\delta^- = $ the relative number of $+$ directed edges in $G^-(\varepsilon)$ and $\kappa^- = $ the $+$ directed edge connectivity of $G^-(\varepsilon)$. The amity or friendliness between $G^+(\varepsilon)$ and $G^-(\varepsilon)$ can be measured in terms of the relative number of positive directed edges $\delta^{+-} = (2M^{+-} + A^{+-})/2g^+g^-$ between $G^+(\varepsilon)$ and $G^-(\varepsilon)$, where M^{+-} and A^{+-} represent the total numbers of M and A dyads between them. Either type of solidarity of the group $G^+(\varepsilon)$ then should be, *ceteris paribus*, a non-decreasing function of Σ^+ and a non-decreasing function of Γ^+ and, for v-solidarity, a non-increasing function of Σ^-, a non-increasing function of Γ^- and a non-decreasing function of Φ^{+-}. We denote the u-solidarity and v-solidarity of the group X by $\sigma_u(X)$ and $\sigma_v(X)$, respectively. If the solidarity $\sigma_w(X)$ of the group X, w $=$ u or v, is greater than, or greater than or equal to, the corresponding solidarity of group Y, $\sigma_w(Y)$, we write $\sigma_w(X) > \sigma_w(Y)$ or $\sigma_w(X) \geqslant \sigma_w(Y)$, respectively.

With respect to a fixed measure of Γ^+ and Γ^- and fixed measure of Φ^{+-}, $\sigma_w(G^+(\varepsilon))$ is maximum when Σ^+ is maximum and $G^+(\varepsilon)$ is an M-clique and, if w $=$ v, Σ^- is minimum, $G^-(\varepsilon)$ consists entirely of N dyads and the intergroup relation between $G^+(\varepsilon)$ and $G^-(\varepsilon)$ is M^*. Likewise, $\sigma_w(G^+(\varepsilon))$ is a minimum when Σ^+ is minimum and $G^+(\varepsilon)$ consists entirely of N dyads and, if w $=$ v, Σ^- is maximum, $G^-(\varepsilon)$ is an M-clique and the intergroup relation between $G^+(\varepsilon)$ and $G^-(\varepsilon)$ is N^*. Let H_1 and K_1, H_2 and K_2, and $H_\emptyset$ and $K_\emptyset$ be macrostructures from the respective protomodels $S1\varepsilon$, $S2\varepsilon$ and $S\emptyset\varepsilon$ where, with respect to members, $H_1 = H_2 = H_\emptyset$ and $K_1 = K_2 = K_\emptyset$, and where, with respect to the sets of + directed edges, $H_{\varnothing} \subset H_2 \subset H_1$ and $K_{\varnothing} \subset K_2 \subset K_1$, and let J_3, J_4 and $J_{\varnothing}$ be intergroup macro-relations from the respective intergroup process models $S3\varepsilon$, $S4\varepsilon$ and $S\varnothing\varepsilon$ where, with respect to the sets of + directed edges, $J_3 \subset J_4 \subset J_{\varnothing}$. Suppose that Σ^+ and Σ^- are fixed, $G^+(\varepsilon)$ is a fixed H_x from $\{H_{\varnothing}, H_2, H_1\}$, N_y^* is a fixed intergroup relation J_y from $\{J_1, J_2, J_{\varnothing}\}$, and $G^-(\varepsilon)$ is a fixed K_z from $\{K_{\varnothing}, K_2, K_1\}$ so that the total macrostructure exhibits either H_x alone or $H_x J_y K_z$, for $x, z = 1, 2, \varnothing$, $y = 3, 4, \varnothing$. Now, since there is no $G^-(\varepsilon)$ and hence no intergroup relation between $G^+(\varepsilon)$ and $G^-(\varepsilon)$ in $+Sx\varepsilon$, we may define by convention that $\sigma_v(+Sx\varepsilon) = \sigma_u(+Sx\varepsilon)$ and $\sigma_u(+Sxyz\varepsilon) = \sigma_u(+Sx\varepsilon)$. Reversing the first equation and also combining the two equations we see that the u-solidarity of any $G^+(\varepsilon)$ can be expressed in terms of $\sigma_v(+Sx\varepsilon)$. Then, since $\sigma_w(Sxyz\varepsilon)$ is either $\sigma_v(+Sx\varepsilon)$ or $\sigma_v(Sxyz\varepsilon)$ we have the following inequalities for the levels of v-solidarity of $G^+(\varepsilon)$ with respect to the given structures H_z, J_y, K_z, and measures of Γ^+, Γ^- and Φ^{+-}, for all $x = 1, 2, \varnothing$, $y = 3, 4, \varnothing$ and $z = 1, 2, \varnothing$:

$$\sigma_v(Sxy\varnothing\varepsilon) \geqslant \sigma_v(Sxy2\varepsilon) \geqslant \sigma_v(Sxy1\varepsilon), \tag{6.1a}$$

$$\sigma_v(Sx\varnothing z\varepsilon) \geqslant \sigma_v(Sx4z\varepsilon) \geqslant \sigma_v(Sx3z\varepsilon), \tag{6.1b}$$

$$\sigma_v(S1yz\varepsilon) \geqslant \sigma_v(S2yz\varepsilon) \geqslant \sigma_v(S\varnothing yz\varepsilon), \tag{6.1c}$$

$$\sigma_v(+S1\varepsilon) \geqslant \sigma_v(+S2\varepsilon) \geqslant \sigma_v(+S\varnothing\varepsilon), \tag{6.1d}$$

$$\sigma_v(+S1\varepsilon) \geqslant \sigma_v(S1\varnothing\varnothing\varepsilon), \tag{6.1e}$$

$$\sigma_v(+S2\varepsilon) \geqslant \sigma_v(S2\varnothing\varnothing\varepsilon), \tag{6.1f}$$

$$\sigma_v(+S\varnothing\varepsilon) \geqslant \sigma_v(S\varnothing\varnothing\varnothing\varepsilon). \tag{6.1g}$$

A partially ordered set (poset) which graphically shows all of the inequality relations implied by (6.1a)–(6.1g) appears in Figure 9.10.

We may also want to postulate that σ_v is a strictly increasing function under certain strict inequality conditions on cohesion and friendliness with Σ^+ and Σ^- held fixed, e.g., *ceteris paribus*:

$$\sigma_v(Sxyr\varepsilon) > \sigma_v(Sxyz\varepsilon), \quad \text{if } x \neq \varnothing \neq y \text{ and } \Gamma^-(K_r) < \Gamma^-(K_z), \tag{6.2a}$$

$$\sigma_v(Sxqz\varepsilon) > \sigma_v(Sxyz\varepsilon), \quad \text{if } x \neq \varnothing \neq z \text{ and } \Phi^{+-}(J_q) > \Phi^{+-}(J_y), \tag{6.2b}$$

$$\sigma_v(Spyz\varepsilon) > \sigma_v(Sxyz\varepsilon), \quad \text{if } y \neq \varnothing \neq z \text{ and } \Gamma^+(H_p) > \Gamma^+(H_x), \tag{6.2c}$$

$$\sigma_v(+Sp\varepsilon) > \sigma_v(+Sx\varepsilon), \quad \text{if } \Gamma^+(H_p) > \Gamma^+(H_x), \tag{6.2d}$$

$$\sigma_v(+S1\varepsilon) > \sigma_v(S1\varnothing\varnothing\varepsilon), \quad \text{if } J_{\varnothing} \neq M^* \text{ and } K_{\varnothing} \text{ is strongly connected} \\ \text{by + directed edges}, \tag{6.2e}$$

$$+S1\varepsilon \rightarrow S1ØØ\varepsilon \rightarrow S1Ø2\varepsilon \rightarrow S1Ø1\varepsilon$$
$$\downarrow \qquad\quad \downarrow \qquad\quad \downarrow \qquad\quad \downarrow$$
$$+S2\varepsilon \rightarrow S2ØØ\varepsilon \rightarrow S2Ø2\varepsilon \rightarrow S2Ø1\varepsilon$$
$$\downarrow \qquad\quad \downarrow \qquad\quad \downarrow \qquad\quad \downarrow$$
$$+SØ\varepsilon \rightarrow SØØØ\varepsilon \rightarrow SØØ2\varepsilon \rightarrow SØØ1\varepsilon$$

corresponding entries: $\Downarrow$

$$S14Ø\varepsilon \rightarrow S142\varepsilon \rightarrow S141\varepsilon$$
$$\downarrow \qquad\quad \downarrow \qquad\quad \downarrow$$
$$S24Ø\varepsilon \rightarrow S242\varepsilon \rightarrow S241\varepsilon$$
$$\downarrow \qquad\quad \downarrow \qquad\quad \downarrow$$
$$SØ4Ø\varepsilon \rightarrow SØ42\varepsilon \rightarrow SØ41\varepsilon$$

corresponding entries: $\Downarrow$

$$S13Ø\varepsilon \rightarrow S132\varepsilon \rightarrow S131\varepsilon$$
$$\downarrow \qquad\quad \downarrow \qquad\quad \downarrow$$
$$S23Ø\varepsilon \rightarrow S232\varepsilon \rightarrow S231\varepsilon$$
$$\downarrow \qquad\quad \downarrow \qquad\quad \downarrow$$
$$SØ3Ø\varepsilon \rightarrow SØ32\varepsilon \rightarrow SØ31\varepsilon$$

FIGURE 9.10.   Poset of agreement–friendship v-solidarity structures, with $G^+(\varepsilon)$ oriented to $\mathscr{I}$, under the nesting conditions specified with equations 6.1a–6.1g. (Arrows go from macrostructures $G^+(\varepsilon)$ which have more v-solidarity to those which have less.)

$$\sigma_v(+S2\varepsilon) > \sigma_v(S2ØØ\varepsilon), \quad \text{if } J_Ø \neq M^* \text{ and } K_Ø \text{ is strongly connected}$$
$$\text{by } + \text{ directed edges,} \qquad (6.2\text{f})$$

$$\sigma_v(+SØ\varepsilon) > \sigma_v(SØØØ\varepsilon), \quad \text{if } J_Ø \neq M^* \text{ and } K_Ø \text{ is strongly connected}$$
$$\text{by } + \text{ directed edges.} \qquad (6.2\text{g})$$

For fixed Σ^+ and Σ^-, if the strengths of cohesiveness of $G^+(\varepsilon)$ and $G^-(\varepsilon)$ and of the friendship level between them change from one model to the other so that either (i) the cohesions of $G^+(\varepsilon)$ and $G^-(\varepsilon)$ both increase or both decrease, or (ii) the cohesion of $G^+(\varepsilon)$ increases and the friendship level between $G^+(\varepsilon)$ and $G^-(\varepsilon)$ decreases, or vice versa, or (iii) the cohesion of $G^-(\varepsilon)$ and the friendship level between $G^+(\varepsilon)$ and $G^-(\varepsilon)$ both increase or both decrease, then we do not have a basis for making a simple comparison of the relative solidarities of $G^+(\varepsilon)$ for these models. For example, we are not able to establish such a simple comparison between models $S131\varepsilon$ and $S232\varepsilon$, $S131\varepsilon$ and $S241\varepsilon$, and $S241\varepsilon$ and $S232\varepsilon$.

We note that the above inequalities are not universally valid for all pairs of structures from a pair of process models. That is, there may be pairs of structures for which an inequality is reversed. For example, if $H_Ø$ is the $G^+(\varepsilon)$ in a macrostructure from process model $SØ32\varepsilon$ and H_2 is the same from process model $S232\varepsilon$, where $H_Ø$ has four members connected cyclically by four M dyads with one A dyad and one N dyad, and H_2 has four members with five pairs connected by an A dyad and the sixth by an M dyad, the $M/A/N$ structure $H_\emptyset$ has $\delta^+ = 9/12$ and $\kappa^+ = 4$ while the M/A structure H_2 has $\delta^+ = 7/12$ and $\kappa^+ = 3$. By (6.2c), $\sigma_v(S\emptyset32\varepsilon) > \sigma_v(S232\varepsilon)$, since $3 \neq \emptyset \neq 2$ and $\Gamma^+(H_\emptyset) > \Gamma^+(H_2)$, even though $G^+(\varepsilon)$ has gone from an M/A structure to an $M/A/N$ structure, a transition in which, by (6.1c), the solidarity does not increase. This shows that the solidarity strength relationship between some pair of macrostructures from two models need not carry over to another pair of macrostructures from those same models. Finally, we note that the u-solidarity of a group is an increasing function of both Σ^+ and the level of cohesion in the group.

It is not difficult to devise a functional formula for the solidarity of $G^+(t)$ at time t, which depends on the absolute strengths Σ^+ and $|\Sigma^-|$, the levels of cohesion of $G^+(t)$ and $G^-(t)$ and the friendliness between $G^+(t)$ and $G^-(t)$ as discussed above for $t = \varepsilon$. Such a formula is not unique. Whether there are further properties that a solidarity function should have, which will further delimit the class of candidate functions, is an open question and will depend on the further development of the theory. As with the choice of measure of cohesion, which function best represents the "robustness of existence" becomes an empirical question.

7. A METHODOLOGICAL APPROACH TO USING THE MODELS

The macrostructure at time t of a sufficiently small group $G^+(t)$, oriented positively to a set $\mathscr{I}$ and in a social environment $G^-(t)$, may be determined by a complete survey sample of all members of the total group $G(t) = G^+(t) \cup G^-(t) \cup G^0(t)$. In such a survey each member of $G(t)$ is asked the equivalent of the following questions:

(1) What is your orientation and strength of orientation towards $\mathscr{I}$ $(+, -$ or 0 and its absolute value)?
(2) To which members of $G(t)$ do you send a positive affect relation and to which do you not? i.e., which members of $G(t)$ are your friends and which are not?

On the basis of the results of this survey the members of $G(t)$ can be partitioned into

$G^+(t) = \{g \text{ in } G(t): S(g) > 0\}$, $G^-(t) = \{g \text{ in } G(t): S(g) < 0\}$ and $G^0(t) = \{g \text{ in } G(t): S(g) = 0\}$.

At this point decisions need to be made regarding which variables go into the measure of solidarity and how these variables are measured. For example, we may decide that the solidarity level of $G^+(t)$ should be obtained directly from the survey data in terms of empirical strengths $\{S(g)|g$ in $G^+(t)\}$ and $\{|S(g)||g$ in $G^-(t)\}$, the empirical cohesions of $G^+(t)$ and $G^-(t)$, and the empirical friendliness between $G^+(t)$ and $G^-(t)$. Here an additional decision regarding which cohesion measure to use presents itself. Alternatively, we may decide that the data warrants another approach to the measures of cohesion of $G^+(t)$ and $G^-(t)$ which may be more robust and which gets at their structures as well.

For example, using the main ingredients of the statistical method developed by Holland and Leinhardt (1970) a triadic analysis can be carried out. Here the censuses of the three dyad types M, A, and N and of the sixteen triad types of Figure 9.1 are first obtained for each of the groups $G^+(t)$ and $G^-(t)$, assuming $G^0(t)$ is benign and can be ignored. Controlling for the numbers of M, A, and N dyads in each of these groups, the expected number and standard deviation of each of the sixteen triads is computed. Comparing the number of actual appearances of a triad type to its (expected number) -1.96(standard deviation), allows the determination of whether that triad appears at chance frequency or greater and is declared a permitted triad, or else at less than chance frequency and is declared a forbidden triad, in the groups $G^+(t)$ and $G^-(t)$. The sets of permitted triads $P(G^+(t))$ and $P(G^-(t))$ are potential micromodels for two macromodels $\Xi_{G^+(t)}$ and $\Xi_{G^-(t)}$. Each macromodel will have at least one macrostructure which has the best fit to the affect structures of $G^+(t)$ and $G^-(t)$, respectively, and the cohesion levels of these best fit structures may be taken as the cohesion values of $G^+(t)$ and $G^-(t)$, respectively.

If the survey sample is not complete and the sample size is much less than the size of $G(t)$ then a determination of the structure of the sample $G_s(t)$ and of the solidarity of $G_s^+(t)$ may not yield an accurate representation of the structure and solidarity of $G(t)$, since these characteristics may be quite sensitive to the possible variation of the corresponding characteristics in the uncollected data. In particular, the adequacy of the extrapolation of the group cohesion and inter-group amity results, or of a group structure determination based on triadic analysis, from a sample to the total group, has not yet been determined.

If $G(t)$ is a large population, of size $\gg 80$, then the empirical inter-personal data collected will very likely have many "do not know" responses, which should be coded as 0s, which indicates that the set of basic triad types should be Ψ of size 138. If a complete survey sample of G is possible then either the direct approach or an extended triadic analysis based on Ψ (cf. Kishida, 1990) may be taken. Here it appears that the characterization of solidarity will require the investigation of many more microprocesses, protomodels and macrostructures than can occur in an analysis based on Θ.

8. THE LARGER CONTEXT FOR SOLIDARITY

We have focussed on the feature which seems central to solidarity, namely, the presence of a set $\mathscr{I}$ of important issues, ideals, beliefs, goals, principles, values or special persons which a subgroup G^+ of members of the larger group G supports and which a subgroup of others G^- opposes. These commitments to $\mathscr{I}$ by the individual members of G^+ serve as ties which indirectly bind the members of G^+ to each other, this subgroup's cohesiveness being reinforced by the interpersonal ties of affect, esteem, trust, etc., which are generated concurrently or subsequently. The opposition to $\mathscr{I}$ by the members of G^- does not automatically induce indirect ties within G^-. However, in the case where G^- actively opposes $\mathscr{I}$ this negative commitment to $\mathscr{I}$ amounts to hostility, which can indirectly bind the members of G^- to each other. This small schema, consisting of a partitioned group $G = G^+ \cup G^- \cup G^0$, the set $\mathscr{I}$ and the adherence relation S (where $S(a_j) = s_j$ for a_j in G) which relates the members of G to $\mathscr{I}$ at various signs and levels, may be expanded to include other proposed features associated with the solidarity of a group and which are part of the context for that solidarity. Because a detailed exposition will require much more space than is available here we confine our remarks to a brief skeleton discussion.

Thus, for example, we may include Collins' *ritual interaction* behavior (Collins, 1981; 1994) by adding a set of specific behaviors $\mathscr{R}$ (a_i performing at level b_i for a_i in G^+) which heighten members' emotions about and reinforce their commitments to $\mathscr{I}$, consequently reinforcing their interpersonal affect, which reinforces the solidarity of the group overall. Here the ritual interactions of a member, as well as other prescribed individual behaviors (a_i performing at level p_i^+ for a_i in G^+) such as contributing to the common good are ordained by the ideals, values, etc., in $\mathscr{I}$ and are in turn a public announcement of the member's commitment to $\mathscr{I}$, which induces others to present their public announcements of commitment to $\mathscr{I}$ by also performing their ritual interactions. The common publicly known commitments to $\mathscr{I}$ then induce or reinforce interpersonal cohesion as discussed above. The members' contributions $\mathscr{C}$ to the production of the group's *common goods* $\mathscr{G}$ (a_j contributing at level c_j for a_j in G^+) available to the individual members of G^+ can have a similar effect. Thus, ritual interactions, as well as contributions to the production of the group's common goods, become part of the set of *prescribed behaviors* $\mathscr{B}^+$ for the group G^+, these behaviors being positively ordained (+ relation) by the items in $\mathscr{I}$.

In addition, there is usually a set of *proscribed* behaviors $\mathscr{B}^-$ which are negatively ordained by $\mathscr{I}$ (− relation). These behaviors erode members' commitments to $\mathscr{I}$ and consequently decrease their interpersonal affect, which lowers the solidarity of the group overall. Here proscribed behaviors of a member, observed by others and negatively ordained by the ideals, values, etc., in $\mathscr{I}$, are an announcement of the member's non-commitment to or dishonoring of $\mathscr{I}$, which tends to decrease the interpersonal affect which links this member to others. Thus, publicly observed non-commitments to or dishonorings of $\mathscr{I}$ tend to decrease the interpersonal cohesion of the group.

These ingredients together with the relations between them may again be expanded to a yet larger schema which allows a formalization of Hechter's rational action theory for solidarity, where agents monitor or are apprised of the behaviors of the members of G^+ and invoke the appropriate prescribed and proscribed sanctions against violators, legitimated by prescriptive or proscriptive norms by which a_i is sanctioned at level q_i^+ or q_i^- for a_i in G^-, for not performing or for performing them, respectively. In this schema, common goods are distributed to individual members and sanctions for behavioral transgressions are distributed to members as subtractions from individuals' resources, a_i's resources and distributions being represented by r_i and d_i, respectively, for a_i in G^+. This extended schema appears in Figure 9.11.

9. DISCUSSION

Fararo and Doreian (1998) present a broad summary of the issues arising with the notion of solidarity, in the process raising a collection of important and challenging theoretical problems and proposing specific problems for mathematical sociologists to tackle. Here we have restricted our attention to a formal theoretical development and elaboration of the small schema corresponding to the characteristics under (a), (c) and (b) (by subsumption under (c)) in the conceptual

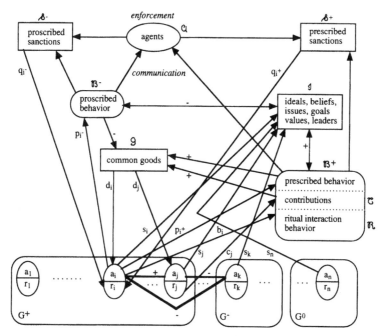

FIGURE 9.11.   An extended schema of solidarity: persons, beliefs, behaviors, contributions, sanctions, common goods distributions and their interrelationships.

scheme of Section 1. As we saw in Section 8 this schema may be
augmented to a larger one which incorporates other issues associated
with the idea of solidarity, for example, Collins' ritual interaction
behavior and the relations and social mechanisms of Hechter's theory
of solidarity.

Here we explore a bit more some issues related to our small schema.
Our development in this paper is an outgrowth of Newcomb's work
on the A–B–X system (Newcomb, 1953; 1956), the author's elaborations of the empirical micromodels for sufficiently small groups and
the microprocesses and micromodels implicated in the A–B–X system
(Johnsen, 1985; 1986; 1989a). It is a detailed working out of the
different possible protomodels and macrostructures implied by our
interpretation of the various triadic microprocesses stemming from the
dynamics of solidarity. Assuming that G^0 has a benign effect on G^+,
we state some comparison conditions that a quantitative solidarity
function should satisfy and, *ceteris paribus*, derive the protomodel comparisons for the different macrostructure combinations for G^+ and G^-

which are nested with respect to their sets of $+$ directed edges. We then give a methodological approach for arriving at the comparative level of solidarity when the group size n is sufficiently small ($n < 80$). A task lying ahead will be to develop the form of the solidarity function to where the function can be applied to groups G with arbitrary structures for its components G^+ and G^-.

We assume the group is sufficiently small to allow for a complete sample survey of the group. When the group has size $n < 40$ it is reasonable to assume that everyone in the group knows everyone else sufficiently well to have either a positive or a negative relation with that person. This justifies the use of the two-valued $+/-$ labeling of the directed edges representing the interpersonal relations in the group and allows an analysis based on the well-known set of 16 basic triads. Between group sizes 40 and 80 the accurate representation of interpersonal relational values by $+$ and "$-$" may be problematical. We can get by if we permit the value "$-$" to represent both "$-$" and "0". Otherwise, and for group sizes $n \geqslant 80$, we should use at least the three values $+/-/0$ for the directed edge relations, which entails a triadic analysis based on at least the set Ψ of 138 basic triads.

In his discussion of "alienation" and "estrangement" Torrance (1977) equates "alienation" to renunciation and separation while letting "estrangement" denote the process by which people become strangers and enemies. At the interpersonal level the first can be represented by the lack of any relationship, while the latter two can be captured by representing the relationship to a stranger by 0 and to an enemy by $-$. Thus, in order to include and differentiate between strangers and enemies we need to use the three labels $+/-/0$ on the directed interpersonal relations, which again requires the basic set of triads Ψ. If in addition we want to distinguish and represent the absence $\emptyset$ of a directed relationship we are led to the use of four labels $+/-/0/\emptyset$, which results in an analysis based on a set of 10 different dyads (4 symmetric and 6 asymmetric) and 720 different triads. Such an analysis could only be useful for analyzing extremely large groups, and would appear to be a forbidding task if a complete survey sample were undertaken.

One might expect that the relative sizes of G^+ and G^- within G should make a difference in the v-solidarity of G^+ independently of other factors. This is not dealt with here, although a preliminary quantification of it seems possible. If G^+ is greatly outnumbered by a hostile and cohesive G^- we expect G^+ to be highly vulnerable to dissolution or fragmentation and to a failure to preserve beliefs, values, goals, special persons, etc., whereas, if a sufficiently solidary G^+ greatly outnumbers a hostile and cohesive G^- we expect G^+ to survive and possibly succeed, although perhaps not without problems. On another note, the v-solidarity of G^+ should also depend on the amounts of resources under the control of the groups G^+ and G^- as a whole and of their individual members (the r_i values in Figure 9.11). There seems to be ample empirical evidence to support this. In a recent example from the classic arena for the manifestation of solidarity, the results of the labor strike at Caterpillar Inc. by the United Auto Workers (UAW) show that the available resources of the company (strong customer sales and an effective cadre of office workers and skilled temporary workers who replaced the strikers) and the relative lack of resources of the union (limited strike funds, little or no support from other unions, and a high level of strikebreaking by its own members; even another UAW local continued to work for one of Caterpillar's suppliers) were sufficient for the company to prevail over the union in imposing its own preferred salary rates, work rules and conditions (Bearak, 1995). The UAW had a limited strike fund and the individual workers had limited family resources to maintain a strike without significant outside income. Typically, other family members had to work and/or the Caterpillar employee had to take part-time work in order for the family to survive. The survival of the union families while remaining in their respective home towns was a necessary condition for the union to remain intact. The union failed, however, to attain its goals with respect to the salary rates and rules and conditions under which its members would work.

   Although we have viewed the model structures at time t or at stasis, we have generated them by incipient triadic microprocesses that shape and change these structures. By combining the microprocesses from the triads involving a fixed pair of persons (vertices), and doing this for all such pairs, one may try to formulate a deterministic or probabilistic dynamic macroprocess models which results from these microprocesses. With regard to interpersonal affect or cohesion, models of varying levels of complexity have been developed by Hubbell et al. (1975), Hunter (1978), Killworth and Bernard (1976), and Holland and Leinhardt (1977). Here, typically, the deterministic or probabilistic value of the relation from i to j at time t is implicitly defined by a differential or difference equation with respect to time. In many cases these models are analytically tractable and lead to macrostructure solutions at time t and at stasis which can be derived and completely specified mathematically. The development of similar types of dynamic models for solidarity seems possible and would be welcome, at least as a foil, for further theoretical and empirical work. All these dynamic models, however, assume a fixed group of individuals G, which is really inadequate to model social groups which change size and composition over time, for example, over generations of UAW union members.

Hechter (1987) has proposed a solidarity function $f(ab)$ in which $a =$ the extensiveness of a group's obligations and $b =$ the rate of members' compliance to these obligations. We consider a group's obligations to be the uncompensated contributions of the members for the benefit of the group. Both of these are represented in Figure 9.11 by the personal ties of the members of G^+ to the three-tiered box of prescribed behaviors $\mathscr{B}^+$, which includes personal contributions and ritual interaction behavior, and to the box of proscribed behaviors $\mathscr{B}^-$. Note that in this extended schema we are positing that these obligations (prescribed and proscribed behaviors) are directly ordained by $\mathscr{I}$. Because of this, conscientiously meeting all the obligations entailed by $\mathscr{B}^+$ and $\mathscr{B}^-$ can serve as an indicator for adherence to $\mathscr{I}$. This seems reasonable when one realizes that much of a_i's prescribed and proscribed behavior will usually be highly visible to and hence easily monitored by the agents of enforcement and sanctioning in the group. Thus, Hechter's rational choice version of solidarity appears to be representable within the extended schema of Section 8.

Within Durkheim's classification we have been formalizing solidarity in its "mechanical" form and in its "organic" form based on institutionalized individualism (viewed as an item in $\mathscr{I}$: "the individual is sacred" is a Parsonian value; cf. Fararo and Doreian, 1998). The residual mode of organic solidarity, based on the division of labor, complementarity and structural interdependence, is not really captured by our small schema. It may, however, be captured by the extension discussed in Section 8. There the prescribed actions $\mathscr{B}^+$ and proscribed actions $\mathscr{B}^-$ are ordained or implied by the items in $\mathscr{I}$, while all other actions $\mathscr{B}^0$ are optional. If $\mathscr{I}$ includes subsets $\mathscr{I}_*$ (special laws, rules, values, norms, persons, etc.) for special subgroups G_*^+ of G^+, and $\mathscr{B}^+$ and $\mathscr{B}^-$ include corresponding special subsets of prescribed and proscribed behaviors $\mathscr{B}_*^+$ and $\mathscr{B}_*^-$, respectively, to all of which all members of G^+ subscribe, we then have a schema for solidarity based on complementarity and structural interdependence. This complementarity and structural interdependence would need to be accepted within the group, where the members come to consensus that this differentiation is for the good of the entire group because it convincingly exploits the efficiencies of the division of labor and leads to increased generation or conservation of individual resources.

Finally, we have the questions of how solidary groups emerge and change over long periods of time. Suppose we start with a pre-existent solidary group G^+ with respect to a set $\mathscr{I}$. A child born into a family having some members in G^+ will be exposed to a microprocess of "friendship induces agreement with respect to $\mathscr{I}$" with such members. When that child adheres to $\mathscr{I}$, either then or later, the result is another member recruited to G^+. A member g of G who is unrelated to G^+ but who is attracted to and begins to adhere to or believe in $\mathscr{I}$ will come into association with members of G^+, after which a microprocess of "agreement with respect to $\mathscr{I}$ induces friendship" will occur which then socially integrates g into the structure of G^+. Now suppose that there is no pre-existent solidary group associated with a set $\mathscr{I}$. Any set $G^{\wedge}$ of members of G (possibly a single person) who formulate an $\mathscr{I}$ and adhere to it are the seeds from which a solidary group G^+ may emerge. Here certain persons begin to adhere to $\mathscr{I}$ based on prior friendly associations (friendship and kinship) by the initial microprocesses of "friendship induces agreement with respect to $\mathscr{I}$", which in turn may reinforce the friendship in G' via "agreement with respect to $\mathscr{I}$ induces friendship", thus socially integrating G' as a solidary structure G^+ in G. These members become the founders. After this beginning the group, in order to survive, must recruit others. These may be other friends and relatives of the founders, which become members of G^+ by processes of "friendship induces agreement with respect to $\mathscr{I}$" or converts obtained by processes of "agreement with respect to $\mathscr{I}$ induces friendship", as discussed above.

A very good example of successful survival and growth which proceeded along these lines is given by the Mormons (The Church of Jesus Christ of Latter-Day Saints), founded in 1830 by Joseph Smith with a small group of friends and relatives G^+ (cf. Encyclopaedia Brittanica, 1911). A very good example of non-survival is afforded by the religious group G^+ of Shakers (The United Society of Believers in Christ's Second Appearing), founded in the 1770s by Ann Lee, again with a small group of friends and relatives (cf. Encyclopaedia Brittanica, 1911). Three of the items in this group's set $\mathscr{I}$ were celibacy, Christian communism and separation from the world. Although their communism was an economic success and they had an associated non-communal order of sympathizers, members had no descendants from whom further full members could be recruited to G^+. After a period of growth in the late 1700s the group entered a long period of decline, marked by repeated establishment and abandonment of communities, to where it is now virtually extinct. There is an irony furnished by this example, namely, that an otherwise solidary group may include in its set $\mathscr{I}$ one or more items which, when honored, can work against the long term survival of the group.

ACKNOWLEDGEMENTS

The author wishes to express his thanks and appreciation to the members of the University of California, Santa Barbara, Social Networks Seminar for their feedback during the presentation of this material. Special thanks are owed to Dorwin (Doc) Cartwright, Noah Friedkin, John Sonquist and Greg Truex for helpful critical comments and suggestions which led to important improvements in the substance and exposition of the final version of the paper.

REFERENCES

Abercrombie, N., Hill, S. and Turner, B.S. (1994) *Dictionary of Sociology*, 3rd edition. London, U.K.: Penguin Books Ltd.

Abrams, P. and McCulloch, A. (1976) *Communes, Sociology and Society*. Cambridge, U.K.: Cambridge University Press.

Baldwin, P. (1990) *The Politics of Social Solidarity*. Cambridge, U.K.: Cambridge University Press.

Bardis, P.D. (1985) *Dictionary of Quotations in Sociology*. Westport, CT: Greenwood Press.

Bearak, B. (1995), Five part series of articles on the United Auto Workers strike at the Caterpillar company, *Los Angeles Times*, vol. 114: 14–18 May. Los Angeles, CA: Times Mirror Company, A1.

Borgatta, E.F. and Borgatta, M.L. (eds.) (1992) *Encyclopedia of Sociology*, vol. 4. New York, NY: Macmillan Publishing Company.

Boudon, R. and Bourricaud, F. (1989) *A Critical Dictionary of Sociology* (selected and translated by Peter Hamilton, ed.). Chicago, IL: The University of Chicago Press.

Cartwright, D. (1968) "The nature of group cohesiveness", in Dorwin Cartwright and Alvin Zander (eds.), *Group Dynamics: Research and Theory*, 3rd edition. New York, NY: Harper and Row, pp. 91–109.

Cartwright, D. and Harary, F. (1956) "Structural balance: A generalization of Heider's theory". *Psychological Review*, **63**: 277–293.

Collins, R. (1981) "On the microfoundations of macrosociology", *American Journal of Sociology*, **86**: 984–1014.

Collins, R. (1994) *Four Sociological Traditions*. New York, NY: Oxford University Press.

Davis, J.A. (1963) "Structural balance, mechanical solidarity, and interpersonal relations". *American Journal of Sociology*, **68**: 444–462.

Davis, J.A. (1967) "Clustering and structural balance in graphs". *Human Relations*, **20**: 181–187.

Davis, J.A. (1970) "Clustering and hierarchy in interpersonal relations: Testing two graph theoretical models on 742 sociomatrices". *American Sociological Review*, **35**: 843–851.

Davis, J.A. and Leinhardt, S. (1972) "The structure of positive interpersonal relations in small groups", in Joseph Berger et al. (eds.), *Sociological Theories in Progress*, vol. 2. Boston, MA: Houghton Mifflin, pp. 218–251.

Durkheim, E. (1888) "Introduction to the Sociology of the Family", in Mark Traugott, (ed.) (1978) *Emile Durkheim on Institutional Analysis*. Chicago, IL: University of Chicago Press, pp. 205–228.

Encyclopaedia Britannica (1911), 11th edition. Cambridge, U.K.: Cambridge University Press.

Fararo, T.J. and Doreian, P. (1998) "The theory of solidarity: An agenda of problems", Chapter 1 in Patrick Doreian and Thomas J. Fararo (eds.), *The Problem of Solidarity: Theories and Models*. (this volume).

Fortes, M. (1945) *The Dynamics of Clanship among the Tallensi*. London, U.K.: Oxford University Press.

Hechter, M. (1987) *Principles of Group Solidarity*. Berkeley, CA: University of California Press.

Heider, F. (1946) "Attitudes and cognitive organization". *Journal of Psychology*, **21**: 107–112.

Holland, P.W. and Leinhardt, S. (1970) "A method for detecting structure in sociometric data". *American Journal of Sociology*, **70**: 492–513.

Holland, P.W. and Leinhardt, S. (1971) "Transitivity in structural models of small groups". *Comparative Group Studies*, **2**: 107–124.

Holland, P.W. and Leinhardt, S. (1977) "A dynamic model for social networks". *Journal of Mathematical Sociology*, **5**: 5–20.

Hubbell, C.H., Johnsen, E.C. and Marcus, M. (1975) *Structural Balance in Group Networks*. Monograph Series: No. 2, Institute for the Interdisciplinary Applications of Algebra and Combinatorics. Santa Barbara, CA: University of California, July.

Hunter, J.E. (1978) "Dynamic Sociometry". *Journal of Mathematical Sociology*, **6**: 87–138.

Jary, D. and Jary, J. (1991) *The Harper Collins Dictionary of Sociology*. New York, NY: Harper Collins Publishers.

Johnsen, E.C. (1985) "Network macrostructure models for the Davis-Leinhardt set of empirical sociomatrices". *Social Networks*, **7**: 203–224.

Johnsen, E.C. (1986) "Structure and process: Agreement models for friendship formation". *Social Networks*, **8**: 257–306.

Johnsen, E.C. (1989a) "Agreement-friendship processes related to empirical social macrostructures", in Manfred Kochen (ed.), *The Small World*. Norwood, NJ: Ablex Publishing Corporation, pp. 239–279. (Revision of Johnsen (1986) above)

Johnsen, E.C. (1989b) "The micro-macro connection: Exact structure and process", in Fred Roberts (ed.), *Applications of Combinatorics and Graph Theory to the Biological and Social Sciences*. New York, NY: Springer, Berlin, pp. 169–201.

Johnson, A.G. (1995) *The Blackwell Dictionary of Sociology*. Cambridge, MA: Basil Blackwell Inc.

Killworth, P.D. and Bernard, H.R. (1977) "A model of human group dynamics". *Social Science Research*, **5**: 173–224.

Kishida, A. (1990) *A Random Graph Approach in Structural Balance*. Ph.D. Dissertation, University of California, Irvine, CA.

Loewy, E.H. (1993) *Freedom and Community*. Albany, NY: State University of New York Press.

Mann, M. (ed.) (1984) *The International Encyclopedia of Sociology*. New York, NY: The Continu Publishing Company.

Marshall, G. (ed.) (1994) *The Concise Oxford Dictionary of Sociology*. Oxford, U.K.: Oxford University Press.

Mitchell, G.D. (ed.) (1979) *A New Dictionary of the Social Sciences*. Hawthorne, NY: Aldine Publishing Company.

Newcomb, T.M. (1953) "An approach to the study of communicative acts". *Psychological Review*, **60**: 393–404.

Newcomb, T.M. (1956) "The prediction of interpersonal attraction". *American Psychologist*, **11**: 575–586.

Newcomb, T.M. (1961) *The Acquaintance Process.* New York, NY: Holt, Rinehart and Winston.

Newcomb, T.M. (1968) "Interpersonal balance", in Robert P. Abelson et al. (eds.) *Theories of Cognitive Consistency: A Sourcebook.* Chicago, IL: Rand-McNally, pp. 28–51.

Ostrom, E. (1990) *Governing the Commons.* Cambridge, U.K.: Cambridge University Press.

Sobrino, J., S.J. and Juan Hernández Pico, S.J. (1985) *Theology of Christian Solidarity* (translated from the Spanish by Phillip Berryman). Maryknoll, NY: Orbis Books.

Stang, D.J. and Wrightsman, L.S. (1981) *DICTIONARY of Social Behavior and Social Research Methods.* Monterey, CA: Brooks/Cole Publishing Company.

Tamney, J.B. (1975) *Solidarity in a Slum.* Cambridge, MA: Schenkman Publishing Company.

Torrance, J. (1977) *Estrangement, Alienation and Exploitation.* New York, NY: Columbia University Press.

Young, F.W. (1965) *Initiation Ceremonies.* Indianapolis, IN: Bobbs-Merrill Company.

10 GROUP FORMATION IN FRIENDSHIP NETWORKS[1]

EVELIEN P.H. ZEGGELINK

University of Groningen, The Netherlands

1. THE EMERGENCE OF FRIENDSHIP GROUPS

A major part of human behavior occurs in groups. Many different kinds of groups and probably even more definitions of human groups exist (among others: Freeman, 1992; Homans, 1950; Shaw, 1981). In the field of social networks in particular, many researchers have attempted to provide a formal definition of such groups (among others: Alba, 1973; Luce and Perry, 1949; Mokken, 1979). We focus on naturally emerging and freely forming small social groups, friendship groups in particular. From all different kinds of groups, these are most difficult to define, because they lack any pre-defined assignment of members (such as in experimental groups, task-oriented groups, problem-solving groups, therapeutical groups, groups in decision making processes and so on (Mullen, 1987)). The motives for group membership concern some form of satisfaction of social needs and related drives that are purely voluntary. A group that emerges accordingly is a very important aggregation from the view of its individual members. How it provides them social identity, and how their behaviors, attitudes, and opinions are shaped by the group are processes frequently studied in the field of social psychology and social networks (Erickson, 1988; Mullen and Goethals, 1987; Tajfel and Turner, 1986). In these studies, however, how these groups come into existence is ignored usually. We think that in order to understand how group membership influences individuals, it is at least as important to understand how the group in one way or the other has been 'constructed' by the same individuals. The emergence of such groups, and especially its related structural characteristics, is the main problem we address here.

Groups are not static entities but change over time. Some theorists (Mullen and Goethals, 1987) argue that these dynamics may actually be necessary not only for a group to be considered as a group but also for its understanding. Nevertheless, in the literature only very little attention has been devoted to the dynamic aspects of groups. Within the generally acknowledged sequence of group dynamics, consisting of forming, storming, norming, performing, and adjourning, most researches have focused on the three middle stages (Shaw, 1981). Too little focus has been directed on the aspect of group formation and emergence. When studying the aspects of storming, norming, and performing, two lines of research can generally be distinguished. One line focuses on the individual as the level of analysis, the other focuses on the group as a whole. In the applications of social network analysis, a similar distinction exists. Dependent on the focus of the research, tools exist to either measure locally structural properties of the individual in the group or network (e.g. point centrality), or to measure globally structural characteristics of the group or network (e.g. density, degree of transitivity). A combined approach, in both fields, in which the individual is the main acting unit, but behaves within, is influenced by, and influences his or her own social context, is seldom found.

Fararo and Doreian (1998, Chapter 1) recognize the same lack in the field of mathematical models of social processes and they consequently present a stimulating argument that asks for a set of general dynamic mathematical models that account for both the structural processes and the generation of solidarity among freely forming, and other, human groups. This argument includes a general distinction in three types of mathematical models, with different focuses of attention on social structure, that have been constructed in the literature so far: 1. Models that examine how a, given and not-varying, structure constrains or shapes social processes (e.g. influence processes of opinions within groups); 2. Models for the static analysis and definition of structures (e.g. group definition in social network terms); 3. Models that study how a structure emerges or changes over time (e.g. the emergence of a leader within predefined groups). The present author has been involved in the development and analysis of so-called individual oriented models of friendship network evolution. These are mainly a representative of the third type of models, but also incorporate the other two foci of attention (Zeggelink, 1993; 1994; 1995). These models attempt to explain macro (sociological) phenomena on the basis of micro behaviors of individuals and thereby explicitly take the restrictions and opportunities provided by the macro level into account.

With this approach, a preliminary model of group formation has been developed that attempts to predict the emergence of groups in friendship networks (Zeggelink et al., 1996). The groups are characterized simply by pure network structure: the distinction between the relative denseness within and sparseness of friendships outside the group defines the existence of a group. In this model these groups emerge 'accidentally' from initially dyadic friendships only, just by the fact that a number of friendships together show a large contrast with the rest of the network structure. This model tries to capture that individuals, in the process of deepening and strengthening their dyadic friendships, become at least acquainted with their friends' friends. When one's friends know each other, it is easier to relate closely and frequently with each of them (Feld, 1981), and common friendships and frequent interaction lead to feelings of 'belonging' together. As such, groups may emerge. In reality, these friendship groups have more characteristics beyond the contrast between structure within the group and between the group and the rest of the population. They are very homogeneous mainly because the initial selection of friends is based on similarity. The homogeneity of the group is further increased by conformity pressures and homophilic selection of new members (Cohen, 1977). Thus, in fact, groups can be characterized by both structure and homogeneity.

However, in this existing model, the initial selection of friends is not based on similarity but is purely random. As a consequence, groups were and could be defined and characterized only by structural features. Furthermore, chances were rather small that groups emerged accidentally from these friendships based on random choice.

An even more important shortcoming is that during and after the establishment process of the group, something beyond structure and homogeneity develops. There is more that represents the so-called 'groupness' or 'entitativity' of the group (Campbell, 1958; Sherif and Sherif, 1964). Or as Fararo and Doreian in Chapter 1 call it, a higher social entity emerges that is defined by the cognitive and affective feelings associated with it by its members. This 'more' leads to group norms and values, group culture, group jokes, and group solidarity. These developments cannot be explained if individual attributes, opinions and attitudes are not taken into consideration. Moreover, these individual characteristics are important determinants for similarity assessments and consequent friendship formation in the first place.

Thus, the existing model of group formation becomes much more interesting if individual characteristics are incorporated that firstly determine the formation of dyadic friendships on the basis of preferences for similarity, and secondly can be changed under the influence of emergent group membership such that the coming into existence of group norms and solidarity can be explained.

Therefore we focus in this chapter on the incorporation of individual attributes, the related preference for similarity in the formation of friendships, and the consequent emergence of groups. How these subgroups subsequently (or simultaneously) create their own identity (by establishing norms, culture and so forth) depends, among other things, on their size, and their connections with other groups or nongroup members. These 'structural' features of the group in the context of a larger friendship network are the main dependent variables that we examine. All other consequences that result from these variables are topics of future research, on which we spend some words in Section 4. As such, this chapter mainly attempts to contribute to problem set #1, the generation of an emergent group (Chapter 1). In order to do so, first the nature and philosophy behind individual oriented models is explained in Section 2. In Section 3, we present the most relevant theoretical literature on group formation. Section 4 presents our new model on the basis of this literature. In Section 5 results based on simulation are shown and a discussion is given in Section 6.

2. MICRO–MACRO MODELS OF NETWORK EVOLUTION

Social networks (Wasserman and Faust, 1994) should play a crucial role when studying processes of group dynamics. In our context, the social network is a friendship network and our goal is to explain the dynamic evolution of its structure mainly in terms of (sub)groups. The friendship network consists of a set of individuals and the possible, non-static, friendships between them.

Groups are often referred to as self-regulating entities. The view and the behavior of the individual with respect to his or her group or other groups is usually of minor importance in studies of group processes. However, individual behavior has its impact on group structure and composition. Therefore, in contrast to most existing approaches, in our individual oriented approach, it is the individual who decides whether or not to establish friendships, whether he or she wants to belong to a group, individuals build and constitute the group. A group does not behave, but an individual does. Although the individuals themselves make the choices to initiate, maintain or dissolve relationships, the (larger) friendship network structure or the macro level can be seen as the 'unintended' or 'unconscious' effect of individual behaviors at the micro level because for them the final results of their actions are incalculable. The examination of these dynamic phenomena is not simple because causes and consequences of the network are difficult to separate. On the one hand, individuals actively construct the network by forming friendships. On the other hand, they simultaneously 'react on' it because it provides and limits the opportunities for their choices. As such it seems as if these choices are 'determined' by the network.

In our individual oriented models, this mutual interaction is taken into account directly, made possible by using object oriented programming techniques and simulation of interacting individual behavioral rules that explicitly 'use' information of the macro level (Stokman and van Oosten, 1994). Individuals are assumed to show 'bounded rational' behavior with respect to initiating, maintaining, and breaking off friendships. This is represented in so-called tension functions that individuals attempt to minimize within the limits of rationality. These boundaries are determined by the limited amount of information and restricted capability of 'imagination' (anticipation or strategic foresight) of every individual: An individual does not have complete information such that he or she is able to make the optimal choices. Incomplete information occurs partly because an individual does not fully perceive all relevant characteristics of other individuals and the network structure. Moreover, an individual will never have complete knowledge on what others will do, and can only partly anticipate on them. This is crucial because the actual reduction of tension as a result of the attempt to minimize tension not only depends on the individual's own actions but also on the (unknown, possibly simultaneous) actions of the other individuals. In this way, the network, as it exists at a certain moment, indirectly influences individual behavior. It also has its direct effects. The structure of the network 'determines' the availability of individuals as friends, their positions in the network, and the number, sizes and composition of friendship groups (and thereby availability).[2]

3. GROUP FORMATION IN NETWORKS

3.1. Defining a Group

Literature shows (among others: Shaw, 1981; Mullen and Goethals, 1987) that a friendship group can in general be characterized by an observable amount of interaction (physical proximity) between its (similar in one or more aspect) members whereby potentially even more friendships between the individuals, if not already present, are developed (Salzinger, 1982). The individuals are aware of the existence of the group and its members, and are motivated to join the group. A common goal is not always necessary but a group is generally perceived as a unity in the sense of sharing a common fate.

In our view of the idea that groups emerge as a result of individual behaviors, it is especially important to know how people, either within or outside a group, recognize groups. Freeman et al. (1988, 1989) show that the rule people use is approximately the following: An individual is assigned to group J if he or she interacts, on the average, more with others in J than with others not in J. It is the large number of friendships within as well as the small number of friendships outside the group that is distinctive (Sailer and Gaulin, 1984). Thus, in terms of network structure only, the most outstanding aspect of a group is the large contrast between the number of friendships within and the number of friendships outside the group (Reitz, 1988).[3] There must be a minimal degree of cohesiveness for a group to continue to exist, or even to come into existence. The relatively high degree of interaction leads to feelings of 'belonging together' and 'closeness', and finally to the 'more', referred to as entitativity and groupness in Section 1.

A definition that can be used within the model should therefore capture the contrast between the structural character of the group itself and the structure between itself and other groups or individuals. Given these structural aspects of groups, the best graph theoretical definition of group existence within a network is the LS set because it simultaneously considers both the internal and external friendships of the group members (Luccio and Sami, 1969; Seidman, 1983; Borgatti et al., 1990). An extensive discussion on the appropriateness of the LS set can be found in Zeggelink et al. (1996). We use the following notation and definitions.

Let $G = (V, E)$ be an undirected graph with vertex set V and edge set E. $G' = (V', E')$ is a subgraph of G if its vertex set V' is a subset of V, and E' consists of all edges of E that are incident with vertices in V'. The number of vertices in a subset V' of V is denoted $|V'|$ and is called its size.

For the translation into sociological terms, graph corresponds with (friendship) network, edge corresponds with friendship, and vertex with individual. Subnetwork is the sociological counterpart of subgraph.

Definition 1 A cutset S of a connected graph is a set of edges of G such that its removal from G disconnects G: $G - S$ is disconnected. The number of edges in a cutset that has the minimum number of edges, is called the edge connectivity $\lambda(G)$ of G.

The edge connectivity $\lambda(v, w)$ of the pair of vertices v, w is the minimum number of edges that must be removed to disconnect them. $\lambda(V') = \min\{\{\lambda(v, w) \,|\, v, w \in V'\}\}$ is the edge connectivity of V', where V' is a subset of V.

Definition 2 The number of edges joining two subsets V_1 and V_2 of V is denoted $\alpha(V_1, V_2)$. The external edges of a subset V' of V are the edges joining vertices of V' with vertices of $V - V'$. The number of external edges of a subset V' is denoted $\alpha(V') = \alpha(V', V - V')$.

Definition 3a A subset L of the vertex set V of a graph G is an LS set if and only if for any proper subset K of L, $\alpha(K, L - K) > \alpha(K, V - L)$.

Thus, an LS set is a set of vertices L in which each proper subset has more edges to its complement within L than to the outside of L. An alternative definition is:

Definition 3b A subset L of V of a graph G is an LS set if for any proper subset K of L, $\alpha(K) > \alpha(L)$.

According to these definitions, an LS set with $\lambda = 1$ can exist only if it is disconnected from the rest of the graph.[4] At least one vertex of such an LS set can become disconnected if just one edge would be removed. Therefore we consider only LS sets with $\lambda > 1$ to have any meaning as a 'group'. Every individual vertex and V itself are trivial LS sets. All other LS sets are called non-trivial LS sets. They cannot partially overlap but they can contain each other.[5] The most relevant property of LS sets is their close internal structure compared to the loose connectedness to the outside represented by the relatively high value of λ: members have many direct or indirect friends in common which contributes to the reinforcement of every friendship. We therefore assume that the higher the value of λ in a group, the stronger the 'group feelings' of its members. However, LS sets cannot be characterized by edge connectivity alone because LS sets with equal edge connectivity can have different sizes and different structures when of equal size. Another important characteristic is the low value of α which represents that an LS set does not contain any individual or subgroup with more 'linkage' outside the group than within the group. It is a measure of distinctiveness: the smaller α the more distinct the group.

Thus, in structural terms, a group can be characterized by its size $|L|$, its 'uniqueness' or isolatedness ($\alpha(L)$) and its 'closeness' ($\lambda(L)$). These are the main features that we study, as they are probably very relevant determinants for subsequent maintenance or dissolution of the group and other group processes.[6]

3.2. The Processes towards Group Formation and Growth

How does such a group, defined as an LS set, emerge from individual choice regarding friendship formation? Being a member of a group provides the individual with some sense of belonging, and the presence of other group members satisfies his or her needs for affiliation. Such groups are not predefined or pre-existing, but first have to arise themselves. They are not purposively constructed but evolve as a natural result of overlapping dyadic friendships among a set of individuals. As the definition of LS set shows, this overlap needs to fulfil the requirements of a relatively large contrast between density of friendships within and density of friendships outside the group. Before this 'overlap' can be examined, dyadic friendship formation has to be modelled. Then, as soon as groups have arisen, the consequent behavior of individuals as group or as non-group members can be taken into account.

Proximity, contact, and interaction are the first prerequisites for interpersonal attraction and subsequent friendship formation. Proximity enables contact and interaction, such that individuals get to know each other better and learn about the characteristics of the other to judge on attractiveness. The most important factor of attraction is similarity with regard to certain, not all, characteristics of the other individual.[7]

Social comparison theory (Festinger, 1954; Goethals and Darley, 1987) is an appropriate theory for explaining both the formation of friendships, and the tendency of individuals looking for group membership. According to this theory an individual has a drive to evaluate his or her abilities and opinions that affect his or her behavior. In the absence of any objective non-social standards, an individual evaluates them by comparing with abilities and opinions of others, and chooses, if possible, individuals who are close to his or her own abilities and opinions. Thus, an individual chooses those who are similar to him or her, also because it is easier to treat someone as an equal (as a friend) if he or she is similar to you.

Suppose for now that groups have emerged. Schachter (1959) already mentioned that the pure individual need for affiliation explains the individual's desire to belong to a group. Being just a member of a group provides the individual rewards, a sense of belonging, and once again the ability to compare oneself with others. As such, social comparison theory also offers an explanation for the fact that individuals want to associate with others, prefer to be member of groups of individuals who are similar to themselves, and thereby is also important for the explanation of the 'development' of groups that are not formed from external constraint but from individual choice. Furthermore, in order to bring about similarity and homogeneity within groups, pressures toward uniformity arise. Social comparison theory states that action is taken to reduce opinion or ability discrepancies when they exist. These discrepancies can be reduced in several ways: by changing one's own opinions (social influence) or abilities (competition), by trying to change those of others, or by ending comparison with 'too' dissimilar others. These elements of social influence: changing one's own or group members' opinions reinforce similarity and homogeneity within groups and may as such lead to the emergence of group norms and group solidarity. Since these processes take place simultaneously with the emergence and formation of the group, the generation of solidarity possibly amplifies group formation.[8]

4. THE MODEL

Given the theoretical considerations in Section 3, we will now formulate the individual behavioral rules. In order to capture the main tendencies of pure friendship – and group formation, the initial situation is that of a closed population of g mutual strangers.[9]

The behavioral rules of individuals concerning the establishing of friendships are based on tension minimization with respect to so-called issues. An issue being any kind of dimension with respect to friendships one has an opinion about, and one thinks is changeable by one's own actions (Hoede, 1990). An individual's state with regard to the presence and configuration of friendships is summarized in his or her tension, and every individual always tries to reduce his or her tension with respect to the issues.

Definition 4   Let z be the number of issues, and let $\Delta_{ip}(t)$ be the ith actor's tension with respect to the pth issue at time t, and let w_{ip} be the importance of the pth issue to the ith actor. Then the general form of the tension function for the ith actor at time t is given by:

$$\Delta_i(t) = \sum_{p=1}^{z} w_{ip} \Delta_{ip}(t), \tag{1}$$

where w_{ip} of each issue and the Δ_{ip} functions are chosen to be non-negative. Usually tension Δ_{ip} is given by some function of the difference between the evaluation of an ideal (preferred) state and the evaluation of the current state, according to actor i, on issue p.

An individual applies so-called myopic behavioral rules: He or she can only imagine what happens at the next point in time as a result of his or her own actions. The actual result of his or her own actions depends on the unknown actions of the other individuals. Every individual therefore assumes that the actions of the others are such that his or her own actions will lead to minimally attainable tension values.

Positive choices are the main type of 'ties' in this model and they represent the willingness to establish a friendship with the individual to whom the choice is directed. An individual may make as many choices as he or she would like to make in accordance with the issues that are relevant. A friendship is assumed to exist as soon as choice is mutual. An individual can also send negative messages (Note the difference between choice and message). These messages are used mainly for modelling convenience and do not have any direct 'negative' meaning: they represent that the sending individual does not want to be friends with an individual that chooses him or her. This does not necessarily mean that he or she has a negative attitude towards that individual, but represents simply that he or she is not open to form another friendship.

Another important element in this context is that individuals do not wait infinitely long for a reciprocated positive choice or a negative message from someone they want to be friends with, i.e. asymmetric positive choices tend to be withdrawn. This behavior is modelled by giving all individuals a so-called 'waiting period': the maximum amount of time that they will not withdraw an unreciprocated choice.[10] We perceive the act of exceeding individual i's waiting period by individual j as similar to the act of individual j sending a negative to message to i. Both represent no urgent desire of j to become friends with i. More on this topic will be discussed after Figure 10.1.

Every individual at least perceives all positive choices and negative messages that are directed towards him or her and also knows the total number of individuals in the population and their relevant individual attributes. Moreover, it is plausible to assume that an individual is able to observe whether he or she is a group member or not (see Section 3). If so, other group members and their friends are known.

The model is based on three issues. The first issue is necessary to capture every individual's need for affiliation and the fact that this may differ among individuals. It represents every individual's specific need for social contact (the number of friends):[11]

$$\Delta_{i1}(t) = |df_i - f_i(t)|,\qquad(2)$$

where $df_i \leqslant g - 1$ is i's desired number of friends and $f_i(t)$ is i's actual number of friends at time t.

Section 3 shows that another relevant aspect of friendship formation is similarity. The second issue thus becomes characteristics of (potential) friends. Individual i compares his or her own values on the relevant individual attributes with those of individual j, with whom he or she has a friendship or who is considered a potential friend. The smaller the difference between their values on these attributes, the more similar the two individuals are, the more satisfaction they obtain from the (potential) friendship relation (and thus the smaller the tension).[12] In this evaluation, some attributes will be more important than others. We assume that all attributes can be captured by one aggregate attribute (constant in time),[13] and that individuals use a linear distance function to measure the discrepancy between values. Let w_{i2} be the relative importance for individual i of the characteristics of friends in general versus the importance of the number of friends. Now, assuming that 'similar' friends lead to larger tension reductions than non-similar friends, and $f_i(t)$ is again the number of friends of individual i at time t, the following tension function represents both the first and the second issue:

$$\Delta_{i2}(t) = \left| df_i - \sum_{j=1}^{f_i(t)} (1 - w_{i2} |x_i - x_j|) \right|.\qquad(3)$$

This tension function is not of the general form (1) because the total number of friends appears both in the tension related to the first issue, number of friends, and the second issue, characteristics of friends. If $w_{i2} < 1$, characteristics of friends are less important than the number of friends (if $w_{i2} = 0$, characteristics are irrelevant, and tension function (2) is obtained). If $w_{i2} = 1$, the characteristics of friends are equally important as the number of friends. If $w_{i2} > 1$, characteristics of friends are more important than the number of friends.[14]

We assume $w_{i2} < 1$. For dichotomous individual attributes (e.g. gender), x_i equals 0 or 1, function (3) becomes simpler: $\Delta_{i2}(t)$ decreases maximally if a friendship is established with a similar individual ($x_i = x_j$). It decreases less if a friendship is established with a dissimilar individual ($x_i \neq x_j$).

So far, we have introduced two issues that are relevant in the formation of friendships: the number of friends, and the characteristics of friends. The third issue subsequently becomes the group. In real friendship formations, individuals cannot observe when a group can readily be formed. It is only as a side effect of having friends in common that groups get a chance to develop. We assume that once an individual is a group member in terms of LS sets, he or she tries to guarantee the future of that group but also takes care of his or her non-group goal (number and characteristics of friends). As such, the model remains individual oriented in which the structure of the friendship relations within one's group may become relevant in the 'calculation' of one's individual behavior, but in which groups themselves do not have explicit preferences, and thereby do not show any particular behavior. However, the fact that every individual group member tries to assure that the group structure 'strengthens' may be considered as some form of striving for group interest, and is closely related to the emergence of group solidarity by preferences for group members above non-group members (see later).

We briefly present the derivation of the tension function related to the group issue.[15] Let $L_i(t)$ be the smallest, if possible, non-trivial LS set to which i belongs at time t. If a non-trivial LS set exists, i is called a group member. If no non-trivial LS set exists, $L_i(t)$ is defined as the trivial singleton set containing just i, and i is a non-group member. $\lambda = \lambda(L_i(t))$ and $\alpha = \alpha(L_i(t))$ are the edge connectivity and the number of external edges of $L_i(t)$, respectively. We will omit the subscript i and the arguments t and $L_i(t)$, where possible.

If an individual is a group member, his or her group sense is stronger the smaller his or her and the group's total number of external friendships, and the larger his or her and the group's total number of internal friendships. The simplest definition of tension is concerned with the total number of external friendships of all group members, α, and attributes this value to every single group member. Similarly, λ is an overall representative of tension with regard to the internal structure. Tension should decrease with decreasing α or increasing λ.

However, LS sets of different size can have equal values of α and λ. If $\alpha(L) = \alpha(M)$ and $|L| > |M|, L$ might be considered as the group with less tension because for the smaller group M chances are higher that the group will no longer be an LS set if the same extra number of external friendships is established than for the larger group L.

For equal λ, it is more difficult to compare different group sizes because edge connectivity is not defined only with respect to friendships within the group. Since the precise functional shape of the tension component is not so relevant for the derivation of behavioral rules, the only specified properties of the tension component are that it increases with increasing α, with decreasing λ, and with decreasing $|L|$. Moreover, the total tension should be larger for non-group members than for group members. Therefore, the next tension function is defined

$$\Delta_{i3}(t) = (g-1)^2 - \frac{\lambda(L_i(t))|L_i(t) - 1|}{\alpha(L_i(t)) + 1} \tag{4}$$

where $L_i(t)$ is the smallest, if possible non-trivial, LS set to which i belongs.

Groups arise 'by chance', and not until then, as $|L_i(t)| > 1$, is this tension component relevant for group members. The value $(g-1)^2$ assures non-negative tension values. Let w_{i3} be the relative importance for individual i of the group in comparison with the importance of the number of friends. We assume that w_{i2} and w_{i3} are equal for all individuals $(w_2, w_3 \geqslant 0)$. Accordingly, the total tension function becomes:

$$\Delta_i(t) = \left| df_i - \sum_{j=1}^{f_i(t)} (1 - w_2 |x_i - x_j|) \right| + w_3 \left((g-1)^2 - \frac{\lambda(L_i(t))|L_i(t) - 1|}{\alpha(L_i(t)) + 1} \right). \tag{5}$$

The general situation of an individual i now is as follows. At a certain moment in time, he or she has a number of friends ($f_i(t)$ reciprocated friendship choices), makes a number of unreciprocated friendship choices, receives a number of unreciprocated friendship choices, and receives or sends a number of negative messages. For the decisions on behavior regarding friendship formation, it is relevant to know who the senders and receivers of these choices and messages are. Moreover, their individual attributes and their positions in the network are of importance. As such, i divides the other individuals j into six main mutually exclusive classes. The division is illustrated in Figure 10.1. Positive choices are represented by regular (bold) arrows. Since we assumed that the act of i receiving a negative message from j is perceived similarly to

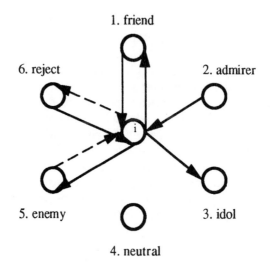

FIGURE 10.1.   Ego's (*i*'s) division of all other individuals.

j exceeding *i*'s waiting period, they are both represented by a broken arrow. A negative message can be sent only in the presence of a positive choice in the opposite direction. So can the waiting period of *i* only be exceeded by *j* in the presence of a positive choice from *i* to *j*. Therefore these positive choices are presented too. A negative message (broken arrow) thus never exists on its own. Consequently, mutual negative messages are without any meaning and cannot appear.[16]

1. friends   = {*j* | *j* sends a positive choice towards *i* and receives a positive choice from *i*}.
2. admirers = {*j* | *j* sends a positive choice to *i*, and *i* does not reciprocate (yet)}.
3. idols   = {*j* | *j* receives a positive choice from *i*, and *j* does not reciprocate (yet)}.
4. neutrals = {*j* | *j* does not choose *i*, and *i* does not choose *j*}
5. enemies = {*j* | *j* has sent/sends a negative message to *i* (or has waited too long to react on *i*)}.
6. rejects   = {*j* | *j* has received/receives a negative message from *i*/ *i* exceeded *j*'s waiting period}.

Except for the class 'friends', all other class names are only for convenience and do not have any relevant sociological meaning!

Within the classes of potential friends, classes 2–4, a subdivision is made according to the others' attributes and/or position in the network. Since we assumed that there is only one relevant dichotomous individual attribute, an individual is either similar or dissimilar to individual i.

I. similars $= \{j \mid x_i = x_j\}$,
II. dissimilars $= \{j \mid x_i \neq x_j\}$.

The subsequent distinction into group members, external friends, and non-group members is only of importance if i him or herself is a group member. The relevance of this distinction will become clear once the behavior of group members is introduced. For group member i, who belongs to group L_i:

a. group members $= \{j \mid j$ is not a friend of i but belongs to $L_i\}$
b. indirect external friends $= \{j \mid j$ is not a friend of i, j does not belong to L_i, but j is a friend of one or more of the members of $L_i\}$,
c. non-group members $= \{j \mid j$ is not a friend of i, nor a group member of L_i, nor friends with any of the members of $L_i\}$.

For all i, $\Delta_i(0) = d f_i$. The general idea is that an individual's tension will reduce if a friendship is established. His or her behavior with regard to friendship choices will depend on the configuration of the classes presented in Figure 10.1. Since individuals have only limited information and limited capability to foresee strategically, the strict form of the tension function cannot be applied to calculate the best ways to minimize it. Therefore, we assume that they use some relatively simple heuristics.

Tension is reduced when a friendship is established. It is reduced more if it is established with a similar individual. For group members it is reduced even more if λ increases or α decreases. In this way, once individuals are group members, they try to guarantee the future of that group. Non-group members do not seek explicit group membership in this model, although Section 3 suggests that they do, especially if the group 'is similar' to themselves. As a first simplification, we assume however that the behavior of non-group members is equal to the behavior that would follow from tension function (3), in which only the first two issues are relevant (Zeggelink, 1995). The derivation of behavioral rules for group members is much more difficult because it is not straightforward how λ, α or $|L|$ will be changed as a result of one's own actions. These values heavily depend on actions of the other individuals. Therefore, only the aspect that group members attempt to achieve smaller values of α and larger values of λ in the process of establishing the desired number of friends is used.

- We assume that for every individual i the number of friends is so important that i will never establish more friendships than the desired number of friends. Consequently i's total number of friendship choices always equals df_i, if possible.
- Both group- and non-group members, will never withdraw reciprocated choices because tension would increase (w_2 and w_3 are relatively small with regard to the importance of the number of friends). Consequently, once established, friendships are maintained. If $f_i(t) = df_i$, i has no impetus to act. However, other individuals observe that i does not need any more friendships, therefore it is justified to assume that i will send a negative message to those individuals j that still try to initiate a friendship with him or her.
- In a similar way, if j receives a negative message from i, j knows that tension will never be reduced by keeping a choice extended to i and thus withdraws this choice and places i in class 5.
- If at a certain moment in time i's number of friendship choices (including the reciprocated ones) is smaller than df_i, i will add choices. In one step, more than one choice may be added. For the addition of choices, i follows his or her preference order.
- Rejects and enemies are not potential candidates for friendship. The class of rejects is empty until i has the desired number of friends or once i has been the least patient individual in the waiting equilibrium. Rejects are not considered as candidates because they once withdrew a choice towards i or because i waited too long to react.[17] Enemies have shown, in one way or the other, not to be very willing to establish a friendship with i. Choices to enemies are always withdrawn and never remade because they reacted negatively or waited too long to react to a friendship attempt.
- For a non-group member i, tension is reduced with certainty (and maximally) if i chooses an admirer who is similar to him or her.[18] This preference for admirers holds only when new choices have to be added.[19] Therefore, in principle and if possible, i makes friendship bids to similar individuals, and similar neutrals are preferred over non-similar admirers. Next in the preference order are non-similar admirers and non-similar neutrals. If the difference between actual and desired number of friends is larger than the number of individuals in the category that i wants to choose from, i chooses

randomly from this category. Consequently, as a result of the limited availability of individuals in classes 2 and 4, at a certain moment in time, the number of choices may be smaller than df_i.

- If i is a group member, the extra subdivision into group members, indirect external friends and non-group members within the classes of potential friends becomes important.[20] Indirect external friends are individuals who are not i's friends but friends with one or more of his or her fellow group members. Those are the individuals that determine the value of α. Within class 2 an individual distinguishes admirers that are group members (2a), admirers that are indirect external friends (2b), and admirers that are non-group members (2c). A same distinction is made in classes 3 and 4. Choices do not yet exist to individuals in class 3. A group member takes into account that λ might increase when he or she establishes a friendship with a group member who was not his or her friend yet. This leads to a preference for individuals in 2a over individuals in 2b and 2c. Analogously, individuals in 4a are preferred over those in 4b and 4c. Within this ordering, similar individuals (I) are preferred over dissimilar individuals (II) (representing that $w_3 > w_2$).

- In contrast to behavior of non-group members, a group member i will also replace choices to idols according to the above preference order, i.e. choices towards idols in classes 3b or 3c will, if possible, be replaced by choices towards individuals in 2a or 4a, and in this preference order (2-Ia, 2-IIa > 4-Ia, 4-IIa > 3b, 3c). For the purpose of increasing λ, we also assume i prefers individuals in class 4a over those in 2b and 2c (4-Ia, 4-IIa > 2b, 2c).

- Another way to reduce tension for a group member is by reducing α. α might be reduced (not with certainty) with a similar increase in group size $|L|$ by the establishment of a friendship with an indirect external friend (b-classes).[21] So, these individuals are next in the preference order, and a group member prefers them in order of the number of group members they are friends with. The higher this number, the large the probability that α will decrease with a simultaneous increase in group size. This number is more important than the similarity aspect. If however, this number is equal for a similar and a dissimilar individual, the former is preferred. Again, a group member will also replace choices towards individuals in class 3c to indirect external friends (2b > 4b > 3c).

- For the purpose of decreasing α, individuals in class 4b are preferred over those in 2c.

Since individuals 'observe' (by receiving negative messages) when they cannot establish anymore friendships, an equilibrium situation in which no individual has an impetus to make any new choices, will always emerge with these behavioral rules. This situation will be characterized by the fact that all individuals cannot directly lower their tension any further as a result of the configuration of friendships in the network.

5. SIMULATION RESULTS

5.1. Simulation Design

Relevant input parameters of the model are population size g, the distribution of desired numbers of friends df_i across the population, and the degree of heterogeneity with regard to the dichotomous characteristic x_i.

The most important output parameters concerning the network structure are the number of groups (LS sets), their sizes, their internal (λ) and external structure (α), and the mean number of friends (d) for individuals in the equilibrium network. With regard to the groups that emerge we are especially interested in their size. The size of a group is one of the main determinants of its functioning and appearance because it relates to the range and complexity of the field of interactions within the group. Observations of groupings among pedestrians, freely playing children, public gatherings and so on, show that group size of freely forming informal groups varies from 2 to 7 (Bakeman and Beck, 1974; James, 1951).

We present results of simulation for populations of size $g = 10$. We assume that every individual desires 4 friends: $df_i = 4$ for all i. The degree of heterogeneity is determined by the number of individuals that have $x_i = 1$ or $x_i = 0$. Let n_1 be the number of individuals with $x_i = 1$; $n_2 = g - n_1$ is the number of individuals with $x_i = 0$. The smaller the difference between n_1 and n_2, the more heterogeneous the population. We examine the situations $n_1 = 5$, $n_1 = 6$, $n_1 = 7$, $n_1 = 8$, $n_1 = 9$, $n_1 = 10$ and call the set of individuals with $x_i = 1$, the majority.

5.2. Equilibrium Network Structures

For every value of n_1, 100 runs of simulation are executed, and different types of equilibrium networks emerge. A type of network is a network where the structure of friendships within the minority, and between the minority and the majority is unique, but the structure within the majority may slightly vary.

The distribution of network structures depends on the value of n_1. Disregarding the individual attributes, common structures do emerge. In Figures 10.2–10.7 and in Table 10.1 that follow, these common structures are represented by a letter. Individuals with $x_i = 1$ are represented by black nodes, those with $x_i = 0$, by white nodes. Friendships between similar individuals are represented by bold lines and are called intra-category friendships, those between dissimilar individuals are represented by dotted lines and are called inter-category friendships. Groups (LS sets) are represented within circles. If LS sets are contained within one another, we consider only the smallest LS set and do not count the larger LS set of which it is a subset, as an LS set.

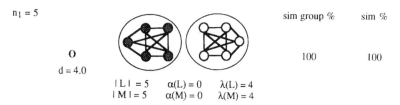

$n_1 = 5$

O

$d = 4.0$

sim group %   sim %

100   100

| $\|L\| = 5$ | $\alpha(L) = 0$ | $\lambda(L) = 4$ |
| $\|M\| = 5$ | $\alpha(M) = 0$ | $\lambda(M) = 4$ |

FIGURE 10.2.   Equilibrium structure $n_1 = 5$.

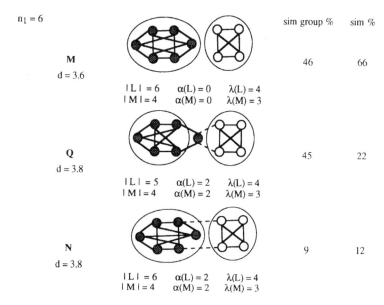

$n_1 = 6$

M

$d = 3.6$

sim group %   sim %

46   66

| $\|L\| = 6$ | $\alpha(L) = 0$ | $\lambda(L) = 4$ |
| $\|M\| = 4$ | $\alpha(M) = 0$ | $\lambda(M) = 3$ |

Q

$d = 3.8$

45   22

| $\|L\| = 5$ | $\alpha(L) = 2$ | $\lambda(L) = 4$ |
| $\|M\| = 4$ | $\alpha(M) = 2$ | $\lambda(M) = 3$ |

N

$d = 3.8$

9   12

| $\|L\| = 6$ | $\alpha(L) = 2$ | $\lambda(L) = 4$ |
| $\|M\| = 4$ | $\alpha(M) = 2$ | $\lambda(M) = 3$ |

FIGURE 10.3.   Equilibrium structures $n_1 = 6$.

In the following, we will refer to the model developed here, as the simgroup model. The model that does not deal with the group issue, but is based on tension function (3) is called the similarity model. We present pictures of 'all' possible emergent network structures for every value of n_1 in order of frequency of occurrence. We summarize a structure in terms of the presence of LS sets and present the frequency of occurrence with both the simgroup model and the similarity model next to it. If similarity is not relevant, but the group issue is, results for $n_1 = 5$ to $n_1 = 9$ are self-evidently similar to those of $n_1 = 10$.

Figure 10.2 shows the trivial equilibrium network that consists of two cliques of 5 individuals of the same category, that emerges when $n_1 = 5$. Every individual is able to find the total number of 4 desired friends among similar individuals ($d = 4$). No inter-category friendships exist (note that for both LS sets $\alpha = 0$).

For $n_1 = 6$, results are less trivial. Three different types of equilibrium networks emerge that are shown in Figure 10.3. All three structures also emerged with the similarity model, but with different probabilities. The mean number of friends in equilibrium is either $d = 3.6$ or $d = 3.8$. The first structure (M) consists of two disconnected LS sets that are made up of individuals of the same category. This network emerged far more frequently with the similarity model (66%). With the simgroup model, the group aspect is more relevant and structure M emerges with approximately equal probability as structure (Q). The reason being that some of the members of the 'black' category at a certain moment in the process of friendship formation constitute a group, and as a consequence 'stick within or close' to their group when making friendships. As a result of these actions, one member of their own category cannot find anymore similar friends and chooses friends in the other category. This one individual from the majority category does in this case neither belong to the larger group nor to the smaller group, and functions as a bridge person between the groups by his 2 intra- and 2 inter-category friendships. In network (N), two individuals of the majority have different friends in the minority. We see that the two individuals in the majority who have an inter-category friendship are friends with each other. With the similarity model, this would always be the case because if they would not have been friends, they both could have had a reduction of tension by becoming friends such that tension with respect to characteristics of friends would decrease. With the simgroup model in which also group structure is important, this does not necessarily hold (see Figure 10.4).

$n_1 = 7$

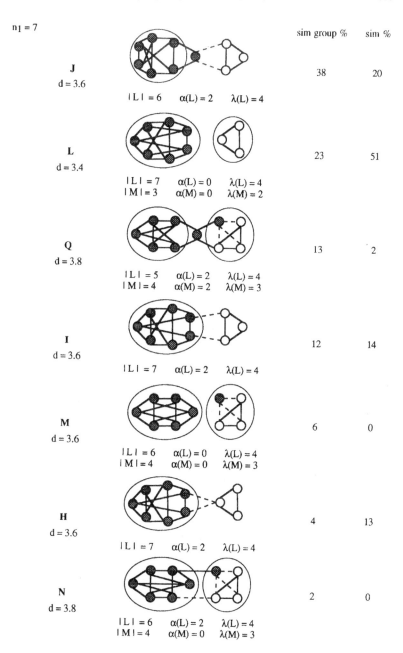

			sim group %	sim %
J			38	20
$d = 3.6$				
	$|L| = 6$ $\alpha(L) = 2$ $\lambda(L) = 4$			
L			23	51
$d = 3.4$				
	$|L| = 7$ $\alpha(L) = 0$ $\lambda(L) = 4$			
	$|M| = 3$ $\alpha(M) = 0$ $\lambda(M) = 2$			
Q			13	2
$d = 3.8$				
	$|L| = 5$ $\alpha(L) = 2$ $\lambda(L) = 4$			
	$|M| = 4$ $\alpha(M) = 2$ $\lambda(M) = 3$			
I			12	14
$d = 3.6$				
	$|L| = 7$ $\alpha(L) = 2$ $\lambda(L) = 4$			
M			6	0
$d = 3.6$				
	$|L| = 6$ $\alpha(L) = 0$ $\lambda(L) = 4$			
	$|M| = 4$ $\alpha(M) = 0$ $\lambda(M) = 3$			
H			4	13
$d = 3.6$				
	$|L| = 7$ $\alpha(L) = 2$ $\lambda(L) = 4$			
N			2	0
$d = 3.8$				
	$|L| = 6$ $\alpha(L) = 2$ $\lambda(L) = 4$			
	$|M| = 4$ $\alpha(M) = 0$ $\lambda(M) = 3$			

FIGURE 10.4.

$n_1 = 7$

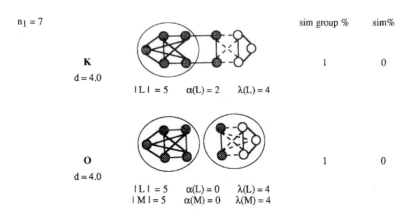

sim group %   sim%

K
$d = 4.0$

| L | = 5 $\alpha(L) = 2$ $\lambda(L) = 4$

O
$d = 4.0$

| L | = 5 $\alpha(L) = 0$ $\lambda(L) = 4$
| M | = 5 $\alpha(M) = 0$ $\lambda(M) = 4$

FIGURE 10.4.   Equilibrium networks $n_1 = 7$.

Figure 10.4 shows a division of equilibrium networks for $n_1 = 7$, where the mean number of friends varies between $d = 3.4$ and $d = 4.0$. Only five (J, L, Q, I, H) of these nine structures emerged with the similarity model. Like with the $n_1 = 6$ situation, the completely disconnected structure consisting of groups that represent the majority and minority, emerged most frequently with the similarity model (51%). The others also emerged with different distributions of probabilities with the simgroup model. The difference in frequencies for structures $Q(13–2)$ and $M(6–0)$ is most striking. These structures are interesting for the fact that groups emerge that contain both members of the majority and the minority. If two individuals in the majority have friends in the minority, they do not necessarily need to be friends with each other because the group aspect is more important than the similarity issue (N). This is in contrast to results with the similarity model in which such majority individuals with inter-category friendships would always be friends with each other.

A similar distinction is made for $n_1 = 8$. Now 11 different equilibrium structures emerge, only four (I, G, F, E) of them would emerge with the similarity model, and again with completely different probabilities. Also, with the similarity model, the majority disconnected from the minority emerged far most frequently (52%) whereas it appears much less often with the simgroup model. Chances are much higher with the simgroup model that group formation takes place within the majority $(n_1 = 8)$ itself (J, Q, M, L, O, N, K). Moreover, and as a result of the process just mentioned, more inter-category friendships emerge with the simgroup model. The mean number of friends in equilibrium varies between $d = 3.4$ and $d = 4.0$.

$n_1 = 8$

sim group %   sim %

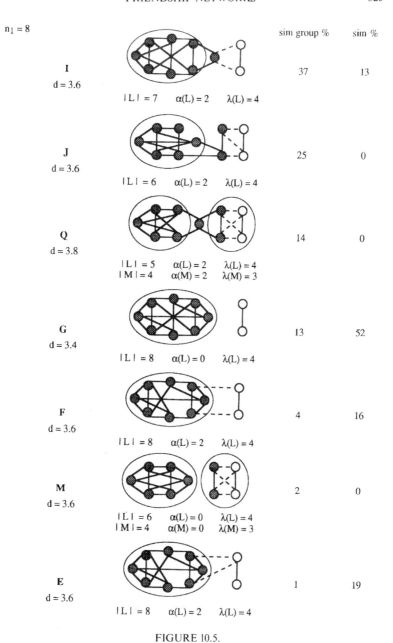

I
d = 3.6

$|L| = 7$ $\alpha(L) = 2$ $\lambda(L) = 4$

37   13

J
d = 3.6

$|L| = 6$ $\alpha(L) = 2$ $\lambda(L) = 4$

25   0

Q
d = 3.8

$|L| = 5$ $\alpha(L) = 2$ $\lambda(L) = 4$
$|M| = 4$ $\alpha(M) = 2$ $\lambda(M) = 3$

14   0

G
d = 3.4

$|L| = 8$ $\alpha(L) = 0$ $\lambda(L) = 4$

13   52

F
d = 3.6

$|L| = 8$ $\alpha(L) = 2$ $\lambda(L) = 4$

4   16

M
d = 3.6

$|L| = 6$ $\alpha(L) = 0$ $\lambda(L) = 4$
$|M| = 4$ $\alpha(M) = 0$ $\lambda(M) = 3$

2   0

E
d = 3.6

$|L| = 8$ $\alpha(L) = 2$ $\lambda(L) = 4$

1   19

FIGURE 10.5.

$n_1 = 8$

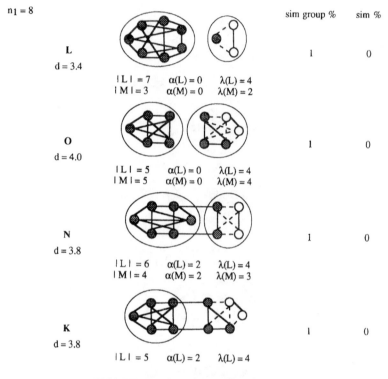

sim group %   sim %

L
$d = 3.4$

$|L| = 7 \quad \alpha(L) = 0 \quad \lambda(L) = 4$
$|M| = 3 \quad \alpha(M) = 0 \quad \lambda(M) = 2$

1   0

O
$d = 4.0$

$|L| = 5 \quad \alpha(L) = 0 \quad \lambda(L) = 4$
$|M| = 5 \quad \alpha(M) = 0 \quad \lambda(M) = 4$

1   0

N
$d = 3.8$

$|L| = 6 \quad \alpha(L) = 2 \quad \lambda(L) = 4$
$|M| = 4 \quad \alpha(M) = 2 \quad \lambda(M) = 3$

1   0

K
$d = 3.8$

$|L| = 5 \quad \alpha(L) = 2 \quad \lambda(L) = 4$

1   0

FIGURE 10.5. Equilibrium networks $n_1 = 8$.

A similar story can be told for $n_1 = 9$. Figure 10.6 shows all possible equilibrium structures. Only three (F, C, D) of these 10 structures would emerge with the similarity model. These structures are those with one group consisting of just majority members.

Finally we present all possible 15 equilibrium structures that emerged when $n_1 = 10$. Since similarity cannot play a role when all individuals have the same value on the relevant individual attribute, results for the model when $n_1 = 10$ are equal to those in which only the group aspect is relevant (Zeggelink et al., 1996). This model will be called the group model. The similarity model in this case produces the same results as a pure random choice model in which only the issue number of friends is important (tension function 2). Only three (D, A, B) of all 15 structures emerged with the similarity model (= random choice model for $n_1 = 10$).

$n_1 = 9$

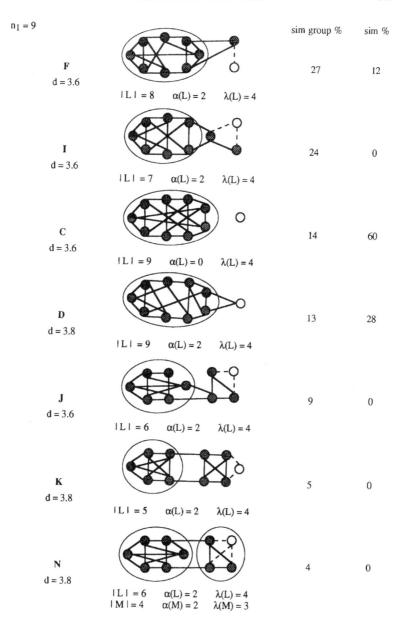

	sim group %	sim %
F $d = 3.6$	27	12
I $d = 3.6$	24	0
C $d = 3.6$	14	60
D $d = 3.8$	13	28
J $d = 3.6$	9	0
K $d = 3.8$	5	0
N $d = 3.8$	4	0

F: $|L| = 8 \quad \alpha(L) = 2 \quad \lambda(L) = 4$

I: $|L| = 7 \quad \alpha(L) = 2 \quad \lambda(L) = 4$

C: $|L| = 9 \quad \alpha(L) = 0 \quad \lambda(L) = 4$

D: $|L| = 9 \quad \alpha(L) = 2 \quad \lambda(L) = 4$

J: $|L| = 6 \quad \alpha(L) = 2 \quad \lambda(L) = 4$

K: $|L| = 5 \quad \alpha(L) = 2 \quad \lambda(L) = 4$

N: $|L| = 6 \quad \alpha(L) = 2 \quad \lambda(L) = 4$
$|M| = 4 \quad \alpha(M) = 2 \quad \lambda(M) = 3$

FIGURE 10.6.

$n_1 = 9$

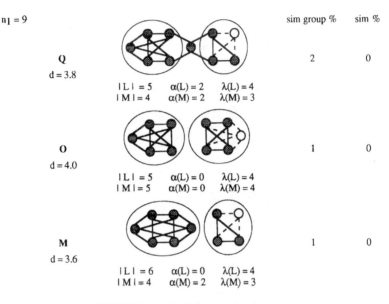

FIGURE 10.6.   Equilibrium networks $n_1 = 9$.

In Table 10.1, we present an overview of all different network structures in terms of groups. In column (1), the related common structure as shown in Figures 10.2–10.7 is given, column (2) shows the total number of groups in the equilibrium structure, column (3) represents the mean number of friends of individuals, d, in the population, columns (4) and (7) give the size of the first and second LS set (if present) respectively, columns (5) and (8) show the value of λ of the first and second LS set respectively, columns (6) and (9) show the value of α of the first and second LS set respectively, and columns (10)–(15) show the frequencies with which the corresponding network structures in equilibrium occur with distributions $n_1 = 5$ to $n_1 = 10$ of the dichotomous characteristic. In column (16) the total percentage of occurrence over all different values of n_1 is presented.

The total number of different network structures is 17, of which 15 emerged with the pure group model for $g = 10$ (is simgroup model with $n_1 = 10$). If we omit structure O from the analysis because it is a special case when $n_1 = 5$, we see that structures I, J, and Q emerge most frequently. Structure I contains one group of size 6 with two external friendships to 2 of the remaining 4 individuals in the population who do not constitute a group of their own. Structure J contains one group

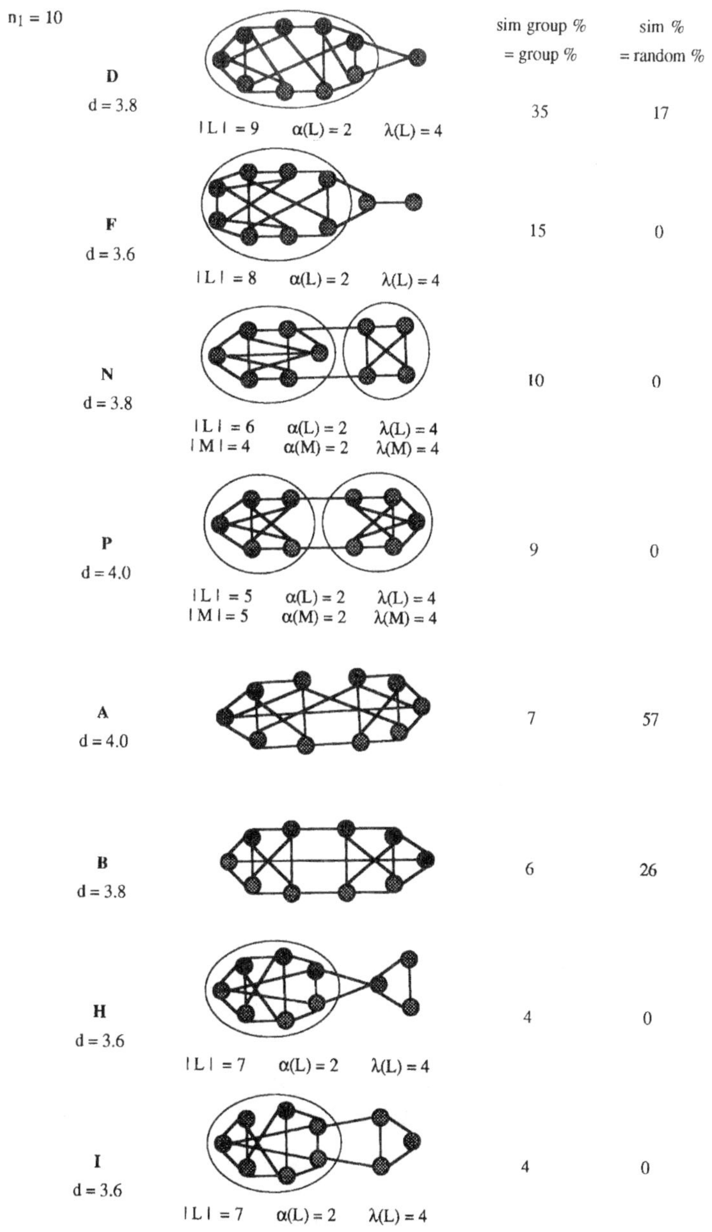
$n_1 = 10$
sim group %
= group %
sim %
= random %
D
d = 3.8
|L| = 9 α(L) = 2 λ(L) = 4
35
17
F
d = 3.6
|L| = 8 α(L) = 2 λ(L) = 4
15
0
N
d = 3.8
|L| = 6 α(L) = 2 λ(L) = 4
|M| = 4 α(M) = 2 λ(M) = 4
10
0
P
d = 4.0
|L| = 5 α(L) = 2 λ(L) = 4
|M| = 5 α(M) = 2 λ(M) = 4
9
0
A
d = 4.0
7
57
B
d = 3.8
6
26
H
d = 3.6
|L| = 7 α(L) = 2 λ(L) = 4
4
0
I
d = 3.6
|L| = 7 α(L) = 2 λ(L) = 4
4
0

FIGURE 10.7.

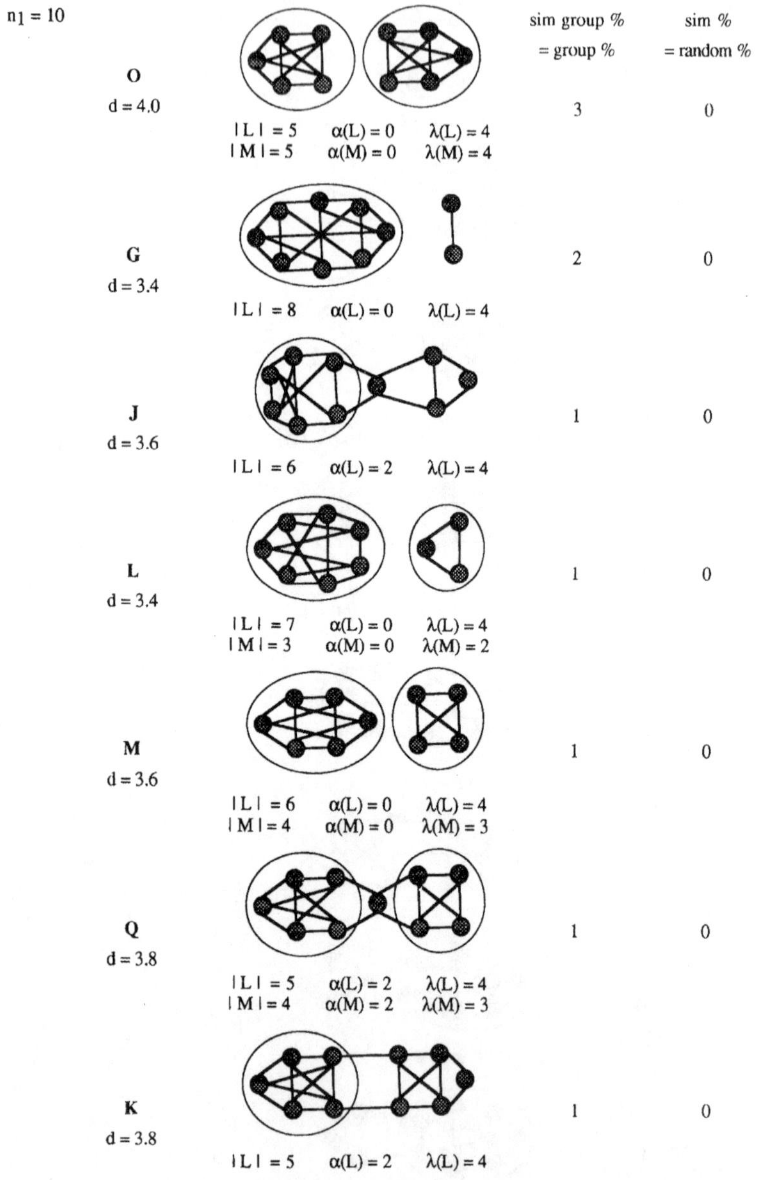

$n_1 = 10$

	sim group % = group %	sim % = random %

O
$d = 4.0$

$|L| = 5 \quad \alpha(L) = 0 \quad \lambda(L) = 4$
$|M| = 5 \quad \alpha(M) = 0 \quad \lambda(M) = 4$

3   0

G
$d = 3.4$

$|L| = 8 \quad \alpha(L) = 0 \quad \lambda(L) = 4$

2   0

J
$d = 3.6$

$|L| = 6 \quad \alpha(L) = 2 \quad \lambda(L) = 4$

1   0

L
$d = 3.4$

$|L| = 7 \quad \alpha(L) = 0 \quad \lambda(L) = 4$
$|M| = 3 \quad \alpha(M) = 0 \quad \lambda(M) = 2$

1   0

M
$d = 3.6$

$|L| = 6 \quad \alpha(L) = 0 \quad \lambda(L) = 4$
$|M| = 4 \quad \alpha(M) = 0 \quad \lambda(M) = 3$

1   0

Q
$d = 3.8$

$|L| = 5 \quad \alpha(L) = 2 \quad \lambda(L) = 4$
$|M| = 4 \quad \alpha(M) = 2 \quad \lambda(M) = 3$

1   0

K
$d = 3.8$

$|L| = 5 \quad \alpha(L) = 2 \quad \lambda(L) = 4$

1   0

FIGURE 10.7.   Equilibrium networks $n_1 = 10$.

TABLE 10.1

Network structures in equilibrium and their frequency of occurrence

(1)	(2)	(3)	(4)	(5)	(6)	(7)	(8)	(9)	(10)	(11)	(12)	(13)	(14)	(15)	(16)
	# groups	d mean # friends	group 1			group 2			n_1						total
			$|L|$	$\alpha(L)$	$\lambda(L)$	$|M|$	$\alpha(M)$	$\lambda(M)$	5	6	7	8	9	10	
A	0	4.0	—	—	—	—	—	—	0	0	0	0	0	7	7
B	0	3.8	—	—	—	—	—	—	0	0	0	0	0	6	6
C	1	3.6	9	0	4	—	—	—	0	0	0	0	14	0	14
D	1	3.8	9	2	4	—	—	—	0	0	0	0	13	35	48
E	1	3.6[a]	8	2	4	—	—	—	0	0	0	1	0	0	1
F	1	3.6[a]	8	2	4	—	—	—	0	0	0	4	27	15	46
G	1	3.4	8	0	4	—	—	—	0	0	0	13	0	2	15
H	1	3.6[b]	7	2	4	—	—	—	0	0	4	0	0	3	7
I	1	3.6[b]	7	2	4	—	—	—	0	0	12	37	24	5	78
J	1	3.6	6	2	4	—	—	—	0	0	38	25	9	1	73
K	1	3.8	5	2	4	—	—	—	0	0	1	1	5	1	8
L	2	3.4	7	0	4	3	0	2	0	0	23	1	0	1	25
M	2	3.6	6	0	4	4	0	3	0	46	6	2	1	1	56
N	2	3.8	6	2	4	4	2	3	0	9	2	1	4	10	26
O	2	4.0	5	0	4	5	0	4	100	0	1	1	1	3	106
P	2	4.0	5	2	4	5	2	4	0	0	0	0	0	9	9
Q	2	3.8	5	2	4	4	2	3	0	45	13	14	2	1	75
									100	100	100	100	100	100	

[a] The LS set of size $|L| = 8$ is contained within a larger LS set of size $|L'| = 9$, with $\alpha = 1$, and $\lambda = 2$.

[b] The LS set of size $|L| = 7$ is contained within a larger LS set of size $|L'| = 8$, with $\alpha = 1$, and $\lambda = 2$.

of size 7 with two external friendships to 2 of the remaining 3 individuals in the population. Structure Q consists of two groups linked by a bridge person who has two friendships with 2 members of each group. One group has size 5, the other has size 4. Although the structures are equal for different values of n_1, the compositions of the groups vary. When $n_1 = 6$, the group of 5 consists of just majority individuals, and the group of 4 of minority individuals (Figure 10.3 Q). When $n_1 = 7$, the group of 5 still consists of just majority individuals, but the group of 4 also contains a majority individual such that homogeneity within this group is smaller (Figure 10.4 Q). This effect is even larger if $n_1 = 8$ and the group of 4 consists of two majority and two minority individuals (Figure 10.5 Q). The composition of the groups that emerge, may have important consequences for its functioning and stability.

Individuals who do not have the desired number of friends, more often do not belong to a group than individuals who have the desired number of friends (e.g. E, H, J), Nevertheless, individuals having less friends than desired can belong to LS sets (e.g. L, N, Q). Moreover, when LS sets are present, usually all individuals with the desired number of friends belong to LS sets. If they do not belong to LS sets, they usually occupy a bridge function between groups and non-group members, or simply between groups (e.g. I, J, Q).

The number of LS sets in equilibrium varies between 0 and 2. In Table 10.2 we present the distribution of the number of groups in the equilibrium networks and their corresponding frequency of occurrence with the different degrees of heterogeneity. Only non-overlapping (distinct) groups are counted. The situation for $n_1 = 10$ is a little deviant because the similarity issue cannot play a role. Aside from that situation, we see that the probability that 2 groups emerge increases

TABLE 10.2
The number of groups in equilibrium networks

# groups	n_1						total
	5	6	7	8	9	10	
0	0	0	0	0	0	13	13
1	0	0	55	81	92	62	290
2	100	100	45	19	8	25	297
	100	100	100	100	100	100	

with increasing heterogeneity (decreasing $n_1, n_1 \geqslant 5$). An equilibrium in which 3 groups emerged did not occur. The reason is that we defined groups to exist if their size was at least $|L| = 3$. In a population of size $g = 10$, the presence of 3 groups would therefore be exceptional, particularly because every individual in principle tries to establish 4 friendships.

More interesting is the size of groups in the equilibrium network. Sizes of LS sets vary between 3 and 9. Since we assumed LS sets to be defined only when $\lambda > 1$, the minimal group size is $|L| = 3$. The maximum non-trivial group size in a population of $g = 10$ individuals is $|L| = 9$. In Table 10.3 we present all possible group sizes and their frequency of occurrence in the different situations. Results here should be interpreted carefully because of the difference between an equilibrium structure in which only 1 group is present and a structure in which two of them exist.

We see that groups of size $|L| > n_1$ never emerge. This can be explained by the importance of the similarity issue for the individuals in combination with our choice of $df_i = 4$ for all individuals. Since n_1 was always larger than df_i, all majority individuals could in principle find the desired number of friends within their own category. Another side effect of $df_i = 4$ is the fact that groups of size $|L| = 5$ emerge most frequently. However in contrast to results of the similarity model, groups with sizes smaller than the majority size do emerge relatively frequently.

It is also important to realize that a large and a small group often emerged in co-presence. The group that is established first, indirectly causes the other individuals to 'construct' a group as well. If the size

TABLE 10.3
Group size and frequency of occurrence

group size $|L|$	n_1						total
	5	6	7	8	9	10	
3			23	1		1	25
4		100	21	17	7	12	157
5	200	45	16	17	9	26	313
6		55	45	28	14	12	154
7			39	60	24	9	132
8				18	27	17	62
9					27	35	62

difference between the minority and majority is small however, the two groups may emerge approximately simultaneously.

We finally present the mean number of friends in equilibrium (and standard deviation) in equilibrium for all degrees of heterogeneity together with a measure of segmentation within the network in Table 10.4. The segmentation index is an appropriate summary measure of the distribution of distances, because it allows for comparisons between networks with different densities (Baerveldt and Snijders, 1994). An undirected network is considered to be more segmented if the distances between individuals who are not directly connected, are on the average larger.[22]

The mean number of friends in equilibrium is larger with the simgroup model than with the similarity model, in particular for $n_1 = 7$ and $n_1 = 8$. The reason has been explained earlier. Since within the majority group formation tends to take place, some individuals of the majority 'go' to the minority for their friendships. As a result, with the simgroup model it becomes easier for those in the minority to establish more friendships. More inter-category friendships emerge with the simgroup model.

As a consequence, for small degrees of heterogeneity ($n_1 = 8, 9, 10$) the degree of segmentation is relatively larger with the simgroup model. It is not just structures with a split between the majority and the minority that usually emerged with the similarity model, but more structures are possible with the simgroup model. The majority itself may become more segmented too. For the larger degrees of heterogeneity ($n_1 = 6, 7$), the same process leads to smaller degrees of segmentation, because the population as a whole becomes 'closer connected' by the inter-category friendships.

TABLE 10.4
Mean number of friends and segmentation for simgroup and similarity model

	d mean # friends (s.d.)		S segmentation (s.d.)	
	simgroup model	similarity model	simgroup model	similarity model
5	4.0 (0.0)	4.0 (0.0)	1.0 (0.00)	1.0 (0.00)
6	3.7 (0.1)	3.7 (0.1)	0.73 (0.16)	0.78 (0.16)
7	3.6 (0.1)	3.5 (0.1)	0.59 (0.14)	0.61 (0.15)
8	3.6 (0.1)	3.5 (0.1)	0.50 (0.12)	0.46 (0.13)
9	3.7 (0.1)	3.7 (0.1)	0.36 (0.13)	0.24 (0.06)
10	3.8 (0.1)	3.9 (0.1)	0.27 (0.22)	0.07 (0.06)

6. DISCUSSION

Although the validity and quality of the simgroup model presented here can only be assessed when confronted with empirical data, we think that we can conclude that it provides already some interesting guidelines towards the construction of a dynamic theory of group emergence. In contrast to earlier models that for example considered only a similarity issue, or a group issue, the combination of these two provided intuitively more realistic results. There is more than just a preference for similarity that 'causes' group formation, but one cannot do without it because it is a very important drive leading to initially necessary overlaps among friendships before groups can even come into existence.

One of the advantages of the simgroup model presented here is that from an initial situation of a majority and a minority category with respect to a dichotomous individual attribute, a friendship network may emerge that does not necessarily represent that same majority and minority. Groups may emerge that are of different sizes than the initial majority and minority. Some individuals may not belong to any of the groups that emerge, they may in that case function as a bridge person. Also groups may be constituted by both members of the majority and the minority. As such, based on the group size, a new 'majority' and 'minority' may emerge.

Some drawbacks of the present model are that there is too much emphasis on the need for social contact. An individual always attempts to establish the desired number of friends and never establishes more friendships than desired. Another element concerning this number of friends is the impossibility of friendship dissolution. As a result, the group aspect does not live up to its promise because the number of friends for an individual is always much more important than his or her group 'state'. Groups that emerged may disappear again because individuals who lack friends continue looking for friends disregarding the possible collapse of the group. By this we mean to say that when individuals continue to establish friendships outside the group, α may become that large, that the group is not a group any more because there are 'too many' external friendships for the set of individuals to be an LS set. Moreover, group members may want to dissolve friendships with those who inhibit a possible future existence of the group. In general these will be individuals that are not group members themselves (indirect external friends, see Figure 10.1).

The model becomes also more realistic if we would consider some variable that represents an individual's available time or energy instead of some abstract variable representing individuals' need for social contact. As such, we could deal with the aspect that friendship and group maintenance requires time and energy, and thereby also becomes a restriction for group growth. It becomes more difficult to maintain all friendships, and negative feelings about the group may emerge. Smaller groups are usually evaluated more positively than larger groups by its members.

Within this perspective group syntality theory from the field of social psychology provides us with some interesting viewpoints (Shaw, 1981). It deals for instance with one special form of group energy (synergy), called maintenance energy. Maintenance energy is necessary to keep the group in existence and is related to aspects of the individual's self-interest versus group interest, the trade-off between individual benefits obtained from the group, and the individual costs that have to be paid. Syntality theory can also help us to explain what the importance of the homogeneity of the group is with regard to maintenance energy (how individual attributes go together).

We have distinguished different types of individuals or group membership from the perspective of an individual (Figure 10.1). This distinction can easily be extended to a distinction in prospective members (non-group members), new members, full members (core or periphery), partial members (for instance bridge persons) or ex-members, to provide a better understanding of the group's dynamics (Moreland and Levine, 1984). Moreover, within the view of the emergence of solidarity, next to direct friendships in the group, a solidarity relationship can be defined as a relationship that connects two persons regardless of the fact whether they are friends or not but when they are members of the same group for instance (Fararo and Doreian, Chapter 1).

The model becomes closer connected to the other problem sets of Chapter 1, by extending this 'purely structural' simgroup model with elements that represent the direct influence from the group to the individual in terms of change of certain individual properties. Our general idea for this purpose is that first the process of group emergence should be captured. Subsequently, individual attributes, like attitudes, should not only be considered in the process of similarity judgements, but should be taken into account in influence processes. An individual's attitudes are influenced through his or her friendships. Within groups such influence processes are reinforced because there are relatively many friends with similar opinions that participate in the influence process. As a result, the contrast between groups tends to become even larger and group feelings, attitudes, and norms arise. These group variables on their turn flow back to the individual group members, and thereby affect individual behavior within the group.

We finally want to comment that another topic that has been given even less attention than the emergence of groups is the break-up or disappearance of groups. Why are some groups more stable than others? The definition of LS set shows that the disappearance of a group can be translated in the changing values of λ and α of the group. Group size is a very important factor here, in determining the relevance of interaction within groups and between groups. It is relevant in the first place to distinguish, also within groups, the possible distribution in dyads, triads, tetrads, and so forth (Lindsay, 1972; Simmel, 1902). It furthermore appears that groups that consist of individuals with similar attitudes are usually more cohesive than groups with individuals with less similar attitudes. An important and interesting extension for future research therefore is modelling the dissolution of groups.

NOTES

1. This chapter was prepared while the author was a visiting postdoctoral fellow in 1994 at the University of Illinois, Urbana-Champaign IL, and in 1995 at the School of Social Sciences, University of California, Irvine CA. This stay was subsidized by the Netherlands Organization for Scientific Research (NWO, S 50–384).

   The author wishes to thank Tom Fararo and Patrick Doreian for fruitful comments on an earlier version of the manuscript.
2. Such a direct influence from the network to the individual can also be found in the mechanisms beyond group formation: individuals 'are changed' by their group membership. Group pressures exist towards adherence to group norms and attitude change (Mullen and Goethals, 1987).
3. As such, it is important to realize that a three-person group of individuals i, j, and k has a different sociological meaning than a triad consisting of the dyadic pairs i and j, i and k, and j and k, who all interact with each other but never interact simultaneously (Wilson, 1982). The former 'real' group's structure may however, and usually does, result from the latter.
4. Note that we do not say that all LS sets disconnected from the rest of the graph have edge connectivity $\lambda = 1$.
5. Although overlapping group membership does occur in reality, friendship groups are usually mutually exclusive.
6. Another interesting property of groups possible to examine, is the degree of homogeneity because of the introduction of individual attributes.
7. Similarity does not always determine attraction. Complementarity, e.g. need complementarity, also plays a role.
8. These processes relate closely to those in the field of social identity theory (Tajfel and Turner, 1986) which says that individuals try to maintain a high level of self-esteem by comparing with specific groups, and avoid comparing with specific other groups. The main difference with social comparison theory in its purest form is that social identity theory is concerned with intergroup comparisons and social comparison theory focuses more on interpersonal comparisons.

9. No individual enters or leaves the population, but this assumption can easily be adapted. Aside from this restriction, all other steps in model building will be as general as possible.

10. To avoid the problem of interpersonal comparisons of waiting periods, we introduce a so-called 'waiting equilibrium'. This is the situation (configuration of states) that all individuals wait for reactions of other individuals in the form of reciprocated friendship choices or negative messages, but no individual does make such a choice or send such a negative message because he has no impetus to do so. We assume that the minimal waiting period of all individuals is larger than the time the process needs to reach this waiting equilibrium. To keep the process running, one randomly chosen individual (the most impatient), will withdraw (randomly one of) his or her unreciprocated choice(s).

11. The need for social contact is not the only relevant variable. Available time and energy also determine how many friendships an individual is able to maintain. We will return to the time aspect later and assume for now that all these variables are captured in the parameter called desired number of friends.

12. It should be realized that similarity also results from friendship because individuals tend to 'influence' each other such that they become more similar once they have become friends. This process is comparable to the group pressures towards more homogeneity within a group of friends.

13. Since we assume that individual attributes are constant over time, it is not possible to deal with the simultaneous aspects of the generation of norms and solidarity (as a result of social influence) and group formation in a way that is described at the end of Section 3.2. In future extensions of the model variable individual attributes will be considered to account for such processes.

14. A more general function is necessary when allowing for m individual attributes that may change over time, and when considering non-linear distance functions. The weight attached to an issue is called the salience of that attribute (Stokman et al., 1994). Let i's value on the bth individual attribute at time t be $x_{ib}(t)$ and let $s_{ib}(t)$ be the salience attached to that attribute at time t by individual i. $x_{ib}(t)$ and $s_{ib}(t)$ are continuous variables on the interval $[0,1]$, and

$$\sum_{b=1}^{m} s_{ib}(t) = 1.$$

If the power q represents the shape of the distance function, the most general tension function is:

$$\Delta_i^*(t) = \left| df_i - \sum_{j=1}^{f_i(t)} \left(1 - w_{i2} \sum_{b=1}^{m} s_{ib} |x_{ib}(t) - x_{jb}(t)|^q \right) \right|.$$

15. This is more extensively discussed in Zeggelink et al. (1996).

16. It is very important that the negative messages in this model represent no urgent desire to form a friendship with another individual. They do not represent any dislike relationship between the individuals concerned, as it is usually the case in social network representations. Would we allow for such a negative relationship with the meaning of dislike, the model as it is presented here would become completely different and potentially more interesting. Negative relationships between individuals could inhibit the formation of groups containing both individuals. Moreover, negative relationships could be used to emphasize differences between groups.

17. This is an assumption that may not mimic reality but suffices as a first rule of behavior.

18. This preference is justified from the fact that people are attracted to those who like them.
19. At first sight, it seems to make sense to replace existing choices to idols with choices to admirers in order to obtain a reciprocated choice with certainty. However, if every individual does so, this effect is lost because in the next step an admirer may have become a neutral.
20. Initiating the first friendship with an individual outside the group can be quite risky for a group member when his group has strong norms regarding 'out group behavior'. An individual takes the judgements of his group subconsciously into consideration when deciding whether to become friends with a non-group member. As a result, group members make more choices within the group than out of it: new friendships that group members develop remain within the group (Granovetter, 1982; Salzinger, 1982). If group members do establish new friendships outside of the group, these new friends will not self-evidently become members of the group, but will be more easily accessible potential candidates for friendship for other group members and later on group membership. These individuals become indirect external friends if they not already were. It is also imaginable that the internal 'outseeker' is isolated from the group or destroys the complete existence of the group.
21. If i him or herself would have an external friendship, he or she could dissolve this friendship (withdraw the friendship choice) and try to establish a new one with a group member. Since this seems a rather rude way of behaving, i does not withdraw friendship choices to friends. This limits the way to reduce α.
22. An important criterion for this index is tnus the threshold where a distance becomes to be considered as large or long. For friendship networks a distance 1 implies friendship and it is proposed to mark that distance as very close. Distance 2 between two individuals implies a common friend and may represent close. Analogously, 3 is defined to be intermediate, and 4 or more is long. Subsequently, a friendship network is supposed to be strongly segmented when most distances between the individuals are either 1 or larger than or equal to 3. Distance 2 should not occur frequently when the network is to be considered segmented.

REFERENCES

Alba, R. 1973. "A graph-theoretic definition of a sociometric clique". *Journal of Mathematical Sociology* 3: 113–126.

Baerveldt, C. and T. Snijders. 1994. "Influences on and from the segmentation of networks: hypotheses and tests". *Social Networks* 16: 213–232.

Bakeman, R. and S. Beck. 1974. "The size of informal groups in public". *Environment and Behavior* 6: 378–390.

Borgatti, S., M. Everett, and P. Shirey. 1990. "LS sets, lambda sets and other cohesive subsets". *Social Networks* 12: 337–357.

Campbell, D. 1958. "Common fate, similarity and other indices of aggregates of persons as social entities". *Behavioral Science* 3: 14–25.

Cohen, J. 1977. "Sources of peer group homogeneity". *Sociology of Education* 50: 227–241.

Erickson, B. 1988. The relational basis of attitudes. In B. Wellman, and S. Berkowitz (eds.) *Social Structures: A Network Approach*. Cambridge: Cambridge University Press.

Fararo, T. and P. Doreian. 1998. The theory of solidarity: An agenda of problems. Chapter 1 in P. Doreian and T.J. Faroro (eds.), *The problem of solidarity: Theories and Models*. Gordon and Breach. (This volume)

Feld, S. 1981. "The focussed organization of social ties". *American Journal of Sociology* 86: 1015–1035.

Festinger, L. 1954. "A theory of social comparison processes". *Human relations* **7**: 117–140.

Freeman, L. 1992 "The sociological concept of 'group': an empirical test of two models". *American Journal of Sociology* **98**: 152–166.

Freeman, L., S. Freeman, and A. Michaelson. 1988. "On human social intelligence". *Journal of Social and Biological Structure* **11**: 415–425.

————. 1989. "How humans see social groups: a test of the Sailer–Gaulin models". *Journal of Quantitative Anthropology* **1**: 229–238.

Goethals, R. and J. Darley. 1987 "Social comparison theory: self-evaluation and group life". In B. Mullen, and G. Goethals (eds.) *Theories of group behavior.* New York: Springer-Verlag.

Granovetter, M. 1982. "The strength of weak ties: a network theory revisited". In P. Marsden and N. Lin (eds.) *Social structure and network analysis.* Beverly Hills, CA: Sage Publications.

Hoede, C. 1990. "Social atoms: kinetics". In J. Weesie and H. Flap (eds.) *Social networks through time.* Utrecht: ISOR.

Homans, G. 1950. *The human group.* New York: Harcourt Brace.

James, J. 1951. "A preliminary study of the size determinant in social group interactions". *American Sociological Review* **16**: 474–477.

Lindsay, J. 1972. "On the number in a group". *Human Relations* **25**: 47–64.

Luccio, F. and M. Sami. 1969. "On the decomposition of networks into minimally interconnected networks". *IEEE Transactions on circuit theory* **16**: 184–188.

Luce, R. and A. Perry. 1949. "A method of matrix analysis of group structure". *Psychometrika* **14**: 94–116.

Mokken, R. 1979. Cliques, clubs, and clans. *Quality and quantity* **13**: 161–173.

Moreland, R. and J. Levine. 1984. "Role transitions in small groups". In V. Allen and E. Van de Vliert, (eds.) *Role transitions: explorations and explanations.* New York: Plenum.

Mullen, B. 1987. "The study of group behavior". In B. Mullen and G. Goethals (eds.) *Theories of group behavior.* New York: Springer-Verlag.

Mullen, B. and G. Goethals (eds.) 1987. *Theories of group behavior.* New York: Springer-Verlag.

Reitz, K. 1988. "Social groups in a monastery". *Social Networks* **10**: 343–357.

Ridgeway, C. 1983. *The dynamics of small groups.* New York: Sint Martens Press.

Sailer, D. and S. Gaulin. 1984. "Proximity, sociality and observation: the definition of social groups". *American Anthropologist* **86**: 91–98.

Salzinger, L. 1982. The ties that bind: the effect of clustering on dyadic relationships. *Social Networks* **4**: 117–145.

Schachter, S. 1959. *The psychology of affiliation.* Stanford: Stanford University Press.

Seidman, S. 1983. "LS sets and cohesive subsets of graphs and hypergraphs". *Social Networks* **5**: 92–96.

Shaw, M. 1981. *Group dynamics: the psychology of small group behavior.* New York: McGraw-Hill.

Sherif, M. and C. Sherif. 1964. *Social Psychology.* New York: Harper and Row.

Simmel, G. 1902. "The number of members as determining the social form of the group". *American Journal of Sociology* **8**: 1–46.

Stokman, F., H. Hangyi. and E. Zeggelink. 1994. "Social networks and principles of self-organization" *Paper presented at the Social Science Information Technology 94 Conference.* Amsterdam, December 7–9.

Stokman, F. and R. Van Oosten. 1994. "The exchange of voting positions: an object oriented model of policy networks". In B. Bueno de Mesquita and F. Stokman (eds.) *Decision making in the European Community: models, applications, and comparisons.* New Haven: Yale University Press.

Tajfel, H. and J. Turner. 1986 "The social identity theory of intergroup-behavior". In S. Worchel and W. Austin (eds.) *Psychology of intergroup relations*. Chicago: Nelson-Hall Publishers.

Wasserman, S. and K. Faust. 1994. *Social network analysis: Methods and applications*. Cambridge: Cambridge University Press.

Wilson, T. 1982. "Relational networks: an extension of sociometric concepts". *Social Networks* **4**: 105–116.

Zeggelink, E. 1993. *Strangers into friends: The evolution of friendship networks using an individual oriented approach*. Amsterdam: Thesis Publishers.

Zeggelink, E. 1994. "Dynamics of structure: an individual oriented approach". *Social Networks* **16**: 295–333.

Zeggelink, E. 1995."Evolving friendship networks: an individual oriented approach implementing similarity. *Social Networks* **17**: 83–110.

Zeggelink, E., F. Stokman, and G. Van de Bunt. 1996. "The emergence of groups in the evolution of friendship networks". *Journal of Mathematical Sociology* **21**: 29–55.

Part V

Assessment

11 SOCIAL NETWORK CONCEPTIONS OF GROUP SOLIDARITY*

BARRY MARKOVSKY

University of Iowa

There is only one condition under which it is sensible to argue that a given definition of *group solidarity* is preferable to others: when it is a component of a theory whose explanations and predictions about empirical phenomena are superior to those of alternative theories. Such a theory may treat solidarity as a determinant that explains variation in other phenomena; or other factors may be invoked to explain variation in solidarity; or both. Whichever the case, no scientific value inheres in defining solidarity this way or that, for definitions alone do not *explain* anything. Worse, it is far too common in our discipline to find candidate definitions for given terms being evaluated using arbitrary criteria that as often as not filter out potentially useful but counter-intuitive candidates, and admit those with intuitive appeal only because they feel warmly familiar or were espoused by an "authority" or a skilled rhetorician.

Inherent limitations on what can be accomplished by atheoretical definitions alone make the present contribution a modest one. Still, it improves upon most previous attempts to define group solidarity. These have been nebulous at best, and efforts to explain solidarity have been hindered by that nebulousness.[1] In general, clarifying definitional issues makes solutions to theoretical problems more transparent and it is in that spirit that this chapter was written. I will begin by working through some of the definitional issues, then make comparisons with alternative perspectives from this volume, highlighting what I think are advantages of the conceptualization of solidarity that I offer.

To foreshadow my conclusions, I will suggest a way of thinking about solidarity that, compared to alternatives, is more about groups and their structures, less about people and their feelings. I also will contend that alternative formulations, in attempting to capture such intuitive, anthropocentric qualities of ostensibly solidary groups, may restrict themselves unnecessarily.

BACKGROUND

The goal of the present work is to develop a conceptualization of solidarity that (1) pares away extraneous semantic baggage, (2) avoids conflating the causes and consequences of solidarity with the thing itself, (3) is sufficiently abstract and general that it will accommodate any type of social configuration that holds together for some span of time, and (4) is sufficiently explicit and fruitful to permit immediate application and testing. Two motives set the work into motion. First, some years ago Edward J. Lawler and I decided that we wanted to collaborate on a project and considered various substantive options. Group solidarity emerged as the most challenging of the problems in which we shared strong, mutual interests. Second, we also shared some strong negative reactions to aspects of Michael Hechter's (1987) monograph *Principles of Group Solidarity* which had appeared recently and made a bit of a splash.[2]

In the work that we first presented in 1988 but only decided to publish more recently (Markovsky and Lawler, 1994), we argued that solidarity required clearer definition and would surely offer greater theoretical utility if not restricted to cost-avoidance and obligation. We scoured the sociological literature on solidarity and the social psychological literature on group cohesion, finding other proposed causes and consequences of solidarity, but no clearer definitions. We suggested that

> ...both concepts [solidarity and cohesion] carry with them numerous intuitively appealing connotations, most of which we readily associate with cohesion, solidarity, or both. This is probably because these connotations are factors that we readily conceive of as causes or consequences. ... Thus, we began by working on definitions that would sidestep the distracting connotations of previous conceptions and theories, highlighting not what leads to or follows from solidarity, but rather the distinctive properties by which it can be identified. [Markovsky and Lawler, 1994, p. 120.]

We drew upon insights from two chapters by physicists published in a volume on social cohesion (Sudarshan, 1981; Silber, 1981). They used terms such as *bonding agents*, *parts* and *wholes*, *constraints* and *chaos*, *states of matter*, and the *emergence* of macro properties from micro conditions. Stopping just short of defining solidarity in social terms, they nonetheless inspired us to pursue a definition that focused on social ties and structures rather than on affective bonds, costs and benefits, or density of group ties. For us this suggested that, to understand solidarity and cohesion, we should specify (1) a few carefully chosen properties of the individuals in the group, (2) certain aspects of the ties between them, and (3) group-wide patterns in those ties (Markovsky and Lawler, 1994, p. 121).

We offered a definition of cohesion based solely on the network concept of *reachability* – the overall proximity of actors in terms of the number and strength of ties between all pairs. The higher the reachability, the higher the cohesion. This notion seemed to do a fairly good job of capturing prior, mostly implicit, definitions. To define solidarity we imposed a further condition: "A solidary group is a set of actors with high cohesion and unity of structure." (Markovsky and Lawler, 1994, p. 123). This captured the two properties that we saw as unique to the state of group solidarity: First, members should be socially close to one another; if not tied directly then at least indirectly through other members. Second, the organization of group ties should be relatively homogeneous, i.e., ties should be distributed throughout the structure in a relatively uniform manner. This implies the absence of any substructures that might be vulnerable, such as via a small number of "cut-points," to calving away from the rest of the structure. Structural heterogeneity implies the presence of fault lines along which a social network is liable to break.

This conception was both more explicit and more general than those which came before. It subsumed not only the rationalistic bases of solidarity that Hechter and others had in mind, but also social ties based on emotional bonds and other "attractive forces" among members. It also allowed solidary groups to have vastly differing macro structures and properties, including forms that may be relatively "liquid" or "crystalline." Some of these ideas were illustrated in the paper with Lawler, then developed further in subsequent work (Markovsky and Chaffee, 1995). The latter integrated assumptions from social identity theory. We argued that identification ties alone could provide a viable basis for a form of group solidarity, and that such ties could strengthen existing solidarity levels in multiplex networks, i.e., networks having more than one type or layer of tie between elements. We also pointed out that if solidarity resides in patterns of social ties, then different types of disintegrative forces – varying in breadth, strength and specificity – would be expected to have differential impact, depending on the relational pattern that provides solidarity to a given set of actors.

Both of these earlier papers emphasized the importance of formalizing a solidarity index. The more I have thought about solidarity, however, the more I doubt that we can get very far by specifying formal definitions without having formal theories. The reasons should become clear below.

KEY TERMS

We start with several basic theoretical elements that deepen and broaden the definitions employed by Markovsky and Lawler (1994) and Markovsky and Chaffee (1995). In particular, although the definition of solidarity still is based on conditions of reachability and structural homogeneity, now it is "relativized." That is, the solidarity of a group is determined by comparing its reachability and homogeneity to those of a referent network.

The terms used in the definitions of a well-constructed theory must be understood by the relevant audience. Some may be defined explicitly, others remain undefined or "primitive" and these must be chosen so as to be already well understood by the targeted audience (Cohen, 1989). I have chosen the primitive terms in these definitions on the basis of their having reasonably widely-shared meanings for network theorists.

>*actor* $(x, y, \ldots)$: a person or collectivity.
>*attractive force* (AF_{xy}): the sum of expected positive consequences for x with regard to y.
>*repulsive force* (RF_{xy}): the sum of expected negative consequences for x with regard to y.
>*tie strength:* $TS_{xy} = AF_{xy} - RF_{xy}$.
>*tie* $x \rightarrow y$ exists iff $TS_{xy} > 0$.
>*reciprocal tie* $x \leftrightarrow y$ exists iff $TS_{xy} > 0$ and $TS_{yx} > 0$.
>*network*: set of actors, each tied to at least one other.
>*cognitive element*: a conception of a putative social object shared by actors in a network.
>*reachability*: the distance between actors in a network.
>*homogeneity*: the absence of discrete substructures in a network.
>*referent network*: a pattern of actors and ties that identifies a class of networks.

solidarity: the reachability and homogeneity of a network relative
to its referent network.

THE (PROVISIONAL) NATURE OF SOLIDARITY

Virtually as abstract and general as the notion of "ties" is the basis I
offer for them: the interplay of *attractive* and *repulsive forces.* These
are the fundamental forces that, in their patterning, will ultimately
determine the shape of the network and all that follows as consequences of that shape. Attractive and repulsive forces are anything
that produce, respectively, positive and negative, or "approach" and
"avoid" consequences for one actor that are associated with another
network element. The attraction or repulsion may be purely utilitarian,
but it also may be emotional. Furthermore, it may range from highly
purposive to completely unconscious. So positive and negative consequences may be direct rewards and punishments, respectively, but
consequences can also be any type of condition, event, or outcome that
represents a preferred or non-preferred state of affairs for the attracted
or repulsed actor.

The definition of *tie strength* recognizes that relational bonds are the
net result of forces that attract and forces that repel. Although for
many theoretical purposes it makes sense to speak of negative ties
among actors in a network, for our purposes, a tie with "negative
strength" makes the same contribution to solidarity as no tie at all.
Within this conceptualization, then, a tie does not exist at all unless it
represents a net surplus of attractive forces over and above repulsive
forces. The alternative does raise some interesting possibilities, however. All else being equal, it may prove useful to conceive of a set of
actors with no ties as having higher *potential* solidarity than a
comparable set with negative ties. More generally, in a network whose
actors manifest a pattern of positive, negative, and absent ties, it may
be reasonable under some conditions to take into account the negative
ties as functioning against group solidarity in a way that the absent
ties do not. This may be useful for a dynamic theory of solidarity that
takes initial tie strengths and tie configurations into account in
predicting later stages of group structure.

The definition of *network* excludes isolates who, by virtue of their
isolation, have no opportunity to contribute to group solidarity.
Although we will continue to use the term "*group* solidarity," implicit
is the notion that any group to which the idea of "solidarity" may be
relevant can be conceptualized as a network – a pattern of social

objects and ties. But networks can extend beyond what we normally think of as social groups, and we also may address the solidarity of these social structures.

The concept of *cognitive element* is not so common in network analysis, but it allows us to include network elements that may be every bit as crucial to group solidarity as living actors. For instance, it recognizes that affective ties to shared symbols may contribute to the integrity of a group, especially (but not necessarily) when that shared symbol is an intersubjective notion of the group itself.

The definition of *solidarity* rests on two general network concepts that can be translated into specific measures: *reachability* and *homogeneity*. One measure of reachability is the mean distance or number of ties separating pairs of actors in a network. Later I will discuss other possibilities. In general, reachability captures the idea that solidarity is enhanced to the degree that actors are tied to one another more directly.

Homogeneity – or lack of heterogeneity – is another general property with many potential indicators. In the context of solidarity, the basic idea is that homogeneity implies a relative absence of any segmentation or patterns of ties in the network. Holding constant the overall density of ties among network members, the more homogeneously those ties are distributed, the more uniform the structure and the more similarly bound are the actors to one another.

The idea of a *referent network* provides a baseline or reference point for determining group solidarity. The researcher must establish one or more explicit, idealized patterns of actors and ties to contrast with empirical cases. If the reachability and homogeneity of a given set of actors and ties fall below the levels measured in the referent, then that set of actors lacks solidarity – at least as a member of that particular referent class of networks. The referent may specify a *minimal* configuration, above which solidarity increases but beneath which solidarity is zero. Alternatively, the referent may specify a *typical* configuration from which solidarity may vary positively or negatively indicating, respectively, a solidarity surplus or deficit.

It would be premature to declare that the "difference" between the actual and referent networks ought to be represented mathematically as a difference formula, as opposed to a ratio, log-ratio, or other form. For now, the difference measure has the nice feature of generating a positive value when a network has a surplus of reachability and/or homogeneity relative to its referent, and a negative number when there is a deficit.

The dual components of the definition of solidarity – reachability and homogeneity – provide omnibus, conceptual guidelines for implementing more concrete measures. Later I will explore some of these measures and, more importantly, consider when we might prefer one measure over another. Already, however, this way of looking at solidarity contrasts with alternative views in consequential ways. Before illustrating these consequences, I will look at several alternative conceptualizations.

CONTRASTING FORMULATIONS

The editors graciously shared with me early versions of most of the other chapters in this volume. Here I review key points from seven that seemed most relevant, and for each I indicate distinctions from the ideas sketched above.

Fararo and Doreian

Fararo and Doreian (Chapter 1) argue that solidarity theories must "...integrate structural and process analysis to study *how structural forms emerge and change*. The very definition of the state of the system needs to be in terms of such forms." As a consequence of this theoretical mandate, the authors "require a combination of an analytic focus on structure, expanded to include emergent part–whole relations, and on the processes generative of changes of state of a system described in terms of possibilities for such relations." Fararo and Doreian want solidarity to span "...*both* a social network with a structural form *and* a higher-order social entity constituted by the cognitive–affective nexus focused on it but, for the actors, transcending it as individuals." Additionally, the authors state that in constructing a more rigorous general theory, "we have to keep in mind both the more recent formulations (of Randall Collins and Hechter) and also older and still useful formulations (such as those of Marx and Homans)." Much of the latter part of Fararo and Doreian's contribution reviews various elements of a number of prior formulations, calling for formalization of those elements and citing as the "final problem" to "assemble the whole set of formal models into the overall formalized theory of solidarity."

While this approach is at once creative and magnanimous, I disagree with much of it. It is not the case that any of the prior theories have provided a conceptualization of solidarity with proven superiority

over alternatives, and so it is unclear why earlier theories must feed
into a more comprehensive and integrative theory. The underlying
problem stems from others employing the rhetorical device of mandat-
ing definitions, relying on their degree of conformity with intuition
rather than clear demonstrations of utility within empirically tested
theories. Fararo and Doreian's ideas are reasonable, but they are
untested, as are those of the people they cite. Therefore, I reject the
prescription that we *must* or *ought to* define solidarity this way or that.

For instance, I find very challenging and appealing the task of
developing the type of dynamic theory of group solidarity that Fararo
and Doreian are seeking. However, I see no warrant to make the very
definition of solidarity dynamic unless doing so can be shown to
permit a more powerful theory, i.e., one that generates hypotheses that
are more precise, general, and accurate. Moreover, dynamics can be
incorporated even with a non-dynamic definition for solidarity,
e.g., solidary patterns or *states* may be reached or modified into other
solidary states through a dynamic process. Occam's Razor suggests
that we might first see how far we can go with a simpler static
definition for solidarity, building in more complex dynamic axioms
only as needed for describing structural changes. This makes the first
task that of defining a state of solidarity, rather than the process by
which solidarity emerges (which still requires a definition for that
which emerges from the emergent process); defining the thing that we
think is changing rather than trying to define a changing thing.

Heise

David Heise (Chapter 6) locates his approach to solidarity within one
of the most micro-level problem areas identified by Fararo and
Doreian: the empathetic alignment of individuals. He sketches "a
provisional description of the key features of empathetic solidarity
wherein emotional and motivational phenomena are central." "Solidarity" receives only lexical definition in Heise's chapter: "A union of
interests, purposes or sympathies among members of a group; fellowship of responsibilities and interests." His main task is not to define
solidarity, however, but to apply Affect Control Theory (ACT) to
explain the emergence of solidarity from interaction. He builds from
Fararo and Doreian's characterization of a solidarity relation S: two
individuals a and b that are in a relation with a central figure p. If aSp
and bSp, then a may infer solidarity with b and vice versa due to their
connections with p. Empathetic solidarity occurs "when a unifies

consciousness with *b* through emotional resonance, and *a* also infers from *b*'s collateral actions that the two of them are allied. In general, this happens when both *a* and *b* have the same relationship with [*p*], and they are experiencing the same emotional event involving [*p*]." "Empathetic consciousness from emotional resonance," and "induction of alliance from observing collateral action" are identified as the two key interpersonal phenomena.

By linking his approach to solidarity so intimately with ACT, Heise guarantees both a benefit and a liability. The benefit resides in the insights that such a theoretical integration affords: To the extent that the integration holds up, the solidarity branch receives strength from the well-developed, well-supported trunk, and the cumulative wisdom in ACT informs the empathetic solidarity process. The cost is that the limitations inherent in ACT – such as the implicit or explicit scope conditions or levels of analysis restrictions endemic to any theory – will be transferred to the solidarity branch unless special provisions are formulated. In this case, the very concept of solidarity, although subject to causes, and capable of effects, beyond the nervous systems of individual people, is defined solely in individualistic terms. This may be fine; we just do not know yet. My suspicion, however, is that if we want to talk about *group* solidarity, then we are going to have to talk about some group properties. We will not necessarily have to locate the causes of group solidarity in group structure. It may even turn out that a parsimonious explanation could be premised on interpersonal dynamics. However, if an approach could set as one of its goals the definition of solidarity as a group property and not as the coincidence or aggregation of self-conscious purposeful individuals, then it is possible that we will learn even more.

Breiger and Roberts

I was optimistic in this very regard when I began reading Breiger and Robert's contribution (Chapter 8). Breiger is well known for his role in the development and use of *blockmodeling* methods for social structure analysis. This technique has great potential for describing the sort of structural heterogeneity that I think may be central to group solidarity. I was even more optimistic to find the authors basing their approach on a kind of reachability criterion: the loglinear model of "quasi-symmetry" applied to generalized social exchange. The model assumes, for instance, that if exchanges flow from and to a given actor in the pattern $i{\rightarrow}j{\rightarrow}k{\rightarrow}i$, then the pattern $i{\rightarrow}k{\rightarrow}j{\rightarrow}i$ will manifest an equal flow. The implication is that the concatenation of such interlocking structures results in a solidary exchange system. By overlaying a blockmodel analysis, regions of such quasi-symmetric exchange can be identified within larger networks. That is, the model would detect blocks of actors within which a common set of quasi-symmetry parameters holds, and whose members further share common types of relations with members of other blocks.

This blockmodeling imagery naturally leads to a higher-level view of the network: blocks resemble actors and relations between blocks resemble exchange ties between actors. Brieger and Roberts devise relatively simple representations of complex multilevel structures by capitalizing on an assumption that also undergirds simple fractal models: Rich and complex structures can emerge from simple rules when different levels of analysis share patterns.

In the end, Breiger and Roberts provide a scheme for representing certain types of patterns among actors and sets of actors engaged in certain types of behaviors. Less obvious is how this defines or otherwise pertains to group solidarity in some more general sense. What, for instance, of Heise's version? Are empathetic and exchange-based solidarities antithetical alternatives? Must one of the views be right and the other wrong? And just what does it mean if a given structure has more blocks or fewer blocks when it comes to assessing its solidarity? It seems that Breiger and Roberts, inspired by Durkheim, find solidarity in variegated, interlocked sets of social relations. However, identifying the quasi-symmetry block structure of a social exchange network does not immediately suggest a metric for solidarity, or a way to describe departures from, or approaches to, such a state.

Collins and Hanneman

Randall Collins' theory of interaction ritual chains is one of the best-known contemporary theories of group solidarity. Collins and Hanneman (Chapter 7) summarize it as follows:

> ...all macro-sociological phenomena (class structures, formal organizations, etc.) can be translated into chains of interaction rituals (IRs). In each encounter, individuals negotiate an IR, which varies in the degree of solidarity and dominance among its participants. These outcomes raise or lower the accumulation of cultural capital (CC) and emotional energy (EE) which these individuals carry away with them; in turn, the match-up of CC and EE in their next encounters determines the success or failure of the next IR, and so

on. Translated into micro-empirical detail, social structures are the shape of just such [IR] chains.

The authors provide further details that fill out the micro-conditions for successful IRs, and they discuss the sorts of causal linkages among actors and social conditions that produce collective emotional intensity, mutual awareness and, ultimately, group solidarity. Hanneman is best known for his computer simulations of social dynamics, and in this collaboration his influence on the direction of Collins' work is clear. Formalizing the earlier IR theory has forced the authors to work through many details that are glossed over in the informal version. The result is sufficiently explicit to permit the execution of dynamic simulations. The down-side is that the simulation is *only* a simulation, relying on the conjunction of quite a few assumptions, thus no better and no worse than any other untested theory. If any of those assumptions are false, the chain is broken and all results are thrown into question. The up-side is that, in contrast to the more classical, discursive approach to explaining highly complex social phenomena, at least these assumptions and arguments are explicit. In making them so, the authors offer clear opportunities to test their theory in rigorous ways.

As with Heise's theory and most others, Collins and Hanneman treat solidarity as a group outcome that exists when members share certain dispositions and behaviors. This is fine, as far as it goes, but still represents another instance of a solidarity theory specifying an effect but taking minimal interest in defining solidarity *per se.* Is the sort of energized-but-focused image that Collins and Hanneman portray the only means by which groups can remain intact? Is it essential that all members of the group share the same heightened emotionality? Might patterns of actors' involvements be relevant, e.g., clusters of zealots or bridge-building facilitators? Or will it be just as fruitful to consider solidarity as a relatively simple, aggregate property – a sort of summary statistic capturing the central tendency of group members? Certainly it depends on the theorist's goals, and on the theory's merits when evaluated against evidence and against alternative theories with shared explanatory goals. However, we cannot hope to evaluate theories with more thoroughly developed conceptualizations of solidarity unless we try to develop some.

Other Formulations: Zeggelink, Johnsen and Lindenberg

Of those chapters made available to me, three others offered notable points of contrast to my own formulation. Evelien Zeggelink

(Chapter 10) uses computer simulations to study the process of friendship network formation. Existing social psychological theories provide the micro-foundations. In the dynamic model, strategic friendship choices allow actors to seek tension reductions with respect to each of an array of issues. Choices take into account affiliation needs, potential friends' traits, and members' interests in maintaining the group. Under different arrays of initial conditions, larger sets of actors break into stable subnetworks of varying shapes and sizes.

Eugene Johnsen (Chapter 9) also builds from a classic social psychological approach: Newcomb's A–B–X system. Somewhat akin to Breiger and Roberts' formulation, Johnsen's identifies nested, hierarchical structures with valued, directed ties between substructures. The approach centers around a set of shared thoughts and discourse among group members pertaining to valued interests, needs, persons, beliefs, etc. The strength of solidarity corresponds to the strength of the positive orientation of members to the central focus, and emerges through what Johnsen calls an agreement–friendship microprocess. Assumptions about the dispositional bases of tie-formations result in (or account for) the emergence of network substructures and patterns of ties among them. The strength of solidarity can then be measured by the strength and valence of ties within and between the substructures, and Johnsen offers some simple measures based on ratios of counts of signed directed ties. The approach distinguishes *solidarity*, which involves shared orientations or commitment to focal issues or persons, from *social cohesion*, which may result merely from interpersonal ties. This accords with Markovsky and Chaffee's (1995) inclusion of an objectified group element in the graph of the network to be analyzed. In our view, however, this element was neither necessary nor sufficient for the existence of group solidarity. In general, Johnson's work provides a valuable formalization of the process by which solidarity emerges within a particular theoretical domain, along with a set of simple indices for measuring solidarity within the range of outcomes that this process can generate.

Siegwart Lindenberg (Chapter 3) attempts to define solidarity "in such a way that it covers the most important intuitive conceptions of the phenomenon." Perhaps realizing that intuition is a rather shaky criterion, he goes on to argue that defining solidarity in terms of sentiment is theoretically unsatisfactory and provides a rational choice alternative. Lindenberg's framing of the problem and his solution are not all that different from Hechter's (1987), though much more fully developed. Solidarity is needed, Lindenberg argues, because people are myopically opportunistic and would otherwise breech the longer-term agreements necessary to achieve interests. This same myopia, however, promotes a framing process whereby saliencies of various outcome sets recede or come to the fore. Thus, the salient benefits that accrue from what Lindenberg calls "sharing groups" – face-to-face collectivities whose members share interests – manage to outweigh the temptations of opportunism by pushing these interests out of the frame and into the background. This is a plausible scenario by which solidary ties of a non-affective nature may form. As with some of the other formulations discussed above, however, it is noteworthy that there is not much "group" in this conception of group solidarity. Determinants and consequences all pertain to the actions and outcomes of individuals.

Discussion of Contrasting Formulations

For the purposes of comparison, it should be worthwhile to identify features of my approach that distinguish it from the others. Perhaps foremost among these is that it avoids an *anthropocentrist trap*. All of the others appear to assume that members conceptualize the group. They may have conscious interests in participating in it, or feelings of attachment toward it, or some other type of relation to it, depending upon the theory. Still, in every case, the relevant entity is always known to the participants and the theories hinge on actors recognizing themselves as a part of something.

This brand of methodological individualism is not preordained, however. Identification with the group, attraction to the group, love of the group, economic interest in the group – these all are viable candidates for "attractive forces" as defined earlier. However, they are not the only sorts of ties or processes that one might imagine to be capable of bonding social actors in relatively stable relational patterns. Furthermore, groups also can be held together by forces acting between substructures – not just between individuals. It is not difficult to conceive of stable patterns of actors where such patterns have analytically discernible causes and consequences, but whose constituents are not aware of the larger patterns they form. It even may be the case that it is these unseen networks which provide the *real* glue holding together society's components.

Second, although some previous formulations allow more than a single, narrowly defined type of social tie, most do not permit anything as general as an "attractive force." At the same time, every formulation posits that *some* type of attractive force holds things together.

A third point that distinguishes the present formulation from many of the others is its lack of commitment to any particular index of solidarity. It requires *some* type of indices for structural nearness or reachability, and for structural integrity or heterogeneity. Within those parameters, however, the type or level of reachability and heterogeneity depend on the theorist's expressed purposes. There will be different kinds of solidarity.

In contrast to most alternatives, my formulation emphasizes defining and analyzing solidarity from a structural standpoint. Most of the other contributors at least recognize that processes which produce solidarity also may leave behind heterogeneous structures, but only Johnsen offers so much as a primitive network-wide index of heterogeneity. I am surprised at the extent to which the sociologists *psychologize* solidarity, examining only the social structural implications of the dispositions and behaviors of individuals, to the exclusion of the potentially structural *nature* and determinants of the phenomenon. Again, there is much yet to be learned at individual and intra-individual levels of analysis, but the knowledge gap at the structural level is even greater.

MEASURES OF SOLIDARITY

In this section I review several measures that implement one or the other part of the bipartite definition of solidarity, noting their unique features along the way. The definition of solidarity underdetermines its measurement in any concrete instance. A major advantage of this is that it facilitates the development of a truly general theory of group solidarity. The disadvantage is that different measures can satisfy both of the definitive properties of solidarity, but may produce contradictory indices for a particular application. The reason, of course, is that different measures are sensitive to different structural nuances. Therefore it is the researcher's burden to specify *a priori* which structural properties are relevant for his/her theoretical purposes and, ideally, why. The best policy is for the theorist to decide what needs to be measured, rather than leaving that critical decision to some prefabricated measure that may have been developed for another purpose.

The other prerequisite for the researcher is to specify the referent network – the archetypal network against which empirical networks are judged. To "identify" the structure means to establish it as embodying the definitive properties for all instances of some *type* or *class* of network structures. Before discussing reachability and homogeneity measures, I must first examine the concept of referent network in more detail.

The Referent Network

To repeat the definition, the *referent network* is a pattern of actors and ties that identifies a class of networks. Several hypothetical examples will illustrate.[3]

> *Friendship circle*: each member of a set of actors has a mutual friendship tie with every other actor in the set.
>
> *Cult*: ten or more followers, each with ties of adoration and social attachment directed toward a leader, and each with ties to at least one other follower.
>
> *Fan club*: One hundred or more members, each of whom is attracted to the public image of an entertainer or group of entertainers, exchange money (dues) for information on that entertainer's group's activities.
>
> *Dating market*: Two sets of actors, each containing potential dating partners for members of the other set.

Each of these simple examples is a kind of structural template against which a given set of empirical actors and ties may be checked. Although common types are used in these examples, there is no requirement that the template describe familiar, naturally occurring formations. The researcher may be interested in the relative solidarity of a social entity that exists outside the awareness of most or all that participate, as when we purchase goods or sell our skills without being cognizant of the structures of the (solidary) economic markets in which we participate. There is also no mandate that the specification of the referent network must be holistic in the sense of capturing all of the actors and ties that may be identifiable within a given empirical instance. However, for purposes of measuring solidarity, the researcher would need to identify actors and ties of given *kinds* on which the solidarity measure is based, including those actors and ties that may be surplus from the standpoint of a particular template. For example, although a cult leader's attachment to followers is not a necessary component of the template, such ties should raise the level of the cult's solidarity beyond the level needed to establish its existence.

Levels of Measurement

The referent network may suggest configurations of clusters, subnetworks, or other corporate entities, as opposed to individual human actors. This can be seen in the dating market example. In such cases, theoretical grounds must determine the relevant measurement level of solidarity, i.e., whether to treat individual persons or sets of people as the unit of analysis upon which the solidarity measure is based.

Consider as an example three clusters of persons with strong, dense affective ties within clusters and a few weaker cross-cluster ties. This is illustrated in Figure 11.1. There are several different ways to describe the degree of solidarity of these 15 people, even without delving into mathematical specifications. First, we might consider the relative strength of interpersonal ties within clusters. Perhaps some theory specifies (1) a referent network having multiple small clusters, "dense" ties within clusters and sparse ties between clusters, and (2) high solidarity produces feelings of *esprit de corps*. This creates a localized definition of solidarity whereby everyone in the network is part of a solidary group, even if the relevant "group" happens not to be the entire structure. Thus, high spirits and positive emotions would be predicted in Figure 11.1. Although this view is myopic from a structuralist perspective, for some purposes it can be perfectly appropriate. For instance, if the clusters are work groups, the ties are friendship bonds, and a researcher wishes to predict satisfaction in the workplace, then this rather constrained version of solidarity would probably suffice.

Suppose instead that the 15-person structure is a search committee for a new university president, and the ties are information flows. The researcher's theory presumes that maximum information sharing optimizes group decisions; the referent network specifies an all-to-all

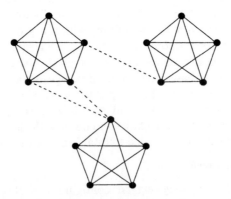

FIGURE 11.1.   Levels of analysis.

structure with maximum possible reachability and complete homo-geneity. These criteria place greater demands on the overall network structure. That is, they specify patterns that need to obtain sim-ultaneously among many actors in the network. Looking again at Figure 11.1, we see that reachability and homogeneity fall off rapidly as soon as we move beyond each actor's within-cluster ties. Although every individual is enmeshed in a highly solidary subnetwork, for analytic purposes he or she is also part of a larger system in which reachability and homogeneity are not so high. Most members are accessible to one another only indirectly because the structure has areas of low density. The clusters may represent informal subcommit-tees whose members share information among themselves more readily than with members of other subcommittees. In this example, the researcher should find poorer decisions in a group structured as in Figure 11.1 than in the case where everyone talks to everyone else.

A third perspective on the same structure involves stepping up a level of analysis to consider the relative degree of reachability and homogeneity among clusters-as-actors. In this case, ties between clus-ters were described as being weaker and fewer than those among individuals, and the hypothetical solidarity measure would find a level of reachability somewhat less than that found within clusters, and less than what may have been specified in an idealized referent network.

Reachability

Reachability was defined as the distance between actors in a network. The upper bound of reachability for a network is its *diameter*, the length of the largest distance (or the *geodesic*) between two actors. For some purposes, the diameter alone can be a very reasonable indicator of reachability, as when the theoretical factor of interest requires only that network members be *x-reachable*, that is, reachable by a path no longer than *x*. For example, diameter provides a crude measure of the departure of an actual friendship clique from its referent described above.

A more structurally sensitive reachability measure takes the mean of the geodesics for all *i, j* pairs in the network, i.e., the mean minimum path distance (*d*) between pairs of actors. Assuming non-directional ties, there are $n(n-1)/2$ paths, the average length of which is given by

$$R = \frac{1}{n(n-1)/2} \sum_{i=1}^{n-1} \sum_{j=i+1}^{n} d_{ij}.$$

Compared to *x-reachability,* this measure will not be so biased due to, say, an offshoot of the central clique consisting of a single path of several tied actors. The *x-reachability* measure would characterize the whole network on the basis of this anomalous segment, whereas the mean geodesic measure would merely combine these peripheral members' reachability scores with those of the more tightly clustered members to form the overall mean.

Technically, it is a misnomer to call the foregoing equation a "reachability" index because it is based on distance, not closeness. Standardizing the index can both restrict its values to a $[0 \dots 1]$ range and change its direction such that larger values reflect increased reachability rather than distance. We accomplish this by obtaining both the maximum and the minimum R for structures that satisfy the referent network criteria, and transforming R as follows:

$$R^* = \frac{R_{\text{Max}} - R}{R_{\text{Max}} - R_{\text{Min}}}.$$

To illustrate, consider again the referent network for cults. The requirements were ten or more members tied to a leader, and each member tied to at least one other member. Suppose that in cults, members experience a kind of closeness to other members via their tie to the leader, net of their direct ties to one another. This notion would be lost if directed ties were used to calculate reachability, so we use nondirected ties for this example. Obviously any network configured exactly as the template satisfies the criteria, but we can imagine other forms that do so as well. For instance, Figures 11.2a and 11.2b also satisfy the referent conditions. Figure 11.2a happens to be the network of lowest reachability that satisfies the referent network requirements, and so $R_{\text{Max}} = 1.73$. That is, the average distance between each pair of actors is 1.73 steps in the network. An all-to-all network would represent the minimum average distance: 1.0. Carrying out the calculations, the reachability index for the referent network (Figure 11.2a) is 0.0, and 0.21 for Figure 11.2b. The more connections we add to the network, the higher this index will go, approaching 1.0 as ties approach maximum density.

There are alternative reachability measures that are sensitive to the direction of ties along each geodesic, and so it is not necessarily the case that all actors in a referent network with directed ties will be mutually reachable. Wasserman and Faust (1994) provide a typology of such connections. We say that i and j are *weakly connected* if they

(a)

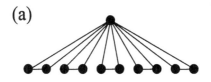

Mean Distance = 1.73
Standardized R = 0

(b)

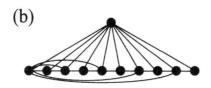

Mean Distance = 1.58
Standardized R = 0.21

FIGURE 11.2.   Reachability in cults.

are connected by a path, irrespective of the direction of ties along the path. They are *unilaterally connected* if, taking directedness into account, either i can reach j, or j can reach i. The two actors are *strongly connected* if i and j can reach each other, though not necessarily via the same set of intermediaries. Finally, i and j are *recursively connected* if the path from i to j is just the reverse of the path from j to i. Four different types of reachability for networks may be defined on the basis of these four types of connectedness for actors. A network is *weakly connected* if all pairs of actors are at least weakly connected; the network is *unilaterally connected* if all pairs are unilaterally connected, etc.

Another property that may be useful for reachability measures is the relative strength of each tie in the path between pairs of actors. In many instances it will make sense to presume that reachability is diminished by the presence of even one weak tie somewhere along a path. For example, a weak tie could indicate an impediment to the flow of information, products, or sentiment. A convenient way to represent this mathematically is to assign each path a value between

0 and 1 representing its strength. To calculate the total strength of flow from actor i to actor j, (1) identify all possible paths that start at i and end at j, (2) calculate the product of the tie strengths along each path, and (3) sum the products.

Given the criteria for the various sample referent networks, it is plain to see why different reachability criteria are needed for different purposes. By their respective criteria, the fact that the cult leader may have ties directed toward members (or others) is irrelevant for determining whether the cult satisfies minimum conditions for solidarity. On the other hand, the theorist may take the position that these non-essential ties nevertheless enhance group solidarity, and so they would be counted in the reachability and homogeneity measures of the actual network that will be compared to the referent network. Rival theories employing these different definitions will have distinct operationalizations, one of which should result in hypotheses that are more robust and precise, and better corroborated in empirical tests.

Homogeneity

Homogeneity presents challenges that do not arise with reachability measures. First, it is a relatively simple matter to devise a network-wide index of reachability merely by aggregating pair-wise measures. There is no such thing as a pair-wise homogeneity index, however, and so there can be no network-wide homogeneity index obtained by simple aggregation.

Second, reachability already is well defined within network parlance. In contrast, homogeneity's meaning is not so clear. Wasserman and Faust (1994) use "heterogeneity" to refer to the variance of the degree indices of individual actors and the variance of pair-wise actor closeness indices. However, whereas these measures are sensitive to the level of homogeneity across characteristics of individual members, they do not screen for higher-level structuring.

Third, homogeneity is not well defined within the present formulation. The "absence of discrete substructures" is an idealized characterization. To allow for *degrees* of solidarity, however, necessitates ways of talking about degrees of departure from this ideal state, i.e., degrees of heterogeneity. But heterogeneity can don various guises, and there is no omnibus method for detecting and quantifying it.

In this section I will discuss two different approaches to measuring network heterogeneity: connectivity analysis and cluster analysis.[4] Both approaches may be useful for conceptualizing certain types of solidarity, and each is sensitive to different forms of departure from homogeneity. Importantly, there are numerous alternatives within each approach, and there are alternative classes of approaches, such as blockmodeling, that detect other forms of heterogeneity.

Connectivity Analysis

One way to extract information on the homogeneity of a network is to examine its vulnerability to the removal of actors or ties. All else being equal, a more homogeneous network is less likely to break into substructures with the removal of any given set of actors or ties. In contrast, a "chunkier" structure's ties are concentrated more in some places than in others, so the removal of one set of elements will more likely result in disconnected subnetworks.

Several network concepts permit a formalized approach to the analysis of connectivity. As the label suggests, a *bridge* is a tie that connects substructures such that its removal results in the disconnection of network components. The idea can be extended to the *L-line cut* – a set of L ties which, when removed, disconnects the network. Note that bridges and L-line cuts are not necessarily weak ties, but from the standpoint of the larger network, they are regions of structural thinness in the network.

Actors, as well as ties, can mediate substructures. An actor is a *cutpoint* if its deletion creates disconnected networks. In a bucket brigade, every actor except the first and last is a cutpoint. A mediator in a labor negotiation may also be a cutpoint in a communication network. The idea also can apply to sets of actors that bind network substructures: A *cutset* is a set of actors that, when removed, creates disconnected networks.

Point- and line-connectivity can provide the basis for network-wide measures of homogeneity. One approach is tantamount to subjecting the network to deepening cuts and tallying the pace of the network's decomposition. Figure 11.3 illustrates such a procedure, which we may call *line-cut heterogeneity*: Start with the network at the top left of the figure. There is one (i.e., $n = 1$) 1-cut ($L = 1$) that cleaves the network. This is indicated in the next network to the right, now redrawn to reflect the tie removal, and labeled with a cut "Depth" of [1]. For each re-drawn figure, the number of ties in a given cut (L) and the number of ways of implementing the L-cut (n) are displayed as an ordered pair (L, n). Continuing the analysis, if another 1-cut could divide one of the two residual networks in the second figure, this would correspond to a

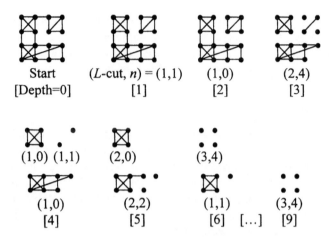

FIGURE 11.3.   Line-cut heterogeneity.

Depth of two. However, no such cut exists. We continue to Depth = 3, which means checking for 2-cuts in the same residual networks. There are four 2-cuts indicated by the ordered pair (2, 4), and we redraw the network with all cuts implemented. At Depth = 4 we may apply a single 1-cut and remove isolates from the previous graph. The other residual structures remain intact because 1-cuts do not affect them. At the next stage, however, there are two 2-cuts in the lower subnetwork. This procedure continues until the network decomposes completely.

The procedure tallies the numbers of new cuts created with each increment in cut-depth. Figure 11.4 graphs these numbers against the depth of each cut, creating a heterogeneity profile for the network. For contrast, the Case 1 network (Figure 11.3) is graphed behind that for Case 2 in Figure 11.4. The distributional properties of these profiles embody a wealth of information on the structural homogeneity of each network, and it is a simple matter to compare parameters across different distributions. By themselves, means are not terribly informative because they can mask large differences across other properties of the distributions. A variance measure, for example, provides information on the variety of substructural levels identified by the analysis. Just as with statistical distributions and densities, the analysis of other distributional parameters can go further still. The skewness of the distribution may be crucial for solidarity analysts. There will be a relatively flat distribution for homogeneous structures, a skewed-left distribution for very brittle or wispy structures, and a skewed-right

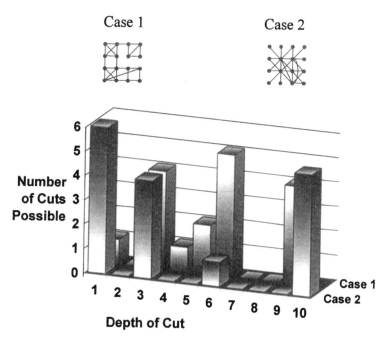

FIGURE 11.4.   Heterogeneity profiles.

distribution for structures having tightly-knit substructures capable of resisting line-cuts. The kurtosis of the distribution also conveys information that can be relevant to solidarity: A structure with a relative excess of midsize substructures would come out higher on a kurtosis index.

With all these possibilities – and I emphasize that this is just one of a variety of approaches that could be devised – it should be evident that analyzing solidarity requires more than an ability to concoct measures. Many other measures are conceivable, and there can be no one index value that will capture all dimensions of homogeneity/ heterogeneity. The researcher must have a theoretical basis for deciding which properties are relevant.

Cluster Analysis

Line-cut heterogeneity unravels networks from the outside in, first by rending the weaker peripheral components, then the stronger inner components, along the way keeping track of the residual clusters until they, too, disappear. In contrast, most procedures for detecting substructures work from the inside out, examining patterns of path distances among pairs of actors. In general, the different measures will provide somewhat different views of a network's homogeneity.

Standard methods for "cluster analysis" markedly differ from line-cut heterogeneity: These are techniques used to divide a set of entities into homogeneous subgroups on the basis of their similarities (Lorr, 1983, p. 1). In the case of actors *in networks,* cluster analysis groups actors on the basis of similarities across some predetermined set of criteria (Wasserman and Faust, 1994). Depending upon the choice of clustering criteria – ideally, a theoretically guided choice – the analysis may yield varying structural images. To illustrate, consider the dual criteria of *cohesion* and *structural equivalence* (Burt, 1982) as bases for determining "similarity." A cohesion criterion looks for sets of actors that have strong, direct ties with one another, whereas an equivalence criterion groups actors according to the degree of similarity of the patterns of their ties to others. To illustrate these distinctions, the network in Figure 11.5 presents the results of

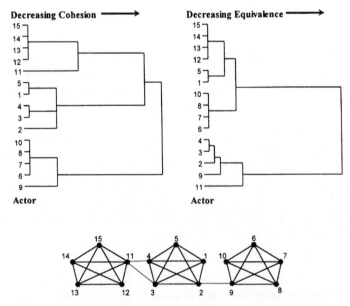

FIGURE 11.5.   Cluster analyses under different similarity criteria.

hierarchical cluster analyses of the Figure 11.1 network under the two different similarity criteria.[5] Actors now are labeled 1–15 in the network diagram at the bottom of Figure 11.5. In the cluster analysis "dendrograms," – subsets of highly similar actors – are indicated by shared membership in a cluster on the far left side, e.g., $\{12, 13, 14, 15\}$ in both diagrams. Higher-level clusters, or "clusters of clusters", are indicated by linked lower-level clusters, such as the connection between clusters $\{1, 5\}$ and $\{3, 4\}$ in the diagram on the left of Figure 11.5. Clusters delimited toward the left of a dendrogram are more homogeneous, and those toward the right are more heterogeneous.

The most prominent features of the cohesion dendrogram on the left side of Figure 11.5 are the three relatively tight clusters, corresponding to the three 5-actor sets in the network diagram. In the $\{11, 12, 13, 4, 15\}$ cluster, actors $\{12, 13, 14, 15\}$ are all structurally identical and equally cohesive, and they form the tightest sub-cluster. Moving to the right in the dendrogram, they are soon joined by actor $\{11\}$ who is very similar to them except for weak network ties to actors 3 and 4. Similarly, the second major cluster, $\{1, 2, 3, 4, 5\}$, shows slight dissimilarities between the sets $\{1, 5\}$, $\{3, 4\}$ and $\{2\}$, but all five join in a relatively strong cluster. The third major cluster, $\{6, 7, 8, 9, 10\}$, is much like the first, with the weak-tied actor $\{9\}$ somewhat distinct from the other four. The remaining "superclusters" are far to the right of the diagram, indicating weaker clustering and greater homogeneity.

The equivalence dendrogram paints a different picture. This time there are two major clusters: $\{1, 5, 6, 7, 8, 10, 12, 13, 14, 15\}$ and $\{2, 3, 4, 9, 11\}$. Note that these do not visually correspond to the most obvious clusters in the network diagram. Rather, they represent two sets of actors distinguished by their patterns of ties. The larger set contains actors whose only ties are strong and intra-clique. All members of the smaller set have strong intra-clique ties *plus* either one or two weak inter-clique ties. Note that the dendrograms also capture fine-grained distinctions among actors within the two major cliques, e.g., $\{2\}$ is somewhat dissimilar from $\{3, 4\}$ because actor 3 and actor 4 each has a weak tie to an actor having two weak ties $\{11\}$, whereas $\{2\}$ is tied to an actor that has only one weak tie $\{9\}$.

In addition to dendrograms, standard output from cluster analysis programs associates criterion values (e.g., calculated distance or cohesion measures) with each cluster, corresponding to the horizontal location of the vertical links in the dendrogram. I re-scaled the horizontal axes for the two analyses in Figure 11.5 so that the tightest clusters (left side) are assigned 0.0 and the cluster including all actors (right side) is assigned 1.0. A summary measure for cluster-based homogeneity can be obtained by tallying the number of "dendrites" or horizontal lines of a given length (measured from the left side), multiplying each such tally by the dendrite length associated with it, summing these across all dendrite lengths, and dividing by the total number of lines tallied. This weighted mean gives us a measure of the mean strength of the clusters in the dendrogram. Lower values indicate more distinct clusters, greater heterogeneity, and thus lower solidarity for the overall structure. Higher values indicate looser clustering, greater homogeneity, and so higher solidarity.

The value of this measure for the cohesion-based image is 0.239, and 0.144 for the equivalence-based image. This quantifies a difference that can be detected visually: The cohesion dendrogram shows clusters forming further to the right as compared to the equivalence dendrogram, indicating looser clusters and more homogeneity. For comparison purposes, assume that the referent network consists of the same trio of 5-actor cliques, plus two additional symmetric ties, 1–6 and 1–11. The cohesion-based measure would be 0.215 and the equivalence measure 0.150. These values indicate that, relative to the referent network, the empirical network has slightly lower solidarity under the cohesion criterion, but slightly higher solidarity for the equivalence-based measure. The differences are slight because the empirical networks and referent network are very similar in this example.

Combining Reachability and Homogeneity Measures

If solidarity is to be a product of both reachability and homogeneity, then the question of how to combine measures of reachability and homogeneity in a single solidarity measure must be addressed. Empirical indicators are theoretically underdetermined in most scientific research. This necessitates imposing – often implicitly – a "measurement theory" to operationalize theoretical terms. Because here I am not proffering a solidarity theory, it would be premature to suggest an appropriate adjunct measurement theory. However, it may be worth mentioning a few implications of some of the more basic and plausible specifications.

The measures of reachability (R) and homogeneity (H) each entails two constituent measures: one for the referent network (R_r, H_r) and one for the empirical network (R_e, H_e). For simplicity, assume that we re-scale each measure x such that $0 < x \leqslant 1$. We must then make two important specifications: (1) the function that compares an empirical network to its referent for both reachability and homogeneity, and (2) the function that combines the two values from (1). These are not independent decisions. For instance, even with the constraint that measures must be non-zero, if we specify solidarity (S) in terms of the ratio of differences

$$S = \frac{R_e - R_r}{H_e - H_r},$$

the function that approaches $\pm\infty$ when homogeneity for the e and r networks are similar, and the potential exists for very small changes in the denominator to create swings from extreme positive to extreme negative solidarity, or *vice versa*. Also, the function is undefined if homogeneity happens to be equal for e and r.

A variety of functions circumvent this problem, but one that may be especially useful is simply the product of the reachability and homogeneity measures, each of which is, in turn, captured as the ratio of the empirical network measure to the referent measure:

$$S = \frac{R_e}{R_r} \times \frac{H_e}{H_r} = \frac{R_e H_e}{R_r H_r}.$$

The multiplicative function captures the assumed joint contribution of reachability and homogeneity to solidarity. Both are necessary; neither alone is sufficient. As specified, however, this function compresses the entire lower range of solidarity (where the empirical network's values are less than those for the referent network) to values between zero and one, whereas the upper range extends from one to infinity. A logarithmic transformation makes the measure symmetric about zero:

$$S = \ln\left(\frac{R_e H_e}{R_r H_r}\right).$$

Now the only remaining problem with this model is its implicit assumption that reachability and homogeneity are weighted equally. Until more is known about the relationship between these two components, it is probably wisest to allow different, empirically determined weights for the reachability and homogeneity components:

$$S = \ln\left\{\left(\frac{R_e}{R_r}\right)^a \times \left(\frac{H_e}{H_r}\right)^b\right\} = a\ln\left(\frac{R_e}{R_r}\right) + b\ln\left(\frac{H_e}{H_r}\right).$$

This form can be rearranged as a linear model for parameter estimation:

$$S = aR' + bH',$$

where $R' = \ln(R_e/R_r)$, $H' = \ln(H_e/H_r)$. Thus, for example, where solidarity is used to predict some other phenomenon, parameters associated with R' and H' may be estimated separately and the relative impact of the two factors on the dependent variable may be determined.

DISCUSSION AND CONCLUSIONS

Defining *solidarity* is a struggle. Anyone who attempts to do so must strike balances among a number of motives. We probably would like "solidarity" to encompass at least some of the meanings already associated with it in the field and, perhaps, in common parlance. But which meanings and to what extent should they be covered? If prior conceptualizations are flawed, then we also would like to improve upon them. For example, we should reduce the risk of tautology by clearly distinguishing the concept from its presumed causes and consequences; and we should reduce the chances of miscommunication by clearly expressing all definitive properties. However, a very tempting solution to the problems of maximizing distinctiveness and communicability is to narrow the definition of the concept, putting these motives at cross-purposes with the first, which demanded a certain degree of breadth. How do we know when a definition affords a concept sufficient degrees of distinctiveness and communicability?

To reiterate a recurring theme one last time, the only way to answer these questions is to work with a theory of solidarity that employs *some* explicit definition of the term in expressing its propositions and derivations. The theory must be subjected to analyses, both logical and empirical, and contrasted with all of its available alternative formulations. This will not be accomplished in the first theoretical go-round or the first empirical test. It must be a long-term project, preferably in competition with alternative formulations. A theory of solidarity will emerge that is both pragmatic and coherent, and undoubtedly will look nothing like what has been presented in this chapter. At the same time, it will of necessity have evolved from a starting point *something* like this one.

NOTES

*Some of this material was presented at the 16th International Sunbelt Social Network Conference, Charleston, SC, February 1996. I am grateful to Tom Fararo and Pat

Doreian for encouraging me to advance this line of theorizing. Valuable feedback was provided by attendees of the Sunbelt Conference, participants of the Iowa Workshop on Theoretical Analysis, and Satoshi Kanazawa.

1. See the review by Markovsky and Lawler (1994).
2. Hechter's basic claim was that solidarity consists of members' compliance to group obligations under the threat of negative sanctions for failing to meet those obligations. Among other things, we contended that (1) Hechter's theory was tautologous because his definition for solidarity included what he also assumed to be its determinants, and (2) sanction-avoidance is but one of many potential bases for solidarity (Markovsky and Lawler, 1994).
3. As with definitions for theoretical concepts, there can be no "right" and "wrong" specification for a referent network. At best, one version may prove more useful than another for identifying empirical cases in multiple empirical tests conducted in service of the theory that employs it.
4. Henceforth I use the term "homogeneity" to mean the degree to which heterogeneity is absent.
5. The analysis was conducted using Burt's STRUCTURE Version 4.2.

REFERENCES

Breiger, Ronald L. and John M. Roberts, Jr. 1998. "Solidarity and social networks." Chapter 8 in Patrick Doreian and Thomas J. Fararo (eds.), *The Problem of Solidarity: Theories and Models.* New York: Gordon and Breach.
Burt, Ronald S. 1982. *Toward a Structural Theory of Action.* New York: Academic Press.
Cohen, Bernard P. 1989. *Developing Sociological Knowledge.* Chicago: Nelson-Hall.
Collins, Randall and Robert Hanneman 1998. "Modeling the interaction ritual theory of solidarity." Chapter 7 in Patrick Doreian and Thomas J. Fararo (eds.), *The Problem of Solidarity: Theories and Models.* New York: Gordon and Breach.
Fararo, Thomas J. and Patrick Doreian 1998. "The theory of solidarity: An agenda of problems." Chapter 1 in Patrick Doreian and Thomas J. Fararo (eds.), *The Problem of Solidarity: Theories and Models.* New York: Gordon and Breach.
Hechter, Michael 1987. *Principles of Group Solidarity.* Berkeley: University of California Press.
Heise, David 1998. "Conditions for empathetic solidarity." Chapter 6 in Patrick Doreian and Thomas J. Fararo (eds.), *The Problem of Solidarity: Theories and Models.* New York: Gordon and Breach.
Johnsen, Eugene C. 1998. "Structures and processes of solidarity: An initial formalization." Chapter 9 in Patrick Doreian and Thomas J. Fararo (eds.), *The Problem of Solidarity: Theories and Models.* New York: Gordon and Breach.
Lindenberg, Sigwart 1998. "The microfoundations of solidarity: A Framing approach." Chapter 3 in Patrick Doreian and Thomas J. Fararo (eds.), *The Problem of Solidarity: Theories and Models.* New York: Gordon and Breach.
Lorr, Maurice 1983. *Cluster Analysis for Social Scientists.* San Francisco: Jossey-Bass.
Markovsky, Barry and Edward J. Lawler 1994. "A new theory of group solidarity." In Barry Markovsky, Jodi O'Brien and Karen Heimer (eds.), *Advances in Group Processes*, Vol. 11. Greenwich, Conn: JAI Press.
Markovsky, Barry and Mark V. Chaffee 1995. "Social identification and solidarity: A revised formulation." In Barry Markovsky, Jodi O'Brien and Karen Heimer (eds.), *Advances in Group Processes*, Vol. 12. Greenwich, Conn: JAI Press.
Silber, Leo 1981. "Group interactions and group behavior in physics," pp. 56–67, in Henry Kellerman (ed.), *Group Cohesion: Theoretical and Clinical Perspectives*, New York: Grune & Stratton.

Sudarshan, E.C.G. 1981. "Cohesion and physical structure," pp. 122–131, in Henry Kellerman (ed.), *Group Cohesion: Theoretical and Clinical Perspectives.* New York: Grune & Stratton.

Wasserman, Stanley and Katherine Faust 1994. *Social Network Analysis: Methods and Applications.* New York: Cambridge University Press.

Zeggelink, Evelien 1998. "Group formation in friendship networks." Chapter 10 in Patrick Doreian and Thomas J. Fararo (eds.), *The Problem of Solidarity: Theories and Models.* New York: Gordon and Breach.

12 SOLIDARITY, SOCIAL STRUCTURE, AND SOCIAL CONTROL

JOHN SKVORETZ

University of South Carolina

INTRODUCTION

Building good theories is difficult under the best of circumstances. It is particularly troublesome when we agree neither on key terms nor on a database of stylized facts to be accounted for by proposed theories. Group solidarity as problem for scientific analysis is a classic example. Fararo and Doreian's introduction describes the various usages and meanings of the term in sociological theory, but other authors, Breiger and Roberts, Johnsen, and Markovsky, for instance, also testify to the multidimensional nature of the solidarity concept. Equally important is the absence of some agreed upon database. Much progress has been made, for instance, in the study of power in networks because there exists a set of stylized facts describing which positions in which networks can extract large or only modest advantages from exchanges with adjacent positions (Skvoretz and Willer, 1993). Were the equivalent available for group solidarity, my task of commenting on the contributions in this volume would be simplified. As it is, my task is similar to that of an anthropologist studying another culture – major dimensions of conceptual variation must be mapped out and, if possible, some order brought to the collection.

I organize commentary around specific reactions to each contributed chapter. I begin with an overview in which I locate the contributions in terms of a few salient features that differentiate among them. As the grouping of the articles in the Table of Contents reflects, the contributions can be differentiated in terms of the relative priority or attention given to costs and benefits (rationality), emotion (affect) and network. First, are cost and benefits of group membership essential to the theory or approach? Second, does theory or conceptualization highlight the importance of affect and emotion? Third, what importance is given to the structuring of communication networks? I then close the chapter with a discussion of how the contributions advance the problem set agenda identified in Fararo and Doreian's introduction. To recall, they list five problem sets, two of which refer to the integration of the other three. The other three problems are substantive: the emergence of groups, the development of the group's corporate obligations, and the compliance of group members with their group's obligations.

DIMENSIONS OF DIFFERENTIATION

A major feature that distinguishes between approaches and theories is the extent to which the costs and benefits of membership are central to the analysis. Naturally, any contribution with an avowedly rational choice perspective falls into the group for whom the analysis of costs and benefits is essential. This group consists of Chai and Hechter, Lindenberg, Weesie and colleagues, and Weidlich and Helbing. Chai and Hechter examine how the costs of compliance can be overcome by the penalties from sanctions. Lindenberg describes how the objectives or goals of actors make some benefits and costs extremely salient to decision making while making other benefits and costs fade into insignificance. Weesie and colleagues calculate the relative payoffs of informally trusting partners in delayed exchanges to deliver the goods vs. using more expensive formal contract methods to insure completion of the exchange. Weidlich and Helbing describe how individuals move between groups and statuses within groups in response to relative cost–benefit ratios of membership.

In these papers, questions of affect and emotion simply do not arise. The image of group solidarity, when the concept is specifically addressed, is cold-blooded. Not all of these contributions specifically address the problem of solidarity *per se*. For instance, for Weesie and colleagues, the central problem is to manufacture trust between autonomous actors in varying institutional environments. While intuitively trust and solidarity are related – we are more likely to trust those with whom we are solidarily bonded – solidarity is not a parametrized influence in their model. Also these papers lack explicit representation of the pattern of social ties linking members of groups and explicit consideration of how variation in the structure of ties may impact on the group's solidarity. The model of Weesie and colleagues is a partial exception since the density of ties among a group of game theoretic equivalent actors (the "buyers") is a parametrized influence on the placement of trust.

A second basis for differentiation is the importance given to affect and emotion in the conceptualization of solidarity. The chapters by Collins and Hanneman and by Heise fall into this group of warm-blooded solidarity images. And, while Johnsen's chapter is classified below in terms of its focus on a group's network of ties, it has a secondary home in this group because the primitive social ties of interest are affective ties of approval and liking vs. disapproval and disliking. Heise's contribution clarifies the social-psychological conditions under which two or more individuals may experience feelings of unity and oneness. These conditions overlap with those Collins stipulates in his theory of interaction rituals – common focus, copresence, common emotional mood – but rather than being postulated, their necessity is derived as an outcome of the interplay between ongoing events and social identities in control of individuals' centers of emotional production. Collins and Hanneman's contribution, on the other hand, glosses the question of how a common mood is produced. Level of common mood and emotional output, among other variables, are simply postulated and their values at various points in time related to one another in a system dynamics formal framework.

The remaining chapters share common focus on the structuring of communication networks in relation to the problem of group solidarity. Breiger and Roberts analyze the structure of social ties based on agreements and disagreements that pairs of individuals in a group have with one another. They do not propose a theoretical model that would generate the agreements and disagreements based on some process parametrized by the group's solidarity. Rather they use a log-linear model of frequency counts, quasi-symmetry, to summarize patterns in the agreement/disagreement data. Johnsen's work focuses on social tie structures that occur in populations under various assumptions about how patterns of agreement are generated from ties of affect and about how ties of affect are generated from patterns of agreement. Zeggelink too examines the conditions under which certain types of tie structures emerge from individual choices of associates, but in her work the choices are not constrained by the orientation of the alters to particular objects or issues. Markovsky concludes this batch of papers on the conceptual and theoretical relations between solidarity and social networks by adopting an explicit definition of a group's solidarity in terms of properties of its communication network.

A THEORY OF THE STATE AND OF SOCIAL ORDER

The assumptions of rational action drive the claims made by Chai and Hechter. Solidary groups form the units of analysis for the problem of state emergence and social order. The calculus of social order among solidary groups mirrors the calculus of solidarity among individuals: as the authors state "attaining solidarity in a group is analytically similar to attaining order in a territory composed of multiple solidary groups; both are instances of the same generic process." As in all rational action theories, the story lies in how costs and benefits are stipulated. Chai and Hechter first reprise Hechter's 1987 theory of group solidarity, examining the cost/benefit structure of individuals coalesced into groups, and then extend the argument to groups coalesced into states.

At the level of individuals coalesced into groups, the problem is how groups insure that individuals comply with corporate obligations to produce the joint goods whose consumption motivates membership. As rational egoistic actors, individuals are motivated to avoid compliance and its costs yet consume their share of the joint goods. For the joint good to be produced some members must comply and so it is the interests of group members to create a group-level control structure to monitor and sanction one another for failure to comply. If the costs of compliance are outweighed by the expected sanctions for failure to comply, members will comply. Yet maintaining such a control structure itself has costs. These costs create additional obligations, the problem of second-order compliance, the need for second-order sanctions that create additional third-order obligations, and so on. Thus for compliance, the expected sanctions for failure to comply must outweigh the sum of the original costs of contribution to the production of joint goods plus the costs of the first, second, third-order, ... costs of maintaining the control structure. Only then will the original joint goods be produced, that is, only then will members comply with their corporate obligations and contribute.

The success of a group in producing joint goods depends critically on the efficiency of group's control structure in producing sanctions per unit input of control contribution, taking into account the chances that noncompliance is detected. To see the logic here, suppose detection is certain. Then to induce compliance, the sanction received for noncompliance must be greater than the sum of the cost of contribution and the (limiting) cost of control. Since it is the contributions to the control structure that produces sanctions, it is clear that the control structure must be a "value-added" process, creating sanctions that have greater (negative) value than the costs that are incurred in producing them. Furthermore, the control structure's efficiency must be even greater when detection is not certain – if detection chances decline to 25%, efficiency must increase by a factor of 4. Chai and Hechter do not offer a theoretical account of the kinds of groups that are likely to be able to establish and maintain such efficient control structures. They do point out, however, that since large groups tend to have lower probabilities of detection, control structures must be correspondingly more efficient.

On the benefit side of the equation, their analysis focuses on how benefits affect the requirements for efficient control structures. Thus the efficiency of control remains at the forefront of their thinking. The idea here is that the benefits an actor receives from her current group relative to the benefits she could receive from other groups establishes her degree of dependence on her group. Positive dependence makes the avoidance of expulsion from the group an additional basis for compliance with obligations. As a control strategy, expulsion is assumed to be costless unlike the sanctions previously analyzed. As a result, for fixed levels of zero-order production costs and control structure costs, greater dependence means that to insure compliance, a smaller expected sanction is necessary. Net of other considerations, greater dependence of members on the group reduces the efficiency with which the group's control structure must operate to produce compliance, that is, reduces the amount of sanctions that must be produced per unit input of control contributions.

If a group solves the control structure puzzle, it is then able to insure that its members comply with zero-order obligations and thus produce the valued joint good. Other things equal, small groups of highly dependent members are more likely to have appropriate control structures than large groups with mildly dependent members. For Chai and Hechter, a group with an effective control structure can behave as a unitary actor because it can control its own members. In the extension to the problem of social order and state formation, this property is important – Chai and Hechter assume that groups that can control their own members can insure that these members do not violate obligations deriving from a higher level of aggregation. By this point in the development of their theory, it is clear that a group's solidarity is defined entirely in terms of an effective control structure. Solidarity is, therefore, a derived notion in their theory and so the problem of solidarity is solved by defining it in terms of effective control structures, but leaving open the question of the conditions under which groups will develop such effective control structures.

These developments are prefatory to the presentation of a theory of the state and of social order. In a nutshell, the theory of social order views the problem as a matter of how preexisting unified groups create and maintain a supergroup (the state) with an effective control structure to insure compliance with supergroup obligations. The problem is analyzed analogously to the problem of insuring compliance of individuals to group obligations. However, in the context of the state, the supergroup obligations are not obligations for contributions from the groups themselves, that is, it is not the compliance of the groups that is at issue, but the compliance of their members with the new obligations deriving from the supergroup or state. Or, put differently, group compliance is defined as the aggregate compliance of all its individual members. Thus the assumption of preexisting groups with effective control structures is necessary for their analysis of social order, but problematic. What guarantee can there be that a group's control structure, efficiently organizing compliance with obligations to produce some joint good, can be generalized to organize compliance with other, perhaps unrelated obligations? At a minimum we need to assume that the obligations organized within a group context are the same obligations with which the state is concerned.

A relevant issue at the group level but not the individual level is the allocation of costs of control as between the supergroup and each individual group. Of particular interest is Chai and Hechter's claim that efficiency of maintaining social order in the society as whole (and measured as control costs per individual) increases with average size of its constituent groups. This result comes about, it is claimed, because holding constant population size, the (infinite-level) aggregated costs of order, denoted by γ_s, has a positive derivative with respect to n, the number of constituent groups. However, it is not clear that this actually follows from the cost logic: basically, the proof hinges on the claim that as the number of groups increases the probability of detecting noncompliance declines. But this claim seems to be in error because as n increases, constituent groups are smaller and in these groups, the probability of detection increases, not decreases. Since γ_s is only implicitly defined in terms of a general function Φ, it is difficult to be certain about this objection. Whether it is correct or not is, perhaps, less important than the fact that such grand questions can be raised in Chai and Hechter's framework.

THE MICROFOUNDATIONS OF SOLIDARITY: A FRAMING APPROACH

Lindenberg's microfoundations of solidarity refer to those conditions and circumstances which enhance the likelihood that ego will display solidary behavior in five different types of situations: need, common good, breach temptation, sharing, and mishap. The solidary behaviors are helping alter, contribute and eschew free-riding, forebear hurting alter even at some cost, divide costs and benefits fairly, and be contrite after inadvertently acting nonsolidarily. The list of situation types is clearly meant to be exhaustive. Furthermore, the more costly the solidary behavior in each of these situations, the greater the degree of solidarity between ego and alter indicated by ego actually engaging in solidary behavior. In each case, ego presumably experiences some costs that are not covered, at least in the short run, or in Hechter's terms as phrased by Lindenberg, ego "contributes private resources without compensation."

Since in the short run, such contributions are irrational, solidary behavior is irrational. In the long run, however, such behavior might have its rewards. In fact, Lindenberg points out that if people were farsighted rational creatures, then solidary behavior would have its compensations and would be just another instance of maximizing behavior. Hence, there would be no puzzle or at least no need to invoke a special concept, solidarity, to deal with behavior in the five situations. But, Lindenberg argues, people are not farsighted optimizers, but myopic suboptimizers. They tend to succumb to short-run temptation at the expense of long-run benefit. Thus solidary behavior remains a puzzle, or rather, what remains puzzling is why individuals do not always fall prey to myopic opportunism.

Lindenberg turns the myopism of actors from a liability into an asset. Because actors are myopic, if the choice situation is "properly" framed, opportunity costs incurred by solidary behavior will be overlooked. Framing is a matter of which goals are active in a choice situation. The active goal frames the situation, meaning that it provides the criteria for ordering alternatives and selecting among them. Other goals that, in general, would provide a different ordering and perhaps enjoin a different choice are pushed into the background of the frame and have only an indirect effect on behavior, an effect that becomes more likely if the framing goal loses salience.

Framing effects are quite general and occur with respect to all types of behavior. So the microfoundations of solidary behavior rest on those conditions that make solidary frames or goals related to solidary behavior highly salient. These conditions are (for the most part) exogenous to the decision maker. Specifically, one of the key conditions that makes a solidary frame highly salient is that ego and alter are comembers of a sharing group, that is, a face-to-face group of people who share in the production and/or consumption of some goods. In such groups, any one person's behavior has both positive and negative externalities for others. In such groups, behaving in a solidary fashion will be useful (to manage negative externalities) and so in such groups, the argument goes, because it is useful and beneficial: first, egos will develop behavioral propensities to produce solidary behavior when appropriate and, second, norms enjoining solidary behavior in regard to comembers will develop. These developments will occur more rapidly and with greater certainty, the greater the amount and value of the goods shared. A second condition produces a weaker form of solidarity and that is a goal to maintain a relationship between ego and alter. The relationship need not be embedded in sharing group. However, it does appear to presume that some goods are shared in the dyadic relationship. But not too much can be shared because the primary orientation of both parties is to personal gain. Solidarity goals become relevant and the personal gain objective is put in the background, that is, loses salience, only when "the pursuit of gain threatens the relationship."

Within the logic of the framing approach, how a frame maintains its salience is a general theoretical question. Lindenberg's discussion of this issue is cast entirely in terms of the maintaining a solidary frame's salience, as if it were especially vulnerable to decay. Relational signals that convey a continued disposition to behave solidarily are held to have some importance in maintenance of salience. But, oddly enough, no attention is directed to the conditions that develop the solidary orientation in the first place, namely, the fact that solidary behavior is useful. If such solidary frames are salient because the behavior they enjoin is useful in many interactions, then so long as these occasions of interaction reoccur regularly, the salience of the frame will remain very high. Relational signaling of intent cannot compensate for the absence of situations in which solidarity behavior demonstrates its usefulness. Thus contrary to Lindenberg's intentions, by his construction, solidary behavior is not especially unstable, absent changes in outside circumstances.

If there is any endogenous destablizing process for solidary behavior, it should be a general process that can affect the salience of any frame. Salience declines if a frame loses power to discriminate between alternatives, that is, when it no longer identifies a large difference between alternatives. In such a case, the frame provides no clear "best" alternative. Thus a solidary frame can lose salience whenever the alternatives are equally good ways of attaining solidarity goals. Suppose two friends each ask for ego's assistance on a particular day. Ego can only help one of them. In either case solidarity motives are advanced (or not) so the solidary frame will lose its salience and ego may decide on the basis of which help will require the lesser expenditure of time and effort. Using a gain orientation this time around may reduce the salience of the solidary frame in later similar situations.

THE MANAGEMENT OF TRUST RELATIONS *VIA* EMBEDDEDNESS

As Weesie, Buskens, and Raub note problems of trust arise in many contexts. The particular problem they explore arises when there is some delay between the moves of two actors with respect to an exchange of goods and services. The delay allows the actor who moves second to default on obligations incurred by accepting payment or goods from the first actor. That is, the second actor can cheat, abscond with the proceeds, and give nothing in return. But if the first actor expects such behavior, then she might insist on a formally enforceable contract, a more costly solution to the problem of the second actor's opportunistic behavior than simply informally contracting with the second actor. Weesie, Buskens, and Raub's analysis of the problem highlights the social dilemma involved: both actors are better off if the first informally trusts the second, but in the absence of additional considerations, rational actors will not behave this way – there is a one-sided Prisoner's Dilemma embedded in the logic of this situation – and the more costly, suboptimal result of formal contracting will be invariably chosen.

The paper explores two ways in which the problem of trust between buyers (actors who move first) and sellers (actors who move second) can be solved in such situations. The first way is called social or structural embeddedness and has two forms – temporal and network embeddedness. Temporal embeddedness means that one play of the Heterogeneous Trust Game (HTG) is usually embedded in a series of plays of the game strung out over time. That is, it is practical to focus concern on behavior in the iterated HTG. Network embeddedness means that buyers are not isolated actors but are embedded (to a greater or lesser degree) in networks of other buyers, from whom they can acquire information about the reputation, i.e., past behavior of a particular seller. As in the analysis of the Iterated Prisoner's Dilemma, the shadow of the future and the spectre of the past change the strategic calculations in a direction favorable to some form of cooperation, in this context, trust.

Trust is enhanced more directly by the second type of consideration, institutional embeddedness. Practically, many particular arrangements can serve as examples of this mechanism but formally they are identical – namely, the seller has the option to form a "commitment" prior to plays of the game, such that the temptation to abuse trust is reduced by a fraction proportional to the size of the commitment. Weesie, Buskens, and Raub do not discuss how such commitments can be made so that the buyer can "trust" that they will be enforced if the seller cheats. Questions of credibility of commitment are simply not addressed and assumed away.

Trigger strategies for playing the ITHG are analyzed. These strategies have the following forms. For the seller, the strategy $\sigma_2(h, \vartheta_2)$ stipulates that the seller makes commitment of size h in the preplay period and honors the trust of a buyer if the temptation to abuse it is below the threshold given by ϑ_2. For the seller, the strategy $\sigma_1(\vartheta_1)$ stipulates that the buyer places trust only if the buyer has no information that the seller has abused trust in the past and if the temptation to abuse trust is below the threshold given by ϑ_1. At issue is the frequency with which trust will be given and honored, the incomplete form of contracting. Basically this is determined by the proportion of times the temptation to abuse trust is below the adopted thresholds. In each play a temptation factor is selected randomly from a known distribution. Therefore, the greater the threshold, the more often will trust be given and honored. The main results of Weesie, Buskens, and Raub are quite straightforward. In the absence of the ability to make commitments, thresholds are higher when (a) the seller has a higher discount rate for future payoffs; (b) there is a greater difference between the sellers payoff for the incomplete contract and his payoff under the complete contract; (c) a buyer is more embedded in the network of buyers; and (d) when the probability of a successive play is higher for both the buyer and the seller. There are no surprises here since each of these factors reduces the incentive for sellers to abuse trust.

If preplay commitments are possible, their effect depends on their cost. Net of other considerations, the more costly a given level of commitment is, the lower is the threshold for the trigger strategies and thus the more often is complete contracting used. As costs decrease, the thresholds increase and so more contracts are incomplete and involve giving and honoring trust. Weesie, Buskens, and Raub describe this situation as one in which exogenous institutional embedding (the complete contract alternative) and endogenous institutional embedding (via preplay commitments) are substitutes for one another, at least with respect to commitment costs. With respect to other parameters of the game, results are unclear and ambiguous. In general, however, structural embeddedness via temporal and network effects and exogenous institutional embedding are clear substitutes for one another. Even in the more complex case permitting preplay commitments, greater structural embeddedness leads to less use of complete contracting.

The role group solidarity plays in this construction is quite minimal. Trust is clearly an outcome variable that we would expect solidarity to affect. That is, members of a highly solidary group are more likely to trust one another in games such as those described by Weesie, Buskens, and Raub than are members of a less solidary group. Such greater trust between comembers could occur for several reasons. The first set of reasons pertains to the interaction structure among members of highly solidary groups; namely, they are likely to have greater network embeddedness (i.e., a greater density of ties between members) and are more likely to encounter each other in the future (more regular and frequent interaction). The second set of reasons pertains to the payoffs experienced by sellers: namely, the temptation to abuse the trust of a comember may be smaller than the temptation to abuse the trust of an outsider or the payoff difference between incomplete and complete contracts is greater if the buyer is a comember since forcing a complete contract is inconsistent with the presumption of trust between group members and thus creates a situation of "imbalance" in psychological terms. Finally, endogenous institutional embeddedness via preplay commitments may be more easily generated *vis-à-vis* insiders than outsiders if the cost function takes into account group membership.

A MATHEMATICAL MODEL OF GROUP DYNAMICS

In Weidlich and Helbing's mathematical model, groups stratified into levels compete for members on the basis of factors that influence the rate at which individuals move from group i and status level h to group

j with status level k. These factors boil down to a catalog of attributes of these states ih and jk which act as pull or push factors on individual movement. The essential equation is

$$v(jk|ih) = \frac{v_0}{d_{ji}^{kh}} \cdot \frac{\exp[v_+(jk)]}{\exp[v_-(jk)]} \frac{\exp[v_-(ih)]}{\exp[v_+(ih)]}.$$

In this equation, v_0 is a baseline rate of movement, the d factor refers to the social distance between states ih and jk, the v_+ factors refer to attractions or pulls to the indicated state, and the v_- factors refer to repulsions or pushes away from the indicated state. Each of these terms is further unpacked into a dizzying array of subfactors: persuasion activity, membership payoffs, membership contributions, membership obligations, costs of admission, etc. Each of these affects the transition rate, net of other factors, in the expected fashion – for instance, if a group increases its cost of admission, the rates of transition into the group are decreased.

The number of assumptions that must go into this construction is quite impressive. Each assumption could, of course, be challenged or altered. For instance, we have the claim that the benefits of membership in status h of group i, denoted b_i^h, derive from only two sources – payoffs, denoted p_i^h, and faith confirmation, denoted f_i – only one of which depends on the status of the individual in group i. Furthermore, payoffs refer to both material and immaterial rewards that depend on status while faith confirmation refers to the immaterial satisfaction obtained because the group confirms an individual's own beliefs and ideas. Also costs of membership take two and only two forms: obligations o_i^h which vary by status and contributions q_i which do not. Questions immediately arise. Is the partition of benefits or the partition of costs truly exhaustive? Why have a faith confirmation factor if the formalism does not specify that individuals have any beliefs? As individuals move from one group to another, do they simply drop or forget their past beliefs and adopt unhesitatingly the beliefs of the new group, thereby capturing the faith confirmation benefit f_j? How can the immaterial nature of obligations be measured?

The solidarity of groups enters into this process of individual transitions from statuses in one group to statuses by affecting benefits. The payoffs from membership in status h of group i depend on the degree of solidarity of group i. The faith confirmation factor depends on the solidarity of all groups in the population. In the first case, solidarity's effect on payoff follows Hechter's hypothesis: solidarity increases the probability that contributions are produced and increases the total benefit that a given level of contribution makes possible. The effect of group j's solidarity on group i's faith confirmation factor depends on a cross-group influence parameter, denoted w_{ij}, which may take on positive or negative values. By definition, a group's influence on its own faith confirmation factor is positive and presumably groups with beliefs contrary to those of group i, will negatively influence group i's faith confirmation factor, while those with compatible or consistent beliefs will positively influence group i's faith confirmation factor. Note that solidarity affects none of the other aspects of the transition rate: solidarity has no impact on the size of obligations, the extensiveness of contributions demanded, the costs of leaving status h of group i, or the costs of admission to status k of group j. Again these are debatable issues: Hechter, for instance, would argue that greater solidarity enables groups to impose more extensive obligations and require greater contributions.

Solidarity is not only an exogenous variable, it is also endogenous in Weidlich and Helbing mathematical model. It is a dimensionless quantity that can take on values between 0 and 1. Its relative rate of change is defined as a difference between two pressures, each of which depends fundamentally on the size of the group:

$$\frac{dS_i/dt}{S_i(t)} = [(\alpha_{0i} + \alpha_{1i}N_i)(1 - S_i)] - [\sigma_{0i}S_i + \sigma_{1i}N_i^2 S_i].$$

The first pressure would increase solidarity up to its maximum in the absence of the second pressure. The rate of increase is a function of the size of group i, denoted N_i. More members mean a greater rate of enhancement in "the sentiments of identity" or the "feelings of commonness" within group i. The counterpressure also depends on the number of group members and the group's current level of solidarity. Dependence on group size is held to reflect the greater ease with which free riding can occur in a larger group. The current level of solidarity impacts negatively on the rate of change in the group's solidarity due to a "saturation" effect, explicated in terms of "limited receptivity of each member of the group for too much ideology."

At equilibrium, the solidarity of group i is a simple function of the size of the group:

$$\bar{S}_i = \frac{\alpha_{0i} + \alpha_{1i}\bar{N}_i}{\alpha_{0i} + \sigma_{0i} + \alpha_{1i}\bar{N}_i + \sigma_{1i}\bar{N}_i^2}.$$

Thus the solidarity of group i depends on the equilibrium size of group i. The equilibrium size of group i depends on the microdynamics of individual transitions from statuses in one group to statuses in another. Thus the solidarity of group i is ultimately dependent on the benefits and costs of group membership, the benefits and costs of admission, and all the other micro influences on individual decision making as these impact on the equilibrium size of the group. But note that group size is not the only determining factor. Solidarity at equilibrium depends also on the trend parameters in such a way that we get the following remarkable result: *empty groups, groups of size 0, can have nonzero levels of solidarity.*

The model offered by Weidlich and Helbing is the most complex of any presented in the chapters in this volume. It is so complex that to even illustrate the consequences of the model for a simple case, two groups each with three status levels, requires the specification of 41 different parameters! In the scenarios, 33 of these are held constant while variation in the other eight is explored. (The eight parameters arise because I assume that the specification of a_2^h, the admission costs of group 2, as a single number means that each of its three levels has the same admissions cost.) Many will find this model simply too complex. They will wonder whether the trends illustrated in the scenarios occur only under the specification adopted for the 33 constant parameters. They will be discouraged by the fact the rate of change in the number of parameters is an increasing function of the number of groups: if we add a third group to the scenarios, we add 22 parameters; if we add a fourth group, we add another 24, bringing the total number of parameters for the four group three status level model to 87. They will be disturbed that, despite the complex structure of the model, it permits groups with no members to exhibit virtually any level of solidarity with the range of acceptable values.

Finally, the Weidlich and Helbing formulation sidesteps the question of emergence, which is at the heart of the solidarity problem. They analyze the problem quite clearly – the value of the null state (00) in which an individual is a member of no group, although 0, is still greater than the value of any other state (jk) because the "the payoff and faith confirmation are $=0$ for the not yet existing groups, but the obligations and contributions already do exist for anyone wanting to initiate a group." In this respect, their model echoes another point of Hechter's 1987 theory of solidarity, namely, that it does not explain how groups come into existence, only that if they do with some measurable level of solidarity, this unity will be reflected in the extent of obligations and the willingness to contribute to group activities. Weiblich and Helbing's opinion on this problem is that it is a problem of small numbers to which their mean value model cannot really apply. That is, the phenomenon they describe are fundamentally stochastic in nature and while the equations they set out may look deterministic, that is only because the model is formulated implicitly in terms of mean values of the true process variables which are stochastic.

CONDITIONS FOR EMPATHIC SOLIDARITY

If group solidarity has an irreducible component of noncalculativity and nonrationality, it resides in the emotional feelings of unity and oneness it engenders among comembers of a group. Heise provides us with an explication of the conditions under which the emotional basis of solidarity is generated. In brief the idea is this: feelings of solidarity with others arise when we see that they have the same emotional response to some stimulus object, called the pivot, that we find ourselves experiencing. In addition, for empathic solidarity to be established, both a and b must be moved to action with respect to p, producing by assumption identical or equivalent behaviors, which give observable evidence that a and b are allies, that is, on the same side. These behaviors may be common vocalizations of approval or disapproval or common body postures, e.g., kneeling vs. standing vs. sitting at particular ritual moments. Finally, a and b must recognize that the other's emotions and actions are "authentic," which occurs when each is aware that the other is observing their emotions and behaviors. (This third proviso is necessary to account for why dramas in which the audience identifies with a character do not create empathic solidarity between the two.)

With few exceptions, the production of empathic solidarity requires that actors have the same social identity with respect to the pivot figure and that they are experiencing the same event with respect to that pivotal figure. This requirement follows from Affect Control Theory as applied to the generation of emotion. Having the same fundamental identity and experiencing the same event leads to the same transient evaluation of that identity and it is the transient evaluation's comparison with the identity's fundamental evaluation that produces emotion. The exceptions to this rule are relationships in which actors can enact the same identity *vis-à-vis* one another, such as sweetheart, and thus can serve as equivalent pivots for one another. Affect Control Theory provides other deductions with respect to empathic solidarity. For instance, it predicts that in the absence of experiencing the same event, actors realizing that they share an identity, e.g., traveler, may have a basis for "provisional" solidarity but only if the identity has a particular evaluative profile. That profile is one in which the identity is evaluated as good, active, and potent or powerful.

Thus empathic solidarity is basically a form of mechanical solidarity: unity and feelings of oneness engendered through likeness. But likeness must be observed in emotion and action and thus in addition to similarity, the production of empathic solidarity requires that certain locational and temporal conditions be met. It is essential that persons be able to observe one another's emotions and actions towards the pivot and so technical details of seating and staging are essential to the production of empathic solidarity among many people simultaneously. Temporally, daily schedules in a group create the opportunity for some subgroups to create empathic solidarity but not others. Heise also recognizes that empathic solidarity decays over time but he does not diagnose this as problem of sustaining emotion. Rather the problem is sustaining the sense of alliance, of joint action, in relation to the pivot. When the relationship to the pivot is not in the foreground – is not the immediate frame of action – then the actors return to other social relationships in which they might be in conflict or competition. This creates the potential to erode the sense of alliance characteristic of empathic solidarity. Thus, in a Durkheimian sense, immersion in the profane world of pragmatic orientations and asymmetric identities tends to erode the sense of unity. Restoration requires periodic immersion in events defined by persons' common relationship to pivots.

Finally, I note that in contrast to the other contributions, this analysis of solidarity brings in considerations of a cultural nature, namely, the social identities actors may adopt in regard to pivots. These identities are cultural schema that predate any occasion in which empathic solidarity may be produced. Hence essential to any further development of Heise's framework would be explicit consideration of how these identities are created and maintained.

MODELING INTERACTION RITUAL THEORY OF SOLIDARITY

Collins and Hanneman's formal model of interaction rituals presented in this paper relies on simple difference equations to describe how quantities basic to Collins' Interactional Ritual Chain Theory change over time in response to exogenous and endogenous influences. These variables are: degree of common focus (F_t), degree of common mood (M_t), level of rhythmic coordination among persons engaged in interaction (R_t), degree of similarity in cultural-membership capital (CS_t), amount of cultural-membership capital stored in interactants memories averaged over interactants (CQ_t), and the emotional energy (E_t) of the group. The equations contain other variables which are introduced in order to make the process "behave." For instance, S_t is the degree of satiation with interaction and CU_t is the average amount of cultural capital not yet used in the current interaction. Both of these variables are introduced to prevent interaction from continuing indefinitely as emotional energy and rhythmic coordination escalate continuously. The model does not posit rational actors nor does it propose to model the behavior of actors. The object of analysis is the interacting group itself. Two examples are given: children at a day care center and faculty at a cocktail party. The variables in the model characterize the group itself rather than specific individual members. In this respect, it is the least methodologically individualistic of the contributions in this volume.

Because of this feature, the model is silent on some basic issues – for instance, how group size would affect solidarity via how it affects the processes under study. The results graphed for the Dean's cocktail party in Figure 5 would hold for a party of 20 faculty or a party of 200. Experience suggests this cannot be true, but the only way to patch the model is by arguing for a change in initial conditions or parameter settings to reflect the differences that group size might introduce. For instance, perhaps the larger group would have a lower initial value of cultural-membership similarity, or higher values of the parameters that govern how fast common focus and common mood dissipate. These changes could be made and a new simulation run to compare its results with those in Figure 5. What we learn, though, depends on the assumption that size has its effects through these changes and not some other factors.

The motivation to undertake some exhaustive comparisons of interesting simulation results is undercut by that fact that the formal statement of the model has problems of interpretability. That is, given the constraints assumed on the range of values a variable can take on, the equation sometimes produce nonsensical results. For instance, the difference equation for common mood using the parameters specified in the simulation is

$$M_{t+1} = M_t + (0.5CS_t + V_t) - 0.01M_t.$$

Here V_t is the extent to which exogenous events produce a common mood and it is assumed to range from 0 (no events contribute) to 1 (events compel all members to share a common mood). Also CS_t ranges from 0 (complete dissimilarity in cultural membership capital) to 1 (complete similarity). The problem is that M_t is also restricted in variation between 0 (randomly distributed member moods) and 1 (member moods are identical). Clearly, there are many assignments of values to CS_t and V_t which makes M_t greater than its theoretical maximum.

One could just dismiss these anomalies and argue that they describe cases that are extremely atypical and not worthy of interest. But the preferred course of action is a careful reformation of the translation of Collins' ideas to avoid such formal inconsistencies. Until such a reformulation is made, pushing the current model further would be unproductive of general insight and understanding – the results hinging too much on careful selection of initial values and parametric quantities.

SOLIDARITY AND SOCIAL NETWORKS

The raw data for the analysis of Breiger and Roberts are a set of actors (Supreme Court justices), a set of issues (opinions) and counts (a) of the number of times that actor i indicates agreement with actor j by joining an opinion that j authors, and (b) of the number of times that actor i indicates dissent with actor j by not joining an opinion that j authors. If the number of issues were equal to one, and we had a measure of friendship between the actors, we would have an example of the kind of situations to which Johnsen's ideas would apply. However, things are rarely so simple in the natural world from which we draw our cases for study. Here we have many issues – in the data examined by Breiger and Roberts there are over 500. Furthermore, the pattern of orientations to issues is more complex. On issues that one member of a pair authors an opinion, it is rarely the case that the other member always agrees or dissents. For instance, Marshall and Brennan author a total of 171 opinions (58 and 113, respectively) and join one another 138 times but dissent from one another 33 times. At the other end of the spectrum, Marshall and White author a total of 133 positions, agreeing with each other five times and disagreeing 128 times. Finally, at stake here is not the development of affiliative ties within subset of Justices, as it would be for Johnsen, but interpreting patterns of interagreement in terms of solidarity related concepts.

Breiger and Roberts' analysis offers no clearly defined measure of solidarity. Rather what they explore is the structure of this group as revealed by various models of quasi-symmetry estimated on the frequency counts of interagreements. Whatever connections they make to the solidarity literature depend on whether a quasi-symmetry model fits agreement data. If the model does not fit, nothing at all can be said about the solidarity of the group in its subgroup aspect (whether it has coherent blocks of actors or not), in its collective representation aspect (whether there is implicit collective representation of a hierarchical image in which actors agree on one another's strengths) or in its individuated aspect (that is, individual departures from the commonly agreed upon strength of each actor). It is unclear whether quasi-symmetry is likely to fit all forms of interagreement counts, or just those from Supreme Court justices. Indeed, it is unclear whether it is essential that interagreement counts be analyzed in order that a quasi-symmetry model can be interpreted in terms of solidarity issues. Are there other types of frequency counts indexed by actors that would serve as well?

The contribution of this paper is limited without a theoretical model to generate a pattern of interagreements that could then be fit by the data model of quasi-symmetry. Such a theoretical model would, perforce, address key issues such as the development and maintenance of subgroups/blocks. The present modeling approach, fitting quasi-symmetry models derived from general methodological techniques to summarize data, illustrate how social association might be patterned, how group hierarchy might be collectively, if implicitly, represented, and how there might be detectable strains between individualizing and collective tendencies, but offer no clues as to when association will be patterned, group hierarchy collectively represented, and strains between individualizing and collective tendencies occur.

STRUCTURES AND PROCESSES OF SOLIDARITY

The basic thrust of Johnsen's work is to describe the triadic structures that emerge in larger groups when various combinations of balancing processes apply to the formation of ties between individuals and from individuals to issues or beliefs. Ties from one individual to another are either positive, to indicate affiliation, or negative, to indicate disaffiliation. Ties from individuals to issues are either positive, indicating support of the belief or issue position, or negative, indicating opposition to the position or belief, or of zero value, indicating no commitment either way. The triadic structures of interest refer to the patterns of ties among triples of actors that are induced by particular combinations of balancing processes.

Four balancing processes are defined in two pairs. The members of each pair are alternatives to one another. For instance, process S1t states that those who agree on an issue tend to be mutual friends. This means that as between two persons, a and b, having the same signed orientation to a belief, induces a positive tie from a to b and also one from b to a. Process S2t relaxes this claim and says that agreement will only tend to produce "some friendship." Specifically, what will be induced by agreement is a positive tie from a to b, or from b to a, or possibly both. Process S1t and S2t cannot both apply to the same population – they are alternative assumptions about the balancing process as it occurs from issues to relations. The other two processes are also alternatives to one another and stipulate how balancing occurs from relations to issues. The processes are not further defined. For instance, in process S2t, we do not know if the same signed orientation to a belief will produce one of the three tie patterns with equal probability or even if from one time point to another, there is a chance that none of the three will form.

Although no explicit process models are given, the idea is that we begin with a population divided into three groups based on their orientation to an issue: G^+, supporters for the belief, G^-, antagonists to the belief, and G^0, neutrals. Overtime and depending on the combination of balancing processes that are assumed, Johnsen's analysis explores the formation of ties within the G^+ and G^- groups as a result of their agreement (and hence constrained by either the S1t or the S2t balancing processes) and the formation of belief orientations in ties that cross group boundaries (and hence constrained by either the S3t or the S4t balancing process). The essential question is the configurations of ties among triples of actors that emerge in "equilibrium" once the balancing processes have worked their magic. For instance, if S1t is assumed, then at equilibrium we get within G^+ and G^- a maximally dense network of mutually positive ties. That is, within each subset, triples of actors have the profile (300), meaning all three ties are mutually positive, none have a positive link one way and a negative one the other (an "asymmetric" tie), and none are mutually negative (a "null" tie).

So the first step of the analysis is descriptive: to classify the set of triad profiles that a combination of balance processes creates at equilibrium. While these triads refer to interpersonal ties between actors, presumably involving actual contact, it is important to recognize that these ties are induced because of actors' orientations to beliefs or issue positions. This is not quite what Fararo and Doreian mean when they propose that a common orientation to the group by its members is a necessary component of group solidarity although it is close. It may be identical to the extent groups are conceived as belief bundles and the membership tie interpreted as support for a particular bundle. However, we then add to the Fararo and Doreian's scheme, the idea deriving from Johnsen's work, that ties between actors can be induced not only the basis of comembership but on the basis of not being members of a particular group. That is, we have the dynamics induced by the SS^{-1} tie, but also the potential for dynamics induced by the $\sim S(\sim S)^{-1}$ tie.

At a later step in the analysis, Johnsen introduces an informal measure for the solidarity of a group, $\sigma(G)$, which can be written as follows:

$$\sigma(G) = f(d_G^+, d_g^+, d_{Gg}^+) \quad \text{where } \frac{d\sigma}{d_G^+} > 0, \frac{d\sigma}{d_g^+} < 0 \text{ and } \frac{d\sigma}{d_{Gg}^+} > 0.$$

The d quantities refer to the density of positive ties either within G, within its countergroup g, or between the two groups. Thus G is more solidary when its density of positive ties is greater, when the density of positive ties in its countergroup is smaller, and when the density of positive ties between the two groups is greater. The first two claims seem unobjectionable, but the third one is problematic: positive ties between actors who have different orientations towards an issue create imbalanced actor-actor-issue triads and subject the actors to "cross-pressure" effects. Rather than enhance each's solidarity with their own group, the effect would be the opposite – to pull them away from those with whom they share an orientation. In any event, Johnsen uses this stipulation to identify which combination of processes lead to structures in which the G^+ group at equilibrium exhibits greater or lesser solidarity.

Johnsen's contribution is both too much and not enough. It is too much in that the range of potential models includes ones that sociologists would simply not seriously entertain. For instance, it would be difficult to justify why one process should apply to tie formation among opponents but another among supporters. For a mathematician, cataloguing all possibilities is standard operating procedure, even if the empirical interpretation is trivial or fantastic. It is not

enough in that the implicit dynamics of realistically conceived processes are at the heart of the paper and at the heart of its potential
contribution to the study of group solidarity. What in-the-small
mechanisms correspond to the global processes of agreement inducing
friendship? How are conflicting directives from different processes
resolved? What role can/do pre-existing ties of association play in the
process of tie building? Is solidarity purely epiphenomenal, i.e., a
particular statistic we chose to calculate on the basis of certain
configurations of positive ties within and among groups? Such questions remain.

GROUP FORMATION IN FRIENDSHIP NETWORKS

Solidarity enters into Zeggelink's model as neither a defined nor
undefined quantity despite the fact that in outline her construction
follows the model building prescription endorsed by Fararo and
Doreian and displayed by most of the papers in this volume. The
prescription is explanatory methodological individualism, namely, the
idea that structural forms of sociation, because they are not agents,
need to be derived from models that involve human activities, actions,
and interactions.

Zeggelink's structural forms are defined as particular clusters of
affiliative ties, "friendships," that exhibit a particular type of cohesiveness. The technical type of cohesiveness is that of an LS set, a set of
individuals such that every subset of these persons has more affiliative
ties to others in the set but not in the subset than to individuals not in
the LS set at all. An LS set is but one of many ways network theorists
can map the common intuition that groups are identified by the
property that there is more interaction or social ties between members
of a group than there is between members and nonmembers. The
generating process involves individuals making motivated affiliative
choices that may or may be reciprocated, establishing ties if choices
are reciprocated.

The model's consequences hinge on the motivations assumed for
individual choices. Individuals try to reduce the discrepancy between
the objective situation they confront and certain desired goal states
along $z = 3$ "issues". An individual takes into account the number
of affiliations she currently has and compares it with the number of
affiliations she desires. She takes into account similarity to self of
current associates along some exogenous attribute (say, gender) and
compares it to the ideal state of complete similarity. Finally, assuming

the current structure of ties places her in one of the structurally cohesive forms of interest, an LS set, she takes into account the size of the LS set and its density of connections and compares this to the ideal state of the entire group constituting an LS set of maximal density. (If she is not in an LS set, then this factor has no influence.) These considerations become relevant to a set of heuristics that individuals are assumed to use to reduce the tension created by discrepancies between these three aspects of the current situation and their corresponding desired states. The heuristics govern to whom individuals will direct an overture of friendship. For instance, reciprocated choices are never withdrawn (that is, affiliative ties, once formed, are stable). Or, when possible, an overture of friendship will be directed to someone similar who has sent a friendship overture (an "admirer") in preference to someone similar but who has not sent such an overture. The idea behind a heuristic is that in the particular circumstances calling for its use, it will specify a choice that will reduce the discrepancy between desired and current states better than any other choice.

The group structures that emerge under these rules vary considerably and exhibit complex dependencies on parametric values of the individual choice process. Group solidarity plays no direct role in the dynamics of this friendship formation process, unless one counts an individual's evaluation of the LS set attribute of a current situation as a solidarity related phenomenon. The evaluation of this attribute is such that motivation to change one's current selection of associates is decreased if the group (LS set) one belongs to (a) has a smaller number of ties to other population members who are not in one's group (i.e., a small value of $\alpha(L_i)$); and (b) has a relatively dense set of ties between members of the group (i.e., a large value of $\lambda(L_i)$). Conversely, one is motivated to change one's selection of associates in a direction that would minimize the ties that one's group has to outsiders – so withdraw unreciprocated choices one has made to outsiders – and maximize the ties internal to the group – extend choices to other group members, perhaps now reciprocating choices sent that were previously unreciprocated. If individuals succumb to these pressures, the group as LS set becomes more unified in the sense of more differentiated from its environment in terms of its external and internal tie structure.

But for Fararo and Doreian, the network of person to person ties is one of two components in the idea of solidarity. The other is that the group itself becomes an object of orientation for its members and thereby creates the potential for a tie between persons devoid of direct interaction – the solidary tie of comembership. In Zeggelink's approach, such a tie could be identified in the LS set evaluation and the associated heuristics that implement this evaluation in the choice of associates. Having a solidary tie to another because they are a member of one's *LS* set enhances the chances that they will be selected (if selection is possible) for direct association over someone to whom one does not have such a tie. The solidary tie is generated by comembership in the *LS* set. Yet, were the selection process unconstrained by other factors, the only effect of such a solidary tie would be to convert it sooner or later into a tie of direct interaction. It has no effect on things that concern other authors: individuals' compliance with group obligations, or the extensiveness of those obligations, in large part because these groups themselves face no external environment and hence no problem of survival.

SOCIAL NETWORK CONCEPTIONS OF GROUP SOLIDARITY

Markovsky recognizes that before we can study some phenomena, we must figure out how to measure its important features. However, we must pick the right features to measure – a precise measure of an object's color will not help us study its rate of fall in a vacuum. Of the various measures of solidarity proposed in the chapters in this volume, Markovsky's are the ones most deliberately focussed on the pattern of communication ties between group members. Furthermore, his discussion brings to light many complexities in how one might measure the solidarity present in a specific network of ties. Matters are not as simple as in Johnsen's proposal, where we compute simple density measures of ties.

In Markovsky's view, there are two essential properties of a group's communication network that must be assessed in order to measure a group's solidarity: reachability, or the extent which members of the group are tied to each other directly or indirectly, and homogeneity, or the extent to which there is an absence of substructures in the group's communication network. Both features refer to properties of a network and not to properties of the individuals, yet unlike Collins' and Hanneman's group variables, it is clear how these properties can be calculated from observations on individuals and their interactions. In particular, it must be emphasized that homogeneity refers not to the fact that individuals are similar along some background social attribute, but to the pattern of ties itself.

A key idea in Markovsky's work is that reachability and homogeneity do not measure solidarity directly but only in relation to the group's "referent" network. Conceptually, a group's solidarity is positive to the extent its actual reachability and homogeneity exceed the reachability and homogeneity of its referent. Similarly, a group's solidarity is negative to the extent its actual reachability and homogeneity exceed the reachability and homogeneity of its referent network. Thus to measure the solidarity of a group, we must identify its referent network and to identify its referent network, we must identify what type of collectivity it represents. Unfortunately, Markovsky offers only examples of these types, for instance, a cult group in which the referent network is at least ten persons who have a tie of "adoration" to the conception of the leader and have at least one tie to another follower. The content of the tie to the other follower is not further specified. What one would like at this point instead is a theoretically grounded typology of collectivities that is mutually exclusive and exhaustive. This is a challenging problem in itself, with many possibilities for arguments of the type "when is a cult not a cult but sect"?

So the question must be asked: why must we use a referent network to measure the solidarity of a group? The referent network is designed to be a baseline, but regardless of the baseline we use, more reachability and more homogeneity is always better, and less reachability and less homogeneity is always worse. All the referent network does is establish the zero point. But surely, this is far more precise than we need to be at the current state of knowledge about solidarity. Markovsky offers no strong reasons for introducing this concept except that without it, "we would be left with the paradox of a measure that purports to determine the solidarity of non-existent groups." Where is the harm in calculating some function of the reachability and homogeneity of an arbitrary collection of individuals and calling the result the "solidarity" of the collection? Surely the result of the calculation is likely to be close to zero, indicating the "group" has no solidarity.

Yet the idea of referent network has some intuitive appeal. One reason why the solidarity of a group should be calibrated relative to groups of its type could be that groups of different types are subjected to different forces of dissolution. Cults, for instance, may require greater degrees of homogeneity and reachability to survive than fan clubs. Where competition is fierce among groups, tight bonds with minimal differentiation between network positions may confer advantage. In this interpretation, then, solidarity is identified as a determinant of survival chances, and if we wish the same level of solidarity in different types of groups to predict the same level of survival chances, calibrating our measures relative to group type is probably a good idea.

CONCLUSION

The theory of solidarity sets an agenda of problems for mathematical sociology. To be clear about these problems, we must be clear about how solidarity as a subject for mathematical theorizing differs from other closely related subjects, in particular, social structure and social control. In their introduction, Fararo and Doreian hold that two inter-related factors are essential to a theory of solidarity: the objectification of the group by its members and their common moral and emotionally based orientation to it. This claim makes the problem of solidarity different from the problem of social structure and the problem of social control. A theory of social structure examines the structured interaction patterns among group members, the social network of the group, and regularities in how the parts are related. A theory of social control addresses the production of compliance/ noncompliance among group members with respect to normative or corporate obligations. Many of the chapters contribute more to the theory of social structure or to the theory of social control than to the theory of solidarity *per se*. That is, some chapters focus on interaction patterns and networks of social relations in abstraction from objectification of the group and the formation of moral orientations. Other chapters analyze conditions under which compliance is more or less likely without giving solidarity any parametric role in the production of compliance, although it may have a definitional role.

In Fararo and Doreian's terms, the agenda of problems set by the theory of solidarity include: the problem of group emergence, modeled "as an interaction ritual process and/or conflict process"; the problem of how norms, conceptualized as corporate obligations, arise in a group/collectivity; the problem of compliance with norms/corporate obligations; and finally, the grand problem of integrating the sub-theories into a comprehensive account of the formation, scope, and impact of group solidarity. It is worth reconsidering how a theory of solidarity would emerge from this agenda of problems. If we knew how groups formed, how norms were created, and how compliance was produced, would we be any closer to our aim of a theory of group solidarity? The answer hinges on whether solidarity plays a role in the formation and structuring of groups, has an identifiable impact on the creation of norms, or is a determinant of compliance and noncompliance. If solidarity plays no role in these processes, rather if theories about these processes do not use the solidarity construct, then we will be no closer to a theory of solidarity for having examined these questions.

Chapters that address the problem of group formation often do so without giving solidarity any special role to play. Zeggelink examines how friendship groups emerge in an aggregate of initially unacquainted individuals. Solidarity, in the specific sense of objectification of membership and moral orientation to the objectified group, plays no part in the formation of these friendship groups. Breiger and Roberts examine how interaction patterns and structure of existing groups might be described, but they give no indication how the group's level of solidarity shapes these patterns and structures. Weiblich and Helbing's solidarity construct influences the payoffs of group membership and thus influences movement from one group to another. But their model is silent on the problem of emergence. Nevertheless, their model does suggest one very important conclusion – rational choice approaches to the solidarity question, Hechter's included, must presume groups exist and cannot account for their emergence. In Weiblich and Helbing's terms, there can be no transitions out of the null state of atomistic individuals because the utility gradient to any other state is always negative.

The other two problems, the extensiveness of corporate obligations and compliance with these obligations, relate to consequences rather than causes of solidarity. Only Chai and Hechter address the second problem, the extensiveness of corporate obligations. However, solidarity does not play a constitutive role in the determination. Extensiveness of group obligations is measured by the cost of producing the joint goods – the greater the cost, the more extensive the obligations. Solidarity refers definitionally to the level of compliance of members with the corporate obligations. Holding constant a group's solidarity, then, there is a tradeoff between extensiveness and dependence of members on the group by virtue of the cost/benefit calculations. As dependence increases, extensiveness can increase, meaning that the same level of compliance can be obtained in a group with more extensive obligations if members are more dependent. But if groups differ in solidarity, they differ by definition in the level of compliance with corporate obligations at all levels of extensiveness.

The third problem, that of compliance, is more central to the rational choice chapters than the others but the contributions lack the special emphasis of Fararo and Doreian on objectification and moral feelings of belonging. To make the connection, consider the role emotions can play in Lindenberg's framing process. In groups where objectification has occurred and moral feelings of belonging are produced, the baseline calculus of cost and benefit is upset as decisions involving comembers are framed differently. Decisions to help another become decisions to help a comember. Objectively higher immediate costs will be born for objectively lower immediate benefits when those who need help are comembers. Trust will be placed and honored at higher thresholds. It is the solidarity feelings themselves that provoke framing in ways advantageous to cooperation with comembers. We may speculate that the connection occurs because of the role emotions play in human information processing. As D'Andrade (1981) has described, emotions and cognition are information processes that operate in parallel. Emotions and feelings, in his view, are reverberating loops that hold information in an active form. Planning and rational calculation occur in cognitive systems while the emotional systems make sure the goal or objective of the planning and calculation is not forgotten. Emotions are essential to the process by which objectives are selected and thus essential to the process of framing.

Thus the chapters advance the agenda of problems set out by Fararo and Doreian but not always in a way that contributes to a better understanding of the causes and consequences of solidarity, *per se*. This outcome is neither surprising nor regrettable. The problem of solidarity is an old one in sociology that has only recently re-emerged on the agenda of sociological theory largely due to Hechter's (1987) influential rational choice framing of the problem. Solidarity has not been a focus of formal theories. Indeed, the whole point of this book was to focus formal attention on the problem. But, not surprisingly, contributors do not approach the problem with a blank slate, but with their own research agenda in mind. These agenda may or may not have an independent emphasis on solidarity and thus, the chapters contribute more or less effectively to the Fararo and Doreian problem agenda.

So where do we stand? I think the first problem on the Fararo and Doreian agenda needs to be reformulated. The problem of group emergence, when conceptualized as the emergence of social structure among an aggregate of actors, can admit of solutions in which solidarity plays no role. A reformulation of the problem is necessary to avoid confounding solidarity and social structure. The essential question is not the conditions under which social structure occurs and transforms an aggregate into a group. Rather, the essential questions are the conditions under which the objectification of the group is likely to occur and the creation of common moral orientation is more or less assured. Answers cannot ignore how the network of ties among group members is structured because some regularities may be more conducive than others to objectification and moral orientation.

By dividing the question of structure and solidarity, we allow for the possibility of non-solidarity groups, groups with socially structured interactions among members but without objectification of membership or without moral feelings of belonging. The division also allows us to sidestep the emergence problem in a theory of solidarity. In such a theory we presume the existence of groups (as structured interaction patterns among individuals) and ask about their variable level of solidarity. In terms of Fararo (1989, p. 137), this strategy allows us to build a theoretical sociology of solidarity, that is, to take on the task of "the construction and analysis of generative theoretical models [of solidarity] such that the dynamics and attractor states of [the solidarity formation process] are shown to depend on social structural conditions." The aim is to explicate how variations in social structure of a group, conceived as a network, generate variations in the degree of objectification of the group and in the level of common moral orientations to it. In this process approach, social structural conditions are parametric, and a group's solidarity is variable. Process models explicate how equilibrium states of solidarity (if they exist) depend on social structural conditions.

The second and third problems can also be approached from this process point of view. Here we are asking for a solidarity theory of extensiveness and compliance with corporate obligations. That is, "the construction and analysis of generative theoretical models [of obligation extensiveness and compliance] such that the dynamics and attractor states of [the extensiveness and compliance process] are shown to depend on" solidarity conditions in the group. In this formulation, solidarity is parametric and the variable conditions are extensiveness of corporate obligations and compliance. Models here should attend to the emotional impact of solidarity on the compliance decision.

Finally, the integration problem brings us full circle. One consequence of complying with extensive group obligations may be that particular kinds of interaction structures are maintained. If these structures, in turn, are conducive to continued objectification of the group and the maintenance of moral orientations, solidarity becomes potentially self-replicating. Thus the problem of integration is not merely a technical exercise in joining together different theories, but rather represents a fundamental fact about the nature of group solidarity: a self-replicating glue composed of social structure *qua* interaction patterns and corporate obligations, and social control via compliant choices motivated by emotion.

REFERENCES

D'Andrade, R. G. 1981. "The cultural part of cognition." *Cognitive Science* **5**: 179–195.

Fararo, T. J. 1989. *The Meaning of General Sociological Theory: Tradition and Formalization.* New York: Cambridge University Press, ASA Rose Monograph Series.

Skvoretz, J. and D. Willer, 1993. "Exclusion and power: A test of four theories of power in exchange networks." *American Sociological Review* **58**: 801–818.

ABOUT THE CONTRIBUTORS

Ronald L. Breiger is Goldwin Smith Professor of Sociology at Cornell University. His research interests include social network analysis; stratification, mobility, and classes; economic sociology; and the construction of social categories.

Vincent Buskens graduated in technical mathematics and technology and development sciences at the Eindhoven University of Technology in 1992. After research visits to Tanzania and the Energy Research Center (ECN), he started his Ph.D. research in 1994 on the effects of network embeddedness on the management of trust.

Sun-Ki Chai is assistant professor of sociology at the University of Arizona. He is the author of the forthcoming book *Choosing an Identity* (Michigan).

Randall Collins is professor of sociology at the University of Pennsylvania. His books include *Conflict Sociology* (Academic Press, 1975) and *Theoretical Sociology* (Harcourt Brace Jovanovich, 1988). *Interaction Ritual Chains*, a collection of Collins' essays developing the theory of rituals, emotions, and social symbols, will be published in 1998.

Patrick Doreian is professor of sociology at the University of Pittsburgh and edits *The Journal of Mathematical Sociology*. His primary interests are social network analysis, generalized blockmodeling, mathematical sociology, dynamic models of social change, societal and global inequality, and network autocorrelation models. He co-edited *Evolution of Social Networks* with Frans N. Stockman (Gordon and Breach, 1997).

Thomas J. Fararo is professor of sociology at the University of Pittsburgh. His primary research interests concern formal and integrative theoretical analysis. His published work includes *Mathematical Sociology* (Wiley, 1973) and *The Meaning of General Theoretical Sociology* (Cambridge University Press, 1989).

Robert Hanneman is professor of sociology at the University of California at Riverside. His main areas of research are the use of simulation in theory construction and large scale organizational systems. He is currently analyzing the evolution of the social structure of salt production in the United States from colonial times to the present.

Michael Hechter is professor of sociology at the University of Arizona. He has previously taught at the Universities of Washington and Oxford.

David R. Heise is Rudy Professor of Sociology at Indiana University and is past editor of *Sociological Methodology* and of *Sociological Methods and Research*. His research interests include variable-oriented quantitative modeling, methodological problems in qualitative research, and the affective and logical foundations of social interactions.

Dirk Helbing is Research Associate II at the Institute of Theoretical Physics at the University of Stuttgart. His primary research interest involves the interdisciplinary applications of statistical physics and nonlinear dynamics to social, biological, and traffic systems.

Eugene C. Johnsen, Professor of Mathematics Emeritus, is an applied research mathematician at the University of California, Santa Barbara. His research efforts lie at the intersection of mathematics and substantive social science, and include work on developing and evaluating models of social structures and processes related to such phenomena as the formation of solidarity.

Siegwart Lindenberg is professor of theoretical sociology at the University of Groningen in the Netherlands. His research interests include the methodology of explanation in the social sciences, theories of action (especially the combination of rational choice with framing), sharing groups and the emergence of norms, and the problems of governance (agency, authority, contractual behavior, revolutions).

Barry Markovsky is professor of sociology at the University of Iowa and director of the Center for the Study of Group Processes. His current work is in such areas as power in exchange networks, social influences on paranormal beliefs, integrating theories of power and status, group solidarity, and the construction and analysis of theories.

Werner Raub is professor of theoretical sociology at Utrecht University. His main research interests are rational choice sociology, including sociological applications of game theory, and organization theory.

John M. Roberts, Jr. is assistant professor in the department of sociology at the University of New Mexico. His interests are in the areas of mathematical sociology, theory and methods for social network analysis, and statistics.

John Skvoretz is Carolina Distinguished Professor of Sociology at the University of South Carolina. His current research projects concern formal models of social networks, status and participation in discussion groups, power in exchange networks, and theoretical studies of action structures.

Jeroen Weesie is associate professor of mathematical sociology at Utrecht University. His main research interests include rational choice theory, mathematical sociology, and statistics.

Wolfgang Weidlich is professor of theoretical physics at the University of Stuttgart. His research areas include quantum physics and quantum optics, statistical physics, and the foundations of sociodynamics.

Evelien P. H. Zeggelink is a postdoctoral associate in the department of statistics and measurement theory at the University of Groningen in the Netherlands. Her main interests are in the fields of mathematical sociology, social networks, dynamics, object oriented modeling, statistical network modeling, and social cognition.

AUTHOR INDEX

SUBJECT INDEX